UNFOR

Reuben
Leona

Colonel Reuben Wells Leonard (1860–1930) was a teacher, civil engineer, militia officer, inventor, businessman, senior civil servant, and philanthropist. In December 1923, he signed the third and final version of the Leonard Foundation trust deed, donating over $500,000 to create a fund for scholarships for Canadian students. The deed begins with a statement of Leonard's belief that the 'White Race is, as a whole, best qualified by nature to be entrusted with the development of civilization and the general progress of the world along the best lines.' It goes on to say that the progress of the world depends on the maintenance of the Christian religion and the independence, stability, and prosperity of the British Empire. The student awards created under the trust were therefore available only to persons who were white Protestants of British nationality or parentage. The Leonard Foundation operated under these terms for over sixty years. When the legality of the trust was questioned in the mid-1980s, an Ontario court ruled that it was valid, and it was not until 1990 that the Ontario Court of Appeal reversed the initial decision and held that the discriminatory qualifications were unlawful.

Unforeseen Legacies is an exploration of Canadian values and beliefs as filtered through the ideologies of Colonel Leonard, the Leonard Trust, and the law governing private discriminatory action. Part biography, part legal and intellectual history, this study investigates Canada's response to issues of race, discrimination, and tolerance of and respect for difference, then and now.

(Osgoode Society for Canadian Legal History)

BRUCE ZIFF is Professor of Law, University of Alberta.

PATRONS OF THE SOCIETY

Aird & Berlis

Blake, Cassels & Graydon LLP

Davies, Ward & Beck

Fasken Martineau DuMoulin LLP

Gowling, Strathy & Henderson

McCarthy Tétrault

Osler, Hoskin & Harcourt LLP

Stewart McKelvey Stirling Scales

Torkin Manes Cohen & Arbus, LLP

Torys

Weir & Foulds

The Osgoode Society is supported by a grant from
The Law Foundation of Ontario.

The Society also thanks the Law Society of Upper Canada
for its continuing support.

Unforeseen Legacies

Reuben Wells Leonard and the Leonard Foundation Trust

BRUCE ZIFF

Published for The Osgoode Society for Canadian Legal History by
University Of Toronto Press
Toronto Buffalo London

© Osgoode Society for Canadian Legal History 2000
Printed in Canada

ISBN 0-8020-4838-2 (cloth)
ISBN 0-8020-8368-4 (paper)

Printed on acid-free paper

Canadian Cataloguing in Publication Data

Ziff, Bruce H.
  Unforeseen legacies : Reuben Wells Leonard and the Leonard Foundation Trust

  Includes bibliographical references and index.
  ISBN 0-8020-4838-2 (bound)   ISBN 0-8020-8368-4 (pbk.)

  1. Leonard, R.W. (Reuben Wells), 1860–1930. 2. Leonard Foundation.
  3. Student aid – Law and legislation – Ontario. 4. Discrimination in
  education – Law and legislation – Ontario. I. Osgoode Society for Canadian
  Legal History. II. Title.

  KE0793.Z54 2000   344.713'0795   C00-931249-8
  KF4235.Z54 2000

University of Toronto Press acknowledges the financial assistance to its publishing program of the Canada Council for the Arts and the Ontario Arts Council.

University of Toronto Press acknowledges the financial support for its publishing activities of the Government of Canada through the Book Publishing Industry Development Program (BPIDP).

For Barb, Hannah, and Eli

Contents

FOREWORD — ix

ACKNOWLEDGMENTS — xi

Introduction — 3

1 Who Was Reuben Wells Leonard? — 12

2 The Leonard Foundation Trust in Context — 52

3 Leonard under Siege — 98

4 After *Leonard* — 136

Epilogue — 163

APPENDIX — 167
NOTES — 187
SELECT BIBLIOGRAPHY — 237
TABLE OF STATUTES — 261
TABLE OF CASES — 263
INDEX — 267

Foreword

THE OSGOODE SOCIETY
FOR CANADIAN LEGAL HISTORY

The purpose of The Osgoode Society for Canadian Legal History is to encourage research and writing in the history of Canadian law. The Society, which was incorporated in 1979 and is registered as a charity, was founded at the initiative of the Honourable R. Roy McMurtry, a former attorney general for Ontario, now chief justice of Ontario, and officials of the Law Society of Upper Canada. Its efforts to stimulate the study of legal history in Canada include a research-support program, a graduate student research-assistance program, and work in the fields of oral history and legal archives. The Society publishes volumes of interest to the Society's members that contribute to legal-historical scholarship in Canada, including studies of the courts, the judiciary and the legal profession, biographies, collections of documents, studies in criminology and penology, accounts of significant trials, and work in the social and economic history of the law.

Current directors of The Osgoode Society for Canadian Legal History are Robert Armstrong, Jane Banfield, Tom Bastedo, Brian Bucknall, Archie Campbell, J. Douglas Ewart, James Flaherty, Martin Friedland, John Honsberger, Kenneth Jarvis, Allen Linden, Virginia MacLean, Wendy Matheson, Colin McKinnon, Roy McMurtry, Brendan O'Brien, Peter Oliver, Paul Reinhardt, Joel Richler, James Spence, and Richard Tinsley. The annual report and information about membership may be obtained by writing: The Osgoode Society for Canadian Legal History, Osgoode Hall, 130 Queen Street West, Toronto, Ontario. M5H 2N6. Telephone: 416-947-3321. E-Mail: mmacfarl@lsuc.on.ca.

Foreword x

The Society is pleased to be publishing *Unforeseen Legacies: Reuben Wells Leonard and the Leonard Foundation Trust* by Professor Bruce Ziff of the Faculty of Law, University of Alberta. With great skill and diligence, Professor Ziff has taken hold of an apparently narrow subject and used it to open up a wide window into some fascinating and neglected themes of the Canadian past.

His subject is a sensitive and controversial one. In 1923 the Canadian mining magnate and philanthropist, Colonel Reuben Wells Leonard (1860–1930), endowed a scholarship fund. The deed creating the Leonard trust asserted Colonel Leonard's belief that 'the White Race is, as a whole, best qualified by nature to be entrusted with the development of civilization,' and restricted awards to persons who were white, Protestant, and of British nationality or parentage.

For over six decades, scholarships were awarded in accordance with the curious and disturbing terms set out by Colonel Leonard in 1923. Over this period, some notable Canadians served on the Leonard Foundation's selection committee. In time, however, controversy swirled around the Foundation and in 1986 the validity of the discriminatory qualifications was called into question. At first instance, an Ontario court found the trust valid, a holding that was reversed four years later by the Ontario Court of Appeal.

In his study of the life of Reuben Wells Leonard, Professor Ziff chronicles the fortunes of the Leonard Foundation Trust in the context of an analysis of shifts in Canadian law and society concerning property rights and discrimination then (*circa* 1923) and now. This book dramatically reminds us of the changes that took place in Canadian values and beliefs between the 1920s and the 1980s. It offers penetrating insights into the extent and nature of societal evolution.

R. Roy McMurtry
President

Peter N. Oliver
Editor-in-Chief

Acknowledgments

For many years I have used the case of *Re Canada Trust and Ontario Human Rights Commission* (known as the *Leonard Foundation* case) as a teaching tool in a course on property law. That decision brings to the fore the power of control immanent in the idea of private property, and shows how the law, in the cause of advancing public policy, can impose limits on the rights of owners to use and dispose of their property as they might wish. More specifically, the case involves an unusual and enigmatic trust document created in 1923 to provide an educational endowment. The trust is full of florid language, which appears peculiar to the modern reader. In part, the deed speaks of advancing the progress of civilization; of the innate superiority of the white race; of the mission of both the British Empire and the Christian religion. In the summer of 1996, I decided to find out more about the author of this amazing text – Reuben Wells Leonard (b. 21 February 1860, d. 17 December 1930). My intention was to prepare a casebook on property and to collect a few pertinent facts about Colonel Leonard to help place the *Leonard Foundation* case in context. To my astonishment, I found no biography; after a few days of rummaging I concluded that very little had been written about him. So began this project. The casebook was put on hold.

Samuel Butler wrote that life is the art of drawing sufficient conclusions from insufficient premises. That has been my task in preparing *Unforeseen Legacies*, given that there is so little primary and secondary material available about Colonel Leonard. I was fortunate to have received research assistance from a variety of sources and in the course of doing so I accumulated numerous debts of gratitude. I would like to acknowledge these here.

To begin, I am grateful for the assistance I received at the various archives (these are listed in the select bibliography) that I visited over the course of the project. Special mention should be made of those who provided help at the National Archives (Carole Sequin), Queen's University Archives (Brian Hubner), St Catharines Public Library Special Collections (Ruth Payne), and the Royal Military College Museum (Ross McKenzie). In addition, both Sandra Wilkins, now head law librarian at the Uni- versity of British Columbia, and Lynne Prunskus, special collections librarian at Brock University, were tireless, creative, and thoughtful in pursuing and unearthing materials. Some items were collected from private sources. I would like to thank members of the extended Leonard family, namely, Valerie Bishop, Susannah Crassweller, and Judith Perry, who kindly made available papers, photographs, and other mementos and who provided insights that steered me in directions that often proved fruitful.

A number of people were kind enough to review the work in progress, including Jim Phillips, David Mills, Peter Oliver, Michiel Horn, James Walker, Martin Friedland, John Honsberger, and David Schneiderman (who not only read the first, extremely rough, version of the book but also collected some materials on my behalf from Chatham House in London). Part of the monograph (in essence, chapter 2) was presented at two workshops held at the University of Alberta and at the 1999 conference of the Australia and New Zealand Legal History Society in Newcastle, New South Wales. I benefited greatly from the comments received at these events.

A research travel grant was awarded by the University of Alberta to undertake the archival work. Funding to hire research assistants was also provided. Colin Feasy, Joyce Chun, Rebecca Sober, and Alison Hayter served in that capacity. The lion's share of the manuscript was written during a study leave granted by the University of Alberta for the 1997–8 academic year. Most of the leave period was spent at the University of Virginia. During the publication phase, I had the pleasure of working with Peter Oliver and Marilyn MacFarlane at the Osgoode Society, and with Jill McConkey and Curtis Fahey at the University of Toronto Press. Ann Wynn provided technical assistance at the University of Alberta. My wife, Barb Strange, who knows far more about Colonel Leonard than she wishes to know, and my children, Hannah and Eli, provided moral support.

Much of the book centres on the origins of the Leonard Foundation and the court case, mentioned above, in which the legality of the trust establishing the Foundation was called into question. Established by Colonel Leonard in 1916, the Foundation continues in operation. Canada Trust serves as the trustee. The Leonard award recipients are selected by a twenty-five-person General Committee, with the assistance of an honorary secretary. I think it is rather important that my relationship with these different constituencies of the Foundation be explained.

I am especially grateful to the honorary secretary, Silvio Sauro, for the encouragement, information, and advice that he provided over the last several years, starting from the moment I approached the foundation (via Mr Sauro) outlining my plans for this study. Canada Trust furnished materials, including copies of the 1920 and 1923 trust deeds and a news-clipping file that proved to be quite useful. The trustee also allowed the 1923 deed to be reproduced in this book. The solicitors for the Foundation provided me with the pleadings relating to the litigation. I had an opportunity to speak with several members of the General Committee on 8 May 1998, at the annual general meeting of the Foundation, where I also made a short presentation. And I received helpful feedback on a draft of the manuscript from two members of the committee, Donald Guthrie and Silvia Lowry (as well as from Mr Sauro).

As part of my research I had hoped to examine the Leonard Foundation records, principally the minutes of the annual meetings and any documents relating to the controversy that is so central to this study. It is my understanding that my request in this regard was considered on several occasions, including at a closed session of the meeting held in May 1998. In the end, however, I was not given access. I believe that the trustee felt, on the advice it had received, that given its obligations, which in law pertain to the trust and the trust alone, I could not be given access to the records. To put matters in the best possible light, I suppose this means that there is still plenty of scope for others to undertake the project of telling the story of Reuben Wells Leonard and the Leonard Foundation Trust.

Bruce Ziff
Edmonton
28 April 2000

Reuben Wells Leonard as Cadet #86, Royal Military College of Canada, circa 1883.
(Courtesy RMC Museum)

Leonard, seated on the far right, working as an engineer in Nova Scotia in 1887.
(Courtesy Valerie Bishop)

Leonard, the blossoming engineer, circa 1895.
(Courtesy St Catharines Public Library)

Lieutenant-Colonel Leonard in military attire, circa 1920.
(Courtesy RMC Museum)

R.W. Leonard in 1923, the year of the Trust.
(Courtesy St Catharines General Hospital)

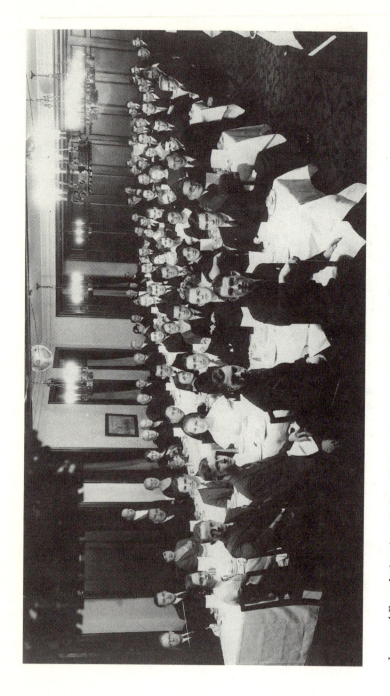

Leonard Foundation Association 6th Annual Dinner, Royal York Hotel, Toronto, 29 November 1933 (three years after R.W. Leonard's death). Arthur Bishop is seated fourth from the left at the head table. To his left is Kate Leonard. (Courtesy Valerie Bishop)

UNFORESEEN LEGACIES

Reuben Wells Leonard and the
Leonard Foundation Trust

Introduction

Colonel Reuben Wells Leonard placed his signature on the third and final version of the Leonard Foundation Trust deed in late December 1923. He had, with this act, donated over $500,000 to create a fund for scholarships tenable across Canada. It was at the time the largest gift of its kind in Canada and, along with a myriad of other benefactions, had served to earn for Leonard a reputation as one of the country's most generous philanthropists.

The deed contains a lengthy preamble that was designed to explain the underlying principles of the trust. It begins with a statement of Leonard's belief that 'the White Race is, as a whole, best qualified by nature to be entrusted with the development of civilization and the general progress of the world along the best lines.'[1] The document also recites that the progress of the world depends in the future, as it has in the past, on the maintenance of the Christian religion, and that the advancement of civilization throughout the world rests upon the independence, stability and prosperity of the British Empire. The Empire, the deed asserts, must remain under the control of British nationals who are not beholden to foreign powers, whether temporal or spiritual. Based on these premises, the student awards created under the trust were available only to white Protestants of British nationality or parentage. Both males and females were eligible, although no more than one-quarter of the funds awarded annually could be given to female recipients.

Odd-sounding, even disturbing as this language may now appear, the Leonard Foundation operated under these terms for over sixty years. Throughout this period, hundreds of scholarships were awarded, the recipients selected by a board of governance that included at various times university presidents, high-placed Anglican clerics, a justice of the Supreme Court of Canada, and a Member of Parliament. What is more, when the legality of the trust was questioned in the mid-1980s, an Ontario court ruled that it was valid. It was not until 1990 that the Ontario Court of Appeal, reversing the initial decision, held that the discriminatory qualifications were unlawful and therefore of no effect.

This book is about Reuben Wells Leonard, the Leonard Foundation Trust, the litigation concerning the validity of the trust's discriminatory provisions, and the judgments rendered in the *Leonard Foundation* case. In this Introduction, I will try to explain why these four objects merit study and how the rest of the work will develop.

Reuben Wells Leonard (1860–1930) led an active life. Over the course of his seventy years he was a teacher, civil engineer, militia officer, inventor, businessman, senior civil servant, and philanthropist. His wealth allowed him an entrée into elite circles in Canada and Great Britain. He counted among his friends and acquaintances prime ministers and governors general of Canada and came to know what he termed 'the big men of London,' people such as Edward, Prince of Wales, T.E. Lawrence, and the members of a group known as the Round Table.

During his lifetime Leonard was a well-known and admired public figure. Nevertheless, seventy years after his death there is no Leonard biography. Despite a renewed interest in Canadian history, and an increase in scholarship pertaining to the period of Leonard's life,[2] no work focusing on him has been undertaken. His contributions were recorded in modest entries in the *Encyclopaedia of Canada* (1935, 1940) and the *Encyclopaedia Canadiana* (1958), as well as in several biographical collections published during this period.[3] However, when the *Canadian Encyclopedia* was released in 1988 there was no entry for R.W. Leonard. He surfaces as a bit player in the stories of other men of his time – in the biographies of Robert Borden, Robert Falconer, Joseph Flavelle, and Lionel Curtis – and in James Kendle's account of the Round Table Movement. Likewise, in the histories of St Catharines, Brantford, Queen's University, Ridley College, Royal Military College, and Wycliffe College, Leonard is mentioned in passing. But there is little else (and, for that matter, virtually nothing about the Leonard Foundation).

It may be that Reuben Leonard has had his due – a few cameo appearances in the annals of Canadian history. Or perhaps the lack of attention is a matter of historiographic circumstance: Leonard's papers, no doubt voluminous, were not archived after his death and have not surfaced since. Family lore has it that his personal secretary, Henry Collins, took the materials with a view to preparing a biography. Collins died impecunious and alone; it is doubtful whether the planned biography was written. Moreover, the chance to draw on living memory to help construct a fuller narrative has now been lost.

Still, the variety of contexts in which the exploits of Reuben Wells Leonard are to be found suggests that a more detailed inquiry would be productive. He was present at critical moments in Canadian history – as a militia officer during the North-West Rebellion of 1885; as the engineer in charge of the building of a major hydro-electric facility at Niagara Falls; as the founding president of Coniagas Mines in Cobalt; as a key figure in the development of the Canadian railway system; as a decorated officer in the First World War; even as a political activist during the Borden administration. His benefactions, in the form of numerous public works throughout the Dominion and in Britain, have left a lasting memorial. Though there is evidence of his life's work, the scattered treatment accorded to Reuben Leonard to date provides an insufficient basis to evaluate his contributions to Canadian society.

In chapter 1, I attempt to chart the major stages in the life of Reuben Leonard. The story is interesting and useful enough in its own right. Here, however, the biographical sketch is designed, primarily, to provide the backdrop for the central subject of this study: an exploration of Canadian values and beliefs as filtered through the ideologies of Colonel Leonard, the Leonard Trust, and the law governing private discriminatory action. In part, this study investigates Canada's response to issues of race, discrimination, and tolerance of and respect for difference, then and now. The examination of R.W. Leonard, and the probing of his curious authorial intentions, are used as a means to explore Canadian society in the first decades of the twentieth century.

In this analysis, the Leonard Foundation Trust deed plays a prominent role. In Chapter 2 the deed is examined in detail. It is, at root, a legal document, creating a charitable foundation (one of the first of its kind in Canada) empowered to administer and distribute trust funds for student bursaries. At the same time, the trust deed is a rich text, one that is capable of being understood on at least three other levels. So, I will argue, it is in part an autobiography, a projection of Leonard's life in this reified form. The deed serves also as a time capsule: inside one discovers an assortment of deeply held values and beliefs of the era in which Leonard lived. Theories of social Darwinism, muscular Christianity, race science, and imperial mission permeate the document. These are all complex ideas, and the manner in which they are invoked in the deed suggests another way in which it may be understood: the trust is a political tract.

In what did Reuben Wells Leonard believe?

Carl Berger's *The Sense of Power* is devoted to an analysis of a form of Canadian nationalism that embraced an imperial vision.[4] It was a patriotism in which collective aspirations about Canada's future were blended with a belief in, and reverence for, the British Empire. At first glance, Leonard seems to personify the image Berger constructed. Steeped in the conventions and myths of the Empire, Colonel Leonard looks Kiplingesque. There is also a faint resemblance with Lorne Murchison, the principal character of Sara Jeannette Duncan's *The Imperialist* (1904). Set in small-town Ontario at the turn of the twentieth century, the novel tells the story of a young man caught up in the blossoming spirit of the Canadian sense of power. Leonard, like young Murchison, became a convert to the idea of imperial federation, which was to become the compass point for the political orientation of both. And, of course, for both it was ultimately to be a lost cause.

Although at first glance Reuben Leonard seems to epitomize this type of nationalist, it would be misguided to suppose that such a characterization is apt. Leonard does not quite fit the mould described by Berger; no one person does. Since the currents of thought in Canada during Leonard's life, on the subjects that mattered most to him, were as varied as at any time in Canada's history, he cannot plausibly stand in as a perfect symbol of his times.[5] What emerges from the present analysis is, predictably, far more complex than such a caricature can portray. One finds a person who adopts the rhetoric of imperial mission. The British Empire served not just the interests of its constituent parts (though it had many practical benefits) but 'mankind' as a whole. Committed to Christian (that is, Protestant) virtues, the Empire was the greatest civilizing power the world had ever known. Leonard harboured concerns about Roman Catholic loyalties and American aspirations. He also believed that the peoples of the world were divided by race, and that in such a world the 'Task of the White Race' (to quote from the trust deed) was to pursue peace, progress, and prosperity. Even though Leonard's thoughts were highly derivative and polemical, they remained potent because they informed the purposes of the Leonard Foundation. In other words, as a man of wealth and privilege, Reuben Leonard was able to impose his rough-hewn ideology through the agency of the Foundation.

As time passed, the world contemplated by the 1923 deed slowly disappeared. This transformation was dramatically illustrated when the litigation concerning the validity of the exclusionary criteria brought the deed into the light of day. In Chapter 3, I endeavour to track the process through which conflict over the trust led first to public debate and in the end to litigation. The setting for this was the development over the preceding fifty years of legal responses to private acts of discrimination. The dispute about the Leonard Trust marks an important staging post in that development. Concern over the restrictive nature of the terms of the scholarships, first raised in the 1950s, intensified in the early 1980s, when the Ontario Human Rights Commission undertook an investigation to determine if the Leonard Foundation, in adhering to the terms of the deed, was thereby violating the province's human rights code. Disagreement within the Foundation was matched by a division of public opinion, as the policy questions raised by the Leonard Trust were debated in the press. The main issue addressed in the media parallelled that at the centre of the legal argument: to what extent should the rights of Colonel Leonard to dispose of his property as he wished be allowed to prevail over other values, in particular, the elimination of discrimination and the promotion of equality? In the result, the Ontario Court of Appeal held that the trust was contrary to public policy and that the discriminatory terms were to be deleted. The way in which this outcome might affect other scholarships was left unresolved.

The story of the life of Reuben Wells Leonard and the Foundation is compelling because it touches on issues that engage our national conscience. It addresses race and discrimination, property rights, private power, and public policy. These are pivotal concepts in contemporary Canada. Chapter 4 contains an examination of how the current law seeks to mediate these conflicting values. The Leonard shadow is cast over the discussion because the ruling in the *Leonard Foundation* case, ambiguous though it may be, has become an important part of the law governing private discriminatory conduct. These problems continue to arise in the setting in which they appear in the Leonard litigation, that is, in relation to discriminatory scholarships and bursaries. In contemporary thought, the pursuit of equality implicates questions concerning the respect for difference and place of multiculturalism, as well as the moral warrant of affirmative action. These issues will also be considered.

When Reuben Wells Leonard died in 1930, his passing was deeply lamented. Canada had lost a distinguished citizen, declared the obituaries published both at home and abroad. He was remembered then, as he had been regarded during his life, as a man who sought to do good in a world in which, to him, right and wrong had sharply tapered edges. In his life he earned a reputation as a scrupulous businessman, a skilled engineer, a decorated veteran, and, above all, a patriot. Regarding his vast fortune as a public trust, he had donated much of it to an array of favoured causes, including schools, universities, hospitals, and the war effort. His generosity was legendary. Among these benefactions, the Leonard Foundation Trust, his largest single gift, has enjoyed a prominent place.

There is now less praise for Leonard and more apology. In the 1980s, as the legality of the Leonard Foundation awards came under scrutiny, Reuben Leonard was vilified in the press as a racist. Some, rallying to the defence of Colonel Leonard, explained that he should be understood as a product of his times, his actions compatible with the temper of that period.[6] The vehicle adopted to pursue his vision (that is, the trust) was 'the one he thought best because of the time in which he lived.'[7] His philanthropy was tainted by attitudes about race that today are treated as repugnant.[8] Canada is now a different and more tolerant nation; naturally, this, too, colours our perceptions of Leonard's contributions.

There is, of course, some merit to this assessment. I will argue that what we know about the views of R.W. Leonard, on such matters as race relations and equality, place him at the extreme end of the scale of beliefs held by those within his peer group. Yet, even so, the Leonard Foundation Trust was not an anachronism in 1923 – perhaps not even in 1953, when it was commemorated in the chapel of Wycliffe College in Toronto, nor arguably in 1959, when a plaque recognizing the Foundation's work was installed at Queen's University. Until the mid-1950s not a single note of public criticism of the Foundation was sounded. That the values encased in the trust could find a congenial home in Canadian social policy and intellectual thought in the inter-war years suggests something about our ignoble legacy of discrimination, prejudice, and intolerance. To explain the trust in this way, deflecting attention away from Leonard, is to appreciate a considerably more unhealthy social order, of which the Foundation can be seen merely as one aspect.

The differences between the perspectives held in the 1920s and those that inform contemporary public policy seem pronounced. In the intervening period, Canadian political and social culture changed. Attitudes about the Leonard Foundation can help to plot that metamorphosis, and juxtaposing the ideologies underlying the trust with those contained in the judgments in the *Leonard Foundation* case provides one measure of that transformation. And it is clear that the harms associated with racism are now treated far more seriously than was the case in 1923. There were at that time no express protections against either private or state-based discriminatory practices. Today there are human rights codes found across the country, together with constitutionally entrenched equality guarantees. However, even in the wake of the *Leonard Foundation* case, the central issue in the litigation, the proper balance of private property and equality rights, remains unsettled. And whether Canada is a more racially tolerant nation is itself a contentious point.

To summarize, this book contains these claims: first, a study of the Leonard scholarship trust yields insights into the evolution of Canadian attitudes touching on such matters as empire, race, religion, education, and philanthropy; second, the life of R.W. Leonard, an instructive (yet previously neglected) figure in Canadian history, provides a context in which the meanings derived from the trust can be understood; third, the changed fortunes of the Leonard Foundation under law demonstrate a shift in the law and public policy concerning principles of equality, racism and private property; and fourth, the questions litigated in the *Foundation* case continue to trouble Canadian law.

The present study is a hybrid: it is part biography, part intellectual history, part legal history, and it concludes with a discussion of contemporary law and policy. Given this unusual combination of fields of inquiry, it is probably useful to say something about where this book fits within existing approaches to scholarship, and on the ways in which it invokes and tries to build upon existing research.

My analysis relies upon several important contributions to Canadian social and intellectual historiography, two of which deserve mention. Reference has already been made to Carl Berger's *The Sense of Power*. I take R.W. Leonard (who is not referred to there) as furnishing a corroboration of Berger's analysis, a blind test of his thesis. Berger's study is not only of value by virtue of the fact that it deals with many of the same questions pursued below: it has also proven to be a pioneering work in the development of Canadian social history.

While *The Sense of Power* is foundational, the present study is not devoted solely to an analysis of imperial thought, important as this may be in understanding both Leonard and his times. It is also about the interrelationship between law, private rights, and public policy. In that regard, this examination of the *Leonard Foundation* case resembles the approach taken by James Walker in *'Race,' Rights, and the Law in the Supreme Court of Canada*,[9] a study of four Supreme Court of Canada decisions in which racial discrimination was central. (Indeed, in that work the *Leonard Foundation* case is mentioned in passing.[10]) Walker employs strategies used by Canadian social historians to examine Canadian law in a creative way. As with the Walker study, I adopt a method in which *local* instances of social phenomena are investigated with the intention of uncovering clues about Canada's past and present.[11]

I also share with Walker an assumption about the utility of treating law as a social barometer. Just as the trust is an artefact of Canadian intellectual thought, so too can the law be seen as a representation of a moment in time. The law is a form of rhetoric, a set of stories, symbols, and visions, which are especially useful because they strive to tell us how conflicting interests ought to be ordered.[12] A caveat should be added, however. Even if it is true that laws are designed to be a practical articulation of social values, the relationship between law and society is dynamic. In essence, there is a dialectic between law, on the one hand, and public policy and public opinion, on the other. Law is reflective of the society that created it and in turn works to mould that society. Because the two interact, determining whether the law informs social values (or vice versa) is sometimes difficult. Moreover, it is by no means clear that a principle of law derived from a decided case (or even from statute) conforms with contemporary points of view. That is especially true of a rule established in some earlier era which has not since been challenged. Some laws become anachronisms yet remain nominally in force.

Even with these qualifications in mind, I believe it is uncontroversial to suggest that Canadian law during the lifetime of Reuben Wells Leonard (and for nearly two decades afterwards) illustrates the following: private property rights were regarded as paramount over the right to equal treatment. Equality, while an important liberal principle, was not protected under law in meaningful ways. In addition, I believe that incongruities in the present law demonstrate the trauma that race issues continue to produce.

Though drawing inspiration and direction from Berger and Walker, the present study also tries to chart new terrain. Despite the substantial growth of Canadian social history in the past thirty years, there is a good deal still to be done. To date, little has been written about Canadian philanthropic practices.[13] The social significance of giving, the development of the modern charitable foundation in Canada, and the interrelationship between charity and the growth of the social safety net are issues that have not been fully explored. Leonard's approach to philanthropy may well be helpful in understanding the role and nature of Canadian philanthropy. Along the same lines, within the recent work on the history of education in Canada (upon which I rely),[14] there is a surprising paucity of scholarship about scholarships. In a field once dominated by institutional histories, there have emerged studies of curriculum design, enrolment patterns, and social practices within schools and universities. The growth and development of student awards should provide insights into such things as patterns of access to education. They are also a symbolic gold mine, expressing, as they often do, conceptions of virtue and excellence. The Leonard scholarship is a case in point. Its stated goal was to equip future leaders of the British Empire with a good education at suitable (that is 'patriotic') institutions. Military or physical training, good character and self-help were part of the description of the educational ideal set out in the trust.

This study examines the 1923 Leonard trust deed in detail, and in doing so I have been guided by earlier efforts at post-colonial discourse analysis. As I see it, what lies at the heart of this field of inquiry is an attempt to expose the ethnocentric bases of imperial discourse, identifying the ways in which language is engaged as a tool of power and hegemony. Portrayals of both self and otherness (and the interaction between the two) form a central concern in the examination of discursive strategies. So far, most of the research in this field has focused on literary texts. The use of this form of analysis in British imperial historiography has been, surprisingly, rather negligible;[15] this is also true in relation to the investigation of Canadian legal texts. Yet an instrument as seemingly mundane as the Leonard Foundation Trust deed can be understood as an element of imperial discourse, its significance in this regard being enhanced by virtue of the fact that it 'does things,' that is, it establishes the constitutional framework of the Foundation and carries the force of law. Hence, I examine the Leonard deed, root and branch, with a view to understanding the narratives encoded within it. In reading the deed, with its talk of the innate superiority of the white race and the role of the British Empire as the steward of 'progress,' one is struck by the confident articulation of timeless truths that have since been abandoned or repudiated. Still, in other ways, namely, as an heirloom of the Canadian polity, it remains durable: for reasons wholly different from those intended in 1923, the Leonard Trust provides a valuable legacy.

1
Who Was Reuben Wells Leonard?

Sara Jeannette Duncan's novel *The Imperialist* is set in a small town that she named Elgin. It was a quiet provincial community in southern Ontario that 'knew two controlling interests – the interest of politics and the interest of religion.'[1] This fictitious place is thought to represent the town of Brantford, Ontario, where Duncan was born in 1861. One year earlier it had been the birthplace of Reuben Wells Leonard. He was one of seven children born to Francis Henry and Elizabeth Leonard (née Catton). The Leonards' paternal ancestors had left England during the period of the Puritan persecution. Fleeing first to Leyden, Holland, they settled in the colony of Massachusetts in 1639; Francis Leonard's father (Reuben) was born there in 1791. Reuben Sr married Julia Anne Wells in Montreal in 1822, and the couple lived in Coburg, Upper Canada, for a time. They moved to what was then the village of Brantford in 1830 and the following year purchased land and built a small house.[2]

THE EARLY YEARS

Life in Brantford for the Leonards was a mix of commerce, public service, and religious devotion. Francis Leonard was a small businessman. He was also active in local government, serving at various times as a school trustee, town councillor, deputy reeve, and reeve in Brantford, as well as warden for the County of Brant. The family was low church Anglican. They worshipped at Grace Church and on Trinity Sunday,

1875, young Reuben took Holy Communion there. He received his secular education in the public school system, graduating from Brantford Collegiate Institute in 1876.

At the age of sixteen, Leonard chose to take up a career in teaching, and he attended the Ottawa Normal School for one year, earning a public school teacher's certificate. The principal thought that he showed promise, owing to his energy and enthusiasm.[3] However, after a brief spell as a teacher in Brant County, Reuben decided that this was not to be his calling. He was accepted into the engineering program at McGill, though he withdrew shortly after the school year began 'for want of the necessary funds to take the course.'[4] Delayed but undaunted, he was accepted at the recently established Royal Military College of Canada in Kingston in 1880.

When Leonard entered RMC his goal was not a career with the military. Only four commissions were offered in a given year, and those who were not interested in a full-time position were able to pursue other academic interests.[5] It was civil engineering that Leonard chose as his field, and he supplemented his studies at RMC with courses in metallurgy and mineralogy at Queen's.

Leonard excelled at RMC, and he blossomed into a tall, fit, self-confident man. When he reminisced about his college days some ten years after graduation, his memories were laden with fondness and melancholy:

How cold even a summer morning can be over on Point Frederick, only those of us can know who used to parade regularly at 6:30 a.m. to be taught swimming by an instructor; but how we enjoyed a plunge off the same bathing-wharf after a hot game of football or cricket! What an enjoyable hour we spent in the winter evenings in the gymnasium, learning fencing, boxing, single stick and gymnastics, under probably the best instructor in Canada! The hard-fought football and cricket matches we played, and the merry dinners in the mess-room in the evening! We shall always remember some of those dinners. The splendid ice-boating and skating in the winter; the sailing and rowing in the summer; the glorious summer days we spent surveying, geologizing, or sketching; the negro minstrels and athletic tournaments; and the annual ball, by which we acknowledged the hospitality and kindness of our many friends in Kingston; the rifle and artillery matches; the riding-lessons; the glee club in the winter, and the songs on summer evenings out in the boats, or on the benches in front of the old barracks, are, for most of us, the pleasantest memories of four very happy years.[6]

In June 1883 Leonard graduated with a first-class certificate, the bronze medalist in a class of nineteen students.[7] He stood first in five subjects and won several college prizes for excellence in athletics and military training: the 'crossed swords' for skill-at-arms; the 'crossed rifles' for shooting; and the 'gilt spurs' for riding.[8]

His time at RMC had prepared Leonard for civilian and military life. On the day of his graduation, Cadet Sergeant Leonard was appointed lieutenant in the Midland Battalion of the Canadian militia. Shortly after leaving the college he took a job as an 'instrument man' and resident engineer with the Canadian Pacific Railway in the Lake Superior district, a position that he held for about two years. In March 1885 word reached Ottawa that Louis Riel had captured Batoche in the North-West Territories and had formed a provisional government. Prime Minister Macdonald mobilized militia units in a swift response to the resistance. At age twenty five, Leonard volunteered for duty, and he joined the force in early April. He served under General Frederick Middleton, the leader of the militia in the field, as a staff officer of transport (holding the rank of captain). Leonard's responsibility was to assist in the transporting of troops westward (a challenging undertaking given that the CPR line had not yet been completed).[9] By early June, Riel had been defeated, and Leonard, along with others who had served west of Winnipeg, received a medal, unceremoniously sent in the mail without the customary personal inscription. He was invited to engrave his name on the medal, at his own expense.[10]

Following this brief tour of duty (103 days) Leonard returned to engineering, spending the next five years working mainly on railway design and construction. For the remainder of 1885 and into the following year he returned to the CPR as a surveying and construction engineer in Ontario and Manitoba. From 1886 to 1890 he worked in the Maritimes for the Cumberland Railway and Coal Company, Spring Hill Collieries, and the Cape Breton Railway. In 1890 he served as an engineer for the New York Central Railway, and in 1891 he was a consulting engineer with the Rutland Canadian Railway.

In 1889, in a brief moment of repose from his professional duties, Reuben Leonard married Kate Rowlands, the daughter of a prominent Kingston family. The two had met while Leonard was at RMC. They were married in Kingston: he was twenty-nine; she was twenty-eight. Their marriage would last for the rest of his life, and in these early years she dutifully travelled with Leonard as he worked on location in central Canada.[11]

In 1892 Leonard's career reached a new plateau – he was hired by the Canadian Hydro-Electric Power Company to be the chief engineer overseeing the construction of a hydro-electric facility at Niagara Falls, Ontario. These were early days in the development of electrical power and this was the most ambitious and logistically difficult project that had been undertaken to that time. It was a major opportunity for the young Leonard, and when the Falls project had been completed Leonard was in demand elsewhere in Ontario. Over the next thirteen years he was engaged in a host of other major works: railway construction in eastern Ontario (the St Lawrence and Adirondack and the Montreal and Ottawa Short Line (1895–9)); iron and nickel development in the Sudbury and Michipicoten districts (1899–90); and hydro-electric plants at DeCew Falls near St Catharines (1902–4), and at the Kakabeka Falls at the top of Lake Superior (1905–6). An emerging authority in those sectors of civil engineering (railways and power), he occasionally presented technical papers on topics related to his work.[12]

Throughout these years Leonard maintained his interest in the military. In 1888 he accepted a position on the management committee at the RMC, and in 1893 was elected president of the Ex-Cadet Club. Occasionally, he delivered papers at the college on subjects such as the principal railway systems in Canada,[13] the railway and shipping industries,[14] and something called the 'gig infantry,' a sulky-like vehicle that Leonard had invented as a cost-efficient and tactically effective means of mobilizing infantry in battle.[15]

More significant, in 1904 Leonard joined the newly formed Canadian Corps of Guides, a small unit that fell under the aegis of the intelligence department of Militia Headquarters in Ottawa. The corps had two main functions. In times of war, it was to provide messengers, cartographers, and scouts who would furnish tactical and operational intelligence in support of the troops in the field. This might include, for instance, patrolling lines of approach and undertaking reconnaissance. In times of peace, its main responsibility was to collect data on Canada's military resources as well as those of foreign powers. In this capacity, it was principally responsible for providing the Canadian military with intelligence designed to assist in the defence of Canadian soil. Among the foreign powers within its purview was the United States.[16] The Corps of Guides was ideally suited to Leonard. Like the gig infantry, the work of the corps involved a synergy of his interests. The corps sought officers who had training in surveying and civil engineering; Leonard was such a person. The regiments were to be mounted; Leonard was an accomplished equestrian. And while RMC graduates who had joined the corps were generally thought of as lax,[17] this was probably untrue of R.W. Leonard. He served as a member of the Corps of Guides militia unit for over twenty years and rose through the ranks: captain (1904); major (1911); lieutenant-colonel (1915). He was a lieutenant-colonel on reserve from 1921 to 1925, when he retired with the rank of colonel.

LEONARD THE MILLIONAIRE

By 1904 Captain Leonard was an established and respected engineer for whom life must have seemed sublime. Yet this was to be just a prelude to the saga of R.W. Leonard the millionaire and philanthropist. The fortune that Reuben Leonard would shortly acquire, and that would indelibly mark his life, was not derived directly from his professional expertise. He earned a comfortable but not spectacular income as an engineer, and his gig infantry, for all of its touted virtues, was never put into production. Instead, he made his money through prospecting and mineral development in northern Ontario. The story is somewhat legendary; indeed, the tale can be found in published accounts of famous Canadian mine findings.[18]

By the turn of the century the mineral potential of the region near what is now Cobalt was becoming known. Some silver veins had been discovered accidentally during the building of the Temiskaming and Northern Ontario Railway in the spring of 1903, and before the end of that year three claims had been staked near the railway right-of-way. As early as 1897, Leonard had shown an interest in mineral prospecting,[19] and while working on location as an engineer he had begun grubstaking, that is, dispatching agents to regions that seemed promising with a view to sharing any claims that were found. After hearing of the silver discoveries in northern Ontario, Leonard decided to prospect there and in May 1904 he sent one Alex Longwell, a recent Queen's graduate, on the understanding that Longwell would receive a 25 per cent interest in whatever he could find on Leonard's behalf.

Longwell came to the Cobalt camp where, by chance, he made the acquaintance of William G. Trethewey, an experienced prospector. Trethewey had come to the region on the advice of Dr Milton Hersey, an assayist in Montreal who had examined sample ores from the 1903 discoveries. Trethewey's initial intention was to buy a property, but he found no one willing to sell and so began exploring the terrain. Within a few days he had made two strikes (known as J.B.6 and J.B.7), both of which were surprisingly close to an early and rather abundant staked site.

Various discovery protocols governed the ownership of such mining claims, and a dispute arose as to whether Trethewey had the best entitlement. On making the first find, he planted a post over the site of the discovery at J.B.7, wrote his name and licence number on it, and also placed a witness tree to mark the spot. Later that same day he made the discovery at J.B.6 and followed the same procedure. However, the practice also required that the discovery be witnessed. That evening he approached Dr Willet Miller (the provincial geologist) and his assistant to act as witnesses. This they agreed to do – provided it could wait until morning. When the party arrived at the site of J.B.6, another stake, purportedly planted the previous autumn, was found.

This 'other' claim was imperfectly marked and looked bogus. However, in face of this, Trethewey resolved that it would be prudent to obtain a ruling on the legitimacy of his discovery. Somebody here was trying to claim-jump, but it might not be entirely clear to the outside world who was first in time. Strapped for funds, and acting on the advice of Dr Miller, Trethewey approached Alex Longwell for assistance. Trethewey was prepared to give a half interest in J.B.6 in return for financial backing in the legal proceedings. Longwell in turn contacted his principal Reuben Wells Leonard for instructions. Satisfied that the claim had merit, Leonard agreed to the arrangement.

It was not until May of the following year that the matter was resolved in Trethewey's favour.[20] Nothing came of the competing claim; no one appeared in court to defend its legitimacy, and evidence presented at the hearing suggested that the putative staking had no validity. In accordance with the agreement, Leonard received a one-half interest in J.B.6. One-quarter of this (that is, a one-eighth interest) was transferred to Longwell. Trethewey gave a one-eighth interest to his brother, and an equivalent share to Dr Milton Hersey (for having proposed the Cobalt prospect in the first place). The brother's share was in turn purchased by Leonard, Longwell, and Hersey for $100,000 and shortly afterwards Trethewey sold his remaining interest in J.B.6 to the Leonard group.

The Trethewey discoveries sparked renewed interest in the Cobalt region, and with a further major strike in August 1906 a silver boom in the region was fully under way. It was one of the most important mineral finds east of the Rockies and by the end of 1906 over 250 companies had been established to search for or operate mines in the area.[21] As of

1910, over 90 per cent of Canada's silver was being supplied from this region, and this yield accounted for 13 per cent of the world supply.[22] Leonard was literally (and figuratively) in the centre of the action. Around the time of the discovery of J.B.6 and 7, a townsite was being surveyed. All of J.B.6 was within the 160 acres that was set aside initially for what was soon to be known as Cobalt Station (later Cobalt). In December 1905 the letters patent to the mines and minerals were granted and shortly afterwards some of the surface above J.B.6 was purchased by the Leonard consortium.

The veins of J.B.6 were rich (more so than those in J.B.7). Not only was there silver but also nickel, arsenic, and cobalt. A mining company was formed in 1906 under the name Coniagas Mines Ltd. The name, coined by Dr Miller, is an acronym composed of the chemical symbols for the four minerals: cobalt (co); nickel (ni); silver (ag); and arsenic (as). A prospectus was issued in the same year and shares in the company were offered. The capitalization was $4 million, derived from the issuance of 800,000 shares with a par value of $5.00 each. R.W. Leonard was the president and general manager of the newly formed company, and Milton Hersey was the vice-president. Alex Longwell also served on the Board of Directors.

Coniagas was a remarkably profitable small mine. In the first year of operation (1906), the company built the necessary facilities for full-scale mining operations, including an ore house, power house, concentrating mill, sleeping and dining camp for 120 workers, and four additional employee lodgings. In that year, the gross value of the ores shipped was reported to be $769,407.26. After the costs of the capital improvements were deducted, there remained a net profit of $624,762.22. Dividends totalling $360,000 were paid, leaving the rest as surplus. In the years that followed, until the First World War, the mine remained highly productive; each year Leonard's annual report to the shareholders spoke of a healthy, vibrant, well-managed company. About 125 workers were employed, many of whom were housed in quarters owned by the company.

In 1908 the Coniagas Reduction Company was formed. That operation, a wholly owned subsidiary of the Coniagas Mines, was established for the purpose of operating a smelting plant in Thorold, Ontario, located adjacent to the Welland Canal just south of St Catharines. The ores from Coniagas were shipped by rail from northern Ontario down to the Niagara peninsula. Ores from other sources were also treated at the smelting plant and, like the mine in Cobalt, it was a profitable venture. Leonard served as the president of Coniagas Reduction, Longwell as the vice-president. Hersey was on the Board of Directors, as was Francis J. Bishop, Leonard's brother-in-law. In 1910 a controlling interest in the Redlington Rock Drill Company was acquired to produce drills for use in the mines.

Reuben Leonard was a hard-nosed capitalist. He resented having to pay tax on the company's profits, and in 1907 he led a lobbying effort that in the end failed to prevent provincial reforms directed toward establishing mineral taxes.[23] He later launched a court appeal (without any greater success) against the assessment made by the town of Cobalt on the Coniagas Mines' earnings.[24] The company also brought an action in response to efforts by the town and nearby businesses to impede the company's surface operations. In 1907 Coniagas had begun trenching on Prospect Avenue in the centre of the townsite. Even before this, it had been using portions of the surface above J.B.6 as a right-of-way. When the surface owners blocked this access, Coniagas sued to establish its rights. The Ontario Court of Appeal validated the use of the right-of-way as a means of access to the J.B.6 subsurface, even though this would interfere with the rights of the other surface owners. However, legislation prevented the use of public streets in this way.[25] All of this earned Coniagas few friends in the community. At the end of 1909, the mayor of Cobalt complained to the electorate that Coniagas had 'tried to crush the town out of existence since its inception by legal suits in the courts; [and] appeals against paying its just rate of taxes.' In sum, claimed the mayor, 'in every way possible it has enroached [sic] on the streets of the town and has caused continual annoyance to the owners of the surface rights that happen to be over their property.'[26]

The head office for Coniagas was established not in Cobalt but 400 miles away in St Catharines. Having found themselves in money in the wake of the early mining successes, the Leonards decided to set up home there. They purchased seven acres of land in the centre of the city where they had built a spacious Tudor-style home. The house had magnificent panelled walls and (in later years) a small movie theatre. The grounds were replete with a domed conservatory, a gardener's house, and a large garage/stable. The estate was known as Springbank. The name was taken from the natural springs found on and near that site; a building called Springbank had been located on the property until it was destroyed by fire in 1903. Nearby was St Thomas' Anglican Church, which became the family's place of worship.

The family soon had a new member. The Leonards had no children of their own, and at the time of the Coniagas windfall they were both in their mid-forties. But they did want a family, someone to succeed to their wealth and to maintain the business. They spoke with Reuben's sister and brother-in-law, Edith and Francis Bishop of Brantford: would Leonard Bishop, their eldest son, wish to live with his uncle and aunt in St Catharines? When it became clear that the nephew preferred to stay with his parents, the same offer was made to his younger brother, Arthur. He was fond of the Leonards, and the thought of living in Springbank, where Uncle Reuben kept horses, appealed to him. So, at the age of twelve, Arthur Leonard Bishop came to live with his relatives. He was enrolled at Ridley, an Anglican finishing school for boys in St Catharines. Arthur boarded at Ridley during the week and spent the weekends at Springbank. After Ridley, he attended Royal Military College. During the summers he worked underground at Coniagas, serving as a general handyman and giving guided tours of the mines. In time, Arthur Bishop became heir to the Leonard fortune.

Only a few years after the find at Coniagas that fortune was already substantial. In 1909 the Montreal *Star* announced that eight Americans and seventeen Canadians had become millionaires from the silver mines of the Cobalt region. Trethewey, Hersey, Longwell, and Leonard were among those listed.[27] R.W. Leonard was becoming known as an able businessman; he accepted a directorship with the Toronto General Trusts Corporation. Although his days as a journeyman engineer were obviously at an end, Leonard maintained an interest in the profession for the rest of his life, serving on the executive of professional societies[28] and presenting papers on a range of engineering issues.[29] However, he was now, first and foremost, a captain of industry. Coniagas was his main professional concern.

It was during this watershed period that Leonard began devoting himself as never before to philanthropic causes. Liberated from the demanding work regimen that he had followed since leaving RMC, he dedicated his energy and skills to a variety of hand-picked causes. He gave part of his time to the church, serving on the board of trustees at St Thomas' (1908) and as the rector's warden (1909–11). In 1910 he was elected vice-president of the Canadian Society of Civil Engineers. Above all else, it was participation in the governance of educational institutions that seemed of greatest importance. By 1911 Leonard was on the Board of Governors of the University of Toronto, Ridley College, Wycliffe College (an evangelical institution affiliated with the university and closely connected with Ridley), and the Kingston School of Mining. In 1913 he was appointed a trustee of Queen's University.

Through his participation on the Board of Governors at the University of Toronto, Leonard became associated with a group known as the Round Table.[30] This organization was the brainchild of a man who was to have a profound influence on the rest of Leonard's life: Lionel George Curtis.[31] Both deserve elaboration.

There are probably few modern equivalents of the Round Table, though in its day it was merely one of a number of Edwardian study groups. (Others included the Royal Colonial Institute, the British Empire League, and the League of the Empire, all three of which Leonard joined.) The Round Table had devolved from the 'kindergarten,' a group of Oxford-educated young men, protégés of Lord Alfred Milner, who played an important role in creation of the Republic of South Africa following the Boer War.[32] In its inception, the Round Table was part reading and social club, part think-tank, part learned society. Whether by design or not, it developed the trappings of a lobby group. Soon after the London group was organized it began to publish a quarterly journal known as the *Round Table*. The purpose of the movement was to provide a forum for political debate among a select group of politically concerned citizens. In essence, this meant discussions about the future of the British Empire, conducted in an ostensibly erudite and urbane fashion by well-educated, well-heeled, well-placed gentlemen.

If Coniagas was the centre of his business life, and St Catharines and St Thomas' his secular and spiritual sanctuaries, the Round Table was the hub of Leonard's intellectual world. He served on the executive of the Canadian group with a number of prominent men. Over the course of his involvement the executive included Sir Robert Falconer, president of the University of Toronto, Sir Edmund Walker, president of the Canadian Bank of Commerce and long-time chairman of the Board of Governors of the University of Toronto, the financier Arthur Glazebrook, the historian George Wrong, Sir Joseph Flavelle and Sir John Willison, publisher and editor of the Toronto *News*, respectively, and Vincent Massey, who was then a young academic at the University of Toronto.[33]

Lionel Curtis, an intense and charismatic individual, became known to all of these men. He was the sort of person who throughout his life worked furtively behind the scenes of important political events (such as the Paris Peace Conference and the establishment of Irish and Indian home rule). In later years he became a lecturer at Oxford on colonial history and was elected a fellow of All Souls College. A man with a powerful intelligence, he crafted grand visions for constitutional reform. In his early years reform of the British Empire was his goal; in later years he was consumed with even broader international questions. The visionary nature of his writing and the zeal with which he sought to convert others to the new orders that he foresaw earned him the moniker 'The Prophet.'[34]

Even prior to the First World War, Curtis had become deeply concerned about the future of the British Empire, perceiving a conflict between the emerging independence of the dominions and the continuation of a strong and united empire. He saw some form of imperial federation as the key to preventing a balkanization of the Empire. Once the London group had been established, Curtis made a series of proselytizing missions to Canada, New Zealand, Australia and South Africa and succeeded in forming a following for the Round Table in all four. The Canadians were quite receptive. By the end of 1914, there were thirty-five chapters across the country, and about 300 members (though these numbers dwindled considerably during the war). In 1910 a list of potential Canadian subscribers to the Round Table was assembled; Leonard was among those canvassed. As with the London group, the dominion-based Round Tables found themselves immersed in issues revolving around the idea of imperial federation that Curtis had staked out assertively as the sole means of preserving the British Empire. Although the Round Table was supposedly not wedded to a particular position on the pressing issues of the day, Curtis's notion of organic imperial union cast a long shadow over the meetings and his writings on the subject were carefully scrutinized. The basic idea found favour, given that the group tended to attract those who, from the start, were partial to the concept of a strong and united Empire: people like Reuben Leonard.

In 1911 Leonard, the erstwhile teacher, engineer, inventor, author, militia officer, entrepreneur, and student of imperial politics, began a three-year stint as a senior civil servant. In the fall of that year, Prime Minister Borden had asked Leonard to accept the post of chairman of the National Transcontinental Railway Commission (NTRC). This he agreed to do, expressing the desire to serve without pay.[35] The commission's function was to oversee the construction of a portion of a new transcontinental railway line (from Moncton to Winnipeg) under an agreement that had been entered into in 1903 between the Sir Wilfrid Laurier's Liberal government and the Grand Trunk Railway. The line was then to be leased to the newly formed Grand Trunk Pacific for a period of fifty years.

This was to be the last major initiative in the construction of Canada's railway infrastructure, and it had been an important component of the

Liberals' railway policy. However, by 1911 the initial plan was faltering. The construction of the Transcontinental had been plagued by graft and incompetence virtually from the outset. Borden's victory in the election of that year meant, of course, that he had inherited Laurier's railway problems.[36] During the final years of the Laurier government, Borden had criticized the Liberals' use of patronage,[37] and the appointment of Leonard's predecessor on the commission, S.-N. Parent, was a case in point. He was a former premier of Quebec who had no technical knowledge of railway construction. Leonard's appointment, made on the heels of the election, allowed Borden to show that the Conservatives were serious about putting qualified personnel in charge of the project. Parent resigned from the commission, but three Laurier appointees remained on the board. In January 1912 the number of commissioners was reduced from four to one, leaving Leonard solely in charge of the project.

Generally speaking, Leonard's appointment was viewed as a sensible and politically astute move. A royal commission struck in 1912 to review the operations prior to October 1911 complained that until the appointment of Major Leonard no member of the commission had any expertise in railway construction or operation.[38] However, the Liberals in Quebec had a different response. Concerned about the declining influence of Quebec in Ottawa following the defeat of Laurier, they asked: 'Why are we losing influence everywhere? Why is the business of the Transcontinental taken to Toronto instead of Quebec? Why was Mr. Parent replaced by Major Leonard?'[39]

Leonard was a 'very energetic and aggressive Chairman,'[40] and over the course of his tenure he was called upon to take a hard stance against both the railway company and the government. He was determined that both should fulfil their contractual obligations to the letter. In one incident, he challenged the government's position on the construction of terminals in Quebec.[41] In another, he reacted sharply in the face of evidence that Grand Trunk was refusing to lease completed portions of the line, as had been agreed.[42] This was a significant moment, because the attempt to resile from the lease obligations – which Leonard was able to prevent – raised concerns in Borden's mind as to whether the Grand Trunk Pacific would be able to run the completed line as a financially viable concern. A decade later it was known that it could not. However, these problems were the exception, not the rule; under the reconstituted NRTC, the line was being built, section-by-section, essentially on time and within budget.

By 1913 Leonard was heavily committed. There was the business of Coniagas and the NRTC, the college and university boards, the Corps of Guides,[43] and his responsibilities on the executive of the Canadian Round Table. He had demonstrated an extraordinary commitment to philanthropy, though to this point it had mainly involved personal service. Apart from a few exceptions, [44] his charitable giving took the form of volunteer work, whether in the aid of education, the church, or, indeed, the government of Canada. All the while, Kate Leonard was similarly engaged, working with such groups as the Victorian Order of Nurses, the Imperial Order Daughters of the Empire, and the St Catharines YWCA (which she helped to found).

Leonard's first attempt to provide a significant financial benefaction went terribly wrong. In late 1913 he offered to provide Queen's University with the monies needed to build a hall of residence to house about 200 men. For the purpose of doing so, he had acquired a six-acre tract of land on the shores of Lake Ontario, adjacent to the campus. It was a tempting offer. There were no student residences at the university at that time, and the growth of the student population was not being met by an increase in affordable private lodgings in Kingston. However, Leonard's plans for the new facility involved more than accommodations: his idea was to endow a military residence on the campus. The goal was to create a program in which the benefits of military training (à la RMC) could be combined with the broadly based education that Queen's could offer. In Leonard's vision, the program and accommodations were designed to prepare Canadian forces to aid in the defence of the British Empire should the need arise.

The initial proposal contained these elements. First, students living in the residence had to be members of the Canadian Officers Training Corps (COTC). To be able to continue in the housing, residents were expected to become 'efficient members' of the COTC after one year. Second, the students would be required to pay board to cover the costs of servants, heating, fuel, maintenance, and so on. Third, places were to be distributed as equally as possible among the different classes and faculties. Fourth, students would be required to perform at least six hours of training per week and attend both lectures on military subjects and an annual training camp. Fifth, the rules of conduct within the residence would be established and administered by an appointed governing board. Finally, it appears that the original plan was that the board was to consist of the principal of the university, the commanding officer in the military district in which the university was situated, and the commandant of the RMC. They were to be duty-bound to administer the residence at all times in accordance with the spirit of the gift.[45]

It was well appreciated that the gift was substantial, being worth somewhere between $500,000 and $600,000 in 1913 dollars. Moreover, the Department of Militia promised to supplement the Leonard donation with a drill hall and armouries on the site. Financial matters aside, there were those who endorsed the objectives that Leonard had in mind. The Montreal *Gazette's* endorsement of the Leonard gift was unequivocal.[46] However, concern was expressed that allowing a donor such a measure of control could set a precedent that the university might later regret. An editorial in the Kingston *Standard* guardedly asked whether the gift would introduce an element of militarism into the university. At the same time, it was said that Leonard's gift would provide a vehicle for 'superb' physical training, as well as much-needed student housing.[47]

In January 1914 the proposal was debated at a meeting of the Board of Trustees. It was decided that it could not be accepted as then conceived. The main stumbling block was not the effect that the plan would have on matters of curriculum; it was instead the composition of the hall's board of governors. The facility was to become part of the university, and so it was felt necessary that the governing body be comprised of a majority of university delegates. A second plan was prepared by Leonard. By letter dated 10 March 1914, he proposed the creation of a board comprised of five people: the principal, one representative each from the Militia Department, the trustees, and the Senate, plus Leonard or his designate. However, he had a change of heart, and on 18 March he wrote to the principal of Queen's, Daniel Gordon: 'I have been thinking over this matter ... and I really can not see any good reason for the objection which some of your people take to the Commandant of the Royal Military College being on the Board.'[48] Hence, he proposed that the commandant of RMC pro tem be added to the complement.

The proposal, including the six-person board, proceeded through the university's governance structure, and at each stage opinion was divided as to whether it should be accepted. Within arts, the largest faculty, a majority of the faculty was opposed to the plan, but it received the endorsement of the faculties of medicine and education as well as the Kingston School of Mining (of which Leonard was a governor). The lack of university control remained the main problem. The principal wrote to Leonard to explain this concern, and a committee was created to work with Leonard on a mutually suitable arrangement. Leonard refused to budge, arguing, among other things, that he should be regarded as representing the interests of Queen's, thus giving the university a majority. The Board of Trustees unanimously supported Gordon's position; it was prepared to accept the five-member board. That decision effectively killed the proposal; in May 1914 Leonard's offer was formally and absolutely withdrawn.

Divisiveness and hard feelings among the faculty at Queen's were the main by-products of this episode. Some faculty members were openly opposed to the entire scheme; others within the university resented the principal's response. For his part, Leonard felt that his generosity had not been appreciated. A brief story in the Toronto *News*[49] brought the friction at Queen's out into the open, much to Gordon's dismay. But the matter did not end there. After the war broke out in August, some members of the faculty scurried to have the matter of the donation reopened. Spearheading this initiative was James Cappon, the dean of arts, who shared Leonard's imperialist leanings and endorsed the proposed scheme. Moreover, Cappon was fearful that Leonard would establish this project, and confer future benefactions, elsewhere. He proposed an interim solution under which the principal and Leonard would share control over the hall until a more permanent arrangement could be devised. Meetings were held with Leonard aimed at effecting a reconciliation. However well-intentioned, these second thoughts served mainly to revive the animosity that had been aroused the first time around. Leonard had lost interest in the idea and seemed to resent having to rehash the matter. Moreover, an inherent problem had been that no endowment for upkeep had been contemplated, and an application for a special grant from the Department of Militia to cover the ongoing costs of operation was denied. As a sop to Leonard, he was offered a position on the Board of Trustees of the university to represent the benefactors; this olive branch was accepted.[50] One last salvo was fired by Dean Cappon. When it became clear that his efforts to reinstate the plan had failed, he wrote to Principal Gordon accusing certain faculty members (the historian O.D. Skelton and the registrar, George Chown, were singled out) of conspiring to sabotage the project from the outset.[51]

Leonard's plans for Queen's were in shambles, but his principal day-to-day concerns, Coniagas and the building of the transcontinental railway line, were both proceeding well. In mid-1914, with the railway works almost complete, legislation had been introduced that transferred increased control to the minister of railways and canals. Leonard saw this as an opportunity to step down and he wrote to the minister, Frank Cochrane, asking to be relieved of his duties at the earliest convenient time.⁵² His hope was to be able to leave for British Columbia in early July to attend to a pressing business matter.⁵³ The nature of this matter and its overall significance to Leonard is not known. In any event, Leonard's request was met and Borden wrote in late June to express his great appreciation for the conscientious job Leonard had performed.⁵⁴ By the end of July, personal affairs and railway construction were overtaken by other concerns. Germany had invaded Belgium, and when Britain's ultimatum for a German withdrawal expired on 4 August, the British Empire, including Canada, was formally in a state of war with the German and Austro-Hungarian empires.

At fifty-four years of age, extensive service for Leonard, even as an officer, was a dubious proposition. He did spend several months in Europe in 1915. However, most of the period from late 1914 to 1918 was devoted to helping the war effort at home. He sat on the executive of the Canadian Patriotic Fund, the Canadian Red Cross, the St Catharines General and Marine Hospital, and he was the chairman of the Lincoln County Victory Loan Campaign. He was a member of the advisory board of Khaki University, which had been formed to provide distance learning for soldiers while in the service. A scholarship was established to assist, among others, the children of returning soldiers. Over a four-year period, Leonard gave an untold amount of money to help the war effort.⁵⁵

Leonard also continued to serve as a member of the Corps of Guides, and in 1915 he was promoted to the rank of lieutenant-colonel in the No. 2 Cyclist Company. The Corps was not mobilized for duty in Europe during the war, though many of its number served in other corps or regiments. Various surveillance duties were carried out within Canada. For example, the corps monitored labour groups that were perceived to be radical. Union-organizing efforts attracted the attention of the corps in places such as Vancouver, Sault Ste Marie, Winnipeg, and Cobalt.⁵⁶ Leonard assisted in this latter regard, advising his superiors that the Cobalt miners' union consisted mainly of aliens: Finns, Poles, Austrians, and Hungarians.⁵⁷ However, his main responsibility with the corps was the monitoring of anti-British activities within the United States.

Even from his perch as a member of the Board of Governors at the University of Toronto, Colonel Leonard saw a role for himself in aid of the war effort. He tried unsuccessfully to have undergraduate dormitories set aside for use by the officers training corps and he pressed the university to provide financial assistance to the families of faculty and staff members of the university wishing to enlist. Ever vigilant for anti-war sentiment, Leonard was indignant about a story that appeared in the

Toronto *Star* in October 1914. The brief article contained comments by Dr Platon Reich, a sessional lecturer in German at Trinity College, questioning the way in which the press and popular opinion had blamed Germany alone for the outbreak of war.[58] Such a viewpoint, published just weeks after fighting had begun, proved incendiary. Shortly after the article appeared, Leonard received a letter from an acquaintance, Colonel John Campbell, who described Reich as an agent of 'William the Bloodstained' being harboured by the University of Toronto.[59]

Leonard attempted to use his influence as a governor to prompt action by the president of the university, Robert Falconer. 'This is not the time for such discussions and the liberties of any men who are inclined that way should be curtailed,' he wrote to Falconer.[60] The president attempted to placate Leonard and Campbell: German faculty members had been advised to keep their own counsel about the war.[61] However, beyond this, nothing more could be done at least in this instance. The constitution of the university did not confer jurisdiction on the president over the faculty at Trinity. Falconer's hands being tied, he was able to avoid acting more directly on the complaint.[62]

Throughout the war years Leonard continued to participate in the Canadian Round Table movement, though in the first years of fighting it met irregularly. In 1916, following the release of Lionel Curtis's controversial plan for imperial reform (*The Problem of the Commonwealth*),[63] Curtis came to Canada to plan strategy with the Canadian executive and to preach the Round Table gospel in an effort to establish new study groups across the country. As the sojourn drew to a close, Leonard offered an annual donation to the Round Table of $1,000; this was much needed and gratefully accepted.[64] Though his support of the Round Table cause was reaffirmed by Curtis's efforts, Leonard felt that more could be done on the Canadian scene:

I hope that this coming winter we will be able to renew the work of the Round Table group, which we formed before the war, but which for various reasons has not met regularly. Every man is now so busy it is difficult to get them to meet regularly, although the War has given a very greatly added interest to all such matters, and I think, generally, the movement of the Round Table is gathering momentum at the moment. I regret that our central group in Toronto is not taking the matter up as energetically or as systematically as, in my opinion, should be done, as there appears to be a tendency to adhere to ... academic study rather than to launch out into an energetic campaign; but I hope that this may be changed shortly.[65]

While the Round Table pondered questions about the future of the British Empire, and sporadically at that, Leonard was engaged with the here and now, that is, with those political issues in Canada concerning the war. He became convinced that it was necessary for a wartime coalition government to be formed. In December 1916 he wrote a letter to the six Toronto newspapers pressing his case. A non-partisan government, he claimed, was necessary for several reasons: to avoid an election which (Leonard asserted) Canadians did not want; to encourage enlistment; and to reduce tensions (concerning conscription) between Quebec and the rest of Canada. He feared that an election 'would embitter a racial quarrel with Quebec which has already gone too far.'[66]

Earlier in 1916, Leonard had joined the national executive of the Win-the-War movement, a pressure group that sought to rally support for Canada's war effort[67] and that favoured conscription and the formation of a union government. At the Win-the-War convention held in early August of 1917, about 800 delegates unanimously passed a resolution, moved by Leonard, calling for a national non-partisan government made up of those who were prepared to engage in a vigorous prosecution of the war[68] and a further extension of the term of Parliament.

A delegation was sent to present the resolution to Borden, who regarded the group as well-meaning but politically naive.[69] Borden did, of course, fully appreciate the value of securing a coalition and by the fall he had adroitly finessed Laurier's rebuff by enlisting the support of Liberal backbenchers and others. Leonard sent a letter to Borden the next day: 'Allow me to congratulate you on your magnificent success in forming a Win this War Cabinet. You have accomplished one of the greatest steps that Canada has yet taken towards good government. Along with most (I think) of the business men of Canada I had begun to despair of our representatives ever emerging from the fog of false issues of petty party politics floating over the slime of party patronage and graft.'[70]

Work at Coniagas continued throughout the war, though operations were affected in a number of ways. By 1914 the company had a payroll of about 150 employees and had issued more than $5 million in dividends. The Coniagas Reduction Company, with a work force of almost 140, was also turning a profit (though the Redlington Rock Drill Company was not). During the first two years of the war, profits from the mining operations dropped. The mine produced cobalt, nickel, arsenic, and silver. Cobalt and nickel came into heavier than normal demand (for use in the production of steel), and arsenic held its pre-war price.

But silver was overwhelmingly the main ore yielded and by far the principal source of revenue for Coniagas. Its main uses being for luxury items, or at least non-necessaries, demand fell in Europe, Canada, and elsewhere. The price of silver, which was 60.55 cents in 1912–13, dipped to 56.75 cents in 1914 and 49.25 cents in 1915. This state of affairs improved in the final years of the war. In 1917 the price approached 80 cents, though this dramatic rise was partially offset by reduced production and increased labour costs.

By 1915 almost one-third of the Coniagas workforce had volunteered for military service; as of 1917 one-half had enlisted. Some joined the British forces, but a substantial number of the miners were of Italian origin and so joined the Italian service. The company undertook to give priority in hiring to those returning from the war, and allowances were provided to the families of married men serving overseas. Many of those who remained pitched in with the wholehearted encouragement and support of the management. The recreation room on the company premises was converted into a Red Cross work room, where socks, bandages, and dressings were prepared by workers and their wives and packed in boxes made by the men from lumber supplied by Coniagas. Donations for the Red Cross and the Canadian Patriotic Fund were collected. Leonard made his position on the war well known to his staff. In late December 1916 each worker was given a Christmas present along with a circular containing this message:[71]

IN THESE TIMES

A PATRIOTIC MAN WILL ENLIST if he is of service age and physically fit, unless he is doing more valuable work for his country in civil life.

A PATRIOTIC WOMAN will work on munitions, or at any suitable employment that shall enable a man to enlist, unless her health or household duties prevent.

OF THOSE WHO DO NOT ENLIST, a PATRIOT will be INDUSTRIOUS and FRUGAL, endeavouring to keep up the Nation's output despite the shortage of labour.

HE, or SHE, will save every cent and invest in War Loans, even the smallest savings, and this will help win this war.

A SLACKER will shirk his work, idle his time, and spend his earnings in enjoyments, motor cars, musical instruments, and various extravagant luxuries. The purchase of such luxuries is particularly unpatriotic if they are imported from other countries, payment for which demands the sending out of money (export of gold), from this country.

A SLACKER, A SHIRKER, an IDLE PERSON, or an EXTRAVAGANT CORPORATION IS A FRIEND OF GERMANY.
IN THESE TIMES you can help win this war and make 1917 the YEAR OF VICTORY.

R.W. Leonard, President

During the war years, the company's annual reports contained an honour roll that listed the names of the Coniagas men who were in the service, along with their rank and deployment. Among the more than eighty soldiers on the roll in the report for 1915 was Arthur Leonard Bishop, a lieutenant in the 2nd Middlesex Regiment, who was listed as having been wounded in action. He had been severely injured on the right side of his head in May 1915, at Fromelles in France. He would survive, and, after an extensive period of convalescence, Bishop returned to active duty. By the end of the war he had received decorations from the Canadian, English, French, and Serbian governments for his service.

Reuben Leonard, the businessman, was involved in the war in other ways. He was a shareholder in several concerns engaged in the production of war provisions. In the face of early reports concerning the lack of munitions in England, he had become part of a syndicate of businessmen that had sought (unsuccessfully) to develop a Canadian plant for the purpose of producing shells: 'Our object was not to make money but to do a public service for the Empire and employ idle men.'[72] That being his perspective, Leonard was incensed by a statement purportedly made by the minister of militia, General Sam Hughes, to the effect that Canadian firms, initially reticent to provide munitions, had become interested in doing so only once it had become apparent that there was money to be made.[73] Leonard wrote to Borden explaining his objections and offering his view that 'if it is General Hughes' wish to check the supply of munitions I cannot see any more efficient method than by publishing such an interview.'[74] Likewise, when a controversy arose relating to the smelting of Canadian nickel in the United States, Leonard assumed the role of advocate on behalf of Canadian industry.[75] It is hard to know if this was merely a self-interested posture. Leonard had been involved in war industries and in 1918 founded a steel production business in Welland, Ontario (Electric Steel and Engineering), so he stood to gain from the growth in domestic steel production. At the same time, he had provided backing to a firm (British-American Shipbuilding) which was under contract to provide cargo and warships to the British government. Leonard lost his entire investment, a risk that he had appreciated at the time of the loan and that he had been prepared to run for the sake of the cause.

Following the armistice, Leonard received two military honours for his wartime efforts: the Colonial Auxiliary Forces Officers' Decoration and the Volunteers' Decoration. He continued as chairman of the Lincoln County Victory Loan Campaign and was appointed to the Canadian Battlefields Memorials Commission, which had been established to oversee the design and construction of the memorials in Europe for Canadian soldiers. Turning his attention to civilian matters, he assumed the presidency of the Engineering Institute of Canada, visiting member branches across the country during his year-long term. In the previous year he had established the Leonard Medal, which was awarded by the institute for scholarly papers on mining subjects. He purchased a three-storey Victorian home in St Catharines which was donated to St Thomas' for use as the Grace Mission. In addition, he became a director of the Western Canadian Colonization Association and a member of the board of the Canadian National Institute for the Blind. Reuben Leonard was, in short, as busy with philanthropic work as he had ever been.

The relative calm that followed the end of the war was disrupted, however, by a serious labour dispute involving Coniagas and the other Cobalt mines. Some forty veterans had returned to the company fold; in short order they had become 'among our most loyal and efficient employees.'[76] Even so, in the summer of 1919 labour relations reached low ebb. A miners' strike brought all production in Cobalt to a standstill from late June until early September; 2,500 workers had walked off the job. The strike was one of a host of industrial disputes that erupted in North America and Europe after the end of the war (the Winnipeg General Strike being the most significant Canadian incident). In Cobalt the workers were seeking a stable base wage, stipulated conditions for the awarding of bonuses, and the setting of boarding rates. However, the central issue in Cobalt was the recognition of the miners' union, the International Mine, Mill and Smelter Workers Union, a Denver-based organization affiliated with the American Federation of Labor. Though the union had been active in the area since 1907, it had never been recognized by the mining firms. There had never been a collective agreement.

Over the years, President Leonard's annual report to the shareholders had typically contained a bouquet for the company's employees. Satisfactory relations with the staff and their loyal service to Coniagas were routinely acknowledged. Yet in 1907 the Western Federation of Miners (which was at that time associated with the International Workers of the World, or Wobblies) succeeded in organizing a strike at Coniagas. Operations were suspended for two weeks, and output was decreased for a further month before the workers were replaced.[77] Likewise, a three-day strike in early 1914 led to the dismissal of about thirty workers, with the remainder 'gladly returning to work on the old terms.'[78] Two years earlier, there had been labour disturbances resulting in violence in the Cobalt and Porcupine camps over attempts to introduce an eight-hour work day. Leonard warned that increased labour costs brought about by such a development would lead, in the end, to a closing of the mine much earlier 'than if the employees were left free to contract with the employers to work as many hours as they please.'[79]

Even if it was true that labour relations had been stable in the past (which is by no means clear), there was no question that by 1919 they were in a fragile state. Overlooking the fact that work stoppages were a nation-wide phenomenon, Leonard accused the Presbyterian, Methodist, and Baptist clergy in the region – men he saw as ill-informed about business matters and themselves underpaid – of precipitating worker unrest.[80]

The strike lasted for seven rancorous weeks. Negotiations were carried on at one level, while red-baiting,[81] racism,[82] claims of outside agitation, and threats of violence operated at another. A group of war veterans was assembled to help bring about a resolution, but it failed in this mission. The Temiskaming Mine Managers' Association, representing the companies, held strong as support for the strike among the miners began to flag. In early September the union executive elected to accept the terms then on the table. The mine managers would recommend to their respective directors an increase in the base wage. There was no improvement on the matter of hours of work or on boarding rates. As to the fate of organized labour in the region, it was proposed that an employees' council be constituted with representatives from each mine. The union had been fended off, though a form of collective bargaining had been recognized. Once the mines were pumped and drained, work was resumed, but some of the mines, near depletion before the strike, were not reopened. Coniagas was one of the first back in operation.

The Cobalt strike set the stage for another Leonard tirade at the University of Toronto.[83] This time the object of his ire was the sociologist Robert MacIver.[84] Educated at Edinburgh and Oxford, MacIver had come to the department of political economy at Toronto from the University of Aberdeen in 1916, and President Falconer, among others at Toronto, considered him to be a first-class scholar. MacIver's political ideology comported with that of some of his colleagues in the department but was not favourably received in other precincts. His calls for the creation of a new social order founded on principles of civic cooperation were decoded by members of the Toronto establishment as a form of socialist dogma, a characterization that was not entirely fair. In the wake of the Bolshevik Revolution and the Winnipeg General Strike of 1919, MacIver's conception of a moral society was threatening to Toronto's business establishment. He garnered his share of press and became widely known for his participation in various labour causes in Toronto.

In contrast, Reuben Wells Leonard believed in free enterprise. While he was prepared to admit that there was a place for organized labour, his opposition to the unionization of miners at Coniagas was unwavering. At the same time, Coniagas was a leading player in the Temiskaming Mines Managers' Association, which had been able to develop a cartel-like alliance that proved too powerful for the union. Leonard was critical of social-welfare measures such as old age pensions and unemployment insurance. He was also opposed to the public ownership of Ontario's power system. Yet he supported state aid for private enterprise (such as the Grand Trunk Pacific project). His schooling in labour relations had been acquired mainly through his experiences at Coniagas. Although, as we have seen, the company's annual reports exuded a sense of respect for the workforce, he had on other occasions offered less generous appraisals. In an address published in 1920 the idea of employee profit-sharing was discounted because, among other things, '[a] great part of what is termed 'common labour' in this country does not understand our language, our laws or our business methods, beyond the signing of a name or marking of a cross on the pay-roll at regular intervals; and the meaning of a stock certificate would be utterly beyond their comprehension.'[85]

Leonard criticized what he saw as the tendency of organized labour to receive the protection of special-interest legislation. The importance of labour and capital to society was not equal. While a given worker assumed personal and familial responsibilities, this could not be treated as equivalent to the contributions and obligations of the owner of the enterprise, upon whose shoulders rested the fortunes of every one of those workers and their families. Moreover, Leonard was convinced that the cause of labour unrest could be located in the provocative actions of union leaders, who concocted problems as a means of securing their own positions.[86] And while he was prepared to accept in principle that gains had been achieved for workers through collective action, he felt that matters had progressed too far, with the result that 'the power of the unions is being exercised unwisely and selfishly.'[87]

These views mixed with the pro-labour writings of Robert MacIver like oil with water (or fire). In January, 1921 Leonard wrote to Edmund Walker, chairman of the Board of Governors at the univerity, to express his concerns about the professor. The letter, depicting MacIver as an agitator who posed a serious threat to the university, was forwarded to President Falconer. On this occasion, it was not as easy for the president to side-step Leonard in the way he had at the time of the Reich complaint. Falconer was utterly unwilling to bridle MacIver, a stance that Walker supported without equivocation. Still, Leonard had to be contended with, somehow. The president's concern was, of course, the danger that academic freedom would be undermined by taking action; or, more to the point, that any attempt to sanction or stifle Professor MacIver would almost certainly fail, with the likely result being that the reputation of the university or Falconer, probably both, would be tarnished in the process. By this time, Falconer had known Leonard for about a decade, through the Toronto Round Table group and the Board of Governors at the university. He thought that he knew how best to appeal to the colonel's better judgment. A letter was written to Leonard. In it, Falconer suggested that the genius of the British people had been enhanced and nourished through discussion. He added that, in his view, the most treasured privilege in the academic world was freedom of thought.[88]

This drew a speedy, angry reply. As Colonel Leonard saw things, 'nearly all our labour and socialistic troubles are fomented by self-appointed leaders from Wales, Cornwall, Scotland and the North of England.' As to the right of free speech: 'If we are to encourage in the University the teaching of one line of extreme, unusual or dangerous doctrine, why not encourage others, such as anti-vaccination, etc. ... or now that Mrs. Besant has played out in India we might bring her over here, or Lenine when Russia should get tired of him.'[89]

As these events were unfolding, Falconer spoke with Professor MacIver to advise him of Leonard's crusade. The president requested and received a short synopsis of MacIver's basic theories in the hope of being able to respond effectively to any further attacks from Leonard.[90] It turned out to be a sensible but ultimately unsuccessful tactic. After reading MacIver's *Labour in the Changing World*,[91] Leonard went on the offensive again. The book has a certain radical tone: the introductory chapter warns that, unless the present warfare between labour and capital is met with changes that improve the conditions of workers, the result will surely be revolution.[92] At the same time, MacIver's reform agenda was surprisingly tame, especially set alongside the events in Russia and the labour unrest occurring throughout North America. The book concludes with several practical proposals, which include maximum working hours, minimum age laws, wage guarantees, occupational health and safety regulations, and so on.[93] Nevertheless, Leonard was furious that MacIver enjoyed free rein within the university, where young students could be so easily influenced and misled. Let the university do the honest thing and appoint MacIver to the 'Chair of Political Anarchy and Social Chaos' was his sarcastic advice to the president.[94]

Falconer, having read the book and armed with MacIver's memo, tried to appease Leonard. He wrote a detailed reply in which he suggested that the political economist was not the extremist that Leonard envisioned but rather a moderate thinker whose work had come under attack from Marxist scholars. In a subtle way, he suggested that Leonard (like himself) might lack the necessary expertise to assess MacIver's theories.[95] In an effort to enlist support, Leonard sought out Edmund Walker and Canon Henry Cody, writing similar letters to both. 'Political economy should be based on actual facts and not on fancy,' he told them. MacIver typified the ethereal scholar locked safely in an ivory tower: 'It is a pity that the seething brain waves of these academic thinkers could not be tempered with some practical knowledge of human nature.' And he complained of the scope that the University of Toronto was giving to 'Marxians and other cranks and lunatics.'[96]

Taking the high road, President Falconer's response to the controversy came in the form of an address on the subject of academic freedom, delivered at Convocation Hall on Valentine's Day, 1922. The paper was a well-crafted exposition on the origins, rationale, and limitations of freedom of expression in academia. The only tangible allusion to the Leonard-MacIver ordeal was the suggestion that those involved in university governance should appreciate the value of a diversity of perspectives. The press coverage tended to stress the limits that should be imposed on participation of faculty members in partisan politics,[97] but this account did not reflect Falconer's efforts to champion the cause of academic freedom.

As for Colonel Leonard, he was not in attendance. On the evening of the lecture he and his wife were in Halifax preparing to sail the next day for the British West Indies as part of a trade mission organized by the Canadian Manufacturers' Association. Leonard and more than a dozen other captains of industry were hoping to take advantage of a new preferential trade arrangement that had been entered into with some of the Caribbean dependencies.[98] On his return in late April he wrote to Falconer about the speech, after having read a published version. It was a fair treatment of the issues, he conceded. In general, the inference he drew was the necessity for considerable caution in the selection of professors. Moreover, Leonard cautioned that faculty members should appreciate that they are not 'omniscient' and so ought to be careful about expressing views, whether in the classroom or in print, that were based on unsound foundations.[99]

Walker had hoped that Colonel Leonard would take the Falconer speech to heart,[100] but he never did relent. Perhaps MacIver was not a threat to the social order, but Leonard was nevertheless doubtful of the professor's competence. When MacIver was appointed head of the department of political economy in 1923, it was in the face of Leonard's objections. When Leonard provided the university with his annual $500 donation he suggested that it be used to help fund a 'Chair in Common Sense' which could be used 'to counteract such nonsense as I have read in MacIver's books.'[101] His tonic for MacIver was a dose of reality about employer/employee relations: 'I seriously think that before a man is qualified to take a position as Professor of Political Economy he should previously have had at least two years of such training as he would get as owner or lessee of a Canadian farm or partner in some manufacturing business where he would be dependent, to some extent, upon hired labour. This would give him actual knowledge of the mental attitude and intellectual possibilities of the different classes of humanity which he could not acquire in a lifetime through the reading of academic books written by men of his same type.'[102]

It seems that the world Leonard found in the aftermath of the war was not much to his liking. The Cobalt strike and the writings of MacIver represented the emergence of a troubling form of militancy. However, that Leonard should have responded as he did to Robert MacIver is not surprising. More revealing, perhaps, is that he was becoming increasingly dispirited with the post-war policies of Prime Minister Borden. He had supported Borden on Union government and worked diligently for him on the NTRC. Now, however, he was dubious about the approach being taken concerning Canadian foreign affairs. The decision to establish a separate Canadian embassy in Washington (a first) was criticized on the ground that it would in the long term serve to undermine the solidarity of the British Empire (a view shared by other hard-line imperialists[103]). Leonard was opposed to Canada's decision to sign the League of Nations Covenant, arguing that it would impose obligations on the nation that it was 'utterly incapable of carrying out.'[104] A number of fellow Round Tablers were organizing the League of Nations Society of Canada, but Reuben Leonard turned down an offer to join its executive committee. Against the League on grounds tied to his views on race, Leonard told Prime Minister Borden that the League was the work of idealists who failed to appreciate 'the radical differences in mental and moral make-up of the different races, which differences are I believe inherent and irradicable [sic].' So great was the gulf that education could not begin to bridge it, except perhaps in the very long term.[105]

Leonard was still staunchly committed to the idea of a strong and united Empire and in this he felt he could still count on Lionel Curtis and the Round Table group as allies. However, Curtis had largely lost faith both in imperial federation as a likely prospect and in the Round Table as an effective vehicle of reform or a platform for his views. His attention and energies were now being directed towards a new project. At the Paris Peace Conference of 1919, which Curtis had attended as part of the British delegation, there was talk of establishing an organization to serve as a non-partisan centre for the study of international relations. Soon afterwards, the British Institute of International Affairs was formed under the directorship of Curtis, its avowed mission being to encourage and facilitate the scientific study[106] of international relations. In 1926 it was granted a royal charter and hence became known as the Royal Institute of International Affairs.

There was a good deal of political support for the development of such an agency, although funding was a major concern from the outset. In the early years the institute had been housed in cramped quarters and had operated on a shoestring budget. Curtis turned to Leonard for support. Once all was done, Reuben Wells Leonard had purchased an historic mansion in St James's Square in the heart of London. The price in 1923 was about $250,000; the current market value must be extraordinary. It was decided that the property, which had been the residence of the Earl of Chatham (Pitt the Elder), Lord Derby, and William Gladstone, would be called Chatham House. Curtis would later claim that this choice of name was Leonard's only stipulation and that the basis for it was that Chatham, the prime minister of England during the Seven

Years' War, had assured that Canadians such as Leonard would live under British not French rule. In fact, as will be seen below, Leonard exerted a good deal of influence before the gift was finalized. (Moreover, the name was decided upon by the institute and presented to Leonard as a virtual fait accompli.[107]) So 'Chatham House' became (and remains) both the home of the Royal Institute of International Affairs and also a term sometimes used to denote the institute itself. To provide for much-needed renovations, a further $40,000 was provided by the Leonards.

There is little question that Lionel Curtis was directly responsible for Reuben Leonard's decision to donate Chatham House. There is less consensus as to precisely how it came to pass. Curtis's account suggests gentle stewardship on his part. In 1922, while the Leonards were in England, the question of benefactions in aid of the Empire had been broached. As Curtis recalled: 'I suggested to them that the greatest need of the British Commonwealth was some institution in which its members could think out its relations with one another, and also with the world at large. This Institute which had sprung into being at the Conference of Paris, might, with proper endowments, fulfill that object. Having made this suggestion, I advised them to consult their great and trusted friend, the Duke of Devonshire. We owe it to the advice and willing assistance which the Duke gave his friends, Col. and Mrs. Leonard, that Chatham House now stands where it does.'[108]

Deborah Lavin, Curtis's biographer, has suggested an account of what transpired that contains elements of urgency, opportunism, and manipulation that are absent in Curtis's recollections. In 1923 the St James property came on the market and an option to purchase it was acquired by the English Speaking Union (ESU), an organization with both American and Commonwealth connections. It proposed sharing the premises with the British Institute as a memorial to Walter Page, the former American ambassador in London. However, the Page family had second thoughts about the purchase and the ESU bowed out, leaving the institute to fend for itself. The time limit set for exercising the option was rapidly approaching. Luckily, though,

[o]nly hours before the deadline Curtis ran across an old Canadian acquaintance, R.W. Leonard, in the street ... The campaign to secure Chatham House for the Institute became a classic of Curtis's disinterested single-mindedness. Leonard was mesmerized by the role Curtis foresaw for the British Institute ('the control of human forces will have to be studied with the same kind of persis-

tence as has been devoted to the study of natural forces'), and on hearing that the Colonial Secretary (the Duke of Devonshire) was writing to the King to commend the scheme to the general patronage of the Prince of Wales, Leonard undertook to present the house to the Prince for the Institute.[109]

The acquisition of the property was not without its difficult moments. With the St James property in hand, Curtis approached the Page family with the idea of establishing a Page library within the institute. Mrs Page agreed, and two beautifully bound volumes of Walter Page's *Letters* were presented for the future library to signify the arrangement. News of the ESU's re-emergence into the picture reached Leonard while he was on a fishing trip with Arthur Bishop at the Tourilli Lodge in the Laurentians. He immediately sent off a cable: 'Suspend all action Chatham House pending receipt of letter dated thirteenth. Leonard.'

The letter was a lengthy and truculent missive. Leonard had a number of misgivings about the way in which the institute was being organized. The composition of the board of trustees was a source of concern: Should Lloyd George be retained? He was, in Leonard's view, 'an exploded opportunist politician who makes beautiful speeches that don't ring true.'[110] There was an advocate of labour on the board; should a counterpart from business also be chosen? However, the main grievance concerned the Page Library. Leonard was opposed to a collaboration with the ESU. He recited what he remembered as having been the understanding reached on this type of cooperative agreement. A partnership with an organization such as the Royal Colonial Institute made more sense to him.[111] But, above all else, one thing was clear: he did not want a memorial to Ambassador Page. There were enough tributes to Americans in England, he complained, citing the memorial to George Washington in Westminster Abbey, the Lincoln monument in Trafalgar Square, and – of all things – the attempted restitution of the remains of Pocohantas. Yet, he added, 'I do not remember any memorial to Sir John A. Macdonald in England.'[112] It would be better, Leonard suggested, to dedicate the library to the overseas dominions and colonies and to decorate it with portraits of Drake, Vancouver, Hawkins, Cook, Nelson, Clive, Sir John A. Macdonald, Botha, Cecil Rhodes, Smuts, Hughes, and so on.[113]

Curtis realized that he had to alter his approach. The plan for the library was abandoned, Curtis assuming the difficult task of explaining the turn of events to Mrs Page and returning the donated volumes to her. By mid-October 1923 Leonard was satisfied with the way that matters stood and title to the property was transferred. An announcement of the gift appeared in *The Times*. The paper reported that the house at 10 St James's Square had been acquired by the British Institute of International Affairs through the generosity of two Canadian donors who wished to remain anonymous.[114] Within a week, however, a decision had been made to make the names public and on 23 October the *Times* reported under the headline 'The Canadian Gift to Britain' that the property had been purchased and donated by Colonel and Mrs Leonard. Colonel Leonard's career was sketched, and Mrs Leonard was mentioned in passing.[115] The Leonards were not entirely happy with the report. On the following day a letter appeared in the paper from Lord Meston, a member of the institute, who took issue with the headline on the benefactors' behalf: the Leonards wished it to be known that they were presenting this historic mansion not to Britain alone but rather to the British Empire.[116]

The official presentation took place on 9 November 1923. The proceedings were on a grand scale and the events of the day were reported in detail.[117] Among the dignitaries in attendance were Prime Minister King, the prime ministers of Australia, New Zealand, and Newfoundland, the Maharaja of Alwar, Sir Joseph Flavelle, the Prince of Wales, and Lord Grey of Fallodon, who presided over the ceremonies. Lionel Curtis was a member of the official party and orchestrated the event. Lord Grey gave the opening speech. He was followed by the Prince of Wales, who, as 'visitor' of the Institute, officially accepted the gift. The expected platitudes of appreciation were exuberantly uttered. At the end of the official program, Lord Curzon conferred the blessings of the Foreign Office. However, before these closing remarks, Reuben Leonard took the podium and presented a short address (the text of which had been reviewed and extensively edited by Curtis). After thanking the Prince of Wales for his kind words about the Leonards' 'modest' role in helping the institute, he provided his views of its purposes and of the significance of the British Empire in world affairs:

To us the British Empire is the greatest of human achievements. (Cheers.) To serve it rightly is to serve mankind. (Renewed cheers.) But to serve it rightly the nations of which it is made up must learn to understand not only their relations to each other but also their relation with foreign countries as well. And it is just this which men and women from all parts of the Empire have undertaken to do since the first foundation of this Institute in Paris three years ago. They have set themselves a task of supreme importance. My wife and I are impressed with the value of the work they have done, and are glad to have had this chance of providing the Institute with a suitable home where it can be carried on to better advantage. To make the results of this work available to the public an endowment will be needed: large perhaps in amount, but trivial when compared with the practical importance of the issues at stake. I have no doubt that whatever is needed for so great a purpose will be forthcoming from the Empire at large. (Cheers.)

After spending some months here, including an extended visit to the Continent, I want to say quite simply that, in my opinion, the people of this country are carrying a load heavier than any other which fought on the same side. For this reason, if for no other, my wife and I are glad to make some contribution to the study of problems vital to us all and I have no doubt that others similarly situated will be glad to do the same. I am sure that his Royal Highness is right in thinking that the value of this house as a place for the study of international affairs is greatly enhanced by its historical associations. As Canadians we can never forget what we owe to Chatham, so we are glad to have done something to have preserved for future generations the house in which he lived, and we hope that in future it will always bear his name as 'Chatham House.' (Cheers.) I can assure your Royal Highness that we are proud to have rendered some service to so great a cause. We heartily wish it all success and again thank you for your gracious words. (Loud cheers.)[118]

Reuben Wells Leonard must have felt like the toast of London. Soon after the ceremony at Chatham House he was invited to attend the official opening of the new Canadian Club facilities in London, where Prime Minister King was the guest of honour. On the Leonards' return to Canada, a dinner was organized by Sir Edmund Walker in honour of their gift.[119] It was also around this time that Leonard, through Curtis, made the acquaintance of T.E. Lawrence, Lawrence of Arabia. By 1923 Lawrence was at work on his account of the desert campaign that had won him such fame. On the matter of publication Lawrence had been urged by Curtis and others that the first edition should be sold by subscription, that is, a certain number of subscribers were to be approached to underwrite the cost of publication and in return they would receive a copy of the work. No books would be offered for general sale; there would be no publishers, booksellers, or (it was hoped) reviews. 'I am aiming at a public that will pay but not read ... and from what one hears the plutocrats should be of that sort,'[120] Lawrence confided to a friend. It was decided that about 100 subscribers would be enlisted to pay 30 guineas each. Today, this would amount to about $1,300 per book.

Predictably, Curtis had sought out Colonel Leonard; he agreed to subscribe, and following his triumphant return to Canada after the Chatham House ceremony he wrote to Curtis to sign on.[121] The colonel threw himself behind the project. He passed on to Lawrence (via Curtis) a copy of Lowell Thomas's *With Lawrence in Arabia*, which had recently been released. Though Lawrence had already seen the book, he wrote to Leonard politely thanking him for the gift. His own account of events, he told Leonard in 1925, 'is, I hope, true.' He added that 'in time you will have your copy ... to judge for yourself how little saint and prophet and patriot and hero of romance I was.'[122] A year later, the first edition of T.E. Lawrence's *Seven Pillars of Wisdom* was completed. Leonard was among the 128 or so subscribers.[123]

In late 1923 the finishing touches were put on a major revision of Leonard's 1916 scholarship trust. In 1916, he had established a fund for the purposes of providing bursaries to the sons of clergymen, teachers, and soldiers. He had augmented the fund in 1920, expanded the number of schools at which the awards were tenable, and provided that a portion of the monies could be awarded to female applicants. By 1923 his vision of the role of the Foundation had grown. In Chapter 2 the details of the 1923 trust deed are examined in detail, though the main elements can be briefly described here.

In 1923 the Leonard Foundation was endowed to a book value of $500,000. The interest from this capital was to be used to provide scholarships at a select number of secondary and post-secondary educational institutions. The awards were bursaries: financial need had to be shown. The goals and premises of the Leonard awards were set out in a series of recitals. Reminiscent of the rhetorical flourishes found in the Chatham House speech, which had been delivered just six weeks earlier, the trust spoke of the need to assist students who showed the promise of becoming leading citizens in the British Empire. Moreover, the peace of the world and the advancement of civilization depended on the independence and prosperity of the Empire. The trust also declared that the white race was best qualified in the main to be entrusted with the advance of civilization, and that progress had, and would, depend on the maintenance of the Christian religion. Hence, the awards were restricted to British subjects, of the white race, who were also adherents of the Christian religion. Because the recipients could owe no allegiance to a foreign power, be it prince, potentate, or pope, Protestants but not Catholics were eligible.

The kernel for the idea of the scholarship was derived, it seems, from the more modest plan of 1913 to establish a residence at Queen's, which was supposed to combine military training with a more broadly based educational experience. The 1923 trust provides that male recipients should normally engage in military exercises, and females were expected to participate in physical training. The Queen's model having been superseded by the more ambitious Leonard Foundation Trust, the lakefront property that was to be the site of the residence was expendable. It was given to the university in 1923 in recognition of the sacrifices that Queen's had made during the Great War. There were no strings attached, though Leonard told the university's principal that the gift was being made 'with full confidence that the university will not fail to render due recognition of and assistance in systematic courses of instruction in military subjects, and in the efficient training of officers for the defence of all time, of Canada and the Empire.'[124]

THE DENOUEMENT

The year 1923 was something of an *annus mirabilis* for Reuben Wells Leonard. His bitter sniping over Robert MacIver's appointment as chair of political economy at the University of Toronto had by year's end been overshadowed by the triumph of Chatham House and the reconstitution of the Leonard Foundation Trust. And R.W. Leonard had become a public figure in Britain and, to some extent, at home.[125] However, the following years were not so kind. At least by 1924, he began to experience the symptoms of what was soon understood to be a neurological disorder. Rumours that R.W. Leonard was near death surfaced in the press, only to be denied. But he had contracted a degenerative disease; over the next six years Leonard became progressively, unrelentingly, paralysed. Leading medical experts were consulted, electrotherapy was tried, and the wells on the grounds of Springbank were re-established so that he could take the waters. Purportedly, he had offered $1 million to any physician who could cure him.[126] However, nothing could be done to stem the tide. Leonard was dying of Parkinson's disease. A man who had previously enjoyed remarkable good health and who from the earliest times loved outdoor pursuits, he was now house-bound. In time, he could no longer walk. In the final weeks of his life, near the end of 1930, he was virtually confined to bed.

The period from 1923 to 1930 was marked by a continuous stream of major benefactions.[127] He provided $100,000 for the building of a YMCA and YWCA in St Catharines. A plan to assist in the building of a new nurse's home at the St Catharines General Hospital, first proposed in 1923, was carried to completion (in an amended form) in 1925. Leonard gave over $100,000 for the construction of a new library at Wycliffe College. Completed in 1929, it is a magnificent example of neo-Gothic architecture, with a carved oak ceiling and floors of Vesuvian terrantine stone. In 1926 money was donated to St Thomas' Church to build a rectory on the site of the Grace Mission. That same year the Leonards became founders of the Art Gallery of Toronto and in the following three years the money they donated to the gallery was used to purchase thirty works by Canadian artists.[128] The Leonards funded the building of an eight-bed hospital in Aklavik, Northwest Territories. At Ridley College, money was provided for a new lower school. A gift of $25,000 was provided as seed money in 1922, but by 1927 the total grant had reached $200,000. The donation was subject to the stipulation that 'no sand or gravel taken from the shores of Lake Ontario should be used in the construction of the building.'[129] He was, it seems, concerned about the erosion of the shoreline in the area.

During this period, Coniagas suffered a major setback, as if in a doleful synchrony with the declining health of its president. In 1924 a fire at Coniagas destroyed the main buildings and facilities. At that time the minerals had almost been exhausted, and it was decided that it would not be profitable to restore mining operations there. Insurance covered the loss and the property was cleared. It was leased in 1928 and later sold. However, the business itself survived. For more than a decade Coniagas had been looking for properties to develop once the original site was exhausted; indeed, it had lasted far longer than had been initially predicted. At the time of the fire, patents were held in relation to more than half a dozen mineral estates, including the Trethewey Mine (J.B.7). And for some years attempts had been made (some costly but unfruitful) to develop gold mines in the Porcupine region. Just weeks after the fire, several sites in that region were consolidated under the name Coniaurum Mines, of which Coniagas held about a 60 per cent interest. This development had a troubled start and did not produce marketable gold ores until 1928. It fell into receivership in 1929, being saved by the infusion of fresh capital by Ventures Ltd., which then held a controlling interest in the company. Through Coniaurum and the other holdings, Coniagas remained a going concern, but it was no longer the robust enterprise it had once been.

In these final years, a host of honours were conferred on the elderly Leonard. He was made lieutenant-colonel in the Lincoln Regiment (to which Arthur Bishop belonged), a counsellor of the Red Cross Society of Canada, the president of Ridley College, and the treasurer of the Banting Research Foundation (all honorary positions). In 1929 the Engineering Institute of Canada awarded the inaugural Sir John Kennedy Medal to Leonard in recognition of his many contributions to the profession. His illness prevented him from accepting the honour in person; Arthur Bishop did so on his behalf. Perhaps the most flattering formal accolade[130] was bestowed by Queen's University, which awarded him an honorary doctorate of laws. The degree was granted to Leonard *in absentia* during a ceremony held in late October 1930. He was near death.

Reuben Wells Leonard passed away at his home early in the morning on 17 December 1930. On the day that he died a banner headline in the Toronto *Telegram* announced: 'Col. Leonard, Philanthropist, Noted Engineer, Dies in St Catharines.' After chronicling Leonard's life, the article concluded, with a bravado found in obituaries of this sort, that Leonard 'was one of Canada's finest citizens.' Likewise, the Toronto *Star* said that he 'exemplified the ideal Canadian – a man who armed with his training as an engineer and soldier, threw all his energies into the creation of railways, electrical power, productive mines and thriving industries.'[131] Across the country, similar homage was paid.[132] On the private front, expressions of grief were sent to Mrs Leonard from the various institutions that Leonard had supported over the years.[133] Dozens of floral gifts and letters of condolence were sent to Springbank. Among these was a telegram from the Prince of Wales: 'I have learned with deepest regret of the death of my friend Colonel Leonard and send you my sincere personal sympathy.'[134]

Leonard had made his mark abroad. An obituary in the New York *Times* described Leonard's philanthropic work and his support of the Empire and Canada's role within it.[135] The Wall Street *Journal*, predictably, spoke of Leonard's fortune, and the Coniagas Mines, which was described (wrongly by this time) as being among the most productive in the world.[136] *The Times* praised Leonard for his life of community service, making special mention of Chatham House.[137] Lionel Curtis wrote an obituary for *International Affairs*, a journal published by the Royal Institute of International Affairs. Among other things, he spoke of the contrast between the modesty of his lifestyle and the generosity of his spirit.[138]

Following a private service at Springbank and a public funeral service at St Thomas', Leonard's remains were buried at Victoria Lawn Cemetery. In the new year steps were taken to settle the estate,[139] and letters of probate were issued without ado in February 1931. The net value of his estate was declared to be in excess of $4.63 million.[140] While such a sum might pale in comparison to the fortunes amassed by the great American industrialists of this era (such as Carnegie, Vanderbilt, or Rockefeller), or the old money of the English upper class, Leonard had been a wealthy man by Canadian standards. He must have seemed even more so in 1931, as the nation was descending ever deeper into the Depression.[141] Moreover, this figure represented merely all that remained of a fortune that for twenty years had been devoted to philanthropic causes.

The will contained few surprises. The Toronto General Trusts Corporation (of which Leonard had been a director for many years) was named as executor and trustee. Kate Leonard received a life estate in Springbank.[142] She was also given most of the personalty in (or around) the home and an annuity of $24,000.00. On her death, the capital used to provide the annuity was to be added to the corpus of the Leonard Foundation Trust, and the fee simple in Springbank was to pass to Arthur Bishop. The rest of the property was to be sold, with the proceeds to be distributed under the terms of an extensive residuary clause. Small gifts were made to relatives from both sides of the family[143] and provision was made for the payment of $50,000 in 'gratuities' (of no more than $10,000 each) to employees.[144] Arthur Bishop was given slightly less than half of this residuary estate. Half of that gift was conferred immediately; the remaining portion was to be conferred when Bishop turned fifty, provided that he had a child living at that time. These stipulations were met in 1945.[145] So, some forty years after being anointed the heir apparent of the Leonard estate, Arthur received his full inheritance.

The remainder of the estate, just less than half of the residue, went towards benefactions. Under the first set of bequests, $340,000 was to be accumulated and divided into seventeen units (hence worth $20,000 each). Under this arrangement, shares were given to Wycliffe College (eight); the Church of England Deaconess and Missionary Training House of Toronto (two); St Thomas' Church (two); St Catharines General and Marine Hospital (one); the Boy Scouts (one), Girl Guides (one); and the Canadian Military Institute (one). Finally, a share was to be paid to Kate Leonard, to be applied towards the completion of charitable benefactions that they had pursued during his life. Any money accumulated under this part over and above $340,000 was to be paid to five educational institutions that had demonstrated the most marked success in connection with the aims of the Leonard Foundation and that showed the most promise of continuing to do so in the future.[146]

A second set of benefactions contained six equal shares of the remainder of the estate. One each was given to the Royal Ontario Museum[147] and the Art Gallery of Toronto (now the Art Gallery of Ontario). One was given to the University of Toronto for undergraduate or post-graduate scholarships (or for such purposes as the trustees or Mrs Leonard should choose after consulting with the Board of Governors of the university). The fourth bequest was to be used for orphans' homes or children's hostels, and the fifth, added just weeks after Leonard received his honorary doctorate, provided for scholarships at Queen's. The sixth share was to be used to generate an annuity for Leonard Bishop.

CONCLUSION

Reuben Wells Leonard's life was like a play in three acts. In the first we see the native of Brantford mature into a civil engineer and military man. Born seven years before Confederation, he became an industrial pioneer. Through his work on railway and energy systems, he participated in the development of Canada's economic infrastructure. Whether it was in the building of the railway, the Niagara Falls hydro-project, or the North-West Rebellion, his life moved in tandem with that of the young nation. In Act 2, one finds Leonard the prospector, industrialist, and magnate. At the age of fifty he had become a millionaire, living comfortably in St Catharines. From there he built the Coniagas Mines from scratch, taking a rich deposit of silver ore and creating a diversified, thriving enterprise. In the course of doing so, he developed the political economy of a resolute and morally certain capitalist. In the final Act, Leonard the elder became a philanthropist and activist, throwing his support and energies towards those causes, of which there were many, that he regarded as worthy. These three phases shade into one another, connected by a set of themes: the importance of religious devotion; the value of education; and the importance of duty and service, military and otherwise, in the aid of virtue.

Within this drama, there were three supporting characters. The first is Kate Leonard, his wife of forty-one years, and, from all accounts, an ideological kindred spirit. She continued on with charitable work for five more years, passing away in September 1935. The second is Arthur Bishop. A top graduate from Ridley, he excelled at RMC and became a war hero. Later Arthur assumed control of Coniagas and took an active role in the Leonard Foundation. He served as the chairman of the Red Cross during the Second World War, was a member of the national executive of the Boy Scouts, and served as the president of the Board of Governors of Ridley College. He became the president of Consumers Gas and sat on the board of directors of a number of business concerns (including Toronto General Trusts).The young boy who came to stay with Kate and Reuben followed in his uncle's footsteps as dutifully as any son could have done.[148]

Finally there was Lionel Curtis. The relationship between Leonard and Curtis was complex. Curtis, directly and through the Round Table, seems to have had a marked impact. His fervour and charm often worked on Leonard as it did with others: 'He wove his proliferating old-boy network out of white Anglo-Saxon Protestant racial and religious sentiment in the Dominions as in Britain. Colonel Reuben Leonard in Canada ... was to place his name and his money at Curtis's disposal.'[149] However, to assume that Curtis controlled Leonard, that Curtis was his political mentor, and that Curtis could count on Leonard's unfailing support is probably to misunderstand the dynamics of this relationship. They were both martinets in their own way; both were used to leading not following. What seems likely is that a symbiosis existed: both Leonard and Curtis knew how to use the other. The quintessential example, but not the only one, was that of the purchase of Chatham House for the use of Curtis's Royal Institute of International Affairs. In return, Leonard was given a window into the world of imperial politics. Their association seems to have been predicated on an implicit pact in which the advancement of their respective interests were the unspoken goals.[150]

Colonel Leonard was highly regarded throughout his life. He was renowned as an excellent engineer and respected for his business integrity (at least outside Cobalt).[151] The success of Coniagas and the rehabilitation of the troubled Grand Trunk Pacific project reinforced his reputation as an able manager. He dedicated a good deal of his life, work, and money in support of the military causes in Canada. Among the Canadian establishment it was virtually *de rigueur* to claim some sort of military pedigree, though most such officers would have been hard pressed to demonstrate a real and substantial commitment to service.[152] This would not, however, be a fair appraisal of Reuben Wells Leonard. He had become a soldier two decades before striking it rich at Coniagas, volunteered for duty in 1885, and remained active in the militia throughout his life. And whatever else may be said about him, his philanthropy and unshakeable sense of duty to Empire gave rise to his reputation as a generous and patriotic citizen.

As in England, Leonard gained access to places of privilege at home. He became known and accepted within the upper echelons of Toronto's and Canada's intellectual, commercial, and political worlds. He came to know some of the important figures of his day – Edmund Walker, Sandford Fleming, Robert Falconer, Joseph Flavelle, the Osler family, prime ministers Borden and King, and two of Canada's governors general, Earl Grey and the Duke of Devonshire. It would have been hard for these men not to have been impressed by R.W. Leonard's engineering accomplishments, business acumen, and extensive philanthropy. Whether this Cobalt millionaire was truly accepted and respected for his outlook on political and social problems is another matter. In a general way, these men shared with Leonard a common patriotic vision, involving both Canada and the Empire. Yet his polemical and imperious style must have accentuated, rather than obscured, a certain lack of insightful political thought. There is little doubt, for example, that his views on academic freedom created difficult moments at Queen's and the University of Toronto. Still, the educational institutions that he favoured understood the benefits of remaining on good terms with this benefactor; they treated him with kid gloves.

At the time of his death, Leonard was perhaps best known for his gift of Chatham House, but there were, and are, many other memorials. In Brantford, at Grace Church, there is a bell tower, a baptistry, and a stained glass window (of the Te Deum) all donated by Leonard. In St Catharines he is remembered at St Thomas' Church (and Grace Mission); at the General Hospital (and the Leonard Nurse's Home); at the Shaver Hospital for Chest Diseases; at the YMCA; and at Ridley College, where one finds the dormitory that he donated in the 1920s and a special scholarship endowment known as the Reuben Wells Leonard Award. The Leonard Hotel and Motel, within which is a down-market diner called Leonard's Coffee Pot, is located in the centre of downtown St Catharines. A walk through the Art Gallery of Ontario reveals the acquisitions made possible by the Leonards' contributions. A gallery and an adjoining rotunda are named after the Leonards; both contain divinity scenes painted by Italian masters. At Wycliffe, the Leonard Library, renovated and rededicated in 1978, remains a memorial. At Queen's, a residence built in 1959 and called 'Leonard Hall' stands at one end of 'Leonard Field,' the lakefront parcel that was once proposed as the site of a residence for COTC candidates. A township in the

Temiskaming area of northern Ontario, not far from the site of the Coniagas Mines, has been named after Leonard. Portraits by the Canadian painter John Russell can be found in Chatham House and Ridley, and one by Kenneth Forbes hangs in Wycliffe.

Yet, for all of this, Reuben Wells Leonard's fame was elsewhere short-lived. Outside the institutions in which he played a role, as governor or benefactor, and the family members who remember their famous, revered, and successful ancestor, few know of Colonel Reuben Wells Leonard, even in St Catharines. For half a century he remained an obscure historical figure until events brought his name back into public circulation. He was, we were to learn, the philanthropist who had established the Leonard Foundation Trust. By the 1980s, the Foundation was embroiled in a controversy over the terms that Leonard had set out in the 1923 trust deed. This dispute was to provide the backdrop against which the contributions of Reuben Wells Leonard – especially the Leonard Foundation – were to be re-evaluated.

2

The Leonard Foundation Trust in Context

At the gala dinner held at the York Club of Toronto in late 1923 in honour of Reuben Wells and Kate Leonard, Canon Henry J. Cody, then chairman of the Board of Governors of the University of Toronto, gave a speech as a tribute to his long-time friends. After praising the Leonards for their magnanimous gift of Chatham House, he turned to another benefaction, the Leonard Foundation Trust. Cody noted that the Foundation, in place since 1916, had assisted many secondary and post-secondary students; and, as he understood it, the scope of the Foundation was soon to be extended.[1] It was on the next day that Colonel Leonard attended at the offices of his solicitors to finalize the new trust arrangement.

The 1916 trust created bursaries open to the sons of clergymen, schoolteachers, and members of the permanent British or Canadian army or navy (or veterans of British Empire wars), the awards to be tenable at Ridley College, Royal Military College, Wycliffe College, and the Royal Naval College in Halifax. In 1920 the size of the trust capital was increased and the list of approved schools expanded. Females were now eligible for awards. In 1923 the trust again underwent substantial revision. Although that deed, as with the predecessor documents, reserved to Colonel Leonard the right to amend the trust further, no changes were made during his life. Provisions in his will called for the corpus to be augmented on the death of Kate Leonard; the money set aside for her annuity was to be added to the trust property.

That 1923 deed begins with a set of recitals, the first four of which set out the philosophical heart and soul of the Leonard Foundation.² They provide that:

WHEREAS the Settlor believes that the White Race is, as a whole, best qualified by nature to be entrusted with the development of civilization and the general progress of the World along the best lines:
AND WHEREAS the Settlor believes that the progress of the World depends in the future, as in the past, on the maintenance of the Christian Religion:
AND WHEREAS the Settlor believes that the peace of the World and the advancement of civilization depends very greatly upon the independence, the stability and the prosperity of the British Empire as a whole, and that this independence, stability and prosperity can be best attained and assured by the education in patriotic Institutions of selected children, whose birth and training are such as to warrant a reasonable expectation of their developing into leading citizens of the Empire:
AND WHEREAS the Settlor believes that, so far as possible, the conduct of the affairs of the British Empire should be in the guidance of Christian persons of British Nationality who are not hampered or controlled by any allegiance or pledge of obedience to any government, power or authority, temporal or spiritual, the seal of which government, power or authority is outside of the British Empire. For the above reason the Settlor excludes from the management of, or benefits in the Foundation intended to be created by this Indenture, all who are not Christians of the White Race, all who are not of British Nationality or of British Parentage, and all who owe allegiance to any Foreign Government, Prince, Pope or Potentate, or who recognize any such authority, temporal or spiritual ...

The operative elements of the trust are faithful to these premises. Hence, the principal requirements for eligibility are that the applicant be a 'British Subject of the White Race and of the Christian Religion in its Protestant form.' There is also an element of financial need (which is not mentioned in the preamble): the awards are available only to those who would be unable to pursue a course of study in one of the designated educational institutions[3] without financial assistance.

The criteria of nationality, race, religion, and need are absolute conditions of eligibility. There are three other factors to be taken into account in the selection. First, although the scholarships are available to males and females, only one-quarter of the funds in a given year were to be allocated to female applicants. Second, the trust provides that the 'physical as well as the mental and moral qualities ... shall be an important prerequisite.' Third, preference is to be given to the sons and daughters of persons fitting into one of six preferred classes. This list was in effect an expansion of the categories of eligibility under the first two deeds. The preferred classes under the 1923 deed are as follows: clergymen; schoolteachers; officers, non-commissioned officers and men, whether active or retired, who have served in His Majesty's military, air, or naval forces; graduates of the Royal Military College of Canada; members of the Engineering Institute of Canada; and members of the Mining and Metallurgical Institute of Canada.

The scholarships are annual awards, capable of renewal. The scholarship holders are expected to take part in athletic or physical exercises, and military or naval training, if available at the institution at which the award is held, and the proficiency of a student in this regard is one factor relevant to the matter of renewal. Award holders are also normally expected to engage in some suitable occupation during the summer vacation, preferably in a job involving physical labour.

The trustees are responsible mainly for the proper management of the trust monies. This aside, the administration of the Foundation is largely assigned to a twenty-five member General Committee. The committee is empowered to create rules and regulations for the governance of the Foundation (provided these are consistent with the trust). They may investigate complaints against a scholarship holder, cancel scholarships, and reinstate these at a later time. An applicant must be nominated by a member of the General Committee, and it selects the scholarship winners. To assist in that process, a five-member scholarship subcommittee was also created by the deed. Under the stewardship of the 'honorary secretary' of the Foundation, the primary function of this subcommittee is to review applications and present recommendations to the General Committee. A list of members of the 1923 General Committee was included in the 1923 deed.[4] It was composed of twenty-four men and one woman, Kate Leonard. She, Arthur Bishop, and Colonel Leonard were entitled to sit on the committee as of right. Nine members were clergymen, twelve were affiliated with educational institutions, and four were members of the Engineering Institute of Canada

The Leonard scholarships were initially available only at a select number of schools, colleges, and universities, and from 1923 onward the designation of the schools was left to the General Committee. Although the power of selection is described as being in the absolute discretion of the committee, it is in fact constrained in several ways. The recitals speak obscurely of the importance of education in 'patriotic Institutions,' which means that the schools selected must 'be free from the dominion or control of adherents of the class or classes of persons ... whom the Settlor intends shall be excluded from the management of or benefits in the ... Foundation.' In addition, preference is to be given to a school, college, or university that prescribes physical training for female students and physical, military, and naval training for male students. The General Committee is empowered to assess the continued suitability of approved schools, and it may periodically review the 'discipline and the ethical, physical and educational standard maintained by each School, College or University.' If an institution falls short of the committee's standards, it may be withdrawn temporarily or permanently from the approved list and the scholarships held at that institution may be suspended or cancelled. Finally, as a guide to his intentions, Leonard set out a list of institutions that had his confidence and approval:[5]

1. Ridley College (St. Catharines, Ontario)
2. Upper Canada College (Toronto, Ontario)
3. St. Andrews' College (Toronto, Ontario)
4. Rothesay Collegiate School (Rothesay, New Brunswick)
5. King's Collegiate School (Windsor, Nova Scotia)
6. Public Schools, High Schools and Collegiate Institutes (and Protestant schools in Quebec)
7. Havergal College (Toronto, Ontario)
8. Edgehill School for Girls (Windsor, Nova Scotia)
9. Nurses Training Schools in Canada (Non-Sectarian)
10. Ontario Agricultural College (Guelph, Ontario); Macdonald Institute (Guelph, Ontario)
11. Macdonald College (St. Anne's, Quebec)
12. Church of England Deaconess & Missionary Training House (Toronto, Ontario)
13. Wycliffe College (Toronto, Ontario)
14. Emanuel College (Saskatoon, Saskatchewan)
15. Anglican Theological College (Vancouver, British Columbia)
16. Royal Military College of Canada (Kingston, Ontario)
17. Royal Naval College of Canada (when re-established)
18. Royal Air College of Canada (when established)
19. The University of Toronto (Toronto, Ontario)
    McGill University (Montreal, Quebec)
    Queen's University (Kingston, Ontario)
    Western University (London, Ontario)
    Dalhousie College and University (Halifax, Nova Scotia)

University of Manitoba (Winnipeg, Manitoba)
University of Saskatchewan (Saskatoon, Saskatchewan)
The University of Alberta (Edmonton, Alberta)
The University of British Columbia (Vancouver, British Columbia)
20. Any University in Great Britain selected by the General Committee.

The scholarship requirements as to race, nationality, and religious affiliation affect other elements of the trust. Members of the General Committee had to meet the same criteria. As mentioned above, a school could not be included within the scheme if it was under the dominion and control of members of the excluded classes. The trust recites Colonel Leonard's hope that former Leonard scholars would establish a club or association to assist unofficially and indirectly in the operation of the Foundation, and also for the purpose of encouraging former holders to provide financial assistance to others within the prescribed class (British, white, Protestant) so that they too might be able to obtain 'the blessings and benefits of an education.'[6] Finally, the trustee was empowered to apply to the Supreme Court of Ontario to seek directions concerning the interpretation or proper administration of the trust. If such action was taken, the deed provided that the judge before whom the application is made had to possess the same restrictive qualifications required to be a member of the General Committee.

THE VALUES EMBEDDED WITHIN THE TRUST

A trust deed, such as that used to create the Leonard Foundation, is, at bottom, a dispositive document. That is, it creates a trust to manage and disperse a fund of money.[7] Reuben Wells Leonard, as settlor, placed title to property valued at $500,000 in the hands of the Toronto General Trusts Corporation. The primary responsibility of the trustee is to invest the trust monies (prudently) in a way that will generate an annual income to be used to provide the scholarships. In aid of that goal, the trustee is given extensive powers to transform the nature of the holdings so as to optimize the income generated by the corpus.

While one can understand the Leonard deed in this purely functional way, it is nevertheless a rather narrow perspective. I see the trust as amenable to at least three other readings. Viewed in one way, it can be treated as an autobiography. Finalized just weeks after the formal dedication of Chatham House, the trust reflects Leonard's life experiences. We see in this trust the colonel who valued physical and military training; the patriot devoted to the cause of Empire; a privileged male who believed in the white man's burden; a Christian philanthropist; the former teacher, school, and university governor who believed in the virtues of education and who, in his youth, was unable to afford university tuition; and the man who believed in the progress of civilization and who saw engineers as enablers. These elements of self-reference are especially pronounced in the list of the preferred classes – the sons and daughters of clergy, teachers, military veterans, RMC alumni, and members of engineering societies. Leonard's offspring (had there been any) would have qualified under all but the first category. Private property is, at times, a medium of self-expression, a reification of identity, a projection of aspects of oneself into the material world.[8] The Leonard Trust deed illustrates this well: it is an epitome of the man himself. The only aspect of Leonard's life that receives no explicit mention is Coniagas. This element is present only in the endowment itself, for the trust fund was derived from the profits drawn from his mining and other business ventures.

The Leonard Foundation Trust can also be treated as a political tract.[9] Leonard's scant writings are fairly unoriginal and heavily polemical; however, he remains important because he was able to insinuate his ideology into Canadian life through the agency of the Leonard Foundation. The trust creates the machinery to administer the political ideology of Reuben Wells Leonard. Because of this feature, his is a political theory with endurance: charitable trusts may last in perpetuity.

One sees in the trust the presence of ideas that enjoyed currency at the time of its creation. For example, Reuben Leonard's views seem to draw on, or are at least consistent with, certain elements of social Darwinism. This is particularly true of his perspective on race, but the congruity extends further. Derived from the work of Charles Darwin,[10] social Darwinism refers to the application of the evolutionary theory of natural selection to, variously, individuals, classes, races, and other communities to explain patterns of hierarchy and to prescribe ways in which the natural evolutionary processes should be facilitated. This prescriptive element took many forms: the term 'social Darwinism' does not stand for a single, cognate theory of social development. While essentially sharing an understanding of human development as mapped out by Darwin, the theories constructed on top of this world-view varied greatly. It had a plasticity that meant that it could be marshalled in support of both laissez-faire liberalism and social reform, as well as vastly different views on race, class, and imperialism.[11]

While the period during which social Darwinism was a force is almost coterminous with the life of R.W. Leonard, whether Leonard can be described as a social Darwinist is not clear. This uncertainty stems from the multivalent nature of this school of thought, taken together with the dearth of information about the man himself. The degree to which social Darwinism was able to affect public policy is also a contested matter. Little is known about the support it enjoyed in Canadian intellectual and social circles. Though there was no Canadian champion of the cause that could be equated with such men as Herbert Spencer in Britain and William Sumner in the United States, its presence can be detected in the writing of such men as Sir George Parkin[12] and William LeSueur.[13] Furthermore, social Darwinism can be seen at work in the emergence of the eugenics movement in Canada (c. 1920–30).[14] Beyond this, the picture is obscure. Yet there appear enough points of contact between the ideas found in the trust, and ideologies commonly placed under the umbrella concept of social Darwinism, to provide a reference point (at least) with which to locate the trust within its intellectual milieu.

Colonel Leonard's political thinking also draws on the work of other contemporaries. His philanthropic outlook accords with that of Andrew Carnegie, the American multimillionaire. Leonard's belief in the importance of pursuing structural imperial unity places him in the company of his Round Table colleagues (such as Lionel Curtis). And it is hard to read the terms of the Leonard Trust without being reminded of Cecil Rhodes and the scholarships that bear his name. The strongest overlap of all between Leonard and his contemporaries seems to be with George Parkin (1846–1922), the imperial federalist.[15] Parkin's writing was infused with generous doses of Christian duty, Canadian patriotism, and imperial jingoism, with a pinch of social Darwinism added for good measure. He was never a member of the Round Table, though he knew the principal Canadian members quite well. He was an acquaintance of Leonard, and the colonel may well have been influenced by his writings.

Despite these similarities, it is well to remember that Leonard was not Parkin; nor was he Rhodes, Carnegie, or Curtis. The framework that emerges from a reading of the trust and other sources reveals a perspective on the world that conforms with that of a number of like-minded men of his time, including Parkin, but in the end amounts to a unique mix, one that at times seems strident even by reference to his cohort group.

Treating the trust as a statement of political theory suggests another way in which the trust can be understood: it is a time capsule. Take the lid off of the document and ones sees the relics of a bygone time. The language of the trust (especially that found in the recitals) contains various literary conventions, and, as just noted, his theories connect with other extant writings. In addition, it can be seen that the trust purports to present timeless truths derived from the lessons of history. By seeking to place the text against the context in which it arose, one can assess the historically contingent nature of these positions.

Progress and Civilization

The first four recitals contain a meta-narrative. Leonard proposes here a world-view in which human history can be seen as a march towards progress. Life on earth was better than it once was, and he hoped that it would become better still. This movement was marked by the gradual refinements that, it was assumed, would lead overall to the advancement of civilization.

In J.B. Bury's *The Idea of Progress*,[16] first published in 1920, it was argued that the ancient cultures lacked an awareness of a deep historical past that might support a theory of gradual progression. Instead, what the early philosophers saw was either degeneration or cyclic renewal. Critics have challenged this thesis.[17] Nevertheless, the starting premise, that is, that the idea of progress is both culturally and historically contingent, so that the search for the immutable laws of progress would prove fruitless, has never been seriously doubted. Some cultures treat history as repetitive, with the unending transition of seasons and the life cycles of plants and animals being suggestive of a world moving in a recurring, not linear, pattern. Furthermore, some conceptions of progress have stressed, to greater or lesser degrees, the importance of Providence; some speak of incremental movement, others of cataclysmic events.

Not all theories of the future adopt a sanguine belief in the continuing improvement of the human condition. Instead, history is seen as conveying a story of degeneration, a fall from grace. Nor is there universal agreement about what counts as a progressive society. One can imagine conceptions of progress that emphasize advances in knowledge, or the flowering of culture, or the degree to which mature political institutions have developed, or, more generally, the extent to which liberty and self-fulfilment have been furthered. Or the benchmarks might be the ways in which the world, or society, has become more moral. Even if a consensus could be reached on the relevant indicia, disagreement might still exist as to whether the consequences of human action should count as a progressive step. Scientific breakthroughs that come at a cost to the environment pose precisely these problems. In short, progress is a contentious concept with a complex history.[18]

Reflecting on the emergence of the ideologies of progress in nineteenth-century England, Peter Bowler has argued that in a culture in which science and reason were ascending over spirituality, 'the idea of progress was imposed on history to create the sense of order that the Victorians craved.'[19] Comforting as this may have been, it also contains a pernicious edge. Belief in the superiority of modern civilization was a key ingredient in Western conceptions of progress. Progress being a value, and civilization being the benchmark, it was possible then to see so-called primitive societies as lagging behind and therefore inferior.

At the turn of the century it was possible for Canadians to embrace a conception of progress tied to the march of civilization. It was plausible to see history as showing how 'mankind' had advanced from primitive societies. The record of Canada's own past was itself inspirational. British North America, with its hardy northern climate,[20] had developed from a wilderness into, first, a cluster of prosperous colonies, then a self-governing dominion ready to assume its share of the imperial mission. The country's progress could be seen in the development of democratic institutions (that is, the establishment of responsible government and later the assumption of nation-status), the emergence of Canadian arts and sciences, and the material well-being that Canadians enjoyed, as well as the technological advances that were being made.[21]

It would have been quite natural for Reuben Wells Leonard to regard improvements in technology as a badge of progress, for he had devoted more than twenty years of his life to the building of railways and hydroelectric facilities. These were not just monumental engineering feats, they were powerful emblems of Canada's possibilities.[22] Drawing on these ideas, he told the 1910 graduating class of engineers at the University of Toronto that, if the twentieth century was to belong to Canada, as Laurier had predicted it would, it was imperative for engineers to play a leading role.[23] The trust tells us that, for R.W. Leonard, the evolution of the world was progressive. There was no golden age to which we should strive to return. He saw the world in which he lived as a 'wonderful and rapidly changing age.'[24]

The Great War, fought between 'civilized' nations, served to undermine the optimism of some. However, Leonard thought that the war had created the necessity for unprecedented improvements, and this had set progress on the right trajectory. At the same time, there was no assurance, no guarantee that nature would continue on this course. Regression, stagnation, and ruin were possible, so that it was necessary to guard against retrogressive action at the hands of agitators. This serves to explain why Robert MacIver was seen by Leonard as so menacing: his preposterous theories, as Leonard saw them, threatened to undo a civilization that it had taken millennia to build.[25] A nurturing of progressive influences was needed. That, patently, is one way of describing the aims and purposes of the Leonard Foundation.

Patriotism, Nationalism, and the British Empire

Reuben Wells Leonard believed deeply in the British Empire. At the opening of Chatham House he described the Empire as 'the greatest of human achievements' and exhorted that 'to serve it rightly was to serve mankind.'[26] The gift of Chatham House was intended as a form of service to the Empire. Likewise, the Leonard Foundation Trust placed the Empire at the centre of the project. The recitals declared that the advancement of civilization depended upon the independence, stability, and prosperity of the British Empire. The awards were designed to assist select children to become 'leading citizens of the Empire.' The British Empire was not, of course, a static institution; nor was Canada's role within it fixed for all time. One wonders, therefore, what Leonard foresaw when he constructed his plan.

In 1911 the English author W.R. Lawson earnestly, if simplistically, posed this question: 'Twentieth-century Canada, what is it to be in the long-run – a British Canada, an American Canada or an independent Canada?'[27] The options were somewhat more complex than Lawson's question suggests. Nonetheless, it is true that, in the decades preceding the Great War, some (such as Goldwin Smith[28]) advocated annexation to the United States; others (including John Ewart[29]) argued for the development of Canadian independence. Most English-speaking Canadians would have opted for what Lawson described as a British Canada, that is, a Canada that remained connected in some fashion to Britain and the Empire. Nothing could be more natural than for an English Canadian to embrace the Empire: Canada was, and should remain in the eyes of many, a dutiful 'imperial daughter.'[30] It was a relationship celebrated in almost every conceivable way. That Canada should be anything other than a British nation was unthinkable.

Two powerful, but somewhat opposing, reasons prompted such

devotion. The first was clothed in the rhetoric of altruism. The British Empire was a bulwark of freedom and an agency of progress and civilization for the world at large. British political culture and governmental institutions stressed democracy and individual freedom. Imperialism had, on this thinking, a normative justification. Thus, John Willison wrote that the British flag 'filled the whole world with its splendour' and meant 'justice and freedom and order and security to millions of mankind.'[31] At the outbreak of the Great War, a Manitoba *Free Press* editorial worried that 'no greater calamity could overtake the world at this time than the break up of the British Empire, the best expression yet obtained of freedom and democracy.'[32] Certainly, Lionel Curtis was not beyond engaging in this type of appeal. Imperial union, he insisted, was not premised on the pragmatic concerns of trade or defence but arose from 'the responsibility which rests on us as trustees of civilisation in its highest form for establishing and maintaining ordinary relations between different levels of human society.'[33] This justification of imperialism revealed a chauvinism that was intertwined with a sense of Christian duty and a view of race hierarchy. It also drew heavily on the conception of progress: the British Empire was the engine of progress, the apotheosis of civilization.

Opponents of the imperial order treated such rhetoric as a smokescreen, designed to obscure the self-interested motivations of British imperialism as it existed in the late nineteenth and early twentieth century. The Empire allowed Britain to hold a dominant position in world politics through a network of holdings spanning the globe which conferred in the aggregate significant economic and military advantages. The Empire was thus Britain's answer to the powers it perceived as a threat to its dominance in world affairs – namely, the United States and Germany. To fall within the imperial umbrella allowed Canadians to enjoy an aspect of this primacy that they knew they could not achieve (not yet, at least) on their own.

The position of the United States, both geographically and politically, played an important part in the formation of imperial support in Canada. Attitudes towards America ran the gamut. Goldwin Smith promoted continental union partially on the basis that it would bring together two powerful Anglo-Saxon nations. Some Canadian imperialists, wholly antagonistic to annexation, could nevertheless see the attraction of that alliance, one in which Canada might serve as an intermediary between the United States and the Empire. The Canadian Round Tablers John Willison, Joseph Flavelle, and Robert Falconer adopted this stance, making the case for Anglo-Saxon unity in the name of world peace.[34] Likewise, George Parkin, affected by his experiences with the Rhodes scholarships, came in time to the same point of view.[35]

The seeds of concern about the United States had been sown by the Loyalists and have remained embedded in Canadian political culture. From one vantage point, the United States was seen as a society in political, moral, and social decay, proof positive that, for all of the American talk of liberty, British political institutions were indisputably superior. This was reason enough to reject annexation, but it did not mean that the American presence could be ignored or its influence negated. Concerns about cultural assimilation and American investment were already part of the landscape by the 1920s.[36] Moreover, an aggressive American foreign policy, which included the idea of manifest destiny, gave some Canadians cause for worry. George Denison warned that Canada should never allow itself to become dependent on the United States; it could not be trusted.[37] In this context, the Empire could be seen as a defence to, or refuge from, American influence. Put another way, Canadian imperialism was a form of anti-Americanism.

In the preceding decade, two events had ushered anti-Americanism to the fore. One was the reciprocity agreement of 1911, which became the central issue in the election of that year. Under Robert Borden, the Conservatives were able to consolidate opposition to reciprocity, especially among Canadian commercial interests. The Conservatives carried the day following an election campaign that invoked the rhetoric of anti-American sentiment.[38] The second event was the late entry of the United States into the First World War. Britain had of necessity become dependent on the Americans through the course of the Great War; the British war debt to the United States was about $3 billion. By every measure, it seemed to some that Americans had profited greatly by the war and suffered little.

Imperial-minded Canadians did not envision or desire colonial subservience. Imperialism did not necessarily imply that Canadian interests should bow to the needs of Westminster. Most imperialists were ardent Canadian nationalists at heart. Carl Berger's ground-breaking work, *The Sense of Power*,[39] seeks to reconcile the apparent dissonance between imperialist thinking and this nationalist spirit in Canada. Berger identified imperialism as a strain of Canadian nationalism. These two ideals went hand in glove. It was therefore understandable that someone such as George Denison could be a founding member of both the Canadian branch of the Imperial Federation League and the Canada First Movement. Those within Canada's business and political elites saw no tinge of servitude associated with being part of the Empire. As matters stood at the beginning of the twentieth century, Canada had plenty to gain by remaining within the imperial fold. Moreover, imperialists often had aspirations about Canada's imperial role. In their mind's eye, Canada was destined to replace England at the epicentre of the British Empire.[40]

The Leonard Foundation Trust lends credence to Berger's thesis. Reuben Leonard was a Canadian to the bone. He lived his entire life in Canada, and his philanthropy was directed in the main at Canadian causes. However, the trust deed speaks throughout of the British Empire. The recitals purport to restrict the Foundation to those of British nationality or parentage and the operative portion of the trust provides that eligible candidates must be British subjects. This was taken to encompass Canadian citizens (among others).[41] The only references to Canada in the document concern the selection of appropriate educational institutions (and even here there was scope to include British universities). To draw from this that Leonard put Empire before nation would be mistaken. One can understand Reuben Wells Leonard as a Canadian nationalist of the type described by Carl Berger. Leonard may not have been a perfect specimen of what Berger had in mind, but the resemblance is nevertheless striking.[42] In essence, the plan embodied in the trust deed was for Canadian schools to prepare men and women – Canadian citizens and hence British subjects – for leadership roles in the Empire.[43]

Leonard adopted the conventions of imperial duty and mission. For him, the British Empire was 'the greatest and most civilizing agency in the world' and in his mind nearly every other nation on earth envied Britain and the Empire.[44] The trust, no less than the Chatham House speech, adopted the discourse of imperial altruism: the Empire served the interests of 'mankind' or 'civilization' as a whole. He saw, too, various material advantages, in relation to trade and commerce and especially in connection with foreign affairs and defence. And he was wary of the United States. He resented the insularity and self-interest of the American people, whom, he claimed, 'were educated to distrust England.'[45] They had joined the war only in 1917, when 'Germany was suing for peace and the U.S.A. practically secured all financial advantage that was obtainable.'[46] The stridency of Leonard's views on this subject surprised Lionel Curtis. It will be recalled that the offer to donate Chatham House to the British (later Royal) Institute of International Affairs was almost revoked once Leonard learned that a library dedicated to the memory of the American Walter Page was being planned. 'His anti-American bias is even deeper than I understood,' Curtis observed in the wake of the Page controversy. 'I think this is in part due to the fact that his special job during the war was watching anti-British plots and operations along the American frontier.'[47] Even before the war Leonard demonstrated a guarded, seemingly irrational, suspicion of the United States. In 1912 he had expressed concern about the number of rail lines and other public works that had been built close to the border. One had to be cautious: 'I do not want to appear as a scare-monger, but troubles occasionally do arise between neighbouring nations, have arisen in the past, and may arise in the future.'[48]

The preponderant hope of English Canada was that the country would forever be bound to Britain in some way. However, there was a broad range of opinion as to the nature of the British connection. Not everyone was as devoted as Reuben Wells Leonard was to the Empire. The evolution of Canadian autonomy both during and after the war led many to appreciate that the status quo ante was no longer sustainable. Canada's emerging stature was seen by some as signifying a move towards independence, the result of which being that the imperial connection would play a diminished, not augmented, role. If so, what seemed likely to result was not a strengthened Empire but rather a looser association of independent states, something along the lines of what came to be called the British Commonwealth. Just what this might mean in practice was not always spelled out. At one end of the spectrum of opinion was the view that the elements that would make this collectivity cohere were the shared heritage and basal values, along with the confluence of self-interest that flowed from these ties.[49]

Others hoped that the war would bring the Empire closer together. The war effort had created a greater synergy in matters of trade and defence than had previously existed. The substantial contributions made during the conflict by the dominions suggested that they would now enjoy a greater role in imperial politics. They had earned as much.[50] Accordingly, some Canadian imperialists sought a reorganization of the British Empire on a formal constitutional basis. Commonly, these proposals called for the creation of some form of 'imperial federation.'[51] The Round Table movement, to which Reuben Leonard belonged, had been formed out of concerns that the movement toward dominion independence would lead to a fatal rupturing of the Empire. And it was thought that the war might well accelerate that process. Much time and effort was devoted by the groups across the Empire to considering ways in which the Empire could be sustained, and imperial federation played a central role in these deliberations. Leonard's imperial theory can be understood in the context of events occurring within imperial reform movements, in general, and within the debates of the Round Table, in particular.

In 1916 Lionel Curtis offered a detailed proposal for imperial federation. His position on what he often referred to as organic union, worked and reworked over the years, was eventually embodied in a monograph entitled *The Problem of the Commonwealth*.[52] The book was divided into two sections. Part I, 'What the Problem Is,' traced the origins of self-government in Britain and the dominions. The problem, as Curtis saw it, related to the limitations that persisted in the areas of defence and foreign affairs. Nations such as Canada, while enjoying plenary control over domestic matters including immigration, had little say on external relations. By the same token, the British government controlled relations between the Empire and the rest of the world, but was shouldering, disproportionately, the costs of defence.

Curtis's panacea (outlined in Part II, entitled 'The Conditions of its Solution') was to establish an imperial parliament that would be responsible to an imperial electorate and would operate under the authority of a written constitution. Finance and taxation in relation to foreign affairs and defence would be within the province of this new body, and to this extent the dominions would surrender sovereignty. Recognizing the contentious nature of this idea, Curtis proposed that the amount to be levied against each participant nation would be fixed by a commission of assessors. In return, the member states would gain a voice on questions of defence and foreign relations. Under the federation, the newly created imperial parliament would be composed of representatives from all of the self-governing dominions. On domestic matters these nations would stand on an equal footing and operate autonomously. Within the federal assembly they would participate in the governance of the Empire as a whole.

The proposal was well written and persuasively reasoned. At the same time, despite its pretensions to the contrary, it contained little that was novel. Imperial reform had been on the table for decades. At least as early as the mid-eighteenth century, forms of imperial union were being advanced, and in British North America calls for imperial union had been suggested from the nineteenth century onwards.[53] A Canadian branch of the Imperial Federation League was established in Canada in 1885 (one year after its English counterpart) to provide a countervail to the annexationism of Goldwin Smith. By 1896 the British Empire League

(BEL) had been formed in Canada to continue the crusade to secure the permanent unity of the Empire.[54] Even Curtis's call for dominion contributions to the treasury was not new. This issue had been raised within the BEL almost twenty years earlier. Drawing on these developments, a well-known aspect of political thought at the turn of the century, Sara Jeannette Duncan used imperial federation as the political motif of her novel *The Imperialist*.[55] In short, many Canadians were well acquainted with the virtues associated with a federal-style government and appreciated the potential for adapting that system to meet imperial needs.

In view of all that had come before, it is somewhat surprising that Curtis's book should have garnered much attention. But it did: *The Problem of the Commonwealth* helped to spawn a revival of interest in imperial federation as a practical means of reform. Of course, the book was placed under intense scrutiny within the Round Table chapters as Curtis had intended. In addition, Curtis's many and varied connections were invoked to ensure that the book received a high profile, especially in England, Canada, and the United States.[56] More important, it became the subject of commentary even before its intended public release.

In 1915 a preliminary version was distributed principally to the Round Table membership and a few prominent politicians (such as Prime Minister Borden and the leader of the opposition, William Lyon Mackenzie King). However, several copies found their way into the hands of the Canadian press. A minor controversy ensued, the main bone of contention being, predictably, the proposal to transfer taxing powers to the imperial parliament.[57] This advance publicity posed strategic problems for R.W. Leonard and the other members of the Canadian executive. There had been plans to expand the membership of the group in Canada but the adverse reaction to the fiscal proposals in the unpublished text was likely, it was feared, to undermine support for the movement.[58] Some in the Canadian group thought it best to publish only part of the original version (the chapters on the problem, leaving out those outlining the solution) as a Round Table publication. A chapter could be added to this version calling for a constitutional convention. Curtis was resistant to the idea, and, contrary to the Canadian plan, it was decided in London that the book would be published under Curtis's name alone, with revisions being introduced to downplay the matters of finance and taxation. He came to Canada in early April and explained this decision to the Canadian executive. *The Problem of the Commonwealth* was released in May, as Curtis was travelling across Canada in an effort to muster support for the Round Table organizations and to explain his proposals.

All in all, the members of the Canadian Round Table were not enthusiastic about Curtis's model; nor were other Canadians, including Borden. In the aftermath of the publication of *The Problem*, the Canadian executive followed through on its plan to try to extend the group's base of support. In February 1917 the Canadian Round Table issued a statement on imperial relations. It urged Canada to undertake its share of the costs of imperial defence and to speak independently on foreign affairs. There was no mention of imperial federation whatsoever, and the statement emphasized the importance of Canada retaining control over its fiscal management. The memorandum called for a meeting of the leaders of the Empire to consider the problem.[59] Shortly afterwards, a forum was held at the University of Toronto, the Canadian group's first public meeting, to explain the workings of the Round Table and to outline the idea of imperial federation. In spite of efforts to the contrary, the Canadian Round Table remained connected to *The Problem* and was increasingly being seen as a pressure group, a not entirely unfair label: it did try to influence Borden on matters of defence and imperial relations. In 1917 Laurier complained that 'Canada is now governed by a junta sitting in London, known as The Round Table.'[60] This was an utter exaggeration.[61] Still, it did conform with perceptions about the Round Table: this supposedly non-partisan group took sides; initially established to discuss a range of views, it looked like a platform for Lionel Curtis; and, ironically, a theory of shared sovereignty over the Empire was apparently being dictated from the metropolis.

What was Reuben Wells Leonard's attitude? Most of the inner core of Round Tablers were inclined to support federal reform models. And in general, Leonard was supportive of Curtis, financially and otherwise. At the end of Curtis's coast-to-coast tour of Canada in the spring and summer of 1916, Leonard had pledged an annual stipend of $1,000. Moreover, he accepted a key premise of Curtis's work, namely, that Britain had shouldered far too much of the burden of defence during the war. On the other hand, Leonard did sign the memorandum designed to distance the Canadian group from *The Problem of the Commonwealth*. He was particularly supportive of Canadian (not imperial) economic policy. Part of his rationale for preserving an imperial allegiance was that it was economically beneficial to Canada. Therefore, surrendering control over fiscal matters would not likely have been acceptable to him.

James Greenlee has suggested that Reuben Leonard was fundamentally a reactionary and that he regarded the British Empire as an 'Anglo-Saxon fortress,'[62] its function being to protect the comfortable world order in which he had lived against the threatening and alien elements emerging from all compass points. This assessment seems essentially sound. Leonard felt that the Empire must endure and that anything else would be unfathomable. But he also realized that imperial relations had to undergo reform to remain viable. In any case by 1924 he appreciated that imperial federation was unlikely to materialize. 'The Round Table,' he told the Toronto *Star*, 'was not committed to Mr. Curtis' view, nor do I think that Mr. Curtis altogether retains his former view. Imperial centralisation may never come. Then again it may come. Who can tell.'[63]

Leonard advocated what he called a 'sturdy partnership' between Great Britain and the dominions for the purpose of advancing their independent goals. This, he thought, would be of greater value to the world than the League of Nations. He saw Canada's support for the League and its assertion of independence in foreign affairs as retrogressive steps. Such action tended to undermine the coherence of the Empire, an outcome that, he despaired, would be 'nothing short of a dire calamity to civilization.'[64] Ever the pragmatist, he explained the virtues of a unified foreign policy in utilitarian terms: 'It would be a pity for Canada to waste her substance on innumerable petty embassies or trade representatives to all the countries of the world. That would drain and dwarf us. The empire is an immense help and saving to us.'[65] Even with his reservations about the League, however, Leonard did allow for the forming of international alliances. Under a partnership with the United States and France, the Empire could assure the peace and prosperity of the world. He felt that, when other nations had been shown to be 'sufficiently trained to be competent,' they could, one-by-one, undertake the duties and guarantees involved in such an international association.[66]

Some idea of what might be meant by a sturdy partnership is perhaps revealed by the language that Leonard invariably chose: he spoke of 'Empire' and not 'Commonwealth.' The latter term is thought to have been first used in relation to the British Empire in the late nineteenth century. By the First World War, it had crept into official usage, Lionel Curtis (and the South African politician Jan Smuts) having helped to popularize the term. To Curtis, it meant the organic union that he had championed so energetically, while for others it began to assume a different connotation. Though the language of Empire persisted for much longer in common parlance, politicians began speaking increasingly of a British commonwealth of nations. This metamorphosis, slow as it was, tracked the growing autonomy of the dominions and the ebbing of the imperial ethos.[67] Of course, the change had threatening undertones because it was taken as signifying a weakening of the British presence in the world arena, something that troubled people like R.W. Leonard. The Leonard Foundation was dedicated to securing the future of the British Empire, not Canada per se and certainly not the Commonwealth. That the Empire was in decline was apparently not something he saw, or at least he was not prepared to acknowledge or concede as much in the 1923 trust deed.

Race

The Leonard scholarships were available only to members of the white race. This is explained by the first recital, which is captioned 'Task of White Race,' that task being the development of civilization and the general progress of the world. Precisely who was meant to fall within the meaning of the term is not specified; perhaps this was thought to be self-evident. No account is taken of the status of a person who might be said to be only partly of the designated 'race.' The pre-1986 application form did not suggest criteria; nor did it require the applicant to make a declaration in this regard. It was presumably left to the General Committee through the interviewing process to determine if a candidate met this qualification.

There are at least four major ideas in the first recital about race and race relations. First, races are amenable to classification, each being identifiable as a cognate type (whether or not these types could be seen as existing within a single species). Second, the differences relate not merely to physical distinctions (such as colour of skin) but to skills, aptitudes, and personality traits. Whites are endowed, for example, with a special capacity for leadership. Third, these differences allow for not just descriptive but normative comparisons. Some races possess attributes that allow for greater achievement in certain domains, so that peoples can be plotted on a scale of racial worth. Fourth, differences among races are the result of *natural* processes. Given all of this, then, if one can define a set of valued goals, then it should be possible to identify those races best able to pursue them. Progress is one such goal, the first recital tells us, which leads to the thesis that the white race enjoys a superior position because of its natural capacity to ensure the progress of the world along the best lines.

None of this was exceptional. By the eighteenth century, the construction of racial typologies had become common. So, for example, the influential work of the Swedish naturalist Carolus Linnaeus suggested that all mankind could be divided into one of four racial groups: white, black, red, yellow. Each of these possessed certain identifiable features: whites were intelligent and creative, blacks were indolent and careless, and so on. Johann Friedrich Blumenbach developed the Linnaean analysis further by describing a fifth racial group (the Malay or 'brown' race) and introducing a notion of hierarchy that was not prominent in Linnaeus's treatment. Many such accounts were published.[68]

Recipients of the Leonard awards might well have been taught principles of race akin to those set out by these scholars. The textbook *Dominion School Geography* (1910), which was used in schools across Canada, contained a description of the peoples of the world. 'The White Race,' pupils were informed, was 'the most active, enterprising and intelligent race in the world.' Within the yellow race was to be found 'some of the most backward tribes of the world' who were, as a rule, 'not progressive.' The red race was 'but little civilized, although a few are beginning to develop industries, such as basketry, pottery, and a little farming.' Those of the black race 'were often impulsive in their actions, but they are faithful and affectionate to any for whom they care.'[69] Likewise, in 1907 members of the Empire Club of Toronto might have heard an address by the Reverend C.S. Eby entitled 'The True Inwardness of the Yellow Peril,' in which the human races were said to be divided into three main groups: 'First there are the uncivilized races, including the blacks of Africa, the tinted peoples of the Pacific Islands, the red man of America and other aborigines scattered everywhere. The second is the civilized, non-Christian races, including the yellow races of Eastern Asia, the brown races of India, the shades of skin and of thought in Western Asia. Thirdly, there are the civilized and Christian races, principally white, and among them the Anglo-Saxons, whose energy and strength would dominate the world.'[70]

Within the complex literature on the subject, the term race was used in a variety of ways, supporting a number of different meanings; whites, Anglo-Saxons, British nationals, even Canadians might be spoken of as a racial group. Typologies differed greatly, though there was a general harmony as to the races that placed highly (whites or Anglo-Saxons and so on) and those that did not (the rest).

The social construction of Anglo-Saxonism was the product of nineteenth-century revisionist thinking under which the English were seen as having been endowed with specific talents. Writing about Britain's past and present began to emphasize the genius of the Anglo-Saxon race in the development of Britain's power and its current standing in world politics.[71] At the heart of this was the conviction, asserted in the Leonard trust deed, that whites possessed a special capacity for leadership.[72] Joseph Chamberlain declared Anglo-Saxons to be 'that proud, persistent, self-asserting and resolute stock, that no change of climate can alter and which is infallibly destined to be the predominating force in the future history and civilization of the world.'[73] In addition, he claimed that 'the British race is the greatest governing race that the world has ever seen.'[74] George Parkin prefaced his analysis of imperial federation with the assertion that a 'special capacity for political organization may, without race vanity, be claimed for the Anglo-Saxon people.'[75]

There remains the question of how this came to be. The Leonard trust declares that the white race has been endowed by nature. Science furnished support for the view that racial differences were inherent, though it was not universally accepted that heredity would necessarily prevail over the effects of the environment.[76] In the nineteenth century, techniques were developed for identifying racial types by reference to the study of skull formations (such as craniology) and by examining other physical manifestations. A central theme emerged that there existed innate differences among races which gave rise to distinct physical, moral, and mental characteristics. The general upshot was that non-white races were shown to have such limited intellectual capacities that they were destined to lag behind in the march of progress. All of this served to enhance the pre-eminent standing of the white race.

Race preoccupied many social Darwinists. Among the early contributions were those of the American palaeontologist Edward Drinker Cope (1840–97). Accepting the Darwinian postulate that man descended from apes, in 1870 Cope advanced a theory of racial hierarchy based on the degree to which a given racial group demonstrated simian traits.[77] Others followed Cope's lead, invoking social Darwinism to reinforce the belief in racial hierarchies. At some level, notions of racial typology and social Darwinism both posed problems for Christian belief systems. Typologists had to account for the existence of what they saw as fixed differences among races in a world in which all humans supposedly trace their origins to Adam and Eve and, therefore, are of common stock. Social Darwinian claims that differences were the product of accidents of nature undercut the idea that all God's creatures were put on earth to fulfil a divine purpose. Despite all of this, such inconsistencies did not seem to trouble Christian social Darwinists. As Darwin's theories gained increased acceptance within the scientific academy, attempts were made to harmonize Darwin's theory with Christian theology.[78] Faith in the progress of civilization formed one common thread.

Theories drawn from race science and social Darwinism served a purpose. As alluded to above, some of this learning suggested that the evident inequality of individuals or groups (whether conceived of as nations, classes, and races, and so on) was inherent. In the struggle for survival the weak would eventually lose, and in consequence the so-called lower races were under threat. The corollary was that those who survived were stronger and better and this in turn explained the growth of Western societies. It took only a small step to come to the view that the ruling elite was rightly in power, or that colonization was proper, even necessary, or that millionaires were to be regarded as the product of natural selection. This way of thinking supported opposition to reforms aimed at the relief of poverty and the regulation of fair working conditions. The principle of natural selection underlying evolutionary progress dictated that inferior peoples, nationalities, and races would be condemned to the bottom of the socio-economic ladder because of their permanent inequality. Those who offered a utopian vision in which the lower races would be encouraged to play a part in the world were ignoring the inescapable effects of obstinate natural forces.[79]

In Canada, theories of race affected political discourse in a number of ways. Canadian imperialists exhibited the same chauvinism as their English counterparts. On the domestic front, race theory informed policies concerning eugenics and the treatment of aboriginal people and other visible minorities. And it was particularly influential in relation to immigration policy. The Canada of the 1920s was not an ethnically diverse society. The 1921 census showed that 55 per cent of Canadians described themselves as being of British heritage; 28 per cent were of French heritage and 14 per cent were classified as 'other European.' All other groups accounted for only 3 per cent of the population.[80] Still, despite the numerical dominance of British-Canadians, increases in non-Anglo-Saxon immigration surfaced as a major concern after the First World War.

As is well known, in this period Canadian public policy was premised on the pursuit of Anglo-conformity (not cultural pluralism, diversity, or multiculturalism).[81] Newcomers to Canada were expected to lose the cultural baggage of the societies from which they had come and to embrace the values of their adopted nation. That being so, a critical concern in assessing the suitability of immigrant groups was the extent to which they were thought to be susceptible to assimilation. Put another way, fears over immigration centred on the dilution of British-Canadian institutions.[82] As R.B. Bennett warned: 'We must still maintain that measure of British civilization which will enable us to assimilate these people to British institutions, rather than assimilate our institutions to theirs.'[83] Fears about the failure of new Canadians to adopt Canadian social values were tethered to concerns that non-British Canadians would or could not be loyal to the British Empire. These were oft-repeated themes.[84] Predictably, the favoured immigrants were British and American; the least preferred were blacks and Asians. The threat of immigration from the Orient, the spectre of alien cultural traditions among peoples incapable of assimilation, led to policies especially antagonistic to immigration from China, Japan, elsewhere in Asia, and Africa.

In Canada during the early part of the twentieth century, theories of inherent racial superiority, with the various corollaries that flowed from these, were common and accepted. The words spoken on racial matters were often caustic,[85] and the rhetorical conventions about race were very different from those that obtain today. It was a time in which, in the course of parliamentary debates, blacks could be referred to as 'niggers'[86] or the epithet 'menace' could be used to describe oriental immigration.[87] In the mainstream press, Jews could be labelled as habitual criminals.[88] These attitudes were not just a matter of political posturing: there is a sad litany of racial prejudice in the Canada of these times, too much to be regarded as exceptional. The treatment of visible minorities, especially blacks, Asians, and First Nations peoples, was deplorable. There were many other groups, including the Ukrainians, Poles, and Jews, that led an oppressed existence in Canada during the period measured by the span of Reuben Leonard's life.[89] Discriminatory practices took many forms, and, as will be seen in the next chapter, there was virtually no recourse in the law against such action.

In Canada, as elsewhere, race science played a role in policy debates.[90] For example, eugenicist writing sometimes focused on traits, such as low intelligence, thought to be common among the immigrant population. The adverse impact of immigration on the regeneration of native-born Canadians was explained on the basis of scientific laws. Hence, W.S. Wallace argued in *Canadian Magazine* that the 'native-born population, in the face of increasing competition, fails to propagate itself, commits race suicide in short; whereas the immigrant population, being inferior, and having no appearances to keep up, propagates itself like the fish of the sea.'[91] New methods of intelligence testing were invoked to validate this outlook. In 1923 Carl Brigham's *A Study of American Intelligence*[92] showed correlations between intelligence and various races: the Nordic races fared best, blacks the poorest.

Several years after Brigham's results were published, Peter Sandiford of the department of education at the University of Toronto released the results of his study of British Columbia school children.[93] He assumed that an influx of immigrants from Britain would enhance the province's average intelligence quotient: 'Obviously, British Columbia is not diluting the intelligence of her population by admitting immigrants from the British Isles, rather is she increasing her average thereby.'[94] What he saw as the 'danger point'[95] was immigration from other parts of Europe, though he also tested children whose families had immigrated from other parts of the world. His initial findings were that oriental pupils scored better than their white counterparts, a result that he found 'profoundly disturbing.'[96] A second test showed white students to be below those of Japanese origin but above those of Chinese ancestry. This was seen as a more encouraging outcome. Sandiford's overall conclusions about the race variable were limited. Although he treated 'coloured immigration' as a vexing problem, he inclined to the view that the climate of Canada, except for British Columbia, would prove too severe for most Asiatic immigrants.[97]

Reuben Leonard's views on race seem to have drawn support from race science and social Darwinism. Even though the Toronto *Star*'s complimentary description of the Leonard Foundation scholarships (in 1924) as being awarded on the basis of 'merit and eugenics'[98] is technically inaccurate, it is nevertheless extremely telling. Leonard saw genetics as infused with racial significance:

We have the much-taught doctrine that 'all men are born "equal,"' which is an obvious fallacy. It is a self-evident fact that there is as great natural inequality – physically and mentally – in the different branches of the human race as in any other species of the animal kingdom. This difference greatly increased by the moral and spiritual inequalities of the human race – is influenced again and emphasized by environment and education from the cradle to the grave. The very men who ignorantly preach that one man is as able as another and as well qualified to rule or hold office – that race and family count for naught – will spare no pains in breeding his live stock to select parents having certain desired characteristics of disposition and physique.[99]

It will be recalled that it was the innate differences that Leonard saw among the different races that explained his pessimism about the League of Nations. This is what he said: 'The League appears to me to have been conceived and drawn up by idealists who do not realize the radical differences in mental and moral make-up of the different races, which differences are I believe inherent and irradicable [sic] ... If I am right, education is useless unless extending over ages of time.'[100]

Describing aspects of racial discourse within Canada provides one setting for Leonard's ideology of race. However, within the context of the Leonard Foundation Trust, race is treated as an *imperial* issue. As we have seen, racial chauvinism was a conventional justification of Empire. The trust conceives of leadership of the Empire as an Anglo-Saxon preserve. The importance of this is revealed through an examination of the relationship between race and the structure of imperial governance, both existing and proposed.

The element of race was critical to many of those interested in imperial federation.[101] In a refurbished Empire, in which power was to be decentred, it was axiomatic that the self-governing dominions would be accorded representation in the imperial parliament. However, there was far more to the Empire than just Britain and the dominions. The range and status of imperially controlled entities defies easy classification. Some holdings were designated as crown colonies (including the Carribean colonies), others as protectorates (such as the East Africa Protectorate), and there were also an assortment of other imperial possessions (including naval stations). Some of these holdings were accorded a limited devolution of lawmaking power over local matters.

In general, the standing of the non-dominions had racial overtones because the template of race fits over top of the categories. The dominions were populated mainly by whites of British stock; one, South Africa, was controlled by a white minority. In terms of demographics, the self-governing states accounted for a mere fraction of the Empire. The rest, that is, those parts actually subject to extensive imperial rule, were predominantly populated by non-whites.[102]

Given this demographic breakdown, one can see that the interface between race and imperial reform emerged whenever the proposed role of the non-dominions was considered. There was considerable disagreement among reformers about these subordinated holdings and other issues concerning the colonies, as is apparent from Seymour Cheng's *Schemes for the Federation of the British Empire* (1930).[103] Cheng reviewed and analysed twenty-three proposals for imperial federation, fifteen of these having been published during what he termed the first phase (1871–1910) and eight during a second phase (1910–30). Among other things, he compared the proposed institutions of governance and the rights of representation to be enjoyed by the different units within the

Empire. Almost all of the schemes treated the dominions differently from other imperial holdings. Members of the former group would be granted full status within the federation; the latter would have some lesser standing or none at all. For instance, under Basil Worsfold's 1916 plan, an extreme one, a distinction was drawn between white and non-white populations. For white states, representation was to be based on population. For non-white states, the number of delegates was to be determined partly as a factor of population and partly by an assessment of the degree of civilization that a given colony had achieved.[104]

Highly revealing are the differences that emerge under Cheng's final category of comparison: 'The Question of India.' The issue of participation was especially vexing in relation to India. The largest British holding by far (its population constituting 70 per cent of that of the Empire), India played a pivotal role in the Empire in relation to defence, manufacturing, trade, and transportation. Not a dominion, nor strictly a colony, India was an empire in its own right. Still, at the apex of control stood the viceroy, the crown's representative. He presided over a complex network of government, which (at the time of Cheng's study) included some delegated authority to local councils. What was to be India's place in the new imperial order?

Some of the schemes did not deal explicitly with India; others suggested that the determination of this sensitive issue be deferred. Of those that offered a plan, the proposals varied considerably. About half of the twenty-three proposals canvassed by Cheng recognized that India should be accorded representation in either a lower or an upper house of some proposed imperial parliament. However, given the size of India's population, it was generally felt that its representation should be based partly on other factors.[105] Four of the proposals rejected the idea of Indian participation. By contrast, under two, India was to have *greater* parliamentary representation than any of the dominions.[106]

Lionel Curtis, whose *The Problem of the Commonwealth* was one of the second-phase proposals surveyed by Cheng, argued that India should initially be treated as a dependency but also that it should be trained for self-government. He maintained that 'the task of preparing for freedom the races which cannot as yet govern themselves is the supreme duty of those who can.'[107] Yet, while Curtis had come to realize the importance of including the dependencies, especially India, there was disagreement among the London Round Table on this point. One member, Lord Brand, rejected out of hand the idea of multiracial governance, confessing that 'I intend that the white man shall always be top dog ... I am not at all sure that this is consonant with mutual citizenship in a Commonwealth.'[108] Edward Grigg (later Lord Altrincham) was of the same view, on the ground that the 'child races [and] lower civilisations [were] the chief menace to the peace of the world.'[109] In sum, among those who wrote about imperial reform, views differed vastly as to the representation to be granted to the non-white regions of the British Empire. On the question of race within the Empire, the English Round Table opinion was also divided. Reuben Wells Leonard could find support for his vision (the white race is best suited for imperial governance) from among this group, though it is at best unclear whether he could claim that his long-term prognosis was the conventional viewpoint.[110]

Religion

Religion played an important role in the life of R.W. Leonard and this is evident from a reading of the trust. The deed recites that the progress of the world has depended and will continue to depend on the maintenance of the Christian religion. The Leonard Foundation scholarships were open only to Christians of the Protestant faith. The sons and daughters of clergymen fell within the preferred class, and over the years this was the most-often invoked special category. There was usually a number of Anglican clergymen on the General Committee of the Foundation. The selection of schools in the initial list was also affected by religious considerations. And as will be discussed in more detail below, the notion of philanthropy, part of the essence of the charitable trust, can be understood as being founded on the fulfilment of Christian duty.[111] Moreover, the trust contains an important feature of imperial discourse in the first part of this century, namely, the intimate link between Christianity and Empire. The fourth recital of the trust asserts that the affairs of the British Empire should remain under the guidance of Christians. As with Anglo-Saxonism, a belief in the superiority of Christianity was bound up with conceptions of Empire.

Carl Berger has suggested that three factors lie at the core of the religious dimension of imperialist thought in Canada.[112] First, the value of the Empire could not be calculated in material terms. As shown above, the rhetoric of Empire was not about trade, defence, and self-interested conquest. Rather, it was an institution with a higher calling. A common refrain in the writings on imperialism is that the Empire was part of God's work on earth. It was a secular instrument that served as a Providential agent, its divine purpose being to advance Christian ideals throughout the world. It was also argued that Christianity was vital to the coherence and unity of the British Empire. In 1908 Canon Henry J. Cody wrote that 'deepest of all, I think, in [the] elements that go to make up the idea of an Imperial unity is the element of a common Christian religion.'[113] And for some, the British Empire was also imbued with spiritual attributes; it was treated as a religion in its own right.[114]

The second factor was the acceptance of the virtue of work and the assumption of sacred obligations. Imperialism was a mission which involved discipline, dedication, and sacrifice. To accept the mantle of imperialism was to realize that one had undertaken a moral responsibility to make the world a better place. To R.B. Bennett, an imperialist was 'a man who accepts gladly and bears proudly the responsibilities of his race and breed.'[115] The British presence in Egypt, he claimed, could be justified on the grounds that 'under the Providence of God we are a Christian people who have given the subject races of the world the only kind of decent government they have ever known.'[116]

Third, within imperialist discourse one finds the logic of social Darwinism and its curious translation into evangelical thought. The ascendancy of the Anglo-Saxon Christian races placed it in a position of control over the weaker races. The world had developed this way for a reason; it was thus God's wish that Christian leadership be exercised.[117] And Christianity was part of the secret of the British Empire's undeniable success.

These ideas find voice through the language of the Leonard Foundation Trust and through the philosophical framework of the document as a whole. Practical consequences also ensued, since restricting eligibility to Protestants eliminated many potential applicants. The 1921 census reported that 56 per cent of Canadians considered themselves Protestant; 44 per cent were therefore excluded by this stipulation.[118] Standing on its own, Leonard's position might be viewed as little more than the type of chauvinism embraced by people such as Bennett and Cody. However, as with the racial qualification, the chauvinism is Janus-like: it can also be understood as an expression of nativism. One group is singled out in the deed: although the recitals speak of the maintenance of Christianity and its importance to the world, Catholics (38.7 per cent of the population of Canada in 1921[119]) were nevertheless precluded from participating in the Foundation.

Roberto Perin has argued that, throughout the first fifty years following Confederation, the Catholic Church in Canada survived within an environment of ethnic confrontation.[120] Indeed, anti-Romanist thought was a recurrent (if not major) theme in Canadian political thought during the period spanned by the life of Reuben Leonard. It was not until the end of the war that anti-Catholic feeling began to wane in Ontario,[121] though it was somewhat more resilient in the west.[122] Over the course of Leonard's life, certain events stand out. In 1876 the Conservative politician Alexander Galt published two pamphlets in which he expressed alarm over the influence that Rome was exerting, invidiously, on political affairs in Quebec and Canada.[123] At around the same time, Charles Lindsey wrote *Rome in Canada*[124] in which a similar thesis was advanced. These fears were shared by others, occasionally in palpable ways: There were some twenty clashes in Toronto between Orangemen and Irish Catholics in the first twenty-five years after Confederation, the most well-known being the Jubilee Riot in 1875.[125]

Anti-Catholic sentiment prompted the creation of Protestant extremist organisations aimed at counteracting Rome's presence. In 1876 the short-lived Protestant Defence Alliance was formed for that purpose. In 1889 the Equal Rights Association was created in an effort to limit the political influence of the Catholic Church and to campaign against the special status being accorded to Catholics within the educational system. Two years later, the Protestant Protective Association (PPA), an offshoot of the American Protective Association, was established in Ontario. Drawing support from the Orange Order, the PPA developed a large membership in the 1890s, though its impact was, in the end, rather negligible.

Such feelings were often bolstered by an accentuated devotion to the British Empire. It is therefore scarcely surprising that the leaders of the PPA, D'Alton McCarthy and George Denison, were also involved in the imperial federation movement.[126] Moreover, the attack on Catholicism was, in large measure, manifested in antipathy towards French Canada. Concerns that were expressed about the preservation of Protestant hegemony in Canada, and the maintenance of a Protestant vision of Canada, translated into fears of French Canadian influence and control. However, the match was not perfect, given that Irish Catholics also suffered under the bigotry directed at Rome.

Catholicism and its adherents were pilloried at every turn.[127] Predominantly Catholic societies were regarded as inferior, even immoral; Catholic immigrants were decried as a burden to the nation; and the teachings of Rome were said to be antithetical to the progress of civilization. A common line of attack concerned the danger of betrayal. Catholics could not be trusted because what Rome ultimately wanted, by whatever means it would take, was political domination. The Catholic clergy demanded 'slavish devotion to a narrow-minded Italian priest' whose religion 'in many cases makes disloyalty a virtue.'[128] Adherence to ultramontane Catholicism involved acceptance of the dogma that the pope was infallible. Because Catholics owed their first duty to the church, under the authority of the pope, they were seen as a fifth column within a secular state such as Canada. The pope being supreme, Roman Catholics could never be beholden to any other regime.

The nativist attack on Catholicism – the fifth-column rationale – captures the central fear of groups such as the PPA. The Roman Catholic Church manipulated the franchise (through bloc voting) as a means of pursuing self-interested goals. A rigid dogma that demanded resolute loyalty and suppressed individual thought thereby allowed the church to assert control. The PPA's avowed function was to rally Protestant forces against the Romanist presence in Canada. Members were required to swear an oath denouncing Roman Catholicism, the pope, his priests, and all his other emissaries, and to pledge to support the cause of Protestantism 'to the end that there may be no interference with the discharge of the duties of citizenship.'[129]

For those inclined towards these views, there was ample evidence to be found. During the Northwest Rebellion, the priests in both the Red River area and the Northwest Territories had supported the rebels; or so it was alleged. After the 1885 uprising (during which, it will be recalled, Leonard had served as an officer), the charges went beyond mere claims of complicity. History will show, it was said, that 'the Romish Church was the "power behind the throne" and Riel the instrument only.'[130] Likewise, during the First World War the conscription controversy in Quebec revived anti-French and anti-Catholic feeling.[131] As enlistment from Quebec lagged, attacks on the integrity of the Catholic Church intensified. English-speaking Catholics outside Quebec, however much they endeavoured to demonstrate their loyalty, were also treated with suspicion and derision.[132] The theme of distrust played out in the federal election of 1917, in which Borden sought a mandate for the newly formed Union government. A contributor to the *Canadian Home Journal* warned that 'Germany's reptile democracy uses many agencies in many lands, and the most important agency that it is today using on Canadian soil is the Roman Catholic Church.'[133] Similarly, the Union candidate Newton Rowell purported to lay bare the Catholic Church's role in undermining the Canadian government: 'We might as well frankly face the issue. There is a Nationalist, clerical and reactionary movement at work in the Province of Quebec which to-day dominates the political situation in that province, and is using this hour of grave national peril to dominate the political situation throughout the Dominion of Canada.'[134]

This strand of nativism finds its way into the Leonard Foundation Trust. Given the function of the trust to further the interests of the Empire, patriotism and loyalty were taken as essential. So, it is said, the holders of the scholarships cannot owe allegiance 'to any Foreign Government, Prince, *Pope* or Potentate'; they cannot 'recognize such authority, temporal or spiritual.'[135] This is the rhetoric of feared betrayal. It parallels the PPA pledge to combat interference with the duties of citizenship and accords with the view that, in a contest between the British monarchy and Rome, 'nine out of every ten [Catholics] would go against the Queen.'[136] While there is no evidence that Reuben Leonard belonged to an organized anti-Catholic faction, it is nevertheless apparent that the trust is part of a tradition of nativist discourse in which Catholics were stigmatized as the enemy within. And just as this posture affected the francophone communities within Canada, so too does the trust. The requirement of adherence to the Protestant faith excludes most French Canadians.

Leonard's treatment of the Protestant/Catholic division within Christianity is obvious. Yet there is also a finer distinction along religious lines drawn in the trust, namely, that which exists between high church and low church (or evangelical) Anglicanism. The development of the modern high church can be traced to the Oxford Movement of the first half of the nineteenth century. In general, low church theology is rooted in the Reformation, while high church theology stresses the historic ties to Catholicism. This fissure is apparent in both the substantive doctrines of these branches and in the manner of observance.[137]

This division within the Church of England quickly became entrenched in British North America. Among other things, it affected the development of private schools and denominational colleges in Ontario. The first Anglican private schools, Trinity College (1851), Trinity College School (1862), and Bishop Strachan School for Young Ladies (1867), were high church. However, 'to the evangelicals the idea of educating a son or daughter at a High Church establishment such as Bishop Strachan or Trinity College School was not merely unacceptable, it was totally unthinkable. Education and religious principles, the Evangelicals believed, must never be set apart ...'[138] In time, Wycliffe College (1877), Ridley College (1889), and Havergal Ladies' College (1894) were founded to provide low church alternatives.[139]

The distinction between high and low Anglicanism was important to the Leonards. Both Grace Church in Brantford and St Thomas' Church in St Catharines are low church. Leonard spent twenty years as a governor of Ridley and Wycliffe; Kate Leonard was associated with Havergal. By contrast, none of their copious benefactions were in aid of high church institutions. Furthermore, one sees this distinction being drawn in the selection of schools as set out in the 1923 deed. In 1923 there were twenty-three universities in Canada. Of these, only six were state-controlled: New Brunswick, Toronto, Manitoba, Saskatchewan, Alberta, and British Columbia. Four were classified as private non-denominational: Dalhousie, McGill, Queen's, and Western. The remaining thirteen were formally affiliated with religious institutions: St Dunstan's, St Francis Xavier, St Joseph's, Laval, Montreal, and Ottawa (Roman Catholic); King's College, Bishop's College, and Trinity College (Church of England); Acadia and McMaster (Baptist); Mount Allison and Victoria (Methodist).[140] The universities selected by Leonard include only those that were state-controlled or officially non-denominational.[141] None of the denominational universities was included in the initial listing because none was low church Anglican. The pattern is similar in relation to the selection of private schools and colleges: Ridley, Havergal, and Wycliffe were included; Trinity, Trinity College School, and Bishop Strachan were not.

Education

A scholarship program is by definition about education, and the support and promotion of learning was a constant in Reuben Leonard's life. He was trained as a teacher and had joined the Board of Governors at RMC just five years after graduation. Over the course of his life he also served as a governor at Ridley, Wycliffe, Khaki University, the Kingston School of Mining, Queen's, and the University of Toronto. He saw education as a critical stepping-stone in life; to be able to pursue one's studies was, in his mind, a blessing.[142]

Though he showed an abiding interest in the matters of education, he was often disconsolate about the state of Canada's educational system. In 1920 he wrote:

We have recently allowed ourselves to be unduly influenced by a few noisy and peculiar people who have been very badly educated ... We have left untaught much fundamental knowledge which should have been taught and we have taught much that should have been left untaught, and there is an apparent lack of national sanity in us.

A few years ago it would have been unnecessary to deal with the fundamentals of our civilization; they were so imbued into our beings that it was almost silly to formulate them into words. We rested securely in the belief that 'Truth is might and will prevail.' Of late, however, so much false teaching and distortion of fundamental truths has been disseminated, and accepted by many, that downtrodden Truth would appear to need the assistance of some Minister of Propaganda if she is to hold her place and prevail before the structure of our civilization is badly shaken.[143]

Leonard had great faith in the efficacy of education. His concerns about the teachings of Professor MacIver were generated by a fear that the professoriate could have a profound impact on the ideologies of students precisely at the time when their political consciousness was at a formative stage. MacIver was worrisome because 'young men who are intrinsically honest themselves cannot comprehend the wiles and misrepresentations of professional agitators who make their living stirring up trouble and advancing all kinds of imaginary grievances.'[144] And when the *Financial Post* published a critique in 1924 of the presentation of communistic lectures at the University of Toronto, Leonard wrote to President Falconer to express his concern, as he had done in relation to MacIver. It was not fair, he thought, 'to subject young men at the most impressionable time of their lives and when their knowledge of world affairs is very limited, to the influence of clever propagandists, paid by the Bolsheviks or other elements whom we consider undesirable.'[145] Leonard thought it crucial that the political views of academics be known before faculty appointments were made and that universities should be on guard for 'any teaching tending to upset a civilization which has been the result of some thousands of years of struggle.'[146]

It is not the value of a good education per se that lies at the base of the Leonard Foundation scholarships. The trust assumes a connection between education and imperialism: it is dedicated to the mission of assisting young men and women who show encouraging signs of becoming leading members of the British Empire. Leonard was not alone in seeing such a causal connection. 'It is of vast importance,' argued George Wrong, 'to get hold of every man who promises leadership and educate him to think imperially.'[147] At the opening of the Manitoba Law School in 1914, Sir James Aikins, long-time president of the Canadian Bar Association, urged the members of the inaugural class to 'aim to be leaders in thought, promoters of the intellectual and moral development of our young nation, so that it may become a strong and forceful leader in the Empire.'[148]

In Britain this perspective gave rise to the emergence of the Imperial Studies Movement.[149] At the Imperial Education Conference of 1923 it was resolved that, in the interests of the solidarity of the Empire it was imperative that support should be given to the teaching of imperial geography and history. In the following year a similar idea was endorsed at the Imperial Studies Conference.[150] Three principal organizations had already emerged to advance this cause: the League of the Empire, the Victorian League, and the Royal Colonial Institute (RCI). These groups tried in their respective ways to affect the course of education at all levels in Great Britain. Leonard supported these initiatives. He was involved in the work of the League of the Empire, serving on its Canadian and Ontario executive committees. He also belonged to the Royal Colonial Institute, which had connections with the London Round Table.[151] In 1913 he became a life member of the RCI, having been nominated by George Parkin and another prominent member, Sir Godfrey Lagden.

The ideals of the Imperial Studies Movement inform, in a general way, the Leonard Foundation Trust. Whatever the impact of that movement, however, it is difficult to resist the conclusion that R.W. Leonard was influenced by another mining magnate and stalwart imperialist – Cecil Rhodes.[152] By 1916 the Rhodes scholarship was already well established as the most prestigious student prize in the English-speaking world. Created by will in 1902, the scholarships were designed to provide full funding for study at Oxford. Rhodes's aim was to select men whose mental and moral qualities suggested that they were likely to aspire to public service. He envisioned that his scholarships would assist in the training of the world's future leaders.

It is implausible that these two men ever met. Rhodes died in 1902, two years before the discovery of the first Coniagas mine. However, Leonard had a few personal connections with Oxford and the Rhodes Trust: in 1923 Lionel Curtis was at All Souls College, and prior to this he had been a don at New College; George Parkin served as the organizing secretary of the Rhodes Trust from 1902 until 1917 and in 1912 he published an account of the Rhodes scholarships.[153]

Like Leonard, Rhodes believed fervently in the greatness of the British Empire. The Empire was the point of departure for the Rhodes Trust and, along with Leonard, Rhodes was certain that its maintenance was of importance to the world at large.[154] Not only did both Leonard and Rhodes believe in the importance of education in achieving their loftier goals, they also held similar conceptions of the well-rounded scholar. Relevant in the selection of a Leonard scholar is the candidate's physical, mental, and moral qualities. For Rhodes, scholastic achievement was important, though he made it clear that he did not want mere bookworms. An interest in the 'manly' sports and qualities such as courage, devotion to duty, selflessness, fellowship, and civic-mindedness were all relevant considerations.

This image of the scholastic ideal is itself rooted in the English public school[155] as it evolved throughout the last half of the nineteenth century. English public schools conceived of their task as the preparation of young men for the responsibilities that privilege would bestow upon them. What emerged as the essential traits of Anglo-Saxon manhood was a mix of virtues captured in large measure by the term 'muscular Christianity.'[156] Thomas Arnold, as headmaster at Rugby in the 1840s, had led the transformation of public school education in Britain. The Arnoldian code was designed to equip young men for imperial leadership. Christian altruism, a sense of fair play, self-discipline, and self-sacrifice were all ingredients. Team sports such as rugby (invented at Rugby) were thought to emphasize these qualities.[157]

Generally speaking, private schools in Canada embraced the central tenets of the English system. Schools such as Rothesay and Ridley as well as others named in the Leonard Trust saw their roles as providing the stock of Canada's and the Empire's finest men and women. As in England, the development of spirit, mind, and body meant that the sites of education included not only the classroom but also the chapel and the playing and drill fields. The rather more Spartan nature of the Canadian private schools and the rigours of Canada's climate allowed for the myths of social Darwinism to inform the pedagogical mission.[158] Only the hardy would endure. The manly sports were prominent here too. If it is true that 'athleticism was an amalgam of Christianity, Darwinism, nationalism and imperialism,'[159] so too can this mix be found in the Leonard Foundation Trust. In addition, the public school ethos stressed the building of character over educational performance, a balance seen in the Leonard awards.

Leonard could also count on the Canadian public-education system to support and sustain his goals in some general sense. The curriculum at the primary and secondary levels focused on notions of character, responsibility, and loyalty to country and Empire. Textbooks dealing with history, geography, and social studies represented Canada as a critical part of the British Empire.[160] In Ontario of the 1920s, for example, Empire Day was enthusiastically celebrated. Each May, the Ontario Department of Education would distribute a pamphlet entitled 'Empire Day in the Schools of Ontario' which contained an inspirational essay by the premier, patriotic songs and poems, and suggestions for studying 'The Greatness of the Empire.'[161] A similar strategy was pursued in Manitoba.[162]

Even with all of this in mind, there is still a tenuous nexus between what Leonard was trying to achieve (the strengthening of the Empire) and his scholarship/bursary awards, especially in relation to university education. Devotion to Empire is not itself a qualification, and no course of study is prescribed by the 1923 trust deed. Moreover, the preferred classes bear no rational connection to the overall objective. Does membership in any of these groups warrant 'a reasonable expectation' (to quote from the third recital of the trust) that Leonard scholars will develop into leading citizens of the Empire? To assess the matter in another way, consider how Leonard's nemesis, Robert MacIver, might have fared under the plan. MacIver appears to have been qualified for the award, and in fact, as the son of a Presbyterian minister, he fell within one of the preferred classes. Raised in the Outer Hebrides, he might well have needed the bursary (he had attended the University of Edinburgh on a scholarship). Was such a candidate what Leonard was after?

Granted, it was not to be expected that each and every selection would necessarily advance the goals of the scheme, and indeed the Rhodes trust suffered from some of the same limitations. However, the Rhodes Scholarships seemed to be constructed more effectively. Rhodes wanted to create connections among recipients, so he mandated that they attend Oxford. Its residential system was a key advantage; so, too, of course, was the fact that it is a world-class university. While the students were encouraged to study at any of the colleges, Rhodes House was built to provide a place for the scholars to meet.

The Rhodes and Leonard scholarships part company in other ways. Under the Leonard Foundation, the racial and religious restrictions were central to the plan. The Rhodes Trust provides that a candidate should not be qualified or disqualified owing to his race or religious beliefs.[163] Because Catholics were not precluded from applying for a Rhodes, more francophones were eligible for a Rhodes than for a Leonard. Those involved in the administration of the Rhodes in Canada appreciated that the awards could be used as a way to respond to anti-imperialist feeling in Quebec. Exposing French Canadians to the Oxonian influence was seen as a way of inducing them to assess the imperial connection in a new light.[164] Therefore, while the Canadian strategy for the Rhodes could be described as conversion, Leonard's approach was one of virtual exclusion.

Rhodes's vision went beyond the Empire. He was among the cadre of imperially minded thinkers who hoped for closer bonds between the British Empire and the United States; so he made provision for American scholarships. This idea was anathema to Leonard. Rhodes scholarships were (and are) awarded to German students.[165] The stated objective was that bringing students from the three great powers together would help to create a tie that would 'render war impossible.' Such an approach would have been totally out of the question to Leonard (as it might have been to Rhodes had his trust been established after 1914).

Although Rhodes and Leonard both placed emphasis on mind and body, Leonard goes one step further. As a rule, Leonard scholars are expected to participate in physical or military training, and the availability of such programs is supposed to be a basis for the selection of institutions. Three military schools were among those listed in the 1923 deed: the Royal Military College of Canada, the Royal Naval College of Canada (when re-established), and the Royal Air College (when established). This element of the trust was a throwback to Leonard's own experience as an engineering student at RMC and his involvement with Khaki University. It was this belief in the importance of indoctrinating a spirit of military imperialism that lay at the heart of another of Leonard's favourite causes, the Boy Scout movement. As early as 1910, he had promoted the integration of military and higher education: 'We should have every man in the University who is physically fit enrolled and given the opportunity of learning to obey before he is called upon to command and of obtaining the first principles of a training that will fit him to help to defend when necessary this Canada of ours, and to keep it for all time a part of the greatest empire the world has seen.'[166]

Perhaps most significantly, this element connects with the failed attempt to establish a student military residence at Queen's University.[167] As with the trust, Leonard regarded that plan as advancing the interests of the British Empire. He felt that it was important that as many men as possible, in an assortment of fields, should be prepared for military action. After the offer was withdrawn and the attempt to revive it was about to collapse, he was disappointed with the attitude taken by the Board of Trustees, which, he said, was 'not what I would expect from wise men having the true interests of the Empire at heart.'[168]

The promotion of military training conforms with developments in education in Canada; it was a part of the culture of Canadian schools and universities before, during, and after the First World War. The rationale was centred not solely on the desire to prepare the citizenry for war but also to provide essential life skills.[169] By the turn of the century, Ontario law permitted classes in military education in public schools, and thirty-three schools in the province had established cadet corps. Such developments were supported by an endowment created by Lord Strathcona in 1909 to encourage physical and military training in schools. In that same year, the Canadian Defence League was established, its mission being, in part, the promotion of systematic physical and military training of young men and women.[170] Officer training was taken up at some universities. McGill established a Canadian Officers' Training Corps in 1912, patterned on the English program created four years earlier. COTC programs were later formed at Western and elsewhere.[171] The outbreak of war focused attention on the role of the university within the Empire. Military training increased, money and supplies were raised for troops in campus drives, and thousands of Canadian university students answered the call to serve in the Canadian Expeditionary Force.

There is also a critical difference between Rhodes and Leonard with regard to gender. Rhodes saw no role for women. The Leonard Trust of 1916 provided awards only for males, but this was changed in 1920: female students became eligible, though no more than one-quarter of the students selected could be female. These revisions were likely motivated by what Leonard saw as the patriotic contributions that women had made in Canada during the war. The approach he adopted in 1920 was continued in the 1923 trust deed, although the capping formula was altered: awards to females in a given year could not amount to more than 25 per cent of the monies available in that year. What does the implementation of this ratio tell us? To put the question another way: In understanding the significance of this stipulation, should we stress the fact that females are included as people likely to become leading citizens of the Empire,[172] or is the dominant consideration the subordinate status that they are assigned by the limitation on awards?

The place of women in higher education was bound up with other issues relating to women's equality (such as voting and property rights). At the time of Reuben Leonard's birth in 1860, there were no universities in Canada that admitted women. The doors of academia were pried open slowly. Although by the 1870s some universities were permitting a select number of women to attend separate classes, it was not until 1872 that women were first admitted into a degree-granting program in Canada. In that year, Mount Allison University in Sackville, New Brunswick, adopted a policy of gender equality. Within the next decade, Acadia, Dalhousie, Queen's, Victoria College, and others followed suit. At Toronto, women were permitted to take the matriculation (that is, entrance) examinations in 1877, and some performed well enough to receive scholarships. However, despite this, they were denied permission to attend lectures, a policy that prevailed until 1884.[173]

In Canada, therefore, the general issue of female access to higher education was past history by the time the three Leonard trust deeds were drafted. By 1925, about 21 per cent of full-time undergraduates and 26 per cent of graduate students were women.[174] The ratio found in the trust (men 75 per cent: women 25 per cent) can be viewed, therefore, as being merely consistent with post-secondary demographics. Nevertheless, while it was to be expected that enrolment rates would change over time, the ratio in the trust was to remain fixed. The trustees were duty-bound to apply the formula (and did so until 1986), and the General Committee could not alter it by exercising its rule-making powers. Moreover, the bursaries were available for secondary education as well. At the high school level, females *outnumbered* males in the 1920s.[175]

The criterion of 'need' also marks an important distinction between the Leonard and Rhodes awards. Financial exigency is irrelevant in the evaluation of Rhodes candidates, while it is essential for a Leonard bursary. The underlying assumption of the latter scheme is that the future leaders of the Empire should not be drawn exclusively from the ranks of the privileged. This, one supposes, was inspired by Leonard's own predicament early in life. He was the promising student from a middle-class Brantford family who rose to become a captain of industry but who had been forced to turn down a place to study engineering at McGill 'for want of the necessary funds to take the course.'[176]

The emphasis on need has a certain egalitarian feel that is intentionally absent from the Rhodes scholarship. However, it is possible to make too much of this difference. The preferred list in the Leonard Trust is geared towards the children of professionals (clergymen, engineers, teachers, and so on) and therefore contains a class bias. Moreover, few Canadians were able to obtain a university degree or even a high school diploma during this period. In 1931, only 3 per cent of Canadians between the age of twenty and twenty-four were enrolled in a post-secondary institution, and the children of professionals were significantly over-represented. Not until well after the Second World War did these figures begin to change. Secondary school enrolment was also far below current rates: in 1921, 27 per cent of females and 22 per cent of males between the ages of fifteen and nineteen were at school. The percentages had increased to thirty-six (females) and thirty-two (males) in 1931,[177] but it was not until the 1961 census that the number of fifteen to nineteen year olds in high school rose above 50 per cent.[178] In sum, even recipients of bursaries to attend school can be seen as part of a select group.

Philanthropy

Throughout his adult life, Leonard demonstrated an abiding commitment to philanthropy. He was known and revered for his generosity, and it was part of the Leonard mythology that few who came to him seeking aid for a worthy cause were sent away empty-handed. The Leonard Foundation Trust was his largest single gift, involving a trust corpus of $1,000,000 as of 1935. In general, the primary object of his bounty was education. In addition to the Leonard scholarships, he provided numerous small gifts to universities and schools as well as funding for major capital projects. He provided the salary for a number of years for a professor of chemical metallurgy, and underwrote the cost of research of the freelance physicist, Wilson Taylor.[179] The gift of Chatham House was, at root, an endowment for the advancement of research. He also donated to cultural causes (such as the Art Gallery of Toronto and the Royal Ontario Museum); to the promotion of health and welfare; to the church; and to the armed forces in both Canada and Great Britain during the First World War.[180] Philanthropy was important to him.

Giving on the scale practised by R.W. Leonard is an activity that is laden with social meaning. In general, Reuben Leonard's manner of being was heavily inscribed with symbols denoting membership in the social strata onto which he was vaulted after the success of Coniagas. His splendid home in St Catharines sat like a manor house at the edge of the old Welland Canal, overlooking the grounds of Ridley College to the south. He was driven around the city in a limousine and he owned a railcar which was used for his various sojourns across the country. He belonged to exclusive sporting and social clubs.[181] Leonard was part of a small circle of wealthy men: by the time that Leonard made his fortune there may have been fifty to sixty millionaires in Canada.[182] Projecting the image of the self-made man, they appeared to personify the Christian values of thrift and industry, tending to see their success as having been acquired by dint of hard work. In the main, they displayed a restrained opulence that projected an aristocratic countenance.[183] And they devoted both time and money to various charitable causes. Men such as Joseph Flavelle, Edmund Walker, Edmund Osler, and Sandford Fleming, who sat with Leonard on the governing bodies of places like Queen's and the University of Toronto, shared the same sense of *noblesse oblige*. Within this world, Reuben Wells Leonard was not the pre-eminent benefactor.[184] He was, however, a major player, and his was one of the first Canadian-based charitable foundations.[185]

The symbolic significance of philanthropy as a status marker cannot explain fully the motivations of Reuben Wells Leonard, whose penchant for service had been established long before he became wealthy. The underlying explanations are certainly more complex. When questioned about this, philanthropists sometimes speak of a sense of civic or religious duty; they see a need to give something back to society.[186] Such claims suggest, among other things, that philanthropy has political import. It is, after all, about the principled allocation of scarce resources, one that is based on some sense of obligation. For captains of industry such as R.W. Leonard, a question arises: How does philanthropy mesh with the central assumption of capitalism that the promotion of public welfare arises through the pursuit of self-interest?

The 'private good theory' of charitable action suggests that the dichotomy between altruism and self-interest is unsustainable because philanthropy is personally beneficial in both the short and the long run. It provides intrinsic rewards such as a sense of self-worth. Extrinsically, philanthropy can be smart business practice by fostering business goodwill (while at the same time reducing taxes). Hence, giving is driven by 'enlightened self-interest.'[187] In a more general way it can serve as a way of legitimizing private wealth.

There are, however, other ways to understand the place of philanthropy inside a liberal democracy with a market economy: philanthropy is based on a belief that it is legitimate and desirable to maintain, through the private sector, a set of institutions whose mission is public. In other words, it rests on a set of assumptions about where state obligations should end and private ones should take over.[188] So, if one were to believe that the government should ensure that post-secondary education should be free to all, it would be misguided to endow a private scholarship. In addition, permitting and encouraging private giving is a recognition of the validity of the use of the power of private property to affect change in the public domain. The selection of worthy causes allows for the promotion of one's political agenda. I have suggested above that the Leonard Trust was an epitome of Leonard's political theories; so, too, can his choice of charity be seen as a manifestation of the political values that he held.

Part of Leonard's philanthropic code involved the acceptance of personal responsibility. He was said to have regarded his wealth as a public trust.[189] This is an important perspective, one perhaps affected by the conception of Christian duty assumed as part and parcel of the British imperial enterprise. At the same time, Leonard had the mindset of a businessman. He resented taxation, which he termed the 'Conscription of Wealth,'[190] and he feared the 'regrettable tendencies of the day toward class legislation and the confiscation of the savings of the industrious and thrifty to give to the shiftless and lazy.'[191] In 1920, during the embryonic days of the Canadian welfare state, he wrote: 'The value of such expedients as Old Age Pensions, Unemployment Insurance, etc., may be overestimated, as they must tend to increase a spirit of irresponsibility and extravagance, to lessen the incentive to thrift, to encourage carelessness in the quality of work performed, and to reduce the sense of filial responsibility. Such results do not tend to advance our civilization. "The hand of the diligent shall bear rule, but the slothful shall be under tribute" – Proverbs XIII, 24.'[192]

Leonard's philanthropy may be founded on a Christian ethic in some general way. However, this is not to say that his views about charity and the politics of social welfare conformed perfectly with those of the church. In fact, by the 1920s the Anglican Church was increasingly engaged in advancing the cause of social reform.[193] Of course, Protestant beliefs could be seen as supportive of commerce and competition;[194] however, as the development of the Social Gospel movement in Canada demonstrates, there was a range of opinion as to how the teachings of Christ might provide guidance for social welfare in Canada. The Anglican-based Social Service Council, for example, adopted a decidedly progressive stance, focusing on labour issues, promoting the very social reforms that Leonard decried, and expressing doubts about the moral integrity of capitalism (that 'evil tree that bringeth forth evil fruit'[195]). Leonard's sense of Christian duty led him to view his social responsibility in a very different way.

Leonard's approach to philanthropy, especially his views on the perceived dangers of social assistance, seem consistent with certain social Darwinian schools of thought. Because competition led to the elimination of unfit individuals, it was imperative that this process not be impeded by providing charity for the unworthy. Both private donation and state regulation should not, on this view, be allowed to alter the course of nature, which would in time winnow out the less fit. A corollary, one that Leonard endorsed, was that success would rightly enure to the benefit of the industrious:

A popular cry of the ignorant, uneducated 'socialist' is: 'Why should the many support the few[?]' All thinking men know that it is the few who have the energy, intelligence, courage and enterprise to overcome the great natural obstacles that frequently lie in the road to success – to explore the unknown wastes of the earth and make them accessible to man, and to delve into the hidden resources of nature ... and who, through their natural and acquired ability to develop and harness nature's great resources to serve the needs of man, are creating industry and the benefits of industry for the great masses of the people ... Achievement along such lines is deserving of honour and distinction, and of the wealth which properly accrues from such accomplishments, for these rewards constitute the foundation stones of the arch of civilization, just as industry, integrity and thrift form the arch stones.[196]

The American philanthropist Andrew Carnegie was of like mind. Carnegie acquired his wealth from steel production and amassed a fortune far in excess of that of Leonard. By 1911, he had formed the Carnegie Corporation to serve as the vehicle for selecting charitable projects. In *The Gospel of Wealth*, Carnegie's philosophy of giving was explained. He maintained that it was essential for a rich man to set an example by living modestly and unostentatiously. He should provide in a reasonable way for those dependent upon him, and, after having done so, 'all surplus revenues come to him simply as trust funds, which he is called upon to administer, and strictly bound as a matter of duty to administer in the manner which, in his judgment, is best calculated to produce the most beneficial results for the community.'[197] However, Carnegie cautioned that a serious obstacle to the improvement of what he obscurely called 'our race' was indiscriminate charity. It was preferable that millions of dollars be thrown into the sea than spent, in the end counterproductively, on the slothful, drunken, or otherwise unworthy.[198]

Leonard's benevolence covered a broad spectrum, as we have seen.

What is noticeably absent, however, are gifts for the relief of poverty, one of the long-standing heads under the law of charitable trusts. At first glance, doling out bursaries to impecunious students seems, at best, an exception to this credo. It is not. Leonard awards are based on a combination of need and merit; much more than empty pockets is required. Moreover, it is far from a free ride: recipients of a Leonard are (still) expected to supplement the money received by working during the summer vacation, at a suitable salary or wage, to defray living and educational expenses. Some form of physical work is to be preferred (arguably a manifestation of the ethos of muscular Christianity). And it was hoped that recipients of the scholarships would in due course help to regenerate the system, through the assistance provided to future recipients by the proposed Leonard Foundation Association of past scholars. Character, austerity, self-help, and the assumption of responsibility were what the bursaries were meant to recognize and foster.

CONCLUSION

To the Christian, the moralist, the philanthropist, no inspiration could be greater than that which might well spring from observing the growing strength of the Empire, and from reflection that this immense energy might be turned in directions which would make for the world's good.[199]

– George Parkin (1892)

In the 1980s, amidst the controversy over the validity of the Leonard Foundation Trust, it was argued that Reuben Wells Leonard and the Foundation must be understood as products of their times.[200] What this was meant to convey was that, while the ideology of the trust strikes the contemporary reader as objectionable, that would not have been the case in 1923. If the trust expresses the ideologies that were prevalent at the time it was created, then the document is an important record. It does seem to provide a verbal portrait of the man. However, the more difficult issue is the extent to which the ideals of Reuben Leonard can be taken as representative of elements of Canadian political culture during his life.

The Leonard Trust conforms in a host of ways with certain ideologies in circulation when the three versions of the trust (1916, 1920, 1923) were drafted. Social Darwinism, for example, provided a safe haven for those who believed in progress and racial inequality and who questioned the efficacy of charity for the poor. Men such as George Parkin and

R.B. Bennett seemed to share Leonard's conception of the triad of Empire, race, and religion. Public discourse about race was also more charged, less subtle, and with fewer latent codes than one finds today.[201] It was possible to hear virulent and hostile language on issues of race and religion in the public discourse of 1923, even on the floor of the House of Commons. This was consistent with the fact that Canadian law and public policy tolerated racist practices in both the private and public domains. As I will endeavour to demonstrate in the following chapter, there was nothing in the Canadian law of the time that cast doubt on the legality of the scholarships.

However, it is well to remember that the intellectual spectrum of this era was wide. For this reason, the temptation to claim that somehow Leonard's beliefs were representative of his times would be misleading. Consider how diverse were the views on race, even those found within the narrow bounds of the groups with which Leonard had some form of connection, such as the imperial federation movement. Additionally, within the intellectual environment of late Victorian and Edwardian Canada, one could find social Darwinists, or devout Anglicans, or imperial federalists who adopted positions on racial equality and the welfare state that were substantially at odds with those of Reuben Leonard. His political theories were a unique blend. Elements of Spencer, Carnegie, Rhodes, Parkin, and others congealed in the trust, yet in critical ways Reuben Leonard was to some extent out of step with the erudite company he kept. His cohorts in the Round Table could share in the chauvinism so apparent in the language of British racial and political superiority. However, it is doubtful whether they saw these ideas through the same filters as Leonard. While Leonard was citing race theory as a basis for rejecting the League of Nations out of hand, Robert Falconer was enlisting the support of many within the Round Table group to found the Canadian League of Nations Society. Leonard's anti-Americanism seems extreme. Believing that the white race was destined to lead the march of progress, his position on the United States ruled out the idea of Anglo-American unity shared by imperialists on both sides of the Atlantic. And even if he could count himself among those Canadian nationalists who favoured imperial federation, it must be remembered that this was itself a marginal position. Despite the raft of federation proposals that emerged during Leonard's life (many of which came from Canada), the idea of organic union did not enjoy much support among ordinary Canadians, especially outside Ontario.

Moreover, the anti-Catholic language of the trust conforms with reactionary elements within Protestantism and beyond. And at the same time that R.W. Leonard was criticizing the emerging social-welfare system, others within Anglicanism were helping to form the social safety net. As Leonard was running the mines at Coniagas or his steel mills in Welland, the assumption that the greatest social benefit results from the pursuit of individual self-interest came under steady attack within Protestantism. While Reuben Leonard was upbraiding Professor Robert MacIver, the Methodist cleric A.T. Moore was suggesting that MacIver's work be required reading for preachers within his denomination.[202] (Indeed, Leonard appreciated this conflict. He decried the support given by the local clergy to the mineworkers in Cobalt and complained of the 'vapourings of labour organizers and socialistic preachers.'[203]) In sum, Leonard's views were not particularly unique, but they were near the extreme end of the scale.

That the Leonard Foundation is predicated on an extreme position can be seen in another way: by reference to the scholarships available in Canada during the period under review. Consider the student awards offered at the nine Canadian universities approved by Leonard in the 1923 deed. Then, as now, the vast majority of academic prizes and awards were purely merit-based. This was emphatically declared in the terms governing the Isbister scholarships, which were endowed at the University of Manitoba for meritorious students of either gender 'without any distinction of race, creed, language or nationality.'[204] A small fraction of the awards discriminated on the basis of gender[205] or nationality.[206] A few scholarships referred to religion, such as the Lieutenant-Governor's Gold Medal in Agriculture at the University of Manitoba, which provided that the recipient must be of 'Christian character.'[207] Some were limited on the grounds of race, for example, an award in law at McGill for students of Anglo-Saxon or Celtic origin.[208] Overall, none of the awards tenable at these universities in 1923 was as restrictive as the Leonard Foundation scholarships. The extent to which the Leonard Foundation Trust discriminated on the grounds of race, nationality, religion, and gender was exceptional.

3

Leonard under Siege

From 1917 onwards the Leonard Foundation offered bursaries to needy students across Canada. In accordance with the trust, annual meetings of the Foundation were held in May. And each year a dinner was held for members of the General Committee and past Leonard scholars. As his health declined in the late 1920s, Colonel Leonard was unable to attend the meetings and in his place Arthur Bishop and Kate Leonard presided over the affairs of the Foundation. All the while, the General Committee went about its business, establishing operating protocols, receiving and reviewing applications, and granting awards. In the exercise of its rule-making powers, a minimum age of fourteen years was set, the number of eligible schools was expanded, and principles were developed to assess whether a candidate was in financial need within the meaning of the trust. Promising candidates were interviewed by members of the General Committee, which was constituted with regional representation in mind. In the early years (at least), the performance of the scholars was carefully monitored. The trustees would routinely request detailed reports concerning the character, conduct, and educational progress of Leonard scholarship holders from the schools at which they were enrolled.[1]

From its modest beginnings in 1917, when seven scholarships were awarded, the Foundation's scope grew, and by 1935 almost 600 Leonard scholars had been selected. In that year, following the death of Kate Leonard, the monies set aside in Colonel Leonard's will to produce her

Table 1: Value of Awards, Awards $, 1917–35

	1917	1918	1919	1920	1921	1922	1923	1924	1925	1926
Average grant to finishing institutions	450	425	303	281	254	259	271	210	206	223
Average grant to secondary schools	400	412	400	440	397	400	378	350	334	329
Average grant to all students	416	415	347	338	347	357	344	295	270	269

	1927	1928	1929	1930	1931	1932	1933	1934	1935
Average grant to finishing institutions	216	213	210	201	184	178	158	162	140
Average grant to secondary schools	294	259	224	208	200	186	164	200	168
Average grant to all students	238	226	215	203	187	179	159	165	145

Table 2: Number of Awards, 1917–35

1917	1918	1919	1920	1921	1922	1923	1924	1925	1926
7	5	5	9	15	16	18	25	27	34

1927	1928	1929	1930	1931	1932	1933	1934	1935
42	52	42	65	43	66	60	28	34

Total: 593

widow's annuity were added to the capital of the trust. The pattern of awards from 1917 to 1935 is set out in Tables 1 and 2.[2]

The average award in 1917 of $450 for students at so-called 'finishing institutions' was substantial. Although the value of individual awards dropped over the next twenty years, the Leonard scholarships remained an important source of funding. In the year that the trust underwent its final revision (1923), the average award to university students was $271. At the time, the cost of living for students at the University of Toronto was estimated to be $650 per year for arts students and $750 for those in medicine.[3] Moreover, there were not many scholarships available in the country. A federal study released in 1939 (the earliest year in which data are available) showed that just 13.7 per cent of undergraduates in Ontario held some form of scholarship, the average value being $121. The numbers were lower in the Maritimes (11.6 per cent; $113) and even more so in the west (6.7 per cent; $89).[4] Looking at the 1935 average of $140.00 for Leonard recipients attending so-called finishing institutions, it is clear that although the awards were far from the generous stipend that they had been in the initial years of the Foundation, the awards still surpass the national figures.

In the 1923 trust deed, Leonard expressed the desire that an association of past award holders be established. In 1928 a Leonard Foundation Association was formed, its stated functions being to foster the aims and ideals of the Foundation, to promote continued interest and fellowship among former holders, and to encourage 'citizenship within the British Empire as a means of furthering a higher standard of world civilization.'[5] Colonel and Mrs Leonard were elected honorary presidents; Arthur Bishop and Canon H.J. Cody were among the honorary vice-presidents. The association published an annual bulletin, which reported on the proceedings at the annual dinner, the summer activities of award holders, and the whereabouts of past recipients.

Over the years, a number of notable men joined the General Committee. Henry Marshall Tory, founder of the University of Alberta, Khaki University, and Carleton, was a member, as was Mr Justice Henry H. Davis of the Supreme Court of Canada, the Right Reverend Walter Barfoot, bishop of Edmonton; General Charles Mitchell, chair of the department of applied science at the University of Toronto; H.C. Griffith, principal of Ridley College; the Reverend Reginald Stackhouse, principal of Wycliffe College and a federal Member of Parliament from 1972 to 1974 and 1984 to 1988, and Canon Cody, who was a member of the General Committee at the same time as he served as the president of the University of Toronto.[6] These men may or may not have shared perfectly the views upon which the Foundation was based, but they were prepared to carry out the regime that Reuben Leonard had put into place.

Throughout the course of the Foundation's existence, the image portrayed in the Leonard Foundation Trust slowly disappeared. The images of Empire, fossilized in the document, are a remnant of a time now long passed. Leonard's vision of the future proved to be utterly misguided: the British Empire is now dead and the sturdy partnership between the dominions and Britain that Leonard had hoped for was never forged. Instead the British Commonwealth emerged in the interwar years, an institution that has now lost virtually all social and political significance. At some date after 1923, one could debate precisely when, the British Empire could no longer plausibly be said to be performing the virtuous role ascribed to it in the recitals of the Leonard Foundation Trust. With its demise, part of the bedrock of the trust, designed as it was to educate the Empire's leading citizens, had been eroded away.

In truth, the disintegration began before 1923. The catalyst was the war, which, far from inducing greater imperial unity, produced an entropy. The move towards independence in matters of foreign affairs, the most critical element of imperial control, demonstrated this transition. At the Imperial War Conference of 1917, a major turning point in this process, it was agreed that the key issues in constitutional reform should be postponed until the war was over. However, it was also resolved that future readjustment should preserve self-government in domestic affairs and recognize the dominions as autonomous nations within the imperial commonwealth. It was understood that these polities should have an adequate voice in relation to foreign affairs and that an effective means for consultation had to be established.

While such a statement of principle might have given impetus to the creation of an organic union, it was the aspect of dominion independence that predominated in later developments. It is perhaps telling that Prime Minister Borden, who had been provided with material on imperial federation by the Round Table group in preparation for the 1917 conference, chose not to raise the issue.[7] Two years later Canada (along with the other dominions) signed the Treaty of Versailles. Shortly afterwards it would send its own representative to the League of Nations. In 1923, the year of the trust deed, the delegates to the Imperial Conference recognized that foreign policy could no longer be conducted unilaterally by Westminster on behalf of the dominions. It was also in that year that Canada signed its first treaty.[8] The Imperial Conferences in 1926 and 1930 continued this process, and the Statute of Westminster (1931) allowed the dominions full reign in the creation of local law. Empire was shading into Commonwealth.

The trust reminds us also of how much Canadian society has

changed, in ways too numerous to recount here. Consider, as a single example, the transformation of Ridley College in St Catharines, the private school located within sight of Springbank. On its grounds stands Leonard House, and across a playing field one finds a building named after Arthur Bishop. At Ridley the ethos of the Foundation was embraced wholeheartedly. Reuben Leonard's will provided that part of the residual estate be given to the five educational institutions regarded by the General Committee as best exemplifying the sprit of the Leonard Foundation. At the annual general meeting of 1936, these schools were selected: they were Havergal, Wycliffe, Toronto, Queen's, and Ridley. The following year the governing council at Ridley decided that the money should be used to fund student awards similar to the Leonard Foundation awards. So an applicant for a 'Ridley' Leonard had to be a British subject of the white race and an adherent to the Christian religion in its Protestant form who without financial assistance would be unable to enter or to continue a course of study at Ridley. It was also necessary that the candidate fit within at least one of the specified classes, which included the sons of clergy, military officers, or old boys of Ridley College. That was 1937. Today Ridley appears to be a far different place. Women have been eligible for admission since 1973 and there is now virtual gender parity in enrolment. Once a male Anglo-Saxon preserve, a stalwart supporter and major beneficiary of Leonard's scholarship program, Ridley now prides (and promotes) itself as a cultural mosaic. In 1993 over 30 per cent of the student body was comprised of non-residents, drawn from thirty-four countries. It is now a place of diversified privilege.

As the Empire disintegrated and the aspirations encoded in the trust lost their meaning, the Leonard Foundation continued nonetheless to pursue its mandate undeterred. It looked like an anachronism, but it remained a source of funding and each year there were about 250 applicants. Every May the General Committee met in Toronto to distribute the available funds. By 1985 the trust was worth about $2 million. By then, some 1,500 Leonard scholars had been selected. Tables 3 and 4 describe the pattern of awards in the years just prior to the litigation.

Resistant to most of what was transpiring around it, the Leonard trust was not immunized totally from the changes occurring in Canadian society. For one thing, it can be seen that the nature of the awards had changed considerably since the initial years of operation. The bursaries were modest in comparison to the early years. In addition, the availability of student loans, a proliferation of other scholarships and bursaries,

Table 3: Number of Students Receiving Leonard Foundation Awards, 1976–85

	Women		Men		Total	Total
	Renewal	New	Renewal	New	Students	Awards in $
1976	35	31	57	46	169	$119,661
1977	39	24	67	42	172	$96,430
1978	26	28	48	43	145	$105,365
1979	28	25	59	36	148	$106,121
1980	27	20	52	33	132	$103,500
1981	22	27	52	28	129	$98,775
1982	37	34	57	36	164	$144,100
1983	27	35	54	39	155	$131,650
1984	33	31	53	47	164	$148,500
1985	13	36	70	38	187	$160,950
Total	317	291	569	388	1,565	$1,215,102

Table 4: Values of Awards ($)

		1984–5	1985–6	1986–7
Women's resident	Renewal	500	450	500
	New	500	450	500
Women's non-resident	Renewal	600	550	600
	New	600	550	600
Men's resident	Renewal	1,100	1,100	1,150
	New	1,100	1,050	1,100
Men's non-resident	Renewal	1,200	1,200	1,250
	New	1,200	1,150	1,200

and inflation had reduced both the utility and profile of the Leonard Foundation Trust awards. But far more important than this were the political changes that were afoot. In time, what emerged was the ascendancy of ideologies that were openly, aggressively, and implacably hostile to those contained in the trust. When the legality of the restrictions contained in the Leonard Foundation trust deed was challenged, what emerged was a showdown between competing values. Among these was the ideology of racial superiority, in its late Victorian or Edwardian forms, and modern liberal conceptions of formal equality. Yet, just as the political and social changes were gradual, so too was the development of the legal reforms aimed at promoting equality and responding to discrimination. It was not until 1990 that these changes overcame the trust.

THE ASCENDANCY OF HUMAN RIGHTS PROTECTIONS PRIOR TO THE *LEONARD* CASE

The rise of anti-discrimination protections cannot be explained by the emergence of a new ideal. The notion of equality lies at the core of liberalism; it can be found as a central tenet of classical theories of democracy, and it forms a central part of Judeo-Christian creed (all are created equal in the sight of God). However, although some conception of equality can be found within Canadian political culture from the outset, little attention was paid to equality norms prior to the Second World War. There were no guarantees of equal treatment under the law,[9] and no grand constitutional declarations about the importance of equality as a founding premise of the country. The word 'equality' does not appear, in any context, in the Constitution Act, 1867. Moreover, the law not only countenanced but provided for gender, racial, and religious inequality.[10] In general, then, equality was a political ideal with little legal significance in Canada. The emergence of equality-based protections, while not signifying the birth of a new sense of justice, represents instead an attempt to infuse conceptions of equality with juridical content. Legal reforms merely gave teeth to the idea, long in circulation, of the equal moral worth of all human beings.

The legal recognition of equality, as with other human rights, involves two distinct issues. Under one, the concern is that action taken by the state might undermine the freedom of its citizenry. The focus is on the governmental power and its potential to deny fundamental individual freedom. In a liberal polity, rights of free speech, assembly, religion, due process, and equality are typically treated as of pre-eminent importance and it is these that tend to attract protection from governmental interference. Measures such as the Canadian Charter of Rights and Freedoms, 1982, as with the Canadian Bills of Rights before it, are designed as responses to the potential of state-based oppression, inhibiting the state from taking action that might infringe a defined set of fundamental rights.[11]

Human rights violations can also arise in the way that people treat each other. The problem for the legal system here is to mediate or regulate private conduct. The discriminatory nature of the Leonard Foundation Trust raises questions that fit within this second category. Reuben Leonard devoted his private property to the charitable purposes defined in the trust. Although the Charter does not circumscribe Leonard's conduct (it not being regarded as state action[12]), it is still possible for the law to respond in some other way, regulating the rights of individuals *inter se*. Human rights codes carry out that function, and, as we will see below, these are not the only legal measures designed to pursue that end.

For the purposes of describing the relevant law, a task undertaken in this section, it is useful to divide private discriminatory conduct into two groups. The first includes discrimination (sometimes overt, at other times covert) in the provision of services, facilities, and housing. One can see that the offering of scholarships might be seen as a type of service, making the developed law on discrimination in relation to services helpful in understanding, even if only by analogy, the law that applies when recipients of the Leonard awards are selected under the 1923 deed. The second type of conduct involves what I call 'documentary discrimination.' I use that term to refer to private dealings in which the discriminatory practice is contained within a document in which property is transferred. This includes wills, deeds of land, contracts, or, as with the Leonard Foundation, a trust. Here, as will be seen, the law governing this type of discrimination varies depending on the type of stipulation at issue.

Discrimination in the Provision of Services and Facilities

Prior to the Second World War, Canadian law imposed few limitations on the rights of businesses to serve whom they pleased or on property owners to sell or lease to whom they pleased. By and large, people could discriminate 'to their heart's content.'[13] On 28 December 1923, the day the final version of the Leonard Foundation Trust was signed, no Canadian province or territory possessed legislation that protected against even the most outrageous discriminatory practices in these settings.

Within a narrow sphere, the common law could be of assistance. By virtue of an ancient principle of English law, which has been received into the law of Canada, innkeepers are under a general obligation to provide their services to the public. The rationale for the principle is that travellers are dependent on the innkeepers for sustenance and safety. In other words, this is an obligation imposed by law in the public interest as a necessary limitation on the private property rights of the innkeeper. Hence, under the common law, innkeepers are obliged to serve all comers unless there are reasonable grounds for refusal (such as the disorderly conduct of the patron). In time, a similar rule was applied to those providing transportation services (common carriers).[14] A refusal premised on discriminatory grounds alone would seem, on its face, to be unreasonable and therefore unlawful, and by 1920 there was at least one judicial decision to this effect.[15]

However, these protections are limited, as is demonstrated by the 1924 decision in the Ontario case of *Franklin* v. *Evans*.[16] In July 1923 one W.V. Franklin was refused service in a restaurant in London, on the explicit grounds that it 'did not serve coloured people.' With the support of the local black community, and in an effort to demonstrate 'to all the world that the majesty of English law will b[r]ook no prejudice,'[17] an action was brought against the owner of the restaurant. The suit failed. The court saw the conduct of the defendant as extremely offensive, and the trial judge said that he was 'touched by the pathetic eloquence of [the plaintiff's] appeal for recognition as a human being, of common origin with ourselves.'[18] Nonetheless, Franklin had no basis for the claim unless it could be established that the restaurant could be placed in the same position as an innkeeper. After a review of the authorities, it was held the common law rule had not and could not be stretched that far. Even though the restaurant was licensed under law, this did not by itself give rise to a duty to serve the public. There was, however, a minor consolation: because of the gratuitously offensive, harsh, and humiliating attitude of the defendant Evans, he was required to bear his own legal costs even though he had prevailed in the case.[19]

In late 1939 the Supreme Court of Canada addressed the same issue under Quebec law in the case of *Christie* v. *York*.[20] There, a tavern owner in Montreal refused service to two men because they were black. It was not disputed at trial that the sole reason for the refusal was the application of tavern policy that blacks were not to be served. The Supreme Court of Canada validated (by a 4:1 majority) the actions of the tavern owner. As in Ontario, it was found that there was no principle under Quebec law that could be invoked to derogate from the defendant's freedom of commerce. As the law then stood, the commercial interests trumped concerns over equal treatment, even in the context of dealings with members of the public. Mr Justice Davis, the sole dissenter (and, as we have seen, coincidentally a member of the Leonard Foundation General Committee), reasoned that the introduction of state regulation of taverns, under which a special privilege to serve liquor is conferred, circumscribed the plenary commercial freedom of the proprietor and gave rise to a general duty to serve the public at large. Within a year, the British Columbia Court of Appeal held that the majority ruling in *Christie* represented the law in the common law provinces as well as in Quebec.[21] So by 1940 it was apparent that the courts were unable – on their own – to fashion an adequate response to racial discrimination in this type of situation.[22]

A sea change occurred following the Second World War. Out of the war came an appreciation of the need to provide a juridical response to prejudice. The United Nations Universal Declaration of Human Rights proclaimed the right of all humanity to equal treatment under law. The war also dramatically altered the politics of race and race discourse. Biological theories had armed the Nazis with a scientific basis from which to assert Aryan superiority, but after the war the scientific program lay in tatters, disgraced by its close association with fascism. In 1950 the newly formed United Nations Educational, Scientific and Cultural Organization (UNESCO) issued a 'Statement on Race' which purported to outline the modern scientific consensus. Revised two years later, the statement begins with the proposition that all men belong to a single species, *Homo sapiens*. Although it was possible to discern a division among the species of Mongoloids, Negroids, and Caucasoids, there was no evidence to support further divisions. It was also declared that there was no reliable way to assess whether traits such as intelligence are best understood as matters of heredity or environment, and therefore it was not possible to validate inscriptions about race and intelligence. Moreover, the statement recites that 'available scientific knowledge provides no basis for believing that the groups of mankind differ in their innate capacity for intellectual and emotional development.'[23] The Universal Declaration of Human Rights was thus consistent with the tenets of scientific thought as proclaimed in the UNESCO statement. The latter ignored the fact that there continued to exist contentious issues among scientists, anthropologists, and experts in other fields. In other words, like the Universal Declaration, the UNESCO statement was at its core a *political* document.

These international developments influenced reform initiatives in Canada.[24] Before the war, limited statutory protections against discriminatory practices in discrete areas had begun to emerge,[25] but the first comprehensive human rights regime was introduced by the Co-operative Commonwealth Federation (CCF) government in Saskatchewan in

1947. The Saskatchewan Bill of Rights provided for protection against state action, including guarantees of freedom of speech, association, assembly, and religion. It also addressed private discriminatory conduct in employment, land transfers, education, and business. Violations were punishable as summary conviction offences.[26] Reform in the other provinces continued in an incremental way over the next fifteen years. For example, the Ontario legislature passed equal pay legislation in 1951[27] and the Fair Accommodation Practices Act in 1954,[28] the latter providing for equal access to lodging, services, and facilities ordinarily available to the public. In 1958 Ontario established an Anti-Discrimination Commission for the purpose of enforcing these protections.[29]

In the 1960s Ontario, in line with other provinces, revised its approach. The various anti-discrimination measures were consolidated and revised in 1962 under a Human Rights Code.[30] Complaints could be submitted to a newly created Human Rights Commission, which could undertake investigations, conduct hearings, impose sanctions, and institute quasi-criminal prosecutions. The code included prohibitions against discrimination on the grounds of race, creed, colour, nationality, ancestry, or place of origin in employment and in the provision of services and facilities to which the public is customarily admitted. The current regime contains prohibitions against discrimination on the basis of race, ancestry, place of origin, colour, ethnic origin, citizenship, creed, sex, sexual orientation, marital status, family status, and handicap.[31] That these measures can be traced to the development of international human rights initiatives is evident in the preamble to the present code. It can also be seen that the 'master-narrative' underscoring the law differs vastly from that found in the Leonard Trust recitals. The contrast is arresting:

Whereas recognition of the inherent dignity and the equal and inalienable rights of all members of the human family is the foundation of freedom, justice and peace in the world and is in accordance with the Universal Declaration of Human Rights as proclaimed by the United Nations;

And Whereas it is the public policy in Ontario to recognize the dignity and worth of every person and to provide for equal rights and opportunities without discrimination that is contrary to law, and having as its aim the creation of a climate of understanding and mutual respect for the dignity and worth of each person so that each feels a part of the community and able to contribute fully to the development and well-being of the community and the Province;

Therefore, Her Majesty, by and with the advice and consent of the Legislative Assembly of the Province of Ontario, enacts as follows ...[32]

The protections seek to prevent discrimination in the provision of 'facilities' and 'services' available to the public. However, these terms are not defined. Prior to the *Leonard Foundation* decision there had been several Canadian rulings that had found that educational programs fell within the scope of the legislation. In one of these, *Rawala et al. v. DeVry Institute of Technology*,[33] a board of inquiry established under the Ontario Human Rights Code held that the code applied to a private educational institution that did not receive public funding. But there were no decided cases on the question of whether a privately endowed scholarship fell within the purview of the Ontario Human Rights Code. At the time of the Leonard litigation, this was an open and contentious question.

Documentary Discrimination

The law governing documentary discrimination has not followed the same course as that relating to access to facilities and services. In the latter context, we have just seen that, prior to the advent of human rights legislation, all that the courts had at their disposal was the principle of reasonable accommodation imposed on innkeepers and common carriers, a doctrine with a limited capacity for expansion. In contrast, the common law has developed a set of principles designed to monitor the legitimate ambit of private transactions. In particular, under the mantle of the doctrine of 'public policy,' the courts have carved out a jurisdiction under which terms in contracts and property transfers can be rendered void. All law is in some measure an expression of public policy, but the term as used in this context has a more limited meaning. This principle (the narrow use of the term) is central to the present study: it was through the application of the doctrine of public policy that the discriminatory provisions of the Leonard Trust were invalidated. Therefore, the nature of this concept merits elaboration.[34]

Public policy is a judicially created doctrine under which courts assume a supervisory power over private transactions, including trusts. The overarching function of the law here is to provide a means whereby private rights are balanced against other pressing social values.[35] The doctrine, probably of fifteenth-century origin, was first invoked in a narrow set of circumstances. The courts resolved, for example, that a contract to commit a crime must be regarded as void. But the scope of the doctrine has expanded considerably. Many of the twentieth-century cases concerning public policy have involved commercial or family law matters. So, for example, a contract in restraint of trade may contravene the doctrine. So may an agreement under which a parent abdicates certain childcare obligations.

The doctrine is indeterminate. Given that public policy (in the broad sense of the term) is in a constant state of flux, so too is the narrow doctrine. As mores shift, so do the contours of permissible private conduct.[36] Therefore, it is essential that the new heads of public policy be capable of judicial recognition or existing heads expanded. Conversely, outdated limitations can be refined or discarded. In addition, in defining the meaning of public policy in a given instance, the courts are not restricted to existing statutory or common law sources. If an issue is covered by statute, there is no need to invoke the ground of public policy at all. The doctrine lives, in essence, in the interstices of cases and statutes, being derived principally from general principles of law, domestic or international, and being informed also by a variety of other sources external to the law itself that are used as benchmarks of acceptable standards of private conduct.

The doctrine of public policy appears to confer on the courts a significant measure of authority to resolve sensitive political matters.[37] That potential is undoubtedly present and the problems inherent in the open-ended nature of the concept have long been appreciated. That is why some courts have warned that public policy is 'an unruly horse,' one apt to lead the rider astray.[38] This is a caution against the danger of judicial hyperactivism. Likewise, in seeking to find an acceptable threshold test of application, it has been said that the courts should intervene only in the clearest cases, where the harm under scrutiny is substantially incontestable. Its invocation should not, it is said, be premised on the idiosyncratic preferences of a few judicial minds.[39] Moreover, while the categories of public policy may not be closed, there is a marked judicial reluctance to break new ground.[40]

Public policy is not the only basis for challenging the validity of a transaction. For example, transfer documents (such as wills or deeds) must be framed in such a way as to meet judicially imposed standards of precision. A transfer failing to meet the requisite standard may thus be found to be 'void for uncertainty.' Such a doctrine pursues a sensible policy goal, since transfers that are obscurely worded can give rise to problems of fairness and enforceability. Within the context of the present study, the rules relating to uncertainty can furnish the basis for a *collateral* attack on discriminatory terms, since they may incidentally render discriminatory provisions void. Racism is thereby ambushed.

The Ontario case of *Re Drummond Wren*,[41] decided in 1945, illustrates several features of this discussion – the plasticity of the doctrine of public policy; the processes used to ascertain public policy standards; and the use of basic principles to found a collateral attack on discriminatory action. The case involved the validity of a 'restrictive covenant,' a device sometimes used as part of land transactions. By virtue of such a covenant, a purchaser of land agrees to be bound by restrictions on the use of the property. A covenant might provide, for instance, that certain lands not be used for commercial purposes. Typically, the covenant is framed so that it will 'run with the land,' that is, so that it will bind not just the present purchaser but all subsequent owners.[42] At one time, restrictive covenants were used in an attempt to restrict ownership or occupation to certain classes or races. For example, a deed registered in 1913 related to land in the Glen Ridge area of St Catharines (a short distance from Leonard's Springbank) provided that the land 'shall not be sold, leased, or occupied by any Armenian, Hungarian, Pole, Italian, Greek or any person of a colored race without the Grantor's written consent.'[43] In time, the legality of these devices came into question, the test case being *Re Drummond Wren*.[44]

The dispute in *Drummond Wren* concerned a residential lot in Toronto that was subject to a stipulation in the deed of transfer that the property could never be sold to 'Jews or persons of objectionable nationality.' Wren applied to the court for a declaration that the covenant was invalid. Mr Justice MacKay granted the order sought, holding, in part, that the covenant was void as uncertain. It was unclear as to who would fall within the definition of a Jewish person; the restriction on persons of 'objectionable nationality' was even more obscure. It was also held that the covenant constituted an unlawful restraint on the right of an owner to transfer property. Additionally – and this is the key point here – it was held that the covenant was void because the discriminatory provisions rendered it contrary to the doctrine of public policy.[45] In ascertaining the state of public policy, the court engaged in a wide-ranging analysis which involved a review of provincial law, international instruments (including the United Nations and Atlantic charters), political speeches (those of Roosevelt, Churchill, and de Gaulle), a declaration issued by the World Trade Union Congress, and, curiously, provisions of the Constitution of the USSR dealing with equality guarantees and prohibitions on racist speech. All of these materials supported the conclusion that the restrictive covenant was contrary to Ontario law:

In my opinion nothing could be more calculated to create or deepen divisions between existing religious and ethnic groups in this province, or in this country, than the sanction of a method of land transfer which would permit the segregation and confinement of particular groups to particular business or residential areas ... It appears to me to be a moral duty, at least, to lend aid to all forces of cohesion, and similarly to repel all fissiparous tendencies which would imperil national unity ... That the restrictive covenant in this case is directed in the first place against Jews lends poignancy to the matter when one considers that antisemitism has been a weapon in the hands of our recently-defeated enemies and the scourge of the world.[46]

The *Globe and Mail* welcomed the decision, describing it as being 'on the noblest level of jurisprudence' and suggesting that it would significantly advance the cause of social equality.[47] By contrast, in an anonymous contribution to the *Fortnightly Law Journal* the wisdom of the court's analysis was trenchantly criticized.[48] The unknown commentator started with the proposition, which was taken as axiomatic, that God had created mankind with varying endowments and attributes. These were genetic differences that were 'probably in accordance with divine law.'[49] As a result, one finds a world in which some races have developed character to the highest degree, such as the Greeks, the Romans, the Normans, the Anglo-Saxons, and the Celts. At the other end of the scale are groups such as the aboriginal Australian, the Hottentot, the Malay, the American Indian, and the races of mixed bloods such as the Mongol-Slavs, whose character has been shown to be static or retrogressive. The unknown author conceived of race science in much the same way as did R.W. Leonard. And, like Leonard, the author maintained that differences in individuals, in strains of blood, and in races could not be overcome through education or by other environment influences. Therefore, attempts to use the law to impose an ideology of equality were destined to fail. Moreover, it was doubted whether the rule applied in *Drummond Wren* could be effective. It would not, it was thought, enjoy public support: people would want to control their neighbourhoods and to select their neighbours. No law could mandate racial tolerance.

In *Re Noble & Wolf*,[50] which arose several years later, the validity of a covenant affecting land was again in issue. The case involved a deed containing a prohibition against the sale of lands to any person of the 'Jewish, Hebrew, Semitic, negro or coloured race or blood.' It also provided that the intention was to limit ownership in the lands to persons of the 'white or Caucasian race.' The affected property was situated near Lake Huron, within a community of more than forty cottage properties known collectively as the Beach O'Pines. The parcels had been created in 1933 and each was sold subject to the same covenant. In 1935 the owners formed the Beach O'Pines Protective Association. In sum, a recreational ghetto had been created. When one of the property holders agreed to sell to Bernard Wolf, a Jew, the restrictions were challenged.

The litigation that ensued differed markedly from that in *Re Drummond Wren*. In that case, no one had appeared to challenge the argument that the clause was invalid, and the Canadian Jewish Congress had intervened to support the applicant. In *Noble and Wolf*, both the vendor and purchaser argued that the covenant was void. Counsel was retained by some forty members of the Beach O'Pines Protective Association to argue in favour of validity. The case became a cause célèbre within the Toronto Jewish community, being seen as a critical challenge to the informal but pervasive anti-Semitic practices that existed throughout the province.

At the first hearing, Mr Justice Schroeder upheld the covenant. The claim that the restrictions on transfer represented a danger to the public interest (the core of the reasoning in *Wren*) was described as fanciful and unreal. There was nothing in this case, nor had there been in *Wren*, that would justify an expansion of the doctrine of public policy to prohibit such restrictions. A five-member panel of the Ontario Court of Appeal agreed. Four separate judgments were issued. Hogg J.A., after a review of the leading authorities on the scope of the judicial power of review under the mantle of public policy, concluded that the matter failed to pass the threshold test: the identified harm was not substantially incontestable. The other judgments were more dismissive of the public policy argument. Hope J.A. suggested that there was nothing in the circumstances to suggest – 'with an atom of reason'[51] – that the covenant was unduly oppressive to the public interest. Indeed, underlying the covenant was the long-accepted principle of freedom of association. Henderson J.A. observed that ways have always existed, and should exist, for people to choose their own friends and neighbours, and he concluded in consequence that the covenants did not infringe any rights whatsoever. Chief Justice Robertson (with whom Aylesworth J.A. agreed) said that to transform the efforts of these property owners from a modest attempt to create a congenial summer colony into a course of action that offends public policy required 'a stronger imagination than I possess.'[52] Furthermore, the law was incapable of producing or imposing racial integration:

Doubtless, mutual goodwill and esteem among the people of the numerous races that inhabit Canada is greatly to be desired, and the same goodwill and esteem should extend abroad, but what is so desirable is not a mere show of goodwill or a pretended esteem, such as might be assumed to comply with a law made to enforce it ... To be worth anything, either at home or abroad, there is required the goodwill and esteem of a free people who genuinely feel, and sincerely act upon, the sentiments they express. A wise appreciation of the impotence of laws in the development of such genuine sentiments, rather than mere formal observances, no doubt restrains our legislators from enacting, and should restrain our courts from propounding, rules of law to enforce what can only be of natural growth, if it is to be of value to anyone.[53]

The court may have been unanimous, but the public reaction was mixed. The Association for Civil Liberties denounced the decision,[54] as did a Toronto *Star* editorial.[55] Rabbi Abraham Feinberg of the Holy Blossom Temple in Toronto alleged that 'the language of the covenant, upheld by the court of appeal, differs only in degree from the dangerous nonsense and blood-worship of naziism.'[56] A public opinion poll conducted following the Court of Appeal ruling indicated that 68 per cent of the respondents claimed that they would not sign an agreement that contained a restriction against the sale or lease of property based on race or colour; 19 per cent were prepared to agree to such a term; 13 per cent were undecided.[57] The *Globe and Mail*, which had applauded the outcome in *Drummond Wren* four years earlier, endorsed the Court of Appeal decision in *Noble & Wolf*, echoing (and quoting) the reasoning of Chief Justice Robertson. It said that, unlike *Drummond Wren*, this was not a case involving the provision of basic shelter. Moreover, 'to assert that any group of people should be forbidden to associate themselves in a perfectly lawful manner, would create problems of a far-reaching nature with all sorts of dangerous implications ... There is much to correct in our treatment of minorities in Canada, but force is not the way to do it.'[58]

An appeal was taken to the Supreme Court of Canada, but the ultimate result of the litigation was an anti-climax. Before the case reached the Supreme Court, the Ontario legislature amended the law to prevent the creation of discriminatory covenants.[59] This did not render the court's ruling moot, since the act was designed to have only prospective effect. However, the court resolved the dispute without regard to the public policy argument. Four (of seven) members of the panel held that the covenant was void for uncertainty; five justices thought that restrictions on the type of occupant (as opposed to, say, the type of *use* intended for the lands) could not be binding on a subsequent purchaser.[60]

The doctrine of public policy, relevant in the context of restrictive covenants, may also affect the validity of gifts made by will. In this context, issues surrounding discriminatory transfers have arisen in the following ways. Property may be given subject to a stipulation that the recipient become or remain a member (or not become a member) of a particular religious faith. Along the same lines, the recipient's entitlement may be conditioned on that person marrying only persons of a specified faith or not marrying persons of some other faith. In Canada, as in England,[61] the traditional view prior to the *Leonard Foundation*[62] decision was that neither condition contravenes public policy.[63] The rationale for this view relates to the importance of respecting private property rights. While it is undoubtedly true that it would be wrong for the state to treat individuals differently on the basis of religion, the same standard has not been seen as applicable to private donors. They are allowed to prefer one religion over another and to act on these convictions in the way that they dispose of property.[64] Moreover, the state has no stake in whether an individual selects a certain religion (or none at all) or who a given person marries.

This is not to say that all such discriminatory provisions have been upheld, for that is not so. Some provisions have failed on the basis of uncertainty (as to the definition of the religious group);[65] others have been found void because they contravene some other facet of public policy. In *Re Hurshman*,[66] for example, property was left to the testator's daughter, to vest in possession on the death of her mother, provided that 'she is not at that time the wife of a Jew.' The court was deeply critical of the sentiments implied by this provision. Although it was said by the court that 'any propensity towards racial discrimination has no place in this country,'[67] the traditional rule permitting religious-based restrictions was grudgingly acknowledged. However, at the time of the testator's death, the daughter was married to a person of the Jewish faith, so that the gift, if valid, might have the effect of inducing her to seek a divorce. There is long-standing authority that a condition that promotes family breakdown contravenes public policy, and this was used as the basis for invalidating the marriage condition in the *Hurshman* case.[68]

Documentary discrimination may also occur in the context of charitable trusts, as the Leonard Foundation Trust itself demonstrates. A charitable trust arises when property is placed in the hands of trustees in order to pursue defined charitable purposes, namely, trusts for the relief of poverty, the advancement of education, or religion, and, as a residual category, purposes regarded as beneficial to the community as a whole. The trust must promote a goal that is beneficial to the public and must be available to a sufficiently broad segment of the public. It is, of course, possible to endow trusts that do not meet these requirements, but charitable trusts receive favourable legal treatment: Income derived from charitable trust properties is normally entitled to various tax exemptions; a charitable trust may exist in perpetuity;[69] and, if the original charitable scheme has become impossible, illegal, or impracticable, a court may be in a position to reconstruct the trust in accordance with a principle known as the *cy-près* doctrine. In other words, when applicable, this doctrine empowers a court to direct that the trust property be applied to some other charitable purpose that resembles as closely as possible (*cy-près*) the original purpose.[70] I stress this aspect of the law of char- ities because, as will be seen below, *cy-près* was instrumental in the re-establishment of the Leonard Foundation Trust in 1990.

Given that a charitable trust may be created for the advancement of religion, it is well established that a trust favouring one religious denomination over all others is valid. In other words, a trust designed to provide an annual payment to, say, the Anglican Church of Canada, or St Thomas' Church of St Catharines, is undoubtedly valid. However, beyond this the law is less certain, for until the *Leonard* decision there was no general judicial guidance on the validity of discriminatory charitable trusts in Canada.

Two English decisions help to shed some light. The first of these, *Re Dominion Hall Trust*,[71] concerned a student residence in the centre of London that had been established prior to the Second World War exclusively for male students of European origin from the British Empire. On 19 June 1945, just weeks after V-E day, the governing body of the charity resolved that a court order should be sought deleting (through *cy-près*) what was referred to as the 'colour bar' (no challenge was made to the gender restriction). Counsel for both the charity and the attorney general, acting on behalf of the public at large, supported the application, and the order was granted. Although it was argued that the terms were contrary to public policy, the court adopted a different line of reasoning.

The court held that the original charitable intent was no longer possible or practicable. It was reasoned that when the trust was initially established (the exact year was not stated), the assumed goal of promoting a community of interest among members of the Commonwealth might have been attained by restricting access to the hall as originally set out. But times had changed, particularly in the face of the war, so that the original restrictions, far from advancing the aims of the trust, 'would be liable to antagonize those students, both white and coloured, whose support and goodwill it is the purpose of the charity to sustain.'[72] It was therefore ordered that the restriction as to European origin be removed (by virtue of the *cy-près* doctrine).

The second English case is *Re Lysaght*,[73] which involved a trust established in 1950 to provide an annual scholarship for medical students. The awards were to be restricted to unmarried male students between nineteen and thirty years of age, who were the sons of doctors and British-born subjects and not of the Jewish or Roman Catholic faiths. The Royal College of Surgeons, which was designated by the testator to serve as trustee, refused to act unless the bar against Catholics and Jews was deleted. Again, no challenge was made on the other grounds (namely, gender, marital status, age, and nationality). Public policy was raised as a basis of attack, but this ground was explicitly rejected. Mr Justice Buckley (in a passage quoted with approval in the first hearing of the *Leonard* case[74]) said this: 'I accept that racial and religious discrimination is now widely regarded as deplorable in many respects and I am aware that there is a bill dealing with racial relations at present under consideration by Parliament, but I think that it is going much too far to say that an endowment of a charity, the beneficiaries of which are drawn from a particular faith, or are to exclude adherents to a particular faith, is contrary to public policy.'[75]

Nonetheless, the application to strike out the religious qualifications, through the application of *cy-près*, succeeded. It was said that the fundamental object of the gift was to provide scholarships for medical students and that the stated religious qualifications were not critical to that goal; they were said to be merely the 'machinery' used to provide funding for deserving students. By contrast, the selection of the Royal College of Surgeons as trustee was treated as vital: the testator chose to confer discretionary powers on the college as the institution best able to carry out the scheme. The refusal of the college to act therefore rendered the gift 'impossible.' Through the removal of those restrictions, effect could be given to the general charitable intent underlying the gift. Reading between the lines, one suspects that the court employed this reasoning as a convenient means to eliminate the discriminatory provisions without departing radically from the basic law governing charitable trusts.[76]

This, then, is where the law stood as of 1986, the year in which the litigation over the Leonard Foundation Trust began. Generally speaking, Canadian law in relation to private discriminatory action was unsettled. The Ontario Human Rights Code provided for protection against discrimination on the grounds of race, religion, nationality, and gender in the provision of facilities and services; however, it was unclear whether this caught privately endowed and administered scholarships. The use of racially based land restrictions had been invalidated by statute in Ontario, but the law permitted certain discriminatory gifts in the context of intergenerational transfers by will. There was no Canadian jurisprudence on the permissible ambit of discriminatory charitable trusts, and the one English court that had considered the question of public policy had rejected this line of reasoning while at the same time finding that the impugned discriminatory terms should be deleted.

THE LEONARD FOUNDATION UNDER SCRUTINY

The first public murmur of discontent was heard in the Ontario legislature during Brotherhood Week, February 1956. Following a brief address by Conservative Premier Leslie Frost, during which he had commended the goals of Brotherhood Week, Donald MacDonald, leader of the CCF, raised the matter of the Leonard Foundation scholarships. He read into the record the underlying principles of the trust as contained in the 1956 application forms (which were drawn verbatim from the first three recitals of the trust deed). The Leonard Foundation scholarships were described by MacDonald as a gross violation of both the values that Brotherhood Week sought to pursue and the policies that had been endorsed by the legislature. He called for the government to investigate.

During the course of the Frost administration, several significant antidiscrimination measures had been introduced. In 1951, as the first wave of reforms appeared, the premier had spoken of Ontario's commitment to the ideals expressed in the United Nations charter, arguing then that the province had acted 'in recognition that all men of whatever race, colour or creed must be accorded equality.'[77] Frost's response in 1956 was different. Evidently aware of the Foundation, the premier dismissed it as anachronistic. The endowment that had been 'established many, many years ago, long before opinions that are held now as correct and true were generally accepted. It was back in the days when such slogans as "No truck and trade with the Yankees" and so on were common.'[78]

No further action was taken. However, for the next thirty years concerns about the trust continued to surface. In 1960, amidst a controversy at the University of Toronto over racist practices in student fraternities, questions concerning restrictive scholarships were raised, and the Leonard Foundation scholarships were singled out.[79] A year later the scholarships were discussed at a meeting of Calgary's city council. It was decided that the aldermen would ask the University of Alberta to remove the University from the list of institutions at which the Leonard scholarships could be held. Other universities were also to be contacted.[80] The only substantive reply to this initiative came from the principal of McGill University, Cyril James. After undertaking to place the Calgary resolution before the McGill Board of Governors (as the letter requested), he stated:

I should ... like to point out to you that the Deed of Donation of the Leonard Trust was executed a good many years ago and that the sentiments expressed in it are those of Colonel Leonard himself. A man presumably has the right to say how his own money is to be used as long as the purposes are not treasonable, seditious, or anti-social. We have at McGill University other scholarships which are exclusively for the use of Jewish students; scholarships that are specifically for the use of Islamic students, some are for French-Canadian students only, and others for students who come from a particular region of Canada. The university has accepted these with pleasure, because each kind of scholarship offers opportunities to particular groups of our Canadian population, and it must always be remembered that each individual donor is trying by his gift to help a particular group of Canadians in whom he has a particular interest.[81]

As the McGill response suggests, the Leonard scholarships were not the only awards that contained eligibility requirements based on race, religion, and so on, and others also fell under scrutiny. In 1951 money was bequeathed to the University of Toronto under the will of Florence L. Cody (the widow of Henry J. Cody) to endow an annual scholarship of $125 at University College. The gift stipulated that recipients of the award must be of 'British stock.' Though concerns were raised about this criterion, the gift was accepted by the University of Toronto and the awards administered in the ordinary course by University College. However, by 1964, the terms of the award had again become contentious. The college, preferring that the terms be altered, by a private bill in the legislature if necessary, asked the Senate Committee on Scholarships to address the issue. Legal advice was sought and the university's solicitors (Cassels, Brock) provided a provisional opinion that it was possible that a court order deleting the criterion could be obtained,[82] and if so this would obviate the need for a private act. In the end a court order varying the trust was granted.[83]

In 1970 McGill University faced a similar problem. In that year McGill had received an endowment under the will of Richard Metcalfe to provide a bursary for medical students. The award was to go to a needy male student who was, among other things, a 'Protestant of good moral character.' Rather than accepting the gift 'with pleasure' (to quote Cyril James), or applying to have the terms altered, McGill declined the bequest and executed a disclaimer, the effect of which was to render the gift void.[84] Likewise, in 1979 the University of Manitoba turned down an endowment of a scholarship designed solely for male students.[85]

As time passed, the universities designated under the Leonard Trust found themselves in an awkward position. Under the procedures outlined in the trust, the awards were normally to be paid to the relevant educational institution and then forwarded to the recipient. Moreover, it was common for the Leonard Foundation awards to be advertised in some way by eligible schools, in some instances in the calender listing of student awards. Typically, the awards were described in general terms; further details were available by writing to the honorary secretary of the Leonard Foundation. Even with this, a university that tolerated the presence of the awards by assisting in its administration could be seen as endorsing the Leonard Foundation. For its part, the Foundation was quite aware that the terms of the awards were provoking concern, and so it began requesting that the application forms not be posted as advertisements. The statement of the underlying philosophy of the Foundation, drawn from the preamble, was dropped from the application form.

The first university to disassociate itself from the Foundation appears to have been Queen's. In 1969 the nature of the scholarships came to the attention of Principal John Deutsch through a discussion with the university padre, Marshall Laverty, who was at the time a member of the General Committee of the Leonard Foundation. By the end of the conversation it had been decided that Laverty would resign from the General Committee. He wrote to the Foundation, expressing his increasing uneasiness about the terms of eligibility.[86] The principal also wrote to the Foundation to advise that Queen's would henceforth not be connected in any way with the scholarships.[87] On the same day, Deutsch ordered that all awards containing discriminatory clauses based on race or creed be reviewed, and as an interim measure references to the

Leonard Foundation scholarships were to be removed from the Queen's calender. The review committee recommended that the university no longer participate in the administration of the awards.[88] Monies were added to the general bursary funds of the university to compensate for the loss of the Leonard awards as a source of support for Queen's students.

Several universities followed Queen's lead, distancing themselves from the Foundation. For example, in 1982, Daniel Lang, assistant vice-president of the University of Toronto, advised the Foundation that the university would no longer assist in the administration of the award monies; a cheque provided by the Foundation was returned.[89] The universities of Alberta, British Columbia, and Western Ontario took a similar stance. The Human Rights Commissions in Alberta and Ontario wrote to the Foundation, as did the human rights branch of the Department of Labour of British Columbia and the Saskatoon Legal Assistance Clinic.

In 1982 the debate intensified. The triggering event was an amendment to the Ontario Human Rights Code that was introduced in late 1981. As we have seen, the code seeks to prohibit discrimination on various grounds in the provision of services and facilities. However, there is no explicit reference to discriminatory scholarships and no special treatment of charitable instruments. Moreover, the prohibition against discrimination applied to services and facilities 'available in any place to which the public is customarily admitted.'[90] The prevailing view was that this latter phrase did not catch the Leonard Foundation: it was not public in the sense contemplated by the code. By contrast, the 1982 amendment provides that 'every person has a right to equal treatment with respect to services, goods and facilities, without discrimination'[91] on any of the prohibited grounds: the reference to discrimination in a public place is omitted, suggesting that a broader reading of what counts as a facility or service is possible. It was now arguable that the Leonard Foundation Trust fell within the scope of the code, and in October 1982 the Ontario Human Rights Commission announced that this issue was under review.[92]

The commission's decision sparked debate. Al Kolyn, the Progressive Conservative MPP for Toronto Lakeshore, raised the issue in the Ontario legislature during Question Period on 22 November:

Mr. Speaker. I have a question for the Minister of Labour. The Ontario Human Rights Commission is currently considering action against the Leonard Foundation for maintaining a private scholarship fund restricted to Canadian university students who are of the white race, of British nationality and of the Christian religion in its Protestant form.

The Leonard Foundation is in good company when it comes to racial, religious and nationality requirements for its awards. The Simon and Rosalie Halpern Memorial Scholarship specifies that recipients must be of the Catholic or Jewish religion. The Murray Brooks Memorial bursaries are designated for students from India, Pakistan and Ceylon. The McGill-Hellenic Club bursaries go to students of Greek descent.

Surely it is a basic right of a citizen, living or dead, to dispose of his property in any way he sees fit. Would the minister agree, given the examples I have cited above, that if the Leonard Foundation scholarship is to be the subject of an inquiry, then so should all other privately administered scholarship funds that have as part of their qualifications and competition requirements specific guidelines with respect to the race, national origin and religion of the applicant?[93]

Russell Ramsay (the minister of labour) replied that he supported the commission's decision to review the implications of the 1981 amendments. Sheila Copps, then Liberal MPP for Hamilton-Centre, pressed the matter further: did the minister agree with the 'incredible statement'[94] made by the member for Lakeshore? The answer was evasive. When the trust was established, Ramsay said, the question of whether its terms were in compliance with the existing law had been considered by the Foundation; moreover, the matter concerned funds provided to individuals, not to a university.[95] Later the minister acknowledged that, though he would abide by the decision taken by the Human Rights Commission, he personally found nothing wrong with a private scholarship scheme such as that of the Leonard Foundation.[96]

The commission's announcement also prompted a debate in newspapers throughout Ontario. A number of stories, editorials, and letters to the editor appeared, most of which were in support of the Leonard Foundation. Two arguments recurred, and these paralleled those advanced in the legislature. The first was that Reuben Leonard was entitled to dispose of his property as he saw fit. Always implicit in this argument, but never expressed, was the view that rights of private property trump concerns about discrimination and racism. The second argument was that it was wrong to single out the Leonard Foundation, given that there were numerous discriminatory scholarships in place in the province and across the country.

In distilling the substance of the claims to these two main points, the tone of the discussion is lost. While some of the discourse was tempered, most was charged and polemical, especially on the second argument – the unfair treatment of the Leonard Foundation. For example, the Orillia *Packet and Times* said this:

There are hundreds of grants for Canadian universities available only to selected people on the basis of race, religion, nationalist [sic] and sex ...

Why is it then that the Ontario Human Rights Commission is considering action only against one private scholarship fund which restricts its grants to students who are 'of the white race, of British nationality and of the Christian religion of the Protestant form'?

They do so because it is very unfashionable these days to be white, Anglo-Saxon and Protestant.

In its idiotic zeal to protect the rights of what it considers to be minorities, the Ontario Human Rights Commission (and a host of other 'protectors of society') have made an oppressed minority of the principal founding people in this country.

WASPs, it seems, must apologize.[97]

Claire Hoy of the Toronto *Sun* wrote a series of columns excoriating what he referred to as the Human 'Wrongs' Commission,[98] a posture found also in a *Sun* editorial written in Hoy's petulant style:

If a black philanthropist wishes to leave scholarships for blacks only, or a donor wishes to give money for women or hunchbacks or Latvians – that is their prerogative.

In fact, that is what makes us especially mad. We have a very strong suspicion that if this was an endowment helping blacks, women or the handicapped, there wouldn't be a murmur from our Human Rights Commissioners. It is because WASPs are a great pariah of our society that this has come up. Well, apart from the obvious fact that there are such things as needy poor WASPs of British nationality, we will not desist from pointing out that even if every WASP lived in Rosedale, a free society should permit a man to leave his money as he sees fit and more importantly, a university to accept it – if they see fit.[99]

The Reverend Reginald Stackhouse, then principal of Wycliffe College and a member of the Foundation's General Committee, expressed concern about the terms of the trust and supported the idea of a revision, though he was unsure as to how this could be accomplished.[100] This position earned him a stern rebuke from Professor David Rayside of the department of political science at the University of Toronto: 'If [Stackhouse] cannot summon up the moral courage to leave his seat on [the General Committee], he might want to consider the propriety of his retaining his office within the university or, for that matter, any office.'[101]

Concerned about whether the Foundation fell within the scope of the revised code (was it a service or a facility?), the commission announced in February 1983 that it would not proceed, and the issue faded temporarily from public view. However, within the Foundation there was a movement afoot to alter the qualifications. In April 1985 Canon Anthony Capon of the Montreal Diocesan Theological College, and a member of the General Committee, told the Montreal *Gazette* that 'I find the provision obnoxious by current standards. And there are a good many of us on the general committee who share that opinion and are working to find ways by which it can be set aside. [But] it is not against the law. People in this day and age would assume that it was contrary to the Charter of Rights and so on. In fact, it isn't because it is a private trust.'[102]

By 1986 the Human Rights Commission was again involved. In January it wrote to the trustees asserting that the Foundation was in contravention of Ontario law and asking that appropriate steps be taken to alter the terms of the trust. Over the years, Canada Trust (which had succeeded the Toronto General Trusts Corporation as the Foundation's trustee) had seen it as its duty to follow the letter of the 1923 deed until such time as a court of competent jurisdiction ruled otherwise. Its reply to the commission reflected this posture: The Leonard Foundation was a private charity and the trustees had received a legal opinion that they were not in breach of the Human Rights Code.[103]

On both the public and private fronts a critical role was played by Reverend Edward Scott, primate of the Anglican Church of Canada and a former Leonard scholar. In late April 1986 he wrote to the trustees urging a review of the terms of the trust before a legal challenge was initiated. Part of his concern was how the present state of affairs might affect perceptions of the Anglican Church. The gospel demanded that discriminatory practices relating to the life of this church be removed, he wrote, and the failure to do so could prompt 'major public relations problems which will hinder the work of the Church.'[104] Likewise, several members of the General Committee, including Anthony Capon and Archdeacon Robert MacRae, were lobbying Foundation members to seek a revision. In addition, the controversy was raised at the General Synod of the Anglican Church of Canada in 1986 and at a meeting of its national executive committee.

The Scott letter was sent just weeks before the annual general meeting of the Foundation. At that meeting the following resolution, moved by Robert MacRae and seconded by Anthony Capon, was placed before the General Committee:

WHEREAS the Church has been and continues to be in the forefront of the struggle for the equality of all people, and

WHEREAS this General Committee has debated the issue of possible racial discrimination in the Trust Deed of the Leonard Foundation, and

WHEREAS it appears that the standards of public acceptance in Canada no longer condone the terms of reference in the Trust Deed concerning racial preference,

BE IT THEREFORE RESOLVED

That the Trustee be directed by this General Committee of the Leonard Foundation to apply to the appropriate Court to have a definitive pronouncement made in the matter of discrimination on the basis of race and sex and, at the same time, to have the offensive terms written out of the Trust Deed but to have the Trust Deed otherwise survive.

The motion, bringing the central issue to the fore, precipitated an intense discussion. There were concerns as to the manner in which the motion was framed: Did the General Committee have the power to compel the trustees to seek a judicial declaration? In addition, while the first clause (which called for a definitive ruling on the legality of the clause) was neutral, the second phrase, asking for the deletion of the offensive terms, presupposed a certain view of what the correct outcome should be. And on the principal question – the contest between private property rights and countervailing policy concerns (such as equality) – there was no consensus. In the end, the motion was defeated, 13 to 7, with 2 abstentions.

While the Foundation grappled with this issue, there were developments of a more general nature occurring in Ontario. In late May 1986 Premier David Peterson unveiled Ontario's *Policy on Race Relations*.[105] The statement announced that the government was committed to equality of treatment and opportunity, and it spoke of the need to create a harmonious racial climate in the province. Overt manifestations of racism 'in any form' would not be tolerated.

The stage was thus set for what Scott and others had foreseen. After years of private discussions with the trustees, the Human Rights Commission decided to take formal action. Under the Human Rights Code, the commission is empowered to initiate proceedings, and on 12 August 1986 Canon Borden Purcell, chair of the commission, filed a complaint alleging the denial of equal treatment with respect to the provision of services and facilities. The Foundation, it was alleged, had discriminated on the basis of race, creed, colour, citizenship, ancestry, place of origin, and ethnic origin. (No mention was made of discrimination on the basis of sex.) Moreover, the code prohibits the publication or display of material that indicates an intention to infringe the non-discrimination protections. The complaint alleged that the Leonard Foundation application form contravened this provision.

The tone of the public discussion was somewhat different from that of 1982. The press coverage might have led one to the view that the tide was turning against the trust. The Toronto *Star* led the offensive. Just prior to the filing of the complaint, it published an article under the title 'Whites-only scholarship is labelled repugnant.'[106] The Reverend Scott was quoted as being opposed to the terms, and so too was Archbishop Michael Peers, Scott's successor as primate. This was followed by an editorial calling for the Foundation to take steps to alter the terms of the awards,[107] and by a story concerning a Japanese-Canadian woman, Edy Goto, who had been denied a Leonard scholarship some fifteen years earlier.[108] The Toronto *Sun* reported on a statement by Dr Bhausheb Ubale, a former member of the Ontario Human Rights Commission, who focused on the discrimination against black students under the Foundation's governing terms.[109] Editorials in *Canadian Churchman* and *The Anglican* urged reform.[110]

However, Leonard was not abandoned. Letters of support for the Foundation continued to appear in the press.[111] Claire Hoy again entered the fray, castigating Scott for not having returned the money he had received from the Leonard Foundation in the 1940s. He reiterated his earlier complaints – first, that the commission was acting duplicitously, and second, that invoking the code would infringe Leonard's property rights:

Keep in mind, this is a private trust fund. If Col. Leonard wanted to leave his money to purple-faced, toad-eating Martians, surely that's his right.

Or it isn't. Not with today's maniacal, reverse-logic concept of equality.

Every single group in society, it seems, is entitled to exclusivity, except white Protestants.

The reason for this is quite simple. Stupid, but simple.

According to human wrong activists, alas, white Protestants are members of a privileged group in our society. They seem to believe that every white Protestant in this country has been privileged, while everybody else, regardless of personal circumstances, has been underprivileged.

Therefore, the illogic goes, white Protestants must be punished.

Had Leonard left his money say, to Third World students, he'd probably be given the Canada Medal posthumously.[112]

Rather than have the question of the legality of the trust reviewed under the Human Rights Code, the Foundation decided to apply for directions from the Ontario Supreme Court, an avenue available to trustees under Ontario law.[113] The trustees sought advice as to whether the exclusionary terms of the trust were contrary to law, by reason that they: (1) were contrary to the Ontario Human Rights Code; (2) were contrary to the common law doctrine of public policy; (3) discriminated on the grounds of race, creed, citizenship, ancestry, place of origin, sex, handicap, or otherwise; or (4) were void for uncertainty.[114] Should all of these grounds fail, the trust would be permitted to stand as originally created. On the other hand, if any basis of attack was made out, an issue would then arise as to the effect of invalidity on the trust. Two outcomes were possible. The terms could be found to be invalid and the entire trust declared to be void. If so, the capital of the trust would then revert to the estate of Reuben Wells Leonard and would pass to the residuary beneficiaries under Leonard's will.[115] Alternatively, the doctrine of *cy-près* might be invoked, the effect of which would be that the trust would be reformed, presumably by creating a more general bursary scheme.

It was proposed by counsel for the Foundation, Donald Guthrie of the firm of Cassels Brock and Blackwell, that counsel be appointed to represent the contingent class of persons eligible to receive scholarships from the Leonard Foundation. The court granted this application, and William Sommerville, of the firm of Borden and Elliot, was appointed for this purpose. The rationale for this action was that the Foundation, in seeking the advice of the court, was not taking a formal position on the questions it had propounded. Nevertheless, court proceedings are adversarial, and so it was important that argument be heard in support of the present terms of the trust. Potential recipients had a stake in preserving the 1923 trust in its original form, and thus an order was sought so that this contingent class would be represented.

By the same token, those who stood to gain should the entire trust fail also had a right to be heard. Therefore, all of the beneficiaries under the residuary clause of the Leonard will, including five family members (descendants of Arthur Bishop), were served with a notice of the proceedings and given an opportunity to be heard. From this group, only the Royal Ontario Museum chose to participate. The motion was also served on the Ontario Human Rights Commission and the Office of Public Trustee, the government agency responsible for supervising charitable trusts.

No special counsel was appointed to represent the class of *excluded* students, and despite the presence of four parties to the action, it was not argued by any one participant that the terms ran contrary to public policy and that those terms should therefore be deleted, leaving the remainder of the trust intact. (That was the final outcome of the litigation.) The Leonard Foundation took no formal stance. The Human Rights Commission confined its submissions to matters relating to its own jurisdiction. The Public Trustee maintained that the trust was valid, and argued in the alternative that if the discriminatory terms were found to be void, they should be deleted while the remainder of the trust be allowed to stand. Counsel for the class of potential beneficiaries took the same stance on the question of validity; alternatively, it was submitted that the entire trust must fail if the impugned terms were invalidated. The Royal Ontario Museum was alone in arguing that the trust was contrary to public policy, though only one paragraph of its written submission was devoted to that ground of attack. Counsel for the museum argued that the trust should fail completely and the trust capital distributed to Leonard's beneficiaries.

The facts of the case were not in dispute, given that the issues concerned the validity of the terms of the trust. The Foundation submitted a detailed affidavit sworn by Jack Cummings MacLeod of Canada Trust, who for many years had been the trust officer responsible for administering the Leonard awards. The MacLeod affidavit, which provided the main factual basis upon which all of the parties relied, outlined the history of the Foundation, the details of its present administration, and critical incidents in the current controversy, as seen through the Foundation's eyes. In addition, William Sommerville provided data on various other discriminating scholarships available in Canada, via an affidavit sworn by William Middleton, an articling stu-

Table 5: Middleton Affidavit Findings on Scholarship Restrictions[116]

Women	133
Aboriginal	30
Men	16
Residence in Canada or specific locale in Canada	28
Ethnicity	21
Origin or residence outside Canada	20
Canadian citizenship or origin	17
Engaged in religious studies or preparing for ministry	15
Attended designated school or school board	15
Religion	12
Francophone	10
Mature Students	10
Nationality	8
Age (other than mature)	8
Family status	2
Anglophone	1
Disabled	1

dent at Borden and Elliot. Middleton had prepared a survey of scholarships tenable at eighteen Canadian Universities (twenty-five were contacted). The affidavit outlines the terms of 279 awards, some of which contained multiple restrictions. Table 5 presents a summary account of the findings.

Arguments in the *Leonard* case were heard over a three-day period in March 1987. On 10 August Mr Justice McKeown released his judgment:[117] The Leonard Foundation Trust was valid. All of the advanced bases of invalidity were rejected.[118]

The court held that the Human Rights Code did not apply to the Foundation: it was not a 'service' or 'facility' within the meaning of the code. The reasoning was rather thin and mechanical. There was no policy analysis of the function of the prohibitions and the ways in which the goals of human rights law should inform an interpretation of the language of the code. In arguing against the applicability of the code, counsel acting for the future recipients presented several general dictionary definitions. So, for example, Webster's defines 'services' as 'the supply of some commodity, as water or gas, accommodation or transport, required by the public.' Similarly, 'service' means 'an act of helpful activity; the rendering of assistance or aid; the performance of duties as a servant; the act or manner of waiting at a table; employment in any duties or work for another or others, or for a government, institution, or the like.' A 'facility' is 'something (as a hospital) that is built, installed, or established to serve a particular purpose.' These definitions were referred to in argument and apparently relied on by the court in finding in favour of validity: nothing in these definitions remotely resembles a scholarship program. In addition, the cases[119] holding that the provision of education can be considered a service under human rights law were distinguished: this line of reasoning had not yet been applied to a trust. 'Therefore,' it was concluded, 'scholarships arising out of a trust are not a service or facility.'[120]

There was a second reason why the Foundation did not contravene the code. Under section 17 (now section 18), an exemption is granted to defined ethnic or religiously based organizations. By virtue of that section, the right to equal treatment with respect to services and facilities is not infringed in cases where 'membership or participation in a religious, philanthropic, educational, fraternal or social institution or organization that is primarily engaged in serving the interests of the persons identified by a prohibited ground of discrimination, is restricted to persons who are similarly identified.' Again, with little elucidation, Mr Justice McKeown held that this section applied to the Foundation. As a result, assuming that the provision of the scholarship constituted a service, it nevertheless fell within the exempt class contemplated by section 17. It was observed that there were numerous other scholarships containing discriminatory restrictions based on such factors as race, ancestry, place of origin, citizenship, creed, gender, and so on.[121] The Leonard scholarship was seen as but one more instance.

These findings effectively disposed of the question of whether the distribution of the Leonard scholarship application forms constituted a discriminatory publication contrary to section 12 (now section 13) of the code. That prohibition is designed to prevent action that would infringe or incite an infringement of the code. The application forms could not produce that result. Given the holding that the Foundation was not acting contrary to the code, the forms, which described the goals of the trust and the grounds for eligibility, could not thereby constitute a published declaration of an intention to violate the equality protections.

Although the trust was not contrary to the Ontario Human Rights Code, it might still run afoul of general principles of public policy, as outlined above. In the court's consideration of this question, a preliminary issue arose involving a somewhat technical point of law. This concerned the role of the deed's recitals in the interpretation and assessment of the document. It was shown in chapter 1 that the Leonard

Foundation recitals are an integral part of a deep ideological bedrock. Nevertheless, as a general rule, trust recitals carry no legal weight. They are, by definition, merely the premises of the trust, in a sense prior to it, and therefore not a part of the working instrument.[122] This exclusionary rule recognizes the difficulty of ascertaining a settlor's motivations, and it underscores the importance of focusing on what the trust actually does (that is, the operative part) rather than on what may have prompted it.[123] There are, however, two established exceptions to the principle that the recitals are not relevant. First, when the trust is ambiguous, the recitals may be resorted to as a way of resolving that ambiguity. Second, where the recitals have been incorporated by reference into the body of the trust, they then are treated as part of the trust. In this latter instance, the recitals would serve double duty, acting both as a preface and as part of the actual scheme of distribution.[124]

It was held that the first three recitals were irrelevant (by virtue of the general exclusionary rule) because they were merely expressions of the settlor's motives. However, part of the fourth recital had been incorporated into the body of the trust (and therefore fell within the second exception). That recital contains Colonel Leonard's belief that the British Empire should remain under the guidance of Christian persons of British nationality who owe no allegiance to a foreign power. It concludes with the declaration that the Settlor excludes from the management of, or benefits in, the Foundation ... 'all who are not Christians of the White Race, all who are not of British Nationality or of British Parentage, and all who owe allegiance to any Foreign Government, Prince, Pope or Potentate, or who recognize such authority, temporal or otherwise.' It was this quoted passage, and this passage alone, that was held to have been incorporated into the operative part of the trust.

Mr Justice McKeown added one final comment on the recitals. He held that, because the British Empire had ceased to exist, the references to the Empire in the recitals were of no effect. In addition, it was concluded that the first three recitals should be regarded as having ceased to operate, having become 'impossible and offensive to today's general community.'[125] However, having excluded the recitals from consideration in relation to the issue of public policy, Mr Justice McKeown's ruling that they would be regarded as offensive, so much so that they had 'ceased to operate,' was irrelevant. Instead, the validity of the restrictions turned on an assessment of the discriminatory qualifications *standing on their own*. In other words, given the ruling that the recitals were not to be considered, the question became this: Is it contrary to the law of Ontario to exclude persons from part or all of the benefits of a charitable trust owing to their race, nationality, national origin, creed, or gender?

The court said no. The cautionary remarks concerning the use of the doctrine of public policy discussed above were endorsed: A finding of illegality should not be based on subjective judicial preferences, but rather should be invoked only in cases where it was accepted that harm to the public might otherwise ensue.[126] The passage from the English decision of *Re Lysaght*, quoted earlier in this chapter, was adopted.[127] The court in *Lysaght* had concluded that, while racial and religious discrimination may be regarded as deplorable, unamiable, and undesirable, it was not contrary to law to establish a charity for the benefit of, say, the adherents of a particular faith. Furthermore, there were countervailing public policy values that were firmly entrenched in the law, namely, the right of freedom of contract and testation. This ground of attack therefore failed.[128]

The Royal Ontario Museum took the case to the Court of Appeal. The Human Rights Commission, the Public Trustee, and the class of persons eligible to receive scholarships under the Leonard Foundation again appeared, the parties adopting the positions that they had taken in the Ontario Supreme Court. The appeal was heard in early September 1989, and the decision was released on 24 April 1990. A panel of three unanimously held that the decision of McKeown J. should be overturned.[129] Robins J.A., with whom Osler J. concurred,[130] delivered the majority judgment; Tarnopolsky J.A. wrote a separate opinion in which he agreed with the result, albeit under a different line of reasoning.

Importantly, Robins J.A. considered the complete set of recitals; he therefore reversed the holding of McKeown J. on this issue. The majority reasoned that the recitals were entirely consistent with the operative part of the trust and were intended to provide guidance to the General Committee in the awarding of scholarships. That was true for the last part of the fourth recital, as McKeown J. had concluded. In addition, there were guidelines to be found in the third recital. There it was asserted that the goal of the awards was to assist those who might become leading citizens of the Empire and who were not compromised by allegiance to an alien power.

In addition, the majority concluded that it would be too limiting to consider only these references. It was held that, as a rule, when the recitals are not clearly severable from the body of the instrument, and where they give meaning to the operative part, the document should be read in its entirety. That was found to be true of the Leonard deed: The elements of the trust were so interconnected that they could not sensibly be divorced from each other. The majority judgment went even further on this point. Mr Justice Robins was prepared to take the recitals into account even if they could be said to represent only the motives of the settlor, on the ground that to treat the operative part in a non-contextual way would be artificial. He said that, while it is true that the Leonard Foundation is a private institution, it has a public dimension, having awarded scholarships to students from a segment of the general population, many of whom would use their awards to attend publicly funded schools. The public or at least *quasi*-public character of the trust suggested that it was proper to consider the stated justifications for the discriminatory terms set out in the deed. Put another way, the public nature of the Foundation suggested that it should be held to a higher standard of conduct than had it been a purely private arrangement.

On the main question (the validity of the qualifications), the majority held that the continuance of this trust, created under terms that were so at odds with contemporary social values, was inimical to the public interest. Two propositions in the deed were stressed. One was the exhortation of the inherent superiority of the white race (as expressed in the first recital). The second was the proposition that peace and the general progress of the world could best be obtained through the education of white, Protestant persons of British nationality (recitals 3 and 4). To state that a trust built on these ideas contravened public policy was said 'to expatiate the obvious.'[131] Furthermore, the idea that one race or religion is intrinsically better was described as 'patently at variance with the democratic principles governing our pluralistic society in which equality rights are constitutionally guaranteed and in which the multicultural heritage is to be preserved and enhanced.'[132] The widespread adverse reaction to the trust was taken as a demonstration of just how far out of keeping with contemporary standards of tolerance and equality the spirit of the Leonard Trust had become. While recognizing the need for a restrained use of the doctrine of public policy, and accepting Leonard's freedom to dispose of his property, the court nevertheless concluded that the public interest would not be served by upholding the trust as originally created.

Just what this might mean for other scholarships was not addressed by the majority. It was said that the court's intervention was mandated by the idiosyncratic nature of the 1923 trust.[133] The Leonard deed was regarded as unique because, though there were other discriminatory awards, none was 'rooted in concepts in any way akin to those articulated here which proclaim [that] some students, because of their colour or their religion, [are] less worthy of education or less qualified for leadership than others.'[134]

With the finding that the trust was contrary to public policy, the other issues pertaining to its validity became moot. It was not necessary for the court to consider whether the trust failed for uncertainty or whether the Leonard Foundation scholarships fell within the scope of the Human Rights Code. The only remaining issue was the effect of invalidity on the continued operation of the trust. Here it was held that the offensive provisions of the scheme could be excised and, under the *cyprès* doctrine, the trust allowed to stand in this revised form. Accordingly, the provisions of the trust that confined the management, judicial advice, schools, universities, and colleges and those who may receive the benefits of the trust on the grounds of race, colour, ethnic origin, creed, or religion and sex were void. While changes in the nature of public policy had rendered the original design impractical, what remained was a charitable trust for the advancement of education (or leadership through education).

Mr Justice Tarnopolsky wrote a separate concurring judgment in which he undertook a review of the leading decisions in the development of the law of private discrimination in Canada, drawing principally on the case law discussed above.[135] Although these cases demonstrated how little the law had responded to discriminatory conduct in the past, this was not seen as determinative. In addition, he outlined a number of post-war legislative and policy initiatives designed to limit discriminatory practices, including the introduction of human rights codes, the equality provisions of the Canadian Charter of Rights and Freedoms, and the Ontario *Policy on Race Relations* of 1986. He also considered three international instruments, all of which had been ratified by Canada and the provinces: the International Convention on the Elimination of All Forms of Racial Discrimination (1965), the Convention on the Elimination of All Forms of Discrimination Against Women (1979), and the International Covenant on Civil and Political Rights (1966). In his view, it was unnecessary to undertake a detailed analysis of these domestic or international measures with a view to seeing if the trust was in direct violation. Instead, they were taken as signposts of modern Canadian public policy, all of which pointed to the conclusion that the trust was contrary to law because it discriminated on the grounds of race (by which he meant colour, nationality, ethnic origin), religion, and sex. This analysis, it should be noticed, does not rely on the recitals at all. Under the reasoning in the minority opinion, the qualifications, on their own, contravened public policy. With the majority, Tarnopolsky J.A. agreed that *cy-près* was available to save the remainder of the trust.

The question of how such a ruling might affect other discriminatory trusts, a matter that Robins J.A. decided to avoid, was addressed in the minority opinion. Under the Tarnopolsky analysis, not all restrictive scholarships would necessarily be rendered invalid. As in other realms, a balancing of competing interests would be required. For example, it was suggested that the Leonard Trust provision establishing the preferred classes was not contrary to public policy. Charitable trusts restricted to those who are in financial need would also be valid. Generally speaking, it would not be sensible to regard scholarship programs created exclusively for women, Aboriginal groups, those with a disability, or of members of other historically disadvantaged groups as invalid. Moreover, given the importance placed on bilingualism and multiculturalism, restrictions based on language would probably be acceptable. Nonetheless, each case would require separate consideration; the context, purpose, and effect of the restriction would have to be assessed under these proposed principles. As in the assessment of equality rights under the Charter of Rights and Freedoms, attention would be paid to the social and historical context of the group concerned.[136] However, excluded from this analysis were family trusts (and wills). They were not to be subjected to the same level of scrutiny as charitable trusts, which were seen as being inherently public in nature.

No further appeal was taken. The Leonard Foundation, having launched the application for directions, chose to abide by the advice it had received under the ruling. None of the other parties, including the class of potential beneficiaries, sought leave to appeal to the Supreme Court of Canada. The Court of Appeal order was that all references to the discriminatory provisions in the 1923 deed were to be removed. The first four recitals were also deleted. What remains today is a framework for the provision of bursaries. The preferred classes, the criteria relating to physical training, suitable summer employment, and so on were unaltered, as were the general powers and duties of the trustees and the General Committee. In addition, the Court of Appeal ordered that the trust be called upon to pay a substantial portion of the legal expenses incurred by the parties to the action. Taking the two hearings together, the cost to the Foundation was about $200,000.[137]

4

After *Leonard*

The Leonard Foundation had suspended operation when the litigation had been commenced in 1986. Following the Court of Appeal decision in 1990, it reconvened under the judicially revised trust. Since that time, significant changes have been undertaken. The grants are now administered under what is termed a 'financial assistance program'; need is the primary concern.[1] Although the original trust contemplated awards at designated public and private schools, as well as colleges and universities, the modern program does not provide assistance for students at the primary and secondary school levels. Instead, the awards are tenable by full-time undergraduates (including those enrolled in a first professional-degree program) at institutions belonging to the Association of Universities and Colleges of Canada. Materials and application forms are available in both official languages, on-line. As seats on the General Committee are vacated (there is no set term of office), diversification has become a factor in replenishing the complement. About half of the present members would not have met the eligibility requirements contained in the 1923 trust.

In 1997 there were 257 applications for assistance. Approximately $150,000 was available and about 125 awards were made. The average grant was therefore about $1,200. In accordance with the terms of the initial trust, renewals are given priority. Moreover, the majority of the applications continue to come from members of the preferred classes, as do the number of awards recommended. Of these, most applications are

Table 6: Leonard Foundation Applicants, 1997

Renewal applicants	77	Recommended	55	72%
New applicants	180	Recommended	73	41%
Total	257			
Preferred groups	183	Recommended	104	
Non-preferred	74	Recommended	24	
Total	257			

Recommendations by nominators

1. Recommended highly	157
2. Recommend	62
3. Not recommended	20
4. Forwarded	6
Not through a nominator	12
Total	257

Preferred group breakdown

Clergy	87
Teacher	56
Military	22
Royal Military College	0
Engineering Institute	9
Mining and Metallurgy	0
None	74
Not recorded	9
Total	257

drawn (as before the litigation) from the sons and daughters of clergy and teachers. Table 6 presents the recommendations of the subcommittee on scholarships for 1997.

The ruling of the Court of Appeal has therefore produced significant change within the Foundation. But its reach extends far beyond this one institution. The decision of Robins J.A., representing the majority opinion in the Court of Appeal, is a legal precedent with relevance to the law governing charitable trusts, privately endowed scholarships, and, more generally, the ambit of the doctrine of public policy. It has served as a standard against which colleges and universities have reassessed the validity of student awards. The *Leonard* case is also used as a teaching tool in some Canadian law schools.

What is more, like the trust, the court rulings are political texts. Chapter 2 of this book contains a detailed analysis of the Leonard Foundation Trust deed. The goal of that discussion was to identify the ideologies that permeated the document. Placing the *Leonard Foundation* judgments alongside the deed invites an assessment of change within the Canadian polity. Accordingly, in this chapter, I will explore the judgments in the *Leonard* case to see what they might tell us about the nature of contemporary Canadian law and society.

Three judicial opinions were rendered in the *Leonard* case: that of Mr Justice McKeown; the majority judgment of Mr Justice Robins (with which Osler J. agreed), and the concurring opinion of Mr Justice Tarnopolsky. Taken together, the judgments and the Leonard trust clearly share a set of beliefs. At a basic level, both the rulings and the trust deed are intended to be dispositions under and in conformity with the law. They acknowledge the rights inherent in the concept of private property. There is a validation of the importance of the promotion of education through philanthropy. The law of charitable trusts is designed to facilitate this type of donative action, and the application of the *cy-près* doctrine allowed the scholarships to be preserved.

The most intriguing area of comparison concerns the concept of equality. Reuben Wells Leonard, as we have seen, did not believe in the equality of races. The idea that people were born equal was, to him, 'an *obvious* fallacy.'[2] Instead, races could be placed on a scale of worth, set by nature. Under this hierarchy, members of the white race were taken to possess the attributes necessary to ensure world peace and the progress of civilization. Social Darwinism and race science could be marshalled in support of these assertions.

The theories of equality found in the *Leonard* judgments stand in marked contrast. Even the judge at first instance accepted that Leonard's views on race had become offensive.[3] In the Court of Appeal, Robins J.A. concluded that 'to say that a trust premised on ... notions of racism and religious superiority contravenes contemporary public policy is to expatiate the *obvious*.' He then said:

The concept that any one race or any one religion is intrinsically better than any other is patently at variance with the democratic principles governing our pluralistic society in which equality rights are constitutionally guaranteed and in which the multicultural heritage of Canadians is to be preserved and enhanced.

The widespread criticism of the Foundation by human rights bodies, the press, the clergy, the university community and the general community serves to demonstrate how far out of keeping the trust now is with prevailing ideas and standards of racial and religious tolerance and equality and, indeed, how offensive its terms are to fair-minded citizens.

To perpetuate a trust that imposes restrictive criteria on the basis of the discriminatory notions espoused in [the] recitals according to the terms specified by the settlor would not, in my opinion, be conducive to the public interest. The settlor's freedom to dispose of his property through the creation of a charitable trust fashioned along these lines must give way to current principles of public policy under which all races and religions are to be treated on a footing of equality and accorded equal regard and equal respect.[4]

If one were to step back from the judgments, a general observation suggests itself. What the case demonstrates is the difficulty that attends issues of equality. This indeterminacy is, in part, manifested by the wholly different analyses found in the three opinions delivered in the *Leonard* case. For all of the steps taken to combat racism (many of which were referred to in the opinions), the Leonard Foundation litigation reveals just how much Canadian law continues to be troubled by racist practices. This is also evident in the public debate about the Leonard Foundation that arose throughout the 1980s. The majority in the Court of Appeal observed that there had been a swell of public criticism of the trust. However, as we saw in chapter 3, the support that the Foundation received in the press suggests that public opinion may have been more divided than was acknowledged by the court.[5]

It is, in fact, difficult to know what the case has actually decided, a further testimonial to the vexing nature of equality questions. Two principal arguments dominated the hearings.[6] One concerned the applicability of the Ontario Human Rights Code; a second dealt with the scope of the doctrine of public policy. On both points we have been left in a quandary, as I will now attempt to illustrate.

APORIAS IN THE LEONARD RULING

Scholarships and Human Rights Protections

It was recognized from the outset that the result in the *Leonard Foundation* case could have implications for a number of other scholarship programs in Canada. The material presented to the court in the Middleton affidavit demonstrated that there were dozens of scholarships that restrict eligibility on the grounds of religion, ethnic origin, sex, language, and so on.[7] The legality of discriminatory scholarships remains a live issue. The number of academic awards has risen exponentially since the founding of the Leonard scholarships in 1916. As in the past, in the vast majority of instances eligibility is based on academic merit or need or some combination of the two. A minority of these contain exclusionary criteria that raise the spectre of a legal challenge. Consider these examples, drawn from university calenders and other student awards publications, all of which were published after the *Leonard* case:

Race, ancestry, ethnic origin, colour
Esso Resources Canada Limited Native Education Award, for Aboriginal (status or non-status), Inuit or Metis students.[8]
Hungarian-Canadian Engineers Association Student Trust Fund, for students of Hungarian origin or descent.
Guru Nanek Award, open to black Canadians born in Nova Scotia.
Canwest Global System Broadcasters, available to a student who is a member of a self-identified visible minority.

Place of origin
The Salim Majdalani Entrance Scholarship, open to a foreign student at the University of Toronto from Lebanon, Syria, Jordan, Iraq, or any other member state of the Arab League.[9]
Bridge Street Scholarship, tenable at Emmanuel College, University of Toronto, for a student from the Third World.

Citizenship
Japanese student scholarships, open to Japanese citizens studying full time in a business or economics program at a Canadian University.

Creed
Herbert S. Sharp Scholarships, open to students at Mount Allison University born in the Maritimes who belong to the United Church.

Sex
Thunder Bay South Jaycettes Entrance Award, for female students attending Lakehead University.[10]
Hanson Rupert D. and Jack C. Memorial Scholarship, available to a deserving son of a returned male member of Canada's Armed Services or to a deserving son of a male member of Canada's Armed Service who lost his life in active service.

Age
The National Council of Jewish Women of Canada (London Section) Award, for female students who are at least twenty-five years old.[11]

Gordon Currie Youth Development Fund, available to students in Saskatchewan who are under the age of twenty-five.

Handicap
McDougall, Mary (nee Outlet) Memorial Scholarship, available to physically handicapped students at the University of New Brunswick.[12]

Sexual orientation
Bill 7 Award, for gay or lesbian students in Ontario.

The fate of scholarship offerings in Canada depends on several factors. Where a scholarship has been established by a governmental agency, the Charter of Rights will apply. As is well known, the Charter contains a guarantee of equality before the law.[13] It is possible that a program founded or administered by a state-controlled educational institution would be regarded as governmental action so as to bring the Charter into play.[14]

Where state action is *not* involved, we have seen that human rights measures may be applicable (in addition to the doctrine of public policy). Unfortunately, the *Leonard* case does not resolve the uncertainty that existed about the scope of the Human Rights Code. It will be recalled that, at first instance, Mr Justice McKeown held that it did not apply. While the McKeown judgment was reversed on appeal, the Ontario Court of Appeal declined to rule on this point, finding it unnecessary to do so. It would be mistaken to assume that the appellate court has overruled McKeown J. on this question, or conversely, that the lower court's finding was implicitly endorsed. The better view is that nothing should be deduced from the Court of Appeal's silence on this question.[15]

In the wake of the *Leonard* case, the Ontario Human Rights Commission issued its *Policy Statement with Respect to Exclusionary Scholarships*.[16] The commission argued that the provision of education is a service within the meaning of the code and that exclusionary scholarships constituted indirect discriminatory action because they affected equal access to education. Therefore, scholarships that discriminate on the basis of the enumerated grounds[17] contravene the right to equal treatment unless they fall within an exemption recognized under the code. Two exemptions are particularly relevant to the type of scholarship being considered here.[18]

The first of these concerns what the Ontario code calls 'special programs.' Section 14 of the code allows for the creation of special programs that are designed to relieve hardship or economic disadvantage, to eliminate discrimination, or to promote equal opportunity. In short, the code permits certain types of affirmative action. In the context of scholarships, the *Policy Statement* suggests that the central question is whether or not a discriminatory qualification 'benefits a group that has been historically disadvantaged in the larger social and political context, and in comparison with other potential applicants.'[19] It was suggested that scholarships in favour of disabled persons, women, and Aboriginal students might well meet this test; those in favour of mature or married students would probably not. More significant perhaps is the commission's contention that many scholarships directed towards members of a specific cultural minority would likely *not* qualify as a special program. Hence, to use examples found in the *Policy Statement*, it would be permissible to provide for a scholarship for students in Italian studies, or even to establish a criterion such as contributions made within the Jewish community, so long as these awards were not restricted to persons of Italian origin or members of the Jewish faith.

The Ontario Human Rights Code also permits discriminatory action in relation to membership or participation in what are termed 'special interest organizations.' This exemption is designed to allow for the existence of cultural or religious associations. Section 18 provides that: 'The right ... to equal treatment with respect to services and facilities, with or without accommodation, is not infringed where membership or participation in a religious, philanthropic, educational, fraternal or social institution or organization that is primarily engaged in serving the interests of persons identified by a prohibited ground is restricted to persons who are similarly identified.'

This provision is important, and its scope of operation is potentially wide.[20] Nonetheless, the *Policy Statement with Respect to Exclusionary Scholarships* states that, as a general matter, the receipt of a scholarship, standing on its own, does not amount to either membership or participation as those terms are used in the section. The situation would be different, the commission argues, in the case of institutions that provided, say, religious education: 'It would be acceptable, for example, for a Roman Catholic institution to restrict its theological awards, on the basis of creed, to Roman Catholics who intend to study for the priesthood, or for a Jewish Hebrew school to declare only Jewish students to be eligible for enrolment. Moreover, such a school may designate scholarships or other financial awards strictly for Jewish applicants.'[21]

It is evident that the *Policy Statement* is a repudiation of the decision of Mr Justice McKeown. It will be recalled that McKeown J. concluded that the Human Rights Code did not apply to the Leonard Foundation, in part, because a scholarship program does not fit within the ordinary meanings given to the terms 'services' or 'facilities.' An accepted canon of construction in the area of human rights legislation is that the protections should be broadly interpreted. While McKeown J. acknowledged that principle, his reading of the code is nevertheless restrictive, depending as it does on ordinary dictionary definitions of the relevant terms. Under the definitions that he cited, education would not seem to qualify as a service, though, as the court recognized, several cases have come to a contrary conclusion. Moreover, under a purposive interpretation it seems sensible to treat student awards as an ancillary service designed to facilitate access to education. This is the reading argued for in the commission's *Policy Statement*, and it seems the appropriate one.

Even adhering to an approach based on usages found in common parlance, the conclusions reached by the High Court in *Leonard* are questionable. One speaks of banks and other lending institutions as providing 'financial services.' This is somewhat analogous to the provision of student bursaries. Along the same lines, decisions rendered under human rights codes across Canada since the McKeown ruling suggest an interpretation of services beyond those contemplated by generic dictionary definitions. The term has been found to include the issuance of a mayoral declaration (such as the announcement of gay and lesbian pride week),[22] a fishing competition,[23] the payment of unemployment insurance benefits,[24] and the provision of insurance coverage.[25] Moreover, it will be recalled that McKeown J. relied on the fact that the Foundation was created under a trust in finding that it did not constitute a facility or service. This cannot be a relevant factor. It is hard to believe, for instance, that a private school that maintained a policy prohibiting the admission of blacks or Jews could be insulated from the Human Rights Code simply by virtue of the fact that it had been created by means of a charitable trust.[26]

Considerably more troublesome is the question of whether the Foundation falls within the definition of a 'special interest organization' quoted above. McKeown J. said that it did, though he did not discuss the question at any length. Looking at that language, one can see some sense in the position that the Leonard Foundation is either a *religious, philanthropic, or education institution* (any one of these will do) that *serves the interests of a group* (that which is identified by Leonard) and that restricts *participation* to those in that same group. The only uncertainty is whether the receipt of a scholarship counts as 'participation' in the organization. As with the definition of the terms services and facilities, the answer lies in the function of this exemption. Its goal is to permit social interaction – to allow similarly situated people to come together in some meaningful way. It contemplates the promotion of group life. If so, it is unlikely that mere receipt of a bursary can be said to constitute participation in the Leonard Foundation. Recipients do not know each other and there is no publication of the names of the award winners. As far as the awarding procedures are concerned, each candidate is treated as separate and independent from all others. Even the Leonard Foundation Association no longer exists, although if it were still in operation this would not necessarily affect the validity of the bursaries. The Leonard awards derive not from that association but rather from the trust.

The Public Policy Issue

We saw in the preceding chapter that the Leonard Foundation Trust was found to be contrary to public policy by all three members of the Ontario Court of Appeal. In the minority opinion of Mr Justice Tarnopolsky, the discriminatory provisions, regardless of Leonard's underlying rationale, were said to be invalid. For the majority, Robins J.A. purported to make the recitals central to the analysis. The assertions of racial superiority in the recitals were anathema to the court; it was patent that this rendered the discriminatory terms of the trust void. Given this approach, one may ask whether the trust would have been upheld absent the statements contained in the recitals. That question is especially intriguing given that the 1916 and 1920 versions of the Leonard Foundation Trust, while containing restrictive criteria, did not include recitals outlining Leonard's theories on race, religion, and Empire. Under a rule in which the proven basis for discrimination is essential to a finding of invalidity, those deeds would have withstood a legal challenge. Indeed, a rule that places reliance on a stated rationale of racial, religious, or gender superiority would be of limited utility. Rarely will such a motivation be explicitly stated, and the present rules on the use of extrinsic evidence severely limit a court from considering evidence of motive not discoverable from the document itself.[27]

However, in my view, the judgment does not purport to lay down such a principle. Robins J.A. refused to address the question of how the law might respond to other discriminatory scholarships. The Leonard Trust was described as unique because of the extraordinary ideological precepts contained in the recitals. With a view to subsequent litigation, what the majority was endeavouring to say was this: 'Although we refrain from drawing a bright line separating valid from invalid scholarships, we are prepared to say that the Leonard trust is on the wrong side of any line that a future court might choose to draw.' The intended implication that one is meant to draw is that the *Leonard* reasons for judgment do not state that claims of (say) racial superiority are necessary to a finding of invalidity. That question is *supposedly* to be left for another day.

I emphasize the word *supposedly* because, although the majority judgment claims to avoid dealing with the validity of 'unexplained' discriminatory action, the order granted in the case reveals an inconsistency on this point. All of the discriminatory provisions in the trust, namely, those relating to race, colour, ethnic origin, creed or religion, and *sex*, were held to be void. The finding in relation to 'sex' is important because there is nothing in the recitals whatsoever concerning the trust's gender preference (that is, that no more than one-quarter of the funds were to be awarded to females). It is, of course, implicit that Reuben Leonard saw males as more deserving of his bounty than females. However, the same implication could be equally drawn about each of the other criteria, even in the absence of the explanations in the recitals. Recitals or no recitals, to have allowed the gender preference to remain would have been seen as incongruous and outrageous. Moreover, while the majority relied to some extent on the public outcry concerning the trust, the focus in the press was on the terms of exclusion, not the recitals. These did not, apparently, come to public attention.

The only reported decision since 1990 that deals with the validity of scholarships appears to adopt a narrow reading of the *Leonard* holding. The case of *Re Ramsden Estate*[28] concerned a 1994 bequest to the University of Prince Edward Island of trust funds to endow student awards. The donor expressed the wish that financial need be a factor and that academic merit not be the governing consideration. It was also the donor's wish that preference be given, if possible, to students intending to enter the ministry. The only mandated requirement was that the recipient be Protestant. When the university expressed concerns about this last criterion, the executors of the estate launched a court application for directions.

The University of Prince Edward Island is created under legislation as a non-denominational and non-political institution. By virtue of the governing statute, it may not accept a gift that is prejudicial to its non-denominational, non-political character.[29] It was held that, under the terms of the Ramsden gift, the university would be required to select among the student body on the grounds of religious affiliation alone, contrary to the statute. That being so, the question then became (as in *Leonard*) whether the gift could be varied under the *cy-près* doctrine.[30] This might have been accomplished by eliminating the religious requirement, but that was not the approach taken by the court. Instead it sought a way of modifying the terms to adhere most closely to the original intention. The identified invalidity arose from the selection of the university as the trustee; this contravened the University Act. That problem would be eliminated if new trustees, independent of the university, assumed the managerial duties, including selecting the recipients. There were already three such scholarships tenable at the university: one available to Catholics; one in which preference is to be given to Protestants or Catholics; and one requiring the holder to be of 'good Christian character.'[31] Because these are all administered by outside agencies, they did not violate the statutory prohibitions.

However, the central issue in *Leonard*, namely, the application of the doctrine of public policy to a charitable trust, was equally germane here, even taking the proposed modifications into account. The court concluded that the *Leonard Foundation* case was distinguishable because the Leonard trust 'was based on blatant religious supremacy and racism.'[32] There was no such basis for the Ramsden gift. Therefore, it was held there was no ground of public policy that would prevent the trust from taking effect, provided it was administered by a body other than the university.[33] As suggested above, it is questionable whether this is a proper reading of the *Leonard* case.

EXPLORING THE DEEPER PROBLEMS

In the preceding section, my goal was to identify ambiguities found in the *Leonard* decision. The uncertainty surrounding the holding is a product of the vexing nature of the legal problem facing the court. The difficulty of the issues at hand, and the overall indeterminacy of the law in this area, explain why the controversy took so long to bubble over and why the trust withstood the first legal challenge only to fail to run the gauntlet on appeal. Putting aside the intricacies of Ontario statute law, and the identification of the precise ruling in the Ontario Court of Appeal judgments, it is possible to understand the *Leonard* case as exposing some important features of the legal treatment of equality in Canada.

There are several reasons why discriminatory conduct is difficult to regulate. One concerns a problem of efficacy – there are limits on the law's capacity to alter beliefs and prejudices in a meaningful way. It is unrealistic to suppose that even stringently enforced equality principles can eradicate deep-seated racial hatred. Another difficulty involves the limits of the forensic process. Proving racial prejudice that runs contrary to provincial human rights protections is often a difficult task. The presence of such a code can itself induce guarded, nuanced conduct, driving discriminatory conduct underground.[34]

Two other problems concerning equality under law are especially evident in the Leonard Foundation dispute. One concerns the way in which we measure the importance of equality against other social values. There are occasions in which the law fails to respond to acts of discrimination on the ground that the public policy costs are too high. The law provides no remedy because the losses are seen as outweighing the gains of a legal response when measured in normative or utilitarian terms. Accordingly, even in cases where it is accepted that it is possible to affect conduct through law (that is, there is no problem of efficacy), and where we know that discrimination has occurred (so that there is also no problem of proof), there are times when no action will be taken because, on balance, it is seen as counter-productive. We may, for example, allow certain forms of racist speech in the name of protecting freedom of expression.

Second, the idea of equality is itself a contested matter, so that just what we are trying to achieve when we use that term to define a social good is sometimes unclear. Principles of equal treatment under law stress the essence of human nature and the need to acknowledge the moral worth of all people. These measures also recognize that discrimination is degrading and disabling. However, this begs questions about the form of equality that societies should strive to achieve. Is the aim equality of opportunity or equality of condition? To what extent can equality be achieved by the unequal treatment of individuals and groups? What is the proper place of affirmative action in Canadian law? To what extent should the law promote, protect, or encourage difference as a value? Or, more generally, in what ways can we distinguish between pernicious and justifiable discriminatory action?

The *Leonard* case touches on these issues: the balancing of equality and other rights, and the contested meanings of equality. These are considered in turn.

Equality v. Other Liberal Values

The International Convention on the Elimination of All Forms of Racial Discrimination (1965) declares that all parties to the convention 'condemn racial discrimination and undertake to pursue by all appropriate means and without delay a policy of eliminating racial discrimination in all its forms.' The convention provides also that all parties undertake 'not to sponsor, defend or support racial discrimination by any persons or organizations.'[35] Although Canada is a signatory to this instrument, there remain instances in which Canadian law chooses to resist responding to prejudicial conduct for the sake of advancing or protecting other accepted values. In the context of the *Leonard Foundation* case, or more generally, in the realm of what I have called documentary discrimination, the countervailing values include freedom of religion and expression and the rights inherent in the concept of private ownership. None of these rights exists in pure-form under Canadian law. There is inevitably a balancing or accommodation of conflicting interests, and a favouring of some of these over others.

Consider the ways in which one might exercise racial or religious preferences. At one extreme one can envision acts that are openly antagonistic to members of racial or religious groups. It is likely that most Canadians deplore the activities of organizations such as the Aryan Nations and would dread being the target of its vitriol of bigotry. For this reason, it is a crime in Canada to promote racial hatred. In addition, human rights statutes prohibit the publication of materials promoting discrimination. Here, equality values have prevailed over claims to free speech.

However, at the other end of a continuum of discrimination, one finds the exercise of preferences that are not only permitted but protected; not just tolerated, but facilitated. The constitutional right to freedom of religion is designed toward that end. At a pivotal point in the Court of Appeal ruling in *Leonard*, quoted above, Mr Justice Robins stated that the trust contravened public policy because it was predicated on notions of racism and religious superiority. To claim that one race or religion is intrinsically superior was said to be offensive to the values of a pluralistic, democratic society.[36] However, in relation to religious belief, this statement may be misleading or wrong. A modern-day R.W. Leonard may prefer low church Anglicanism over any other type of religion. He may feel that its doctrine expresses the true word of God. Moreover, nothing will prevent him from donating money to that cause, even though this means that all other religions on earth will receive nothing from him. Even if he wished to donate to each and every religion known to him, except one, this would be permitted. Likewise, he might wish to endow an educational institution that taught the scripture based solely on specific theological principles. All of this would be sanctioned, protected, and encouraged; his donations would be tax deductible. In these instances, religious freedom would easily prevail over equality under law.

Instead of focusing on freedom of religion or speech as the countervailing values, one can understand the problem as pitting the protection of private property against the promotion of equality. This is the essence of the Leonard Foundation controversy, in which concerns over discrimination were set against the rights of private property. The support for Leonard that appeared in the press was founded on an appeal to property rights as an important liberal value. This was a dominant theme within the public debate over the Leonard Foundation Trust: almost every public defence of the Leonard Foundation contains an argument along these lines. It was said that Reuben Leonard's rights, even more than fifty years after his death, should be respected. Part of the rationale was that to do otherwise would have a chilling effect on philanthropic practice. What the discourse does not reveal is just how complex these concepts can be. The rights of property owners are limited, as one can see in the review of the authorities on discriminatory transfers presented in chapter 3. Both the judge at first instance and the Court of Appeal in the *Leonard* case saw the problem in those terms, that is, as a response, for instance, to equality concerns, the composition of the bundle of rights that constitute property ownership can be altered so as to limit the rights of transfer. Where the judgments at the two levels differ is, primarily, as to how these rights should be ordered.

This dilemma can be illustrated by reference to another continuum. At one end can be placed the well-accepted limits on property entitlements. For example, the ownership of contraband may be prohibited altogether; the possession of certain inherently dangerous objects is also heavily regulated. Some transfers are prohibited (the sale of cigarettes to children) or regulated (the sale of prescription drugs) in the public interest. However, in general, property rights are extensive: by and large, owners are entitled to do whatever they wish with their belongings, even to the extent of destroying their property. Assume, for example, that Reuben Leonard bestowed a gift on some perfect stranger. When asked about this bewildering action, Leonard replied as follows: 'I selected him because he is white, and because I believe that he is a Protestant and of British parentage.' Even after the *Leonard* case there is no basis in law for treating this (outright) gift as invalid. Nor would it be unlawful to confer a gift on the Aryan Nations. What is more, there is a large ambit of offensive discriminatory conduct that is not contrary to human rights protections. People are entitled to decide that whites only may enter their home. In that domain, rights of ownership continue to prevail over the values inherent in equal treatment.

A host of reasons have been advanced to explain why the law confers broad powers and privileges as part of the ownership bundle. Some of the rationales for property are consequentialist. Hence it is sometimes asserted that private property rights allow for economic efficiency and therefore produce material well-being. Property allows for freedom, and it promotes privacy and full human development. Property rights are also sometimes justified as apt rewards for labour and productivity. Although all of these assertions are contentious, they nonetheless serve to fuel the powerful ideological engine of property rights in Canadian law and society.[37] As a result, when other values come into conflict with those underscoring rights of ownership, a strong case for curtailing property entitlements is often demanded.

Bearing this reasoning in mind, one can imagine a modern-day Reuben Leonard marshalling a defence along the following lines: I may express my views on racial or national preferences provided that I do not promote racial hatred or otherwise violate various statutory prohibitions. I may demonstrate my devotion to one religion by a direct donation, though by doing so I effectively discriminate against all other religions. I may destroy all of my savings or indulge in frivolous gifts as much as I wish, though no public good otherwise results. I may choose who may walk on my lawn, and in doing so I may happen to exercise preferences that my neighbours see as racist and therefore inexcusably objectionable. That being so, why is it that the law does not allow me to exercise *the very same preferences* through the instrumentality of the Leonard Foundation?

The answers given in the Court of Appeal rely upon the 'public' dimension of his so-called 'private' foundation. Mr Justice Robins emphasized what he termed the quasi-public nature of the Foundation, a status that arose from the fact that it was a charitable trust, designed (therefore) to benefit the public. Moreover, the awards were tenable at publicly funded educational institutions. Similarly, Tarnopolsky J.A. was careful to distinguish between charitable trusts, such as the one in issue, and family trusts. The rationale for the distinction under each approach is clear: public action is to be assessed in law by reference to a different (that is, more rigorous) standard than that applied to private dealings. In a sense, even Reuben Leonard understood this way of thinking. He regarded his fortune as being held as a 'public trust.' He accepted, therefore, that a sense of public duty attended his actions. Indeed, it is ironic that this very characterization was so instrumental in defeating his 1923 scheme.

The public/private dichotomy is often invoked in legal analysis, especially in relation to human rights issues, but the dividing line between the two is not always clear. This is because the dichotomy is actually deployed in two different ways, producing not two but three categories of conduct. The public/private divide is sometimes used to separate state from non-state action. It is this use that explains why the Canadian Charter of Rights and Freedoms is not directly applicable to the Leonard Foundation Trust. As we have seen, the Charter applies to state (public) conduct. The Foundation is treated as private for the purposes of Charter analysis. The category of private conduct is further bifurcated. One speaks of acts done in the public arena and those done in private. For instance, it is understood that in a market economy resources are primarily allocated by private transactions, not by public authority. However, private enterprise in the marketplace is construed as public when compared to the private domain of the home.[38] The three categories that emerge are therefore as follows: (1) state action; (2) private conduct in the public domain (such as the conduct of private enterprise); (3) private conduct treated as being outside of the public arena (such as family life).

The effect of defining three forms of action is seen in the rules for scrutinizing conduct. With regard to equality concerns, the state is subject to the highest level of scrutiny because it is duty-bound to treat each citizen with an even hand. In contrast, citizens are permitted, indeed invited, to pursue self-interest and to exercise their personal preferences in a host of ways. Between these two realms lies conduct that partakes of both private and public elements, and it is in this region that the debate over the Leonard Foundation occurred. The initial inquiries made by the Ontario Human Rights Commission to the Leonard trustees were met with the response that the Foundation was a private trust.[39] This, of course, is no answer to the commission's jurisdiction to investigate, since its province is the regulation of private discriminatory conduct. In this context, the term 'public' refers to actions ordinarily occurring in a public forum. This is category (2) conduct.

Even if we accept this three-part description, the dividing lines remain imprecise. This is because the private and the public are not really as separate as this above analysis suggests. Rather, they overlap. All discriminatory action regarding private property can be seen, at bottom, as state action. It is sometimes said that property is understood in the law as a set of rights created under law, and that, therefore, absent state sanction and enforcement, property rights vanish. As a result, in allowing property to be used in a discriminatory way, the state is therefore acting complicitously. On occasion this complicity is apparent: consider again the cases of *Franklin* v. *Evans* (1924) and *Christie* v. *York* (1939), which were discussed in chapter 3. Both disputes involved the refusal of services to black patrons. In both, under the law as it then stood, the legal attack on the discriminatory conduct failed. In short, any legitimate private discriminatory conduct will, by definition, receive the backing of the state. In this sense, then, all *private* property dealings have a *public* dimension. Property rights can be seen as a state delegation of the decision-making power (about property) into private hands.

This line of reasoning applies not just to the category (2) type of conduct but to category (3) as well, that is, to private action occurring in a non-public setting. Consider another situation discussed in chapter 3: a testamentary gift conditioned on the recipient adhering to a particular religious faith. We saw in that chapter that these gifts have generally been treated as valid. It was here that Tarnopolsky J.A. felt his reasoning should stop. Family trusts, as he called them, would not be subject to the rigorous rules he proposed for discriminatory scholarships. Similarly, category (3) conduct is generally thought to be outside the reach of human rights instruments.

I am not sure that these limitations make sense. First, a gift subject to a stipulation concerning religious adherence (as in the above example) is subject to legal enforcement. It is therefore public in the sense that the courts will enforce all valid testamentary gifts. And it is only private (in the category (3) sense) if we assume that the recipients of such gifts are denied the status of being members of the public at large. To put it another way, it is not clear that we should tolerate discriminatory action that affects family members to any greater extent than that tolerated in the community at large.

One answer to this issue is sometimes suggested. If a gift is given, say, from father to son, on the proviso that the son does not marry outside the Jewish religion, it is always open to the son simply to disclaim the gift. He need not sacrifice his moral beliefs concerning religious adherence because he can walk away from the 'offer' contained in the bequest. Therefore, no harm is done by allowing such a gift to stand.

My reply to this reasoning is based on an apparent extrapolation of the *Leonard* case. We know that Colonel Leonard could have chosen to destroy his fortune in a bonfire or to make an absolute gift to some person he thought to be a worthy recipient. However, having chosen to endow a scholarship, the law now demands that he adhere to a certain level of fairness. Likewise, where a testator decides to confer a conditional gift on a small set of the outside world (that is, family members), one could argue that he or she is equally bound to comply with an appropriate public policy standard. This closeness of these two situations would, perhaps, be more apparent if another example is given. Imagine a testamentary gift under which a college fund is promised 'to all the members of my family who are white, British subjects, and adherents to the Christian religion in its Protestant form. It is provided also that no more than one-quarter of the monies set aside shall be allocated to female relatives.' In assessing the 'publicness' of such a gift, the difference is purely one of degree. It is not clear to me that, if the Leonard Foundation trust of 1923 is unacceptable, such a family gift should pass muster.

Given this reasoning, the 1996 Ontario decision in *Re Fox Estate*[40] is noteworthy. The case involved an attempt by a mother to disinherit her son because, contrary to her dictates, he had married a woman not of the Jewish faith. In the purported exercise of her powers as executor under the will of her deceased husband, she diverted property otherwise destined to fall into her son's hands. The Ontario Court of Appeal, reversing the trial judge,[41] concluded that Mrs Fox had acted improperly; she had exceeded her powers as executor. Although the case fell within the context of family transfers, one member of the Court of Appeal, Mr Justice Galligan, assessed whether the dictates of public policy could serve as a discrete ground for challenging the mother's action. Drawing explicitly on the *Leonard Foundation* case, Galligan J.A. took it as now settled that it is contrary to public policy to discriminate on the grounds of race or religion. To allow the disapproval of a marriage on the basis of religion was thus 'abhorrent to contemporary community standards.'[42] In the course of argument in *Fox*, a question was posed from the bench as to whether conferring gifts expressly conditioned on marriage within a designated faith would still be regarded as valid. In reply, it was conceded that such a condition would probably no longer be upheld.[43]

Let me summarize this last point. In the *Leonard Foundation Trust* case we see the law resolving a competition between conflicting values. In *Leonard*, a distinction was drawn between public and private action, and this dichotomy was instrumental in the reasoning in both appellate judgments. However, I find the attempt to explain the line between permissible and impermissible discrimination by relying on a distinction between private and public conduct to be unhelpful. What results from such an approach is not a bright line at all but three overlapping categories that obscure rather than clarify what the law should be.

Contested Meanings of Equality

The problem in the law governing equality discussed above pertains to the balancing of conflicting rights. The issue addressed in this section involves competing conceptions of equality. Unlike the contest between equality on the one hand and values external to it (such as property rights) on the other, the dilemma here involves a conflict contained *inside* the concept of equality itself. That problem can be described in this way: Although we live in a world in which no two individuals are or can be equal in every conceivable biological, legal, or other way, the pursuit of equality has nevertheless become an important goal. At the same time, in a multicultural society that aspires to respect and value difference, it is obvious that equality (defined as sameness) may not be a desirable end.

The tension between competing notions of equality can be found in human rights legislation. Anti-discrimination codes tend to stress the common elements of the human condition. As a result, Ontario's law mandates that in the provision of goods and services we must not take account of certain differences. We all need decent accommodation, whatever the colour of our skin or our religious beliefs. In relation to these needs, we are all to be treated as equals. Put another way, what is required by such a law is neutrality. We are being asked to ignore some considerations in the way that we treat people. That demand might encompass intentional acts that demonstrate differential treatment, as well as systemic factors that wind up producing the same result. In both situations, all that such equality rules require is that there be no correlation between our conduct and a prohibited ground of discrimination.

However, neutrality is only one way of conceiving of the idea of equality. If, by contrast, it is considered important that each member of society enjoy certain material conditions in life, neutrality normally will not suffice. An unrestrained egalitarian might argue, for instance, that the law should ensure that each and every one of us can enjoy an equal measure of property or prosperity. A more tempered approach might suggest that the demands of substantive equality are met when, say, everyone is accorded some minimal standard of living. Rather than ignoring differences (that is, acting neutrally), people would have to be treated differently, that is, their present position would have to be assessed and reassessed until the goal of material equality (whatever the specific target may be) is achieved.

It is in relation to the pursuit of this type of equality goal that the idea of affirmative action emerges. Affirmative action occurs when some positive steps are taken in a differential way to achieve some form of equal standing. Often at work here is the appreciation that past acts of discrimination (in effect, prior breaches of the idea of neutrality) can have lasting and harmful effects. Therefore, affirmative action has been used to improve the lot of historically marginalized and disadvantaged groups. To place matters within the context of the present study, it may be observed that both Reuben Wells Leonard and advocates of affirmative action accept the privileged status of the white Anglo-Saxon males. For Leonard, it was both natural and beneficial. Affirmative action is predicated on the view that that privileged position is historically contingent and deeply damaging.

Equality, then, is multidimensional. Even so, it remains an important liberal precept, and in many ways Canadian law is committed to achieving some version (or other) of this ideal. Because equality (choose your meaning) is treated by most people as virtuous, it carries rhetorical weight: It is nowadays hard to be against equality, even though there may be vehement disagreement as to what that term should mean. Given its protean character and its popular appeal, it is understandable that equality-based arguments could be found on both sides of the Leonard Foundation controversy. Both groups felt it useful to resort to equality claims to bolster their respective positions.[44] So the Human Rights Commission alleged that the Foundation was in violation of the equal rights protections found in the Ontario Human Rights Code. Those writing in support of the Leonard Foundation argued that the scholarships should be governed by the same rules that apply to other discriminatory scholarships, such as those open only to South African blacks, Jews, persons of Greek descent, and so on. McKeown J.'s reasons for judgment comport with this point of view. The Leonard Foundation Trust was like other scholarships that discriminated on the basis of race or nationality. The implication to be drawn from his reasons for judgment was that to strike down the Leonard Trust would be to imperil a host of other ostensibly worthy scholarships and bursaries. Again, such is the rhetorical force of the word 'equality' that both camps sought to enlist its support.

However, the reasons of McKeown J., like all of the pro-Leonard arguments that appeared in the press, adopt a 'neutrality' definition of equality. What is called for is the application of a type of 'moral algebra,'[45] one that mandates that dominant and marginalized groups be treated equally. We have just seen that this is only one meaning that can be given to the term. The pursuit of substantive equality through affirmative action was almost totally ignored in the public discourse about the Leonard Foundation. This is surprising since the concept of affirmative action has a firm footing under current Canadian law. With regard to governmental action, the Canadian Charter of Rights and Freedoms contains a basic guarantee of equality before the law. However, this is qualified by an exemption in favour of governmental action directed at the amelioration of conditions of disadvantaged individuals or groups.[46] In addition, generally speaking, provincial human rights codes, such as Ontario's, exempt certain forms of reverse discrimination.[47]

In Canada, as elsewhere, the adoption of affirmative action programs, in employment, education, and elsewhere, has been controversial.[48] At the heart of the critiques is the complaint that affirmative action is, by definition, discriminatory and therefore wrong. The argument is based on the view that the legal conception of equality should be confined to the idea of neutrality; the law should take no notice of differences (such as race or religion). Moreover, it is said that the application of affirmative action can produce harmful and unfair results. In seeking to respond to existing patterns of discrimination, it can serve to confer a benefit on those who have not in fact suffered injustice while at the same time imposing burdens on those who were not responsible for past wrongs. For instance, when an affirmative action policy is applied, the most competent members of a benefited group will receive an advantage at the expense of the most competent members of the non-benefited group. In addition, whether affirmative action is effective in pursuing equality goals is an open question; some complain that it cannot begin to address the entrenched problems of social inequality. Where it is effective, the intended beneficiaries may in time enjoy an undue advantage. As well, affirmative action can be difficult to apply, that is, it is not always easy to identify or prove the specific area of disadvantage and to construct a remedy that responds to that concern, no more and no less. Another claim is that affirmative action can be counter-productive, breeding resentment and hostility against the groups to be benefited and devaluing the accomplishments of those who have received assistance under an affirmative action program. And it is argued that affirmative action leads to mediocrity because merit factors are given subordinate importance.

I believe that it is important to employ devices like affirmative action, though it is, one must concede, a blunt instrument. Problems of application, some of which are described in the preceding paragraph, surface when endeavouring to assess the validity of discriminatory scholarships. What precisely are we seeking to ameliorate? Is it necessary to demonstrate material disadvantage in Canadian society at large? Or in the institution at which the award is tenable? Or in the program of study? In some fields, such as nursing, women have been historically over-represented. Would affirmative action be justified here? Conversely, might this be a case in which scholarships to induce men to enter nursing might be acceptable as a form of affirmative action. Just how Canadian courts will treat these issues as they relate to affirmative action scholarships and bursaries is not yet known.[49]

Is there an element of affirmative action to be found within the 1923 Leonard Trust? It was, in essence, a bursary, financial need being an absolute prerequisite. In the selection of recipients, the General Committee has always treated this consideration as central. That remains true. Hence, an argument can be made that the scholarship can be said to have a valid purpose even having regard to contemporary public policy dictates. Put another way, the trust identifies a marginalized segment of the population, namely *poor*, white, Protestant, British subjects. Viewed in this way (and absent reference to the recitals), the trust is designed to help not a dominant elite but an underclass.

Attractive at first glance, this argument must ultimately fail. The requirement of financial stringency was never challenged in the litigation and remains part of the trust. It was unassailable. That being so, the question that emerges is whether there are grounds for favouring poor white students over poor black ones, poor Protestants over poor Catholics, Muslims, or Jews, and so on. Also, one would want to know why more help should be afforded to needy men than women. It is entirely appropriate to set aside the invidious distinctions while preserving the valid one (poverty). So, if we control for poverty, no justification exists in this instance for favouring Leonard's selected group of poor over the others. Under the scholarship program as reshaped by the court order, white, Protestant, British subjects may still apply for a Leonard award. That aspect of the original design is unaltered, and therefore that segment of Canada's underclass is still aided. What has changed is that they must now compete with a broader range of similarly situated candidates. To put it still another way, one good apple does not save the whole barrel. If it were not so, one virtuous act of charity could work to insulate other elements that are deplorable.

The English and American Experiences

My modest thesis in this chapter is that the treatment of discrimination under law is incoherent, and that when, years from now, legal historians come to examine the *Leonard Foundation* case, they will find this uncertainty to be a telling feature of the law of our times. Other evidence is also available. Consider, for example, the English and American responses to some of the issues dealt with in the Leonard controversy.

Apart from the decision in *Re Lysaght*[50] (which was discussed in chapter 3), there are no reported English decisions concerning discriminatory scholarships. Still, subsequent English developments are instructive. One concerns a revision made to the Rhodes scholarships. As we saw (in chapter 2), the Rhodes was, arguably, influential in the creation of the Leonard Foundation awards. The terms of Rhodes scholarships contain an age stipulation (candidates must be over eighteen but under twenty-five at the time the award is taken up), and they were originally restricted to men. This exclusion as to gender was removed in the mid-1970s, not by virtue of a court challenge, but under the terms of the Sex Discrimination Act, 1975, which conferred a power to delete such terms on the Secretary of State.[51] In effect, the Rhodes was rendered gender-neutral by act of Parliament.

Although such action might suggest that English law now takes a hard line on discriminatory charitable gifts, in fact the reverse is true. Under the first version of the Race Relations Act, passed in 1968, charitable trusts were partially exempt from the legislation. That act provided that the prohibitions against discrimination do not apply to charitable instruments that confer benefits on persons of a particular race, descent, or national or ethnic origin.[52] Only discrimination on the basis of colour was not exempted. The 1976 reform of the legislation continues this approach.⁵³ Therefore, the charitable nature of a trust, far from attracting strict scrutiny (as in the *Leonard* case) serves as the basis for a relaxed anti-discrimination regime. A comparable provision (relating to gender) is contained in the Sex Discrimination Act.⁵⁴ It would appear that the promotion of charitable action, even at the expense of the denial of equal treatment, is the guiding principle.

As one might expect, American law has had more to say about discriminatory conduct. Although the patterns of racism and discrimination in the United States differ greatly from those in Canada, there are nevertheless a number of common elements. Hence, even though the ideology of equality is embedded in American political ideology and discourse, from (at least) the Declaration of Independence onward, it was not until the end of the Second World War that the concept became infused with significant meaning. It was only after 1945 that measures were introduced to limit discrimination in employment and in the provision of services and accommodations. And it was not until after the war that the equal rights guarantees contained in the American Bill of Rights were used effectively against state-sanctioned segregation and other race-based policies.⁵⁵

The American jurisprudence concerning equality rights as they relate to documentary discrimination has been dominated by constitutional considerations. This can be illustrated by the law governing restrictive covenants. We have seen that in Canada the legality of racially restrictive land transfers was determined prior to the advent of the Canadian Charter, and, therefore, without regard to constitutional norms. (Moreover, it is unlikely that the Charter would be found to apply to this type of private transaction.) Instead, under Canadian law, such covenants are ineffective either because they contravene legislation (as in Ontario and Manitoba) or because they will not create an enforceable obligation in accordance with basic land law principles. Arguably, they also contravene the common law doctrine of public policy. By contrast, in the United States such covenants are subject to constitutional constraints. The judicial enforcement of such a covenant is treated as state action, thereby triggering the equality protections of the American Bill of Rights.⁵⁶

Moreover, a broad definition of state action has allowed for the application of the constitutional protection of equality in the context of discriminatory scholarships. As a result, state action may be found when, for example, an agent of the state (such as a school or school board) assists in the selection of candidates or in the administration of the awards. In such instances, the courts have struck down awards that discriminate on the basis of race, religion, and gender.[57] However, it has been held that the advertising of the awards, even coupled with the initial screening and designation of potential recipients by a university, will fall beyond the reach of the Bill of Rights.[58] That would probably be true of the Leonard Foundation. Even assuming that publicly funded schools and universities constitute state actors, their role under the Leonard Trust (in essence, dispersing the scholarship monies to the successful candidates) would not likely attract constitutional scrutiny under American law.

An expansive concept of state action in American law has thus provided a powerful weapon to eradicate discriminatory conduct. However, in those instances in which the constitution cannot be invoked, the scope for discriminatory dispositions is wide. For example, American courts, as with their Anglo-Canadian counterparts, have permitted testamentary gifts containing discriminatory provisions relating to such matters as the religious or marital preferences of a donee.[59] Moreover, when a scholarship is established through a charitable trust, and where there is no state action, challenges to the validity of scholarships based on the doctrine of public policy have generally been ineffective. In some instances, the doctrine of *cy-près* (or a comparable rule known as 'equitable deviation') has been applied to remove restrictions in instances in which the selected trustees refused to administer the gift.[60] In general, then, while the equality protections of the constitution have been accorded an extensive field, the American doctrine of public policy has been allowed to atrophy. In short, were the Leonard Foundation transplanted to American soil, it would probably not be found to be invalid, at least based on the American scholarship case law as it now stands.[61]

Under American law, little scope exists for the application of principles of affirmative action as a constitutional concept.[62] Under the equality protections in the United States constitution, racial and ethnic distinctions are subject to a standard of strict scrutiny.[63] This means, in effect, that racial discrimination will be treated as unconstitutional unless it is based on a compelling state interest and is narrowly tailored to pursue that interest. That standard applies whether or not the impugned program involves affirmative action. Remedying existing effects connected to past discrimination can furnish a sufficiently compelling rationale for state action, so long as the present effects can be linked to specific acts of past conduct. This is a stringent test. Moreover, the requirement of a narrowly tailored response establishes a hurdle that is difficult to surmount. In general, it must be shown that nondiscriminatory approaches are unlikely to work, that undue preference is not being given to the targeted group, and that the program is flexible and temporary.[64]

The 1994 ruling in *Podberesky* v. *Kirwin*,[65] an important decision on the constitutionality of discriminatory scholarships, demonstrates just how exacting the American standard can be. *Podberesky* involved a challenge to a scholarship fund at the University of Maryland at College Park. The awards were available only to African-Americans. The university defended the scholarship on the ground that it was carefully designed to remedy past discrimination. It was not until the 1960s that blacks had in fact attended the College Park campus. The university also maintained that the effects of past discrimination lingered. Evidence was presented to show that blacks remained under-represented at College Park, that graduation rates were low, that the campus was seen by blacks as a hostile environment, and that the university had a poor reputation among the local black community. Despite all of this, the scholarship was found to violate the equality protections of the Bill of Rights. What the evidence failed to disclose, in the court's view, was that the attitudes held by black students and the black community were tied specifically to past practices on campus. It was also found that the scholarships were not narrowly tailored. The data assembled by the university did not convince the court that blacks were in fact under-represented. Nor was it shown that there was a sufficient relationship between the students eligible for the awards and the type of person that had been subjected to the university's discriminatory practices in years past.[66]

Several points emerge from this brief review. The English law demonstrates a balancing of equality and property rights that is very different from the situation in Canada. Under American law, the constitution has proven to be a powerful tool to prevent discrimination by state agents, and this can affect even some charitable trusts. However, if the constitution cannot be invoked (as in the Leonard-type situation), the scope for discriminatory conduct is wider than that permitted under the *Leonard Foundation* case ruling. A narrow conception of affirmative action can adversely affect even those scholarships aimed at responding to systemic discrimination.

CONCLUSION

In this chapter I have tried to explain why the *Leonard* case is of lasting importance in the law. It is, curiously, not the clarity of the holding, not the light that it shines, that makes the case worthy of study, but rather the complexity that it exposes. The Court of Appeal has resolved little about the scope of the common law doctrine of public policy and even less about the meaning of current human rights legislation. In effect, we have seen four different legal solutions to the Leonard puzzle: those offered by McKeown J., Robins J.A., Tarnopolsky J.A., and the Ontario Human Rights Commission. Additional perspectives are added by the English and American experiences. What is revealed by these various approaches, I suggest, is that we have so far failed to understand how to solve the principal problems at issue in the Leonard litigation. Even if it is accepted that the *Leonard* case itself was rightly decided, we still do not know how to order or balance rights of ownership against the pursuit of equality. We still cannot define comprehensively the forms of equality to which we, as a society, should aspire.

Epilogue

In the mid-1990s Charles Chan donated $4 million to endow a scholarship at the University of Alberta, his Alma Mater. The award was available to students from Tai Shan in the People's Republic of China. A story about Chan and his donation in the Edmonton *Journal* in April 1997[1] drew a letter of complaint from one reader:

> I read in *The Journal* ... that a former Chinese university student named Chen [sic], who is now a multi-millionaire, gave the University of Alberta $6.5 million in the past 18 months, including a $4-million scholarship fund 'for Chinese students who wish to train at the U. of A.' Why am I hearing nothing but a deafening silence from the liberal-left politically correct elite? Not a hint of the 'R' (racism) word anywhere.
> Can you imagine the resounding cries of outrage and righteous indignation from the politically correct elite if some white millionaire had set up a scholarship fund for 'white (may even include black, red pink and green) students only.'[2]

This is, of course, a variant of the Leonard Foundation controversy (about which the angry reader was apparently unaware). And it is not the only modern manifestation that connects with the life of Reuben Wells Leonard. I have presented this study as one designed to contrast social attitudes found at the beginning and end of the twentieth century. Yet it is remarkable how many current counterparts can be seen, so much so that the Leonard saga appears in some ways to be an allegory for modern times. Imperial federation never came to be, and the British Empire has disappeared, but initiatives to forge supra-national alliances, such as the North American Free Trade Agreement, are again on the political agenda, just as the fate of the Canadian polity remains at issue. The Coniagas mines are spent, but the struggles of organized labour for industrial democracy in northern Ontario and elsewhere continue. Modern libertarians argue that charity should supplant state social programs.[3] As in Leonard's time, universities recruit business leaders to sit on governing boards. Increased reliance on private-sector financial support for public educational institutions has prompted questions about the integrity of academic freedom. Here one is reminded of the failed endowment at Queen's. The events surrounding the work of Professor Robert MacIver (circa 1921) resonate with existing controversies about political correctness and speech codes on campus. To be sure, this contest has changed in important ways. The Leonard/MacIver contretemps concerned the clash of establishment values with Marxist theories. For R.W. Leonard, the issue was whether MacIver (and his ilk) should be given a platform from which to pollute the minds of Canada's youth. The current debate concerns whether academic freedom can be marshalled to provide a safe house for sexist and racist theories that undermine the position of marginalized groups.[4]

Leonard's theories on race also have modern counterparts. One might be tempted to conclude that the wave of human rights reforms aimed at eradicating discrimination marked the death of the science of racial difference. The events surrounding the litigation might be taken as lending support to that reading. There was, after all, absolutely no defence of the Leonard Foundation Trust on the merits. Nowhere in the public debate, and certainly not in the judgments, does one find any suggestion whatsoever that Leonard's position of the natural endowments of the white race are cogent. Instead it was his rights of private property that were championed.

Despite all of this, the history of the Leonard Foundation does not illustrate the death of race science. The story is not, sadly, a parable of how racism and the ideologies on which it is based have been vanquished. It cannot be, because theories of primordial racial difference are not dead. Rather, nativism, chauvinism, and social Darwinism have been replaced by modern counterparts. The traditions of typology and hierarchy that flourished in the nineteenth and early twentieth centuries recur in new dress.[5] From the 1920s through to the Second World War, the watershed event in the advancement of anti-discrimination reforms, there has been an unbroken string of scientific hypotheses that assert meaningful genetic racial distinctions.[6]

Much of the current literature has involved purported links between IQ and race. In 1969 Arthur Jensen, a professor of educational psychology at Berkeley, maintained that such a correlation existed. His findings, published in the *Harvard Educational Review,* suggest that the differences in IQ performances of blacks and whites in the United States could be attributed principally to heredity.[7] Jensen's contention was, in essence, a modern adaptation of Carl Brigham's 1923 study of American intelligence (referred to briefly in chapter 2). The most prominent recent rearticulation of this point of view is contained in Richard Herrnstein's and Charles Murray's immensely controversial book, *The Bell Curve,*[8] in which correlations between class and IQ, and, inferentially, race and IQ, are claimed. In Canada, J. Philippe Rushton, an associate professor of psychology at the University of Western Ontario, has returned to the analysis of cranial capacity in search of racial correlates.[9] In response to attacks against such research,[10] Rushton has defended the data on IQ testing (which conform with his own research on cranial measurements). Moreover, he has maintained that the scientific case against equality has been effectively mounted: 'For the past thirty years an increasing number of world-class scholars, including those without the remotest taint of segregationism or Nordicist anti-semitism, have published research in the most prestigious academic journals (Nature, Science, Psychological Science, Behavioral and Brain Sciences, Behavior Genetics, and Intelligence) that demonstrably challenges each and every article of the egalitarian dogma. But it was only with the publication of The Bell Curve as a trade book by a major US publisher that this information has made its way to the general reading public.'[11]

The debate about the genetic import of race that *The Bell Curve* has fuelled anew is intense and ongoing;[12] Rushton's confident assertion is, to put it mildly, contestable. It is, of course, beyond the scope of the present study to assess the evidence offered by this new brand of race scientist. But my reason for discussing these developments does not require that type of appraisal. My point is simply that race science has not disappeared;[13] nor is it likely to in the near future, especially now that genetic science has ascended in importance.[14] Indeed, as data from the Human Genome Project are released, one can expect that contentious claims about race will continue to emerge. In the face of evidence suggesting that race is not a meaningful genetic category,[15] claims are already being made that findings generated by the Project prove that there are statistically significant differences among races in relation to intelligence.[16] Moreover, these theories are likely to serve as a prop to support racism and discriminatory action, the role performed by social Darwinism in R.W. Leonard's time.[17] Given these developments, what the outcome of the *Leonard Foundation* case suggests is not that such views have been scientifically repudiated but rather that they have been politically marginalized. While theories of genetic difference survive, race science does not appear to be influential. Rushton is a pariah at Western and in the 1980s he came perilously close to a criminal charge of inciting racial hatred.[18] For the moment, at least, his views and those of his cohort group have little political currency in Canada.

What the Leonard Foundation controversy seems to teach us is that questions about the law's approach to intolerance remain unresolved in Canada. It cannot seriously be doubted that the present response to the harms of discrimination, even if lamentably incomplete, is more robust than it was in 1923. It is, of course, in relation to the law of discrimination that the life of Reuben Wells Leonard can have its most direct impact – through the agency of the *Leonard Foundation* case. That case is arguably the most important decision on the law of public policy in Canada on the question of documentary discrimination. Nevertheless, as we saw in chapter 4, the case forms only a starting point of analysis.

Leonard's work lives on in a way that he would not likely have anticipated. The Court of Appeal ruling in the *Leonard Foundation* case was the first Commonwealth authority in which the doctrine of public policy was used to invalidate the terms of a charitable trust. More generally, as just noted, the case has emerged as a pivotal authority on the law of public policy as it affects property rights in Canada. It is ironic that the Foundation, which is predicated on a belief in the natural superiority of the white race, has given rise to a principle of law that denies the validity of that very claim and that undermines the efficacy of future conduct based on such a belief. The educational trust that Colonel Reuben Wells Leonard first established in 1916 was designed to serve as a permanent benefaction and memorial. Given the resolute way that he seemed to hold his convictions, it is doubtful that he would have anticipated then that his trust would one day be considered repugnant to contemporary public policy. And it is also unlikely that Leonard would have expected that, for all of his charitable endeavours, his life's work would have yielded these enduring legacies – a trust deed containing refracted images of ideological artefacts, and a legal precedent that outlaws the very discriminatory action in which he believed.

Appendix

1. Prefatory Notes

Various parts of the Leonard Foundation Trust deed were deleted by virtue of the order of the Ontario Court of Appeal in *Re Canada Trust and the Ontario Human Rights Commission* (1990) 69 Dominion Law Reports (4th) 321. The deleted parts are reproduced in ***bold italics***. Reference is made in the deed to a schedule 'C.' That schedule contains a list of property settled under the trust. It is not reproduced here.

2. Leonard Foundation Trust Deed (1923)

THIS INDENTURE made in duplicate the *twenty-eighth* day of *December*, in the year of our Lord, one thousand nine hundred and twenty-three,

BETWEEN

REUBEN WELLS LEONARD of the City of St. Catharines, in the County of Lincoln, and Province of Ontario, Esquire, hereinafter called the 'Settlor'

OF THE FIRST PART,

AND

THE TORONTO GENERAL TRUSTS CORPORATION, hereinafter called the 'Trustee,'

OF THE SECOND PART.

Task of White Race

WHEREAS *the Settlor believes that the White Race is, as a whole, best qualified by nature to be entrusted with the development of civilization and the general progress of the World along the best lines:*

Maintenance of Christian Religion

AND WHEREAS *the Settlor believes that the progress of the World depends in the future, as in the past, on the maintenance of the Christian Religion:*

British Empire and Education of Selected Children

AND WHEREAS *the Settlor believes that the peace of the World and the advancement of civilization depends very greatly upon the independence, the stability and the prosperity of the British Empire as a whole, and that this independence, stability and prosperity can be best attained and assured by the education in patriotic Institutions of selected children, whose birth and training are such as to warrant a reasonable expectation of their developing into leading citizens of the Empire:*

Conduct of affairs of British Empire; Persons excluded from managements and benefits of Foundation

AND WHEREAS *the Settlor believes that, so far as possible, the conduct of the affairs of the British Empire should be in the guidance of Christian persons of British Nationality who are not hampered or controlled by any allegiance or pledge of obedience to any government, power or authority, temporal or spiritual, the seal of which government, power or authority is outside of the British Empire. For the above reason the Settlor excludes from the management of, or benefits in the Foundation intended to be created by this Indenture, all who are not Christians of the White Race, all who are not of British Nationality or of British Parentage, and all who owe allegiance to any Foreign Government, Prince, Pope or Potentate, or who recognize any such authority, temporal or spiritual.*

Trust Indenture of 1st Nov. 1920

AND WHEREAS by Indenture of Trust dated the First day of November, 1920, and made between the parties hereto, but subject to the trusts, terms and conditions and provisoes therein contained, the Settlor made provision for Scholarships for selected students in certain Schools, Colleges and Universities in the Dominion of Canada from a fund set aside by him and known as 'The Leonard Foundation,' reserving however to himself powers of revocation in whole or in part of the trusts therein declared of and concerning the trust estate therein referred to or any part thereof or to declare new or other trusts of and concerning said trust estate with similar powers of revocation and declaring new and other trusts as in said Indenture of Trust more particularly defined and referred to:

Supplementing Trust of 1st Nov. 1920

AND WHEREAS the Settlor under and by virtue of all powers and authorities him thereby enabling has decided to enter into this Indenture for the purpose of supplementing and to a considerable extent taking the place of the said Indenture of Trust of the First day of November, 1920, for the objects and purposes hereinafter contained and referred to:

Association of Kate Leonard in management

AND WHEREAS the Settlor has received valuable advice and assistance from his Wife, Kate Leonard, in the creation and administration of the trust in connection with the said Leonard Foundation, and desires that her name should be associated with his in the administration of the said Trust:

NOW THEREFORE THIS INDENTURE WITNESSETH that in pursuance of all powers and authorities him thereby enabling, the Settlor hereby revokes the trusts and powers set out in said Indenture of Trust of the First day of November, 1920, in so far as same are inconsistent with the provisions of this Indenture, and doth hereby declare as follows: -

New Trusts; Leonard Foundation and Scholarships

1. THE trusts hereby declared and the trust property hereby transferred, assigned and set over and all other and additional property included in the trust estate, as hereinafter defined, shall be known as 'THE LEONARD FOUNDATION,' and the Scholarships provided pursuant to the provisions of this Indenture shall be known as 'THE LEONARD SCHOLARSHIPS.'

Educational Institutions entitled to benefit

2. THE Schools, Colleges and Universities in which such Scholarships may be granted and enjoyed, are such one or more of Schools and Colleges in Canada and such one or more of Universities in Canada and Great Britain as the General Committee hereinafter described may from time to time in its absolute discretion select, *but subject always to the requirements, terms and conditions concerning same as hereinbefore and hereinafter referred to and set out, and to the further conditions that any School, College or University so selected shall be free from the domination or control of adherents of the class or classes of persons hereinbefore referred to, whom the Settlor intends shall be excluded from the management of or benefits in the said Foundation:*

Approved Educational Institutions; Schedule 'A'

FOR the guidance merely of the said Committee in making such selection, and in order that the Settlor's intention may be clearly comprehended, the Schools, Colleges and Universities particularly designated in Schedule 'A' hereto annexed and which Schedule is to be considered as part of this Indenture and to be read therewith, are of the respective types which enjoy the Settlor's confidence and approval, and subject always to the discretionary powers of the Committee same are in the Settlor's opinion eligible for selection in which Scholarships hereunder may be enjoyed.

Definition of word 'School'

PROVIDED further and as an addition to the class or type of Schools above designated or in the Schedule 'A' hereto attached, the term 'School' may for the purposes of Scholarships hereunder, include *Public* Schools and *Public* Collegiate Institutes and High Schools in Canada of the class or type commonly known as such in the Province of Ontario *as distinguished from Public Schools and Collegiate Institutes and High Schools (if any) under the control and domination of the class or classes of persons hereinbefore referred to as intended to be excluded from the management of or benefits in said Foundation, and shall* also include a Protestant Separate School, Protestant Collegiate Institute or Protestant High School in the Province of Quebec.

Physical and Military training

PROVIDED further that in the selection of Schools, Colleges and Universities, as herein mentioned, preference must always be given by the Committee to the School, College or University, which, *being otherwise in the opinion of the Committee eligible,* prescribes physical training for female students and physical and military or naval training for male students.

General Committee; 25 members; Schedule 'B'; Power of Settlor to make changes in personnel

THE administration and management of the said Foundation is hereby vested in a permanent Committee to be known as the General Committee, consisting of twenty-five members, men and women *possessed of the qualifications hereinbefore in recital set out.* The names of the first members of the General Committee appear in Schedule 'B' hereto annexed, and which Schedule 'B' shall be considered as a part of this Indenture and be read therewith, reserving however to the Settlor pending the calling of the first meeting of the said General Committee the power to make such changes, if any, as he may desire in the personnel of said Committee, and in case a change or changes therein be made the person or persons whose name or names may be substituted shall be a member of said General Committee as effectually as if his or her name had originally appeared herein.

Chairman of Committee; Appointment of Substitute

THE General Manager or Assistant General Manager, or a Director, for the time being of the said The Toronto General Trusts Corporation, *if possessing the qualifications herein required of a person selected or appointed to assist in the management of the said Foundation,* shall at all times be a member and also the Chairman of the said General Committee and of the Committee on Scholarships hereinafter referred to. The said General Manager, Assistant General Manager or Director, as the case may be, in case of his inability to attend any meeting of the General Committee or Committee on Scholarships may appoint a Director of The Toronto General Trusts Corporation *possessing the said requisite qualifications,* to act in his place and stead, and the Director so appointed shall be considered as a member of the General Committee or Committee on Scholarships during the period of his appointment, and be possessed of the right of voting, including a casting vote, and all of the rights and powers possessed by the person whom he is appointed to represent.

The Settlor, Kate Leonard, and A.L. Bishop Members of Committee

THE Settlor, Kate Leonard the Wife of the Settlor, to whom he is greatly indebted for valuable suggestions, assistance and encouragement in the inception and the successful administration of this Foundation Trust to date, and Arthur Leonard Bishop, a nephew of the Settlor residing at the date hereof at the premises known as 75 Yate Street in the City of St. Catharines, shall, during their respective lives or until they respectively resign or become incapable of acting, be members of the General Committee.

Power of Settlor to appoint successors

THE Settlor reserves the right and shall have the power during his lifetime of appointing by deed his own successor as a member of the General Committee, and he shall also, if either the said Kate Leonard or Arthur Leonard Bishop shall cease to be a member of the General Committee in his (the Settlor's) lifetime, have the power to appoint by deed a successor of the said Kate Leonard and Arthur Leonard Bishop on said Committee.

Filling of Vacancies in General Committee; Settlor's Power to Create Vacancies

SUBJECT to the special powers hereinbefore reserved to the Settlor, or in default of the exercise of such special powers, or in so far as such special powers shall not extend or be capable of taking effect, and otherwise generally, except in the case of the General Manager or the Assistant General Manager or Director of The Toronto General Trusts Corporation for the time being as aforesaid, all vacancies in the membership of the General Committee from whatsoever cause arising, and incapacity or inability to serve as a member of the General Committee shall constitute a vacancy within the meaning of this paragraph, subject as hereinafter provided, shall be filled as they from time to time occur, by a majority of the remaining members of the General Committee, who shall appoint such person or persons as the case may be, *possessing the requisite qualifications as aforesaid.* Provided however and notwithstanding anything in this Indenture contained, the Settlor during his lifetime reserves the right to himself, if he so desires, to create from time to time a vacancy or vacancies in the personnel of said General Committee, and to fill any vacancy or vacancies which may be created in the membership of said General Committee by reason of any cause whatsoever. Pending the filling of a vacancy or vacancies as aforesaid, the members for the time being of the said General Committee or a majority of them may exercise all the powers and perform all the duties conferred upon the General Committee by this Indenture, notwithstanding any vacancy or vacancies which may have occurred therein.

Application to Court to Fill Vacancy

IF a vacancy in the General Committee is not filled for two years after it occurs, pursuant to the above provisions, the Trustee may apply to any Judge of the Supreme Court of Ontario, *possessed of the qualifications herein required of a member of the said General Committee,* to appoint some proper person to fill such vacancy, and the person so appointed shall thereupon be a member of the General Committee.

Decision of majority

THE decision of a majority of the duly authorized members present at any meeting of the General Committee shall in all matters over which it has control, be final and conclusive.

Services gratuitous; Payment of expenses

THE members of the General Committee shall give their services as such gratuitously, but shall be entitled to be paid from out of the net annual income derived from the Trust Estate their actual travelling and hotel expenses, if any, in connection with their attendance at meetings of the General Committee.

Casting vote

THE Chairman at all meetings of the General Committee shall be entitled to an additional vote by way of casting vote in the event of an equality of votes upon questions brought before the said General Committee for discussion or determination.

Minutes of Meetings; Secretary; Minutes prima facie evidence

THE minutes of all meetings of the General Committee shall be taken by a member of the staff of the said Trustee, hereinafter referred to as the secretary, and upon same being read and confirmed at the same or any subsequent meeting of the General Committee they shall be signed by the Chairman and Secretary, and any minutes recorded in the book to be kept for that purpose and noted as having been read and confirmed and signed, as aforesaid, shall be received as prima facie evidence of the acts done, decisions taken and of the statements therein contained.

Duties of Secretary

THE Secretary shall act under the direction of the Chairman of the General Committee in the calling of all meetings of the General Committee and in the performance of his duties as Secretary of the said General Committee. The Secretary shall also serve without personal remuneration.

Care of books, papers &c.

THE Trustee shall provide and shall have the custody and care of the minute book and of all other books, papers and vouchers concerning the trusts hereby created, which shall always be open for the inspection of any member of the General Committee.

Meetings of General Committee

ALL meetings of the General Committee (and of the Committee on Scholarships hereinafter referred to), shall be held at the office of the Trustee in the City of Toronto in the Province of Ontario, and shall in connection with the meetings of the General Committee be called by the Trustee, and in connection with the meetings of the Committee on Scholarships be called by the Secretary of such Committee, by a letter addressed to each member of the Committee in question at his last address furnished to the Trustee, postage prepaid, deposited in one of His Majesty's Post Offices at Toronto. The failure of a member of the General Committee (or of the Committee on scholarships, as the case may be), to receive such a notice shall not invalidate the proceedings taken at the meeting if a quorum of the members be present thereat.

First and subsequent meetings of General Committee

THE first meeting of the General Committee shall be held on the Fourth Friday of the month of May, 1924, and subsequent meetings shall be held at the times or dates fixed or to be fixed, subject to change, by the General Committee.

Special meetings; Quorum of General Committee

A special meeting or meetings of the General Committee shall be called by the Trustee in any year upon the requisition in writing or a majority of the members for the time being of the General Committee. At any meeting of the General Committee seven members thereof shall constitute a quorum.

Powers of General Committee

THE General Committee shall have the following powers: –

(a) *All* powers hereinbefore or hereinafter conferred upon it by this Indenture.

To make Rules and Regulations; Amend &c.

(b) *Additional* power to make such further or other rules regulations or resolutions for the better despatch of business and the administration of the Foundation hereby created as are not contrary to the provisions of this Indenture, with power to alter, modify, amend, vary or repeal the same at pleasure and such rules, regulations or resolutions while in force shall have the same force and effect as though embodied in this Indenture and shall be construed therewith as an integral part thereof.

Selection of Students

(c) *Power* to select students or pupils *of the classes or types hereinbefore and hereinafter described* as recipients of the said Scholarships or for the enjoyment of same, as the Committee in its discretion may decide.

Power over Students; Cancel selections

(d) *Power* to deprive any student or pupil selected as the recipient of a Scholarship under the provisions of this indenture of the benefit herein intended to be provided and to cancel his or her selection at any time, for any cause which the General Committee may in its absolute discretion decide upon.

Restoration of Student

(e) *To* restore a student or pupil to the benefits of which he or she may have been deprived pursuant to the provisions of the preceding clause if the General Committee in its discretion so decide.

Investigation of complaints

(f) *To* investigate all complaints made against a student or pupil selected or proposed as the recipient of a Scholarship under the provisions of this indenture, with liberty to act upon the report of the proper authorities of the school, College or University in which the said student or pupil may be or may have been in attendance, or on such other evidence as the General Committee think sufficient.

Special Committees; Personnel; Settlor's views on Special Committee; Expenses

(g) *To* appoint, in addition to the Committee on Scholarships, which is hereinafter provided for, such Special Committee or Committees as the General Committee may from time to time deem advisable and necessary in connection with the administration of the said Foundation, to regulate procedure for the calling and conduct of the meetings of such Special Committee or Committees, and to assign particular duties to such Special Committee or Committees, and to discharge same when and as the General Committee may see fit, but nevertheless the decision and work of any such Special Committee shall be subject to the approval of the General Committee. The personnel of any such Special Committee need not necessarily in whole or in part consist of members of the General Committee, as in the Settlor's opinion the performance of the particular duties assigned to any such Special Committee and in particular the duty of collecting facts and data in connection with Scholarships in localities outside the Province of Ontario may be safely entrusted to a small Special Committee of persons resident in the particular locality or

Province of Canada, where the particular duties are to be performed, thereby curtailing the expense which would otherwise make serious encroachments on the income of the Trust Estate, the actual travelling and hotel expenses of the members of a Special Committee while engaged in the duties assigned to them shall be paid from and out of the net annual income of the trust estate.

Approve of standard &c. of Schools; Withdraw benefits

(h) *To* consider from time to time the discipline and the ethical, physical and educational standard maintained by each School, College or University. To approve or disapprove of such standard in its absolute discretion. To withdraw either for a limited time or permanently the benefits of the Foundation hereby created from the students or pupils of any such School, College or University whose standard fails to meet with the approval of the General Committee, and from such School, College or University, and to deprive the students or pupils of such School, College or University as well as such School, College or University, of and from further participation in the benefits hereunder and at pleasure to restore the benefits so withdrawn or taken away.

Additional powers

(i) SUCH additional, further and other powers which the Settlor may from time to time during his lifetime by deed under his hand and seal confer on the General Committee.

Committee on Scholarships; Chairman; Hon. Secretary and duties

THE General Committee shall from among themselves select a sub-committee of five persons, other than the Chairman of the General Committee and other than the Settlor and his said Wife, in case they or either of them exercise the right hereafter reserved to them or either of them to become a member thereof, to be designated and known as the Committee on Scholarships. The Chairman for the time being of the General Committee shall always be a member of such Committee on Scholarships, and shall also be the Chairman thereof; and for the efficient operation of said subcommittee an Honorary Secretary thereof shall be appointed by the General Committee with power to define from time to time such Honorary Secretary's duties, powers and authorities. The selection of said Honorary Secretary need not necessarily be from among the members of the General Committee, and he may when so selected, if the General Committee so decide, be a member of such sub-committee.

Quorum

A majority of the members for the time being of the Committee on Scholarships shall constitute a quorum.

Minutes of proceedings of Committee on Scholarships; General Committee may adopt or reject

THE Committee on Scholarships shall meet from time to time as required for the transaction of business and at any time at the call of the Chairman. The minutes of proceedings at the meetings of the Committee on Scholarships shall be kept by the Secretary of the General Committee in a book to be provided by the Trustee for that purpose and of which the Trustee shall have the custody. The said minutes shall be open for the inspection of any member of the General Committee, and they shall be signed by the Chairman and Secretary when read and confirmed. The minutes shall be read at the next annual or special meeting of the General Committee, which may adopt, vary or reject the same in whole or in part, and such minutes shall if adopted in whole or in part and to the extent to which they are adopted by the General Committee become minutes of the General Committee and shall be signed and countersigned as such, and when so signed and countersigned with such notations as may be proper in the circumstances they shall be of the same effect as minutes of the General Committee similarly authenticated.

Right of Settlor and Kate Leonard to membership on Committee on Scholarships

THE Settlor hereby reserves the right to each of them the Settlor and the said Kate Leonard to be a member of the Committee on Scholarships if he or she so desires.

Selected annually

SUBJECT to the provisions aforesaid the members of the Committee on Scholarships shall be selected annually and the members shall be eligible for re-election.

Filling vacancies

SUBJECT to the provisions aforesaid the members of the General Committee shall fill any vacancy which may occur in the Committee on Scholarships whether by reason of death, incapacity or inability to serve or from whatsoever cause arising, by appointing thereto any member of the General Committee or the Honorary Secretary for the time being and any person so appointed shall hold office until the next annual meeting of the General Committee.

Instructions to Hon. Secretary

THE Committee on Scholarships when the General Committee is not in session shall give all necessary and requisite instructions and directions to its Honorary Secretary for obtaining and furnishing of information and for the collection of facts and data in connection with the said Scholarships and applications therefor, and the Honorary Secretary shall give prompt attention to the carrying out and observance of all such directions and instructions.

Further duties Committee on Scholarships

THE Committee on Scholarships shall also take into consideration all suggestions, recommendations and nominations for scholarships, the respective qualifications of all students or pupils nominated and all other questions and matters which could properly come before the General Committee, and through its Honorary Secretary report its findings to the General committee at their annual general meeting or at any special meeting of the General Committee which may be called.

Final decision with General Committee

THE General Committee may accept or reject any report or recommendation of the Committee on Scholarships or of any Special Committee herein provided for, in whole or in part and the final decision on all matters included in or covered by such reports and recommendations shall be with the General Committee.

Object in creating a Committee on Scholarships; Honorarium &c. for Hon Secretary; Expenses of members

THE principal object in providing for a Committee on Scholarships and of its Honorary

Secretary is for the consideration and collection of all facts and data in any way bearing on the said scholarships not entrusted to a Special Committee and the placing of same in proper order before the General Committee and otherwise to expedite and simplify the work of the General Committee. The General Committee is hereby fully empowered to fix an honorarium if it shall deem it advisable, for the Honorary Secretary of the said Committee on Scholarships, in connection with the performance of his duties, as well as the reasonable travelling and hotel expenses of the said Honorary Secretary and of the members of the Committee on Scholarships, and such honorarium shall be paid by the Trustee from and out of the income of the Trust Estate.

Other powers

THE Committee on Scholarships shall have all of the powers and perform all of the duties hereinbefore or hereinafter conferred upon or assigned to it, as well as such further and other powers and duties which the General Committee may from time to time confer and assign to it.

THE classes and descriptions of students of either sex from among which selection for scholarships under the provisions of this indenture is to be made, are as follows: -

Classes and description of Students

SUBJECT to the provisions and qualifications hereinbefore and hereinafter contained, a student or pupil to be eligible for a Scholarship shall be a *British Subject of the White Race and of the Christian Religion in its Protestant form, as hereinbefore in recital more particularly defined*, who, without financial assistance, would be unable to pursue a course of study in any of the Schools, Colleges or Universities hereinbefore mentioned. Preference in the selection of students or pupils for Scholarships shall be given to the sons and daughters respectively of the following classes or descriptions of persons *who are not of the classes or types of persons whom the Settlor intends to exclude from the management or benefit of the said Foundation as in the preamble or recital more particularly referred to*, but regardless of the order of priority in which they are designated herein, namely:

(a) Clergymen,

(b) School Teachers,

(c) Officers, non-commissioned Officers and Men, whether active or retired, who have served in His Majesty's Military, Air or Naval Forces.

(d) Graduates of the Royal Military College of Canada,

(e) Members of the Engineering Institute of Canada,

(f) Members of the Mining & Metallurgical Institute of Canada.

Maximum expenditure for female students

PROVIDE *further that in the selection, if any, of female students or pupils in any year under the provisions of this Indenture, the amount of income to be expended on such female students or pupils from and out of the moneys available for Scholarships under the terms hereof, shall not exceed one-fourth of the total moneys available for Scholarships for male and female students and pupils for such year.*

Discretion of General Committee as to Scholarships &c.; Living and others expenses of Students; Annual Scholarship only; Scholarships to whom payable

SUBJECT always to the provisions of this Indenture, the nomination and selection from time to time of all students and pupils as recipients of Scholarships as hereunder, the selection of the several Schools, Colleges and Universities to which the students shall be allotted and in which they shall pursue their course or courses of study, or the abstaining from making any such selection or selections, and the terms, conditions and regulations governing such students or pupils while in attendance at or associated with such Schools, Colleges and Universities, or any of them; and the amount and terms and time of payment of each Scholarship awarded under this indenture shall be entirely in the discretion of the said General Committee, but the General Committee in fixing the amount of any Scholarship hereunder may take into consideration the living and other expenses of the student or pupil while in attendance and at such School, College or University. Each Scholarship, subject to the powers of revocation herein contained, shall be an Annual Scholarship only, though it may be renewed from year to year by the General Committee, and all payments except as hereinafter provided shall be made to the School, College or University to be disbursed by it for the benefit of the student or pupil so selected. Provided however that in case of a student or pupil selected to attend a *Public* School, Collegiate Institute or High School, as hereinbefore referred to, the amount of the Scholarship fixed by the General Committee for the benefit of such student or pupil shall be paid to the parent or guardian of such student or pupil, or to the student or pupil direct, as the General Committee shall in its discretion decide.

No vested rights

THE Settlor hereby declares and desires it to be distinctly understood that no student or pupil of any School, College or University, however designated or selected under the provisions of this indenture, shall have any vested right in the trust estate or in the income or any part of the income thereof or in the Foundation or Scholarships herein respectively created or provided, so as to be entitled to be absolutely benefitted thereout, as the acts and discretions of the General Committee shall be final and binding upon everyone concerned.

Physical mental and moral requisites; Athletic, Physical, Military, Naval Requisites; Renewal of Scholarships; Engage in suitable occupation during vacation

IN selecting the recipients for the said Scholarships the physical as well as the mental and moral qualities of the student or pupil shall be an important prerequisite, as during his or her attendance at the School, College or University so selected, he or she, unless excused therefrom by the General Committee, will be expected to take part in the athletic and physical exercises, and in addition thereto the military and naval training, if any, which are practised or required to be practised by the students, male and female respectively, of such School, College or University, and if possible to become proficient in one or more of such exercises and proficiency in such exercises shall be a factor (not necessarily a governing factor) in enabling the General Committee to decide whether a Scholarship for a student or pupil shall after the first year be renewed for a subsequent year or years, and as an additional requirement a student or pupil selected as a recipient of a Scholarship under this Indenture shall, (unless for reasons satisfactory to the General Committee the recipient shall be relieved or excused), produce satisfactory evidence that he or she has during his or her summer vacation engaged in some suitable occupation (preferably one involving physical work), at such salary or wage as she or he may be able to procure, and such salary or wage, or, at all events, some portion thereof, should be used to supplement the Scholarship awarded hereunder, in defraying the expenses of the education, maintenance and clothing of such student or pupil.

Formation of Students' Association or Clubs; Purposes of

IT is the Settlor's desire and he wishes the fact to be made known by the General Committee, that the students or pupils who have enjoyed the benefits of a scholarship under the Foundation hereby created as well as under prior Foundations created by the Settlor will form a Club or Association for the purpose of -

(a) Unofficially and indirectly assisting by some means, the operation of the said Foundation and thus aid in its continued success and usefulness, and
(b) Encouraging each other when occasion arises and circumstances will permit, to personally afford financial assistance to pupils and students *of similar classes as in recital hereinbefore described* to obtain the blessings and benefits of an education.

Completion of students' education

FOR the guidance of the said General Committee in arriving at the number of students or pupils, to be selected in any year as recipients of scholarships hereunder, the Settlor declares that in such connection his intention is, that the education of an especially deserving student or pupil, should he or she continue to receive the approval of the General Committee, should be completed through the aid of the Settlor's bounty rather than that such student or pupil should be discharged before his or her education is completed in order to render the scholarship which he or she enjoys available for bestowal upon a new student or pupil in any of the said Schools, Colleges or Universities.

Forwarding Applications

APPLICATIONS for the benefit of a Scholarship must be made through a member of the General Committee, and delivered or forwarded by post to the Honorary Secretary for the time being of the Committee on Scholarships for attention, and until received by the said Honorary Secretary same shall not be deemed to be in the possession of the General Committee.

Hon. Secretaries Duties, re Applications

THE Honorary Secretary for the time being of the Committee on Scholarships shall on or before the first day of April in each year notify each of the then members of the General Committee of the necessity of furnishing the said Honorary Secretary with the names and addresses of his or her nominations of a student or students for the benefit of a scholarship or scholarships hereunder, accompanied with the authorized or official application therefor and with all requisite and necessary particulars respecting such nomination or nominations, on or before the tenth day of May of such year, accompanying such notification by the Honorary Secretary shall be forwarded official application forms as aforesaid.

Notices by Trustees

ALL notices required to be given by the Trustee to a member of the said General Committee or by the Honorary Secretary as aforesaid to a member of the Committee on Scholarships, shall be considered as sufficiently given by mailing same in His Majesty's Post Office, Toronto, addressed to the member of the said respective General Committee or Committee on Scholarships as aforesaid, at his or her last Post Office address furnished to the Trustee or to the said Honorary secretary, as the case may be.

Trust Estate Schedule 'C', $493,062.56

AND WHEREAS the Settlor is the absolute owner and possessor of certain assets or securities of the total par value of (four hundred and ninety-three thousand and sixty-two and fifty-six one-hundredths dollars ($493,062.56), which are particularly described and referred to in the Schedule hereto annexed marked '(C),' and which at the date hereof form all of the trust estate of the said Indenture of First November 1920, and of this Indenture supplementing and to a great extent taking the place of same.

Definition of 'Trust Estate'

AND WHEREAS the words 'Trust Estate' hereinafter used shall be read and construed to include the assets and securities set out and described in the said Schedule 'C' hereto annexed and which are hereby assigned and transferred to the Trustee or intended so to be, and also such additional property, securities or moneys, whether capital or income, as may be received by the Trustee from time to time as part of the Trust Estate, under or pursuant to Indentures of Trust entered into between the parties hereto, whether prior to or subsequent to the date of this indenture, and also such additional property, securities or moneys (if any) as the Settlor may hereafter during his lifetime assign, transfer, make over or pay to the Trustee or which he may bequeath to the Trustee by his last Will and Testament to supplement the Trust Estate, and also any additional property, securities or moneys which the Settlor may assign, transfer, make over or pay to the Trustee or which he may bequeath to the Trustee by his last Will and Testament to supplement the Trust Estate, and also any additional property, securities or moneys which the Settlor may assign, transfer, make over or pay to the Trustee to provide for additional objects, trusts and benefits as the Settlor may in his discretion decide, and which right to supplement from time to time is hereby reserved to the Settlor, and also all property, securities or moneys which in the hands of the Trustee may from time to time represent the securities set out in said Schedule 'C' or supplemental or additional or other property, securities or moneys as aforesaid, or the proceeds of the sale or sales or conversion, exchange or liquidation of the same or any part thereof, and generally all property, securities or money held from time to time under the trusts in this Indenture.

Operative Clause, Assign &c.

NOW THEREFORE THIS INDENTURE FURTHER WITNESSETH that for the consideration aforesaid the Settlor doth hereby assign, transfer and set over unto the Trustee, its successors and assigns, all of the property, assets, securities and moneys particularly mentioned and described in the Schedule hereto annexed and marked 'C' and which Schedule shall be considered as a part of this indenture and read therewith, and which said property, assets, securities and moneys shall in accordance with the aforesaid recital form part of the assets of the Trust Estate, to hold upon the trusts, terms and conditions and for the objects and purposes herein set out of and concerning the same, namely:

Duty of Trustees re Trust Estate; Sale and conversion; Acting on direction of Settlor

1. THE said property, assets, securities and money and such further or additional or substituted property, assets, securities and moneys which may from time to time form part of the Trust Estate shall be retained by the Trustee until their maturity, if any, unless in the meantime the Trustee with the approval of the Settlor during his lifetime or until the Trustee in its discretion after the death of the Settlor shall deem it to be in the interests of the Trust Estate to sell and convert the same or any part thereof and in the event of the Trustee deciding after the death of the Settlor to convert the same or any part thereof before their maturity, if any, such conversion shall be made at such time or times, in such manner, for such price or prices and upon such terms as the Trustee shall in its discretion deem to be in the best interests of the Trust Estate. During the lifetime of the Settlor his consent to or direction for any conversion, sale or exchange of such property, assets or securities or any part thereof shall be sufficient justification to the Trustee for the making of any such conversion, exchange or sale, and its action shall not be open to question.

Non-conversion, Exoneration of Trustees

2. THE Trustee shall not be liable or responsible for loss, damage or depreciation to the Trust Estate or any part thereof arising from the retention of the said property, assets or securities so set out in the said annexed Schedule 'C' or of any further or other or additional or substitutional property, assets or securities which shall come into the hands of the Trustee as part of the Trust Estate as investments of the Trust Estate when it is by this instrument empowered to retain the same, notwithstanding that such property assets or securities are not of the kind in which Trustees are by law permitted to invest trust funds.

Investment of moneys

3. THE proceeds of the conversion of any such property, assets or securities and the capital money forming part of the Trust Estate, no matter how derived, shall during the lifetime of the Settlor be invested and kept invested by the Trustee in such securities, property or assets as the Settlor and the Trustee may approve of and the Trustee shall be justified in investing the capital moneys of the Trust Estate in any securities, property or assets as may be approved by the Settlor during his lifetime, although such securities, property or assets may not be of the class in which Trustees are or may be permitted by the laws of the Province of Ontario to invest trust funds, and the obtaining of the approval of the Settlor to the investment in such securities, property or assets shall free the trustee from all liability and responsibility for loss, damage or depreciation arising from the investment in securities, property or assets other than those in which Trustees are or may hereafter be authorized by the laws of the Province of Ontario to invest trust funds, but from and after the death of the Settlor the Trustee shall invest all capital moneys of the trust estate which may from time to time be awaiting investment in such securities as Trustees are by the laws of the Province of Ontario now or hereafter in force permitted to invest trust funds.

Succession Duty

4. IF after the death of the Settlor it shall be found that the Trust Estate covered by this Indenture is liable or assessable for succession duty under the provisions of the Succession Duty Act of the Province of Ontario, and which liability is not hereby admitted, same shall be chargeable against and payable out of the capital of the said Trust Estate.

Trustees' compensation &c. charge on income; Expenses of Committees charge on income

5. AS a first charge upon the net annual income derived from the Trust Estate to pay to the Trustee compensation or remuneration for its care, pains and trouble in connection with the trusts herein declared and the administration thereof, and all disbursements, costs, charges and expense incurred in connection therewith as herein provided for, as well as expenses of General Sub-Committee and Special Committee, honorarium and expenses, if any, of the Honorary Secretary of the Committee on Scholarships, as hereinbefore referred to, also including taxes or assessments, if any, whether Dominion, Provincial or Municipal, for which such net annual income may be assessable or chargeable.

Trusts, terms &c. governing Trust Estate

6. SUBJECT to the above preferential charges, the following trusts, terms, powers, privileges, directions, conditions and provisions shall apply to and govern the said Trust Testate and the net annual income thereof shall be held and administered by the Trustee in manner following and as in subsequent paragraphs hereof directed, that is to say: -

Notification to General Committee on or before 1st April

7. THE Trustee shall on or before the first day of April in each year notify in writing each member of the General Committee of the approximate amount of net annual income which for the ensuing scholastic year will be available for scholarships as hereinbefore and hereinafter referred to.

Disbursement of net annual income; Payment of scholarships for students in Public Schools, Collegiates or High Schools

8. THE Trustee shall disburse the whole or such part of the net annual income derived from the Trust Estate among the persons, schools, Colleges and Universities in such amounts, at such times, upon such terms and in such manner as the General Committee shall in its discretion consistent with the intention of the Settlor as hereinbefore set out, decide, and the money payable in respect of such Scholarships shall, except as hereinafter provided, be paid to the respective Schools, Colleges or Universities in which the respective student or students, pupil or pupils, are in attendance to be by it disbursed as hereinbefore provided, and the receipt of the proper authority of any of the Schools, Colleges or Universities for payments made to such School, College or University out of the said income shall be a sufficient discharge to the Trustee, who shall not be called upon to see to the application thereof. Provided however that in the event of the selection of a pupil or student for attendance at a *Public* School, *Public* Collegiate or *Public* High School, as hereinbefore provided for, the scholarship awarded towards providing for the education of such pupil or student therein may be paid direct to the student or pupil, or to his or her parent or guardian, whose receipt therefor shall be a sufficient discharge to the Trustee, and who is not called upon to see to the application thereof. In case the disbursements of income of the trust estate by the Trustee in any year in accordance with the directions of the General Committee shall not exhaust all of the said net annual income, then in such event, whenever the same shall happen, the surplus income of any year so remaining in the Trustee's possession shall be available for distribution in any subsequent year or years, in accordance with the directions of the General Committee.

Application to Court for opinion &c.; Intervention of Public Trustee not desirable

9. THE Trustee is hereby empowered at the expense of the trust estate to apply to a Judge of the Supreme Court of Ontario *possessing the qualifications required of a member of the General Committee as hereinbefore in recital set out,* for the opinion, advice and direction of the Court in connection with the construction of this trust deed and in connection with all questions arising in the administration of the trusts herein declared, and on all such applications notice thereof shall be served on the said Official Guardian for the time being of the Supreme Court of Ontario, who shall fully represent all interests, other than that of the Trustee, who may or might by any possibility be in any way affected or concerned in such application, and in the opinion, advice and direction of the Court so applied for, and in particular but without affecting the generality of above, the Settlor hereby declares that the intervention of the Public Trustee of the Province of Ontario in any matters connected with the trusts herein or of the foundation of the Scholarships herein referred to, is not by him considered as requisite or necessary and should be dispensed with.

Trustees' remuneration, disbursements &c.

10. THE Trustee shall be entitled to be paid such remuneration for its services in connection with the administration of the capital and revenue of the trust estate as has been agreed upon between it and the Settlor as set out in a letter received by the Settlor from the Trustee bearing even date herewith, and in addition the Trustee shall also be entitled to reimbursement out of the Trust Estate for all disbursements, costs, charges and expenses made and incurred in and about the administration of the trusts hereby created or intended so to be.

Auditing Trustees' Accounts; County Court Judge, York; Official Guardian

11. WITH reference to the passing and auditing from time to time of the Trustee's accounts in connection with its administration of the said capital and revenue of the trust estate and of the trusts thereof, such duty shall be performed by the Settlor during his lifetime, who for such purpose shall fully represent all interests herein save those of the Trustee and whose findings shall be final and binding upon all such interests and shall not be open to question, but from and after the death of the said Settlor such accounts from the date of the last passing and auditing thereof by the Settlor shall be passed and audited by one of the Judges for the time being of the County Court of the County of York, upon application from time to time of the Trustee, and upon such passing and auditing all persons interested therein other than the Trustee shall be sufficiently represented by the Official Guardian for the time being of the Supreme Court of Ontario, upon whom notice shall be served.

Directions of General Committee exoneration of Trustees

12. THE Trustee shall be absolutely exonerated and freed from liability or responsibility for any act, matter or thing which it may do or suffer or permit to be done at the direction of the General Committee acting within the scope of its powers as laid down in this Indenture.

Settlor's power to altar [sic], vary, &c.; Settlor's power to revoke or alter &c.; Objects as to application of income

13. THE Settlor may at any time during his lifetime, by deed or deeds under his hand, alter or vary any of the provisions herein set out for the administration of the trusts hereby

created and substitute other provisions therefor, or he may wholly or partially revoke or alter all of any of the objects or purposes for which the income of the trust estate is herein directed to be applied, or any of the objects or purposes for which the said income or any part thereof may be rendered applicable under the terms hereof, and may declare that in lieu thereof the said income or any part thereof shall be applicable and such income shall thereupon become applicable for such other objects or purposes, being an object or purpose conducive to the promotion or encouragement of education, as the Settlor may from time to time think proper.

Settlor's general power to revoke &c.; Assign &c. to Settlor

14. NOTWITHSTANDING anything herein contained, it shall be lawful for the said Settlor at any and all times and from time to time hereafter by deed or deeds under his hand and seal to revoke all or any of the trusts declared by the said Indenture of the First day of November 1920, and by these presents, of and concerning the trust estate or any part thereof, and the whole or any portion thereof to repossess and to re-enjoy freed and discharged from the terms of the trusts hereby created, or at the option of the Settlor to declare from time to time or at any time or times hereafter any new or other trust or trusts of and concerning the said trust estate or of any portion thereof, with similar powers of revoking all or any of the said trust or trusts, and in the event of the Settlor declaring any of such trust or trusts to be at an end and that he has no desire to declare any new or other trust to trusts of and concerning the trust estate or any portion thereof, the Trustee shall at the request of the Settlor and upon receiving from him such sum or sums of money to be fixed by the General Committee to pay the scholarship or scholarships of any student or students, pupils, which may at the date of such revocation and cancellation have been selected by the General Committee and who shall have not completed his or her then year's course of education, and the expenses and honorarium, if any, of any Committee, General Management or Special, as hereinbefore provided, which shall not have been previously liquidated, assign, transfer and make over to the said Settlor all of the said trust estate freed and discharged from the terms of this trust, subject always to the payment to the trustee of its remuneration in connection with the said trust estate and of its costs, charges and expenses incurred or for which it may be liable in connection with the same.

Marginal notes shall not affect the construction hereof.

Acceptance of Trust

THE Trustee hereby accepts the burden of the trusts hereby created upon the terms, provisoes and conditions hereinbefore set out.

IN WITNESS WHEREOF the Settlor has hereunto set his hand and seal and the Trustee has set its corporate seal, attested by its proper officers in that behalf.

SIGNED SEALED AND DELIVERED	)	
	)	
IN THE PRESENCE OF	)	R.W. Leonard (sgd.)
	)	
(signature of witnesses)	)	

SCHEDULE 'A'

THIS IS SCHEDULE 'A' referred to in the Trust Deed annexed hereto, dated the *28th* day of December, A.D. 1923, and made between Reuben Wells Leonard, Settlor, and The Toronto General Trusts Corporation, Trustee.

1. Ridley College — St. Catharines, Ontario
2. Upper Canada College — Toronto, Ontario
3. St. Andrews' College — Toronto, Ontario
4. Rothesay Collegiate School — Rothesay, New Brunswick
5. King's Collegiate School — Windsor, Nova Scotia
6. Public Schools, High Schools and Collegiate Institutes, as [described in this] Trust Deed
7. Havergal College — Toronto, Ontario
8. Edgehill School for Girls — Windsor, Nova Scotia
9. Nurses Training Schools in Canada (Non-Sectarian)
10. Ontario Agricultural College — Guelph, Ontario,
    Macdonald Institute — Guelph, Ontario,
11. Macdonald College — St. Anne's, Quebec
12. Church of England Deaconess & Missionary Training House — Toronto, Ontario
13. Wycliffe College — Toronto, Ontario
14. Emanuel College — Saskatoon, Saskatchewan
15. Anglican Theological College — Vancouver, British Columbia
16. Royal Military College of Canada, — Kingston, Ontario
17. Royal Naval College of Canada (when re-established)
18. Royal Air College of Canada (when established)
19. The University of Toronto — Toronto, Ontario
    McGill University — Montreal, Quebec
    Queen's University — Kingston, Ontario
    Western University — London, Ontario
    Dalhousie College and University — Halifax, Nova Scotia
    University of Manitoba — Winnipeg, Manitoba
    University of Saskatchewan — Saskatoon, Saskatchewan
    The University of Alberta — Edmonton, Alberta
    The University of British Columbia — Vancouver, British Columbia
20. Any University in Great Britain selected by the General Committee.

SCHEDULE 'B'

THIS IS SCHEDULE 'B' referred to in the Trust Deed annexed hereto, dated the 28th day of December, A.D. 1923, and made between Reuben Wells Leonard, Settlor, and The Toronto General Trusts Corporation, Trustee.

1. Toronto General Trusts Corporation Representative, — Toronto, Ontario
2. R.W. Leonard (Lieutenant-Colonel) — St. Catharines, Ontario
3. Mrs. R.W. Leonard — St. Catharines, Ontario
4. A.L. Bishop (Lieutenant-Colonel) — 50 Ontario Street, St. Catharines, Ontario
5. Rev. Canon H.J. Cody, — 603 Jarvis Street, Toronto, Ontario
6. Rev. Canon T.R. O'Meara, — Wycliffe College, Toronto, Ontario
7. Mr. H.C. Griffith, — Ridley College, St. Catharines, Ontario
8. Rev. Allen Daniel, — Rothesay Collegiate School, Rothesay, New Brunswick
9. Rev. W. Wallace Judd, — King's Collegiate School, Windsor, Nova Scotia
10. Dr. A.J. MacPhail, D.S.O. — Queen's University, Kingston, Ontario
11. Rev. W.H. Vance, — Anglican Theological College, Vancouver, British Columbia
12. Rev. W.T. Hallam, — Emanuel College, Saskatoon, Saskatchewan
13. Rev. R.B. McElheran — Winnipeg, Manitoba
14. Mr. T.A. Russel, — 162 Walmer Road, Toronto, Ontario
15. Mr. A.M. Overholt, — Principal, Collegiate Institute Brantford, Ontario
16. Mr. Fraser S. Keith, — 176 Mansfield Street, Montreal, Quebec
17. Rev. D. Bruce Macdonald — St. Andrews College, Toronto, Ontario
18. Mr. A.G. Colquhoun — Department of Education, Toronto, Ontario

19. Mr. C.V. Corliss — Mond Nickel Corporation, Coniston, Ontario
20. Mr. W.J. Drope — Lake Lodge School, Grimsby, Ontario
21. Dr. A.S. Mackenzie — Dalhousie University, Halifax, Nova Scotia
22. Dr. H.M. Tory — Council for Scientific & Industrial Research, Ottawa, Ontario
23. Dr. L. Norman Tucker — London, Ontario
24. Rev. R.J. Renison — 45 Charlton Avenue West, Hamilton, Ontario
25. General C.H. Mitchell — University of Toronto, Toronto, Ontario

Notes

Introduction

1 See Leonard Foundation Trust deed (1923) at 1, reproduced in the appendix.
2 See A. Greer, 'Canadian History: Ancient and Modern' (1996) 77 Canadian Historical Review 575.
3 The most comprehensive account of Leonard is in C.G.D. Roberts and A.R.Turnbull, eds., *A Standard Dictionary of Canadian Biography* (Toronto: Trans-Canada 1934–8), vol. 2 at 240–2. See also H. Charlesworth, ed., *A Cyclopaedia of Canadian Biography* (Toronto: Hunter-Rose 1919) at 268–9.
4 C. Berger, *The Sense of Power: Studies in the Ideas of Canadian Imperialism, 1867–1914* (Toronto: University of Toronto Press 1970).
5 See also M. Valverde, *The Age of Light, Soap, and Water: Moral Reform in English Canada, 1885–1925* (Toronto: McClelland and Stewart 1991) at 13.
6 See, for example, 'Bias and the Bequest,' *Globe and Mail*, 29 November 1982, 6 (editorial); L. Smith, 'A benefactor largely forgotten,' St Catharines *Standard*, 21 February 1983. See also 'A Sorry Anachronism,' Toronto *Star*, 12 August 1986 (editorial).
7 *Re Canada Trust & Ontario Human Rights Commission* (1990) 69 Dominion Law Reports (4th) 321 (Ontario Court of Appeal) at 355 (per Tarnopolsky J.A.).
8 Ibid.
9 J.W. St.G. Walker, *'Race,' Rights, and the Law in the Supreme Court of Canada: Historic Case Studies* (Toronto and Waterloo, Ont.: Osgoode Society and Wilfrid Laurier Press 1997). This approach is also adopted in C. Backhouse,

Colour-Coded: A Legal History of Racism in Canada, 1900–1950 (Toronto: Osgoode Society and University of Toronto Press 1999).
10 Supra, note 9, at 241–3.
11 Ibid. at 40. Walker's orientation is, in turn, influenced by the work of the American anthropologist Clifford Geertz. See further C. Geertz, *The Interpretation of Cultures* (New York: Basic Books 1973) and *Local Knowledge: Further Essays in Interpretive Anthropology* (New York: Basic Books 1983), both of which are referred to in Walker, 'Race,' Rights, and the Law.
12 See further J.B. White, 'Law as Rhetoric, Rhetoric as Law: The Arts of Cultural and Communal Life,' (1985) 52 University of Chicago Law Review 684. See also K.B. Nunn, 'Law as a Eurocentric Enterprise,' (1997) 15 Law and Inequality 323.
13 A helpful, though brief, contribution to the learning can be found in M. Bliss, *Northern Enterprise: Five Centuries of Canadian Business* (Toronto: McClelland and Stewart 1987) at 347–9.
14 See, for example, P. Axelrod, *Making a Middle Class: Student Life in English Canada during the Thirties* (Montreal: McGill-Queen's University Press 1990); P. Axelrod and J.G. Reid, eds., *Youth, University, and Canadian Society: Essays in the Social History of Higher Education* (Montreal: McGill-Queen's University Press 1989); A.B. McKillop, *Matters of Mind: The University in Ontario, 1791–1951* (Toronto: University of Toronto Press 1994).
15 See further D. Kennedy, 'Imperial History and Post-Colonial Theory' (1996) 24 Journal of Imperial and Commonwealth History 345.

1: Who Was Reuben Wells Leonard?

1 S.J. Duncan, *The Imperialist* (1904) (Toronto: McClelland and Stewart, ed., 1961) at 58.
2 He is said to have earned a living through trading with the Iroquois nations: C.M. Johnston, *Brant County: A History 1784–1945* (Toronto: Oxford University Press 1967) at 26.
3 Letter of reference, principal (signature indecipherable), Ottawa Normal School, 3 October 1877, St Catharines Public Library, Special Collections. Likewise, James Mills, headmaster at Brantford Collegiate Institute, described Leonard as a 'diligent, keen and successful student': letter of reference, 20 December 1877, St Catharines Public Library, Special Collections.
4 R.W. Leonard, 'The Scope of Engineering in Canada' (1910) 4 Applied Science: Transactions of the University of Toronto Engineering Society (new series) 1, at 4.

5 R.W. Leonard, 'Another Graduate's Views' (1894–5) 4 Canadian Magazine 431, at 432.
6 Ibid. at 432–3.
7 It is typically reported in various secondary sources that Reuben W. Leonard won the silver medal. However, the school records at Royal Military College indicate that he finished third, not second, in his class; W.J. Stewart (#85) won the gold medal, J.I. Lang (#79) the silver. Leonard was promoted within the RMC hierarchy from the rank of corporal to company sergeant-major in June 1882 but was demoted to sergeant in May 1883. The college records do not mention the reasons for the demotion: Personal Correspondence, Ross McKenzie, RMC Museum, 18 April 1997.
8 In his alumnus report, Leonard stated that he had also received an award known as the 'crossed-skids' in 1881 and 1882. This was probably for 'gun laying'; it is not described in the RMC regulations.
9 See further B. Beal and R.C. Macleod, *Prairie Fire: The 1885 North-West Rebellion* (Edmonton: Hurtig 1984).
10 M. Powell to R.W. Leonard, 30 April 1886, Special Collections, St Catharines Public Library.
11 There is little information available about Kate Leonard. Her paternal grandfather immigrated to Canada from the Scottish Highlands and her father was once editor of the Kingston *News*. Her maternal grandfather, James Lesslie, also from the Highlands, established a merchandise and trading business in Kingston and Dundas, Ontario. See further 'Mrs. R. Leonard Passes Away,' *Globe*, 13 September 1935.
12 See, for example, R.W. Leonard, 'The Spring Hill Collieries' (1888) 2 Transactions of the Society of Civil Engineering 404; R.W. Leonard, 'Masonry Pier Moved by Ice and Replaced' (1898) 12 Transactions of the Canadian Society of Civil Engineers 131; R.W. Leonard, 'Railway Fencing' (1903) 17 Transactions of the Canadian Society of Civil Engineers 329; R.W. Leonard, 'Some Experiments on Loss of Heat from Iron Pipes.'
13 R.W. Leonard, 'The Principal Railway Systems of Canada from a National Point of View,' Proceedings of the Royal Military College Club of Canada (1902) 144.
14 R.W. Leonard, 'The Railway and Shipping World,' Proceedings of the Royal Military College Club of Canada (1903) 175.
15 See 'Gig Infantry,' in Proceedings of the Royal Military College Club of Canada (1904) 145; 'Gig Infantry,' in Proceedings of the 25th Annual Meeting of the Royal Military College Club of Canada (1908) 403.
16 See generally D.R. Jenkins, 'The Corps of Guides, 1903–1914' (1996) 5(2) Canadian Military History 88.

17 Ibid. at 96.
18 See, for example, B.F. Townsley, *Mine-Finders* (Toronto: Saturday Night Press 1935) at 55–8; D.M. Le Bourdrais, *Metals and Men: The Story of Canadian Mining* (Toronto: McClelland and Stewart 1957) at 132–3.
19 R.W. Leonard's 1897 diary describes meetings on 5 and 12 February between Leonard and Professor Willet Miller of Queen's (and later the provincial geologist) during which mining prospects were discussed.
20 The court records are not available. Passing reference to this dispute is contained in *Coniagas Mines Ltd.* v. *Town of Cobalt* (1907) 20 Ontario Law Reports 622 (Court of Appeal) at 624–5. See also '"All Sunshine Makes a Desert" Said Cobalt Pioneer Miner,' *Northern Miner*, January 1931. Not all accounts of the Trethewey discovery make reference to the dispute as to title: see, for example, H.P. Davis, *The Davis Handbook of the Cobalt Silver District* (Canadian Mining Journal 1910) at 10ff.
21 G. Lonn, *The Mine Finders* (Toronto: Pitt Publishing 1966) at 33. Longwell staked another claim as agent for Leonard. This property was later sold and developed as the Buffalo Mine.
22 Commission of Conservation (Canada) Lands, *Fisheries and Game, Minerals* (Ottawa: Mortimer 1911) at 409–10.
23 See further S. Young and A. Young, *Silent Frank Cochrane: The North's First Great Politician* (Toronto: Macmillan 1973) at ch. 5, passim.
24 *In re Coniagas Mines Co. & The Town of Cobalt* (1907) 15 Ontario Law Reports 386 (Court of Appeal).
25 *Coniagas Mines Ltd.* v. *Town of Cobalt*, supra, note 20.
26 H.H. Lang, Open letter to the citizens of Cobalt, 27 December 1909, Scrapbook, Cobalt Museum, quoted in D. Baldwin, 'The Development of an Unplanned Community: Cobalt, 1903–1914' (1978) 18 Plan Canada 17, at 20.
27 'Cobalt has made 25 millionaires – steel directors to meet next friday,' Montreal *Star*, 14 April 1909, 12.
28 Leonard served on the Council of the Canadian Society of Civil Engineers in 1905, 1908, and 1909; he was vice-president in 1910 and president in 1919 (by which time it had become the Engineering Institute of Canada). He was also vice-president of the Canadian Mining Institute and the Ontario Mining Association, a member of the Council of the Institute of Mining and Metallurgy (Great Britain), and a member of the American Institute of Mining Engineers.
29 Among these papers are: R.W. Leonard, 'The Scope of Engineering in Canada' (1910) 4(1) Applied Science (new series) 1; R.W. Leonard, 'Nickel-Copper Steel' (1918) 32 Transactions of the Canadian Society of Civil Engineers 361; R.W. Leonard, 'Economic and Strategic Aspects of Enlargement of

the Welland Canal and of Construction of the Georgian Bay Ship Canal' (1916) 30 Transactions of the Canadian Society of Civil Engineers 197; R.W. Leonard, 'The Mining and Metallurgy of Cobalt Silver-Ores' (1919) 2 Engineering Journal 86.

30 See further J.E. Kendle, *The Round Table Movement and Imperial Union* (Toronto: University of Toronto Press 1975); J. Eayrs, 'The Round Table Movement in Canada, 1909–1920' (1957) 38 Canadian Historical Review 1; D. Lavin, *From Empire to International Commonwealth: A Biography of Lionel Curtis* (Oxford: Clarendon Press, 1995) at ch. 6, passim; C. Quigley, 'The Round Table Groups in Canada, 1908–38' (1962) 43 Canadian Historical Review 204.

31 See further Lavin, supra, note 30.

32 See further W. Nimocks, *Milner's Young Men: The 'Kindergarten' in Edwardian Imperial Affairs* (Durham: Duke University Press 1968).

33 Others on the executive were Frank Beer, Hugh Scully, secretary of the Canadian Manufacturers' Association, and H.V.F. Jones, assistant general manager of the Canadian Bank of Commerce. Also associated with the group were Loring Christie and a young historian at the University of Toronto, Edward Kylie.

34 Vincent Massey recalled: 'As an undergraduate [in Oxford] I fell under the influence of Lionel Curtis – influence is too weak a word, for he was the most persuasive and magnetic of men': V. Massey, *What's Past Is Prologue* (Toronto: Macmillan 1963) at 34. See also ibid. at 34–41, passim. 'I know of no man with so big a furnace in his belly. It is so fierce that the fumes overwhelm his brain at times. But it scorches all whom he encounters, and hounds them to greater thoughts and greater deeds': P. Kerr to R. Brand, 1 January 1910, quoted in Lavin, supra, note 30, at 111.

35 It was estimated that his annual income was about $1 million at this time.

36 See generally J.A. Eagle, *Sir Robert Borden and the Railway Problem in Canadian Politics, 1911–1920*, PhD Thesis, Department of History, University of Toronto, 1972.

37 See also R.C. Brown and R. Cook, *Canada: 1896–1921: A Nation Transformed* (Toronto: McClelland and Stewart 1974) at 194.

38 *Report of the National Transcontinental Railway Investigating Commission* (Ottawa: King's Printer 1914) at 5. They found that 'the Transcontinental Railway Commission, and Grand Trunk Pacific Railway, and those having charge of the construction of the railway did not consider it desirable or necessary to practice or encourage economy in the construction of this road': ibid. at 12.

39 *Le Canada*, 26 September 1913, quoted in J.C. Hopkins, ed., *Canadian Annual Review, 1913* (Toronto: Annual Review Publishing 1914) at 284.

40 Eagle, supra, note 36, at 120.
41 See further R.C. Brown, *Robert Laird Borden: A Biography* (Toronto: Macmillan 1975) vol. 1, at 251–2.
42 This dispute is recounted in depth in Eagle, supra, note 36, at 119ff.
43 In 1912 Leonard established an equestrian contest, known as the Guides Challenge Cup, for commissioned officers of the permanent and militia forces of Canada and of the Royal North-West Mounted Police. The conditions of the contest are set out in S.R. Elliot, *Scarlet to Green: A History of Intelligence in the Canadian Army* (Toronto: Canadian Intelligence and Security Association 1981) at 599.
44 These included: the gift of an organ to St Thomas' Church, the provision of a car for the use of the rector, the donation of uniforms to the Cadet Corps at the University of Toronto Schools, and most notably, a capital grant to help found a consumptive sanitorium in St Catharines.
45 'University Students' Residence' (n.d.), Queen's University Archives.
46 'Major Leonard's gift to Queen's,' Montreal *Gazette*, 17 January 1914, 16; 'Major Leonard's gift,' Montreal *Gazette*, 19 January 1914, 10.
47 'Queen's University and the Leonard Gift,' Kingston *Standard*, 25 April 1914, 4.
48 R.W. Leonard to D.M. Gordon, 18 March 1914, Queen's University Archives.
49 'Reorganization of Queen's University with important changes now possible,' Toronto *News*, 16 April 1914. The *News* was owned by Sir Joseph Flavelle and edited by Sir John Willison, both members of the Round Table.
50 R.W. Leonard to G.W. Chown, 22 December 1914, Queen's University Archives.
51 J. Cappon to D. Gordon, 11 January 1915, Queen's University Archives.
52 R.W. Leonard to F. Cochrane, 16 June 1914, Borden Papers, 20590.
53 R.W. Leonard to F. Cochrane, 26 June 1914, Borden Papers, 20591.
54 R.L. Borden to R.W. Leonard, 29 June 1914, Borden Papers, 20593.
55 Among his donations were: a grant of $7,500 to the British government for a biplane, $30,000 for the Duchess of Connaught Hospital in Clivedon, England, $5,500 to the Belgian Relief Fund, and $1,000 towards equipment for a hospital in France.
56 Elliot, supra, note 43, at 54. A detachment of the Corps of Guides was placed on active service to guard the British Columbia coast.
57 R.W. Leonard to Captain A. Coventry, Camp Borden, 1917, Department of National Defence Records, National Archives of Canada, referred to in D. Baldwin, 'A Study in Social Control: The Life of the Silver Miner in Northern Ontario' 2 (1977) Labour/La Travailleur 78, at 103.
58 'Says German case complete,' Toronto *Star*, 14 October 1914, 2. Born in Moravia, Reich was by this time a British subject.

59 J.S. Campbell to R.W. Leonard, 15 October 1914, Falconer Papers, box 34.
60 R.W. Leonard to R. Falconer, 16 October 1914, Falconer Papers, box 34.
61 R. Falconer to R.W. Leonard, 17 October 1914, Falconer Papers, box 34.
62 This incident is placed within the context of academic freedom in Canada during the Great War in M. Horn, *Academic Freedom in Canada: A History* (Toronto: University of Toronto Press 1999) ch. 3, passim.
63 L. Curtis, *The Problem of the Commonwealth* (Toronto: Macmillan 1916). The thesis of the book and the events surrounding its release are discussed in chapter 2.
64 R.W. Leonard to P. Kerr, 12 October 1916, Curtis Papers, Bodleian Library, Oxford University, sent in reply to P. Kerr to R.W. Leonard, 24 August 1916, ibid.
65 Leonard to Kerr, supra, note 64.
66 He added that 'we desire co-operation with Quebec': R.W. Leonard to G. Wrong, 8 December 1916 (enclosure), George Wrong Papers, Ms Coll. 36, Fisher Rare Book Room, University of Toronto. The papers to which the letter was sent were: the *Star*, the *Telegram*, the *Globe*, the *World*, the *News*, and the *Mail and Empire*.
67 'Formation of the Union Government,' in J.C. Hopkins, ed., *The Canadian Annual Review of Public Affairs, 1917* (Toronto: Canadian Annual Review Publishing 1918) at 560. See also 'The Liberals and the War: Sir Wilfrid Laurier's Policy,' in J.C. Hopkins, ed., *The Canadian Annual Review of Public Affairs, 1916* (Toronto: Canadian Annual Review Publishing, 1917) at 417.
68 Resolution of the Win-the-War Convention, 2 August 1917, quoted in 'Formation of the Union Government,' supra, note 67, at 568.
69 H. Borden, ed., *Robert Laird Borden: His Memoirs* (Toronto: Macmillan 1938), vol. 2, at 737ff.
70 R.W. Leonard to R.L. Borden, 13 October 1917, Borden Papers, 73516.
71 Flavelle Papers, MG30, A16, vol. 4, National Archives of Canada.
72 R.W. Leonard to R.L. Borden, 17 June 1915, Borden Papers, 12699.
73 The statement came to Leonard's attention via a report contained in the St Catharines *Standard*: 'General Hughes says Canada will soon have 157,000 men under arms,' St Catharines *Standard*, 16 June 1915, 1.
74 Supra, note 72. Prime Minister Borden conveyed this message to General Hughes: R.L. Borden to S. Hughes, 18 June 1915, Borden Papers, 12701. Borden also wrote to Leonard to express his view that the statements were unfortunate and ill-advised. He did suggest, however, that General Hughes might have been right in his assessment of certain manufacturers who had refused to provide munitions in the early stages of the war. However, he appreciated that 'this ... did not justify the general reflection upon the manu-

facturers of this country': R.L. Borden to R.W. Leonard, 18 June 1918, Borden Papers, 12702.
75 In 1915 he said this: 'There is no special plant required outside of what may be found at Sydney, Hamilton or the Soo, for making nickel-steel. If these works have a demand for bridge stuff, rails or bars of nickel steel, there are no technical reasons why they could not make them now ... There absolutely is no present reason why any of the existing nickel refiners could not establish their works in Canada if they are prepared to sacrifice the few million dollars invested in Wales and New Jersey, and move their technical men to Canada. It is doubtful if the difference in operating costs would be perceptible in the selling price of their products': quoted in J.C. Hopkins, ed., *Canadian Annual Review of Public Affairs* (Toronto: Annual Review Publishing 1916) at 546.
76 President's Address, Annual Report, Coniagas Mines Ltd (1919) at 6.
77 Director's Report, Annual Report, Coniagas Mines, Ltd (1907).
78 'The President's Address,' Annual Report, Coniagas Mines, Ltd (1914) at 6.
79 'The President's Address,' Annual Report, Coniagas Mines, Ltd (1912) at 7.
80 R.W. Leonard to J. Willison, 30 April 1919, Willison Papers, box 25, 18320, National Archives of Canada.
81 See, for example, J.A. McRae, 'Banner of Bolshevism behind strike of miners in northern district,' Saturday Night, 16 August 1919; 'Radicals appear to gain ground in Cobalt strike,' Saturday Night, 6 September 1919, 18.
82 See Baldwin, supra, note 57.
83 It will be recalled that, at the outbreak of war, Leonard had remonstrated about the views of Platon Reich of Trinity College: see the text accompanying notes 58 to 62, supra.
84 For an account of this episode, stressing Robert Falconer's role, see J.G. Greenlee, *Sir Robert Falconer* (Toronto: University of Toronto Press 1988) at 275–84. See also A.B. McKillop, *Matters of Mind: The University in Ontario, 1791–1951* (Toronto: University of Toronto Press 1994) at 366–72; Horn, supra, note 62, at 68–71.
85 R.W. Leonard, 'Retiring President's Address' (1920) 3 Engineering Journal 78, at 80.
86 Ibid.
87 Ibid. at 81.
88 R.A. Falconer to R.W. Leonard, 18 January 1921, Falconer Papers, box 65, University of Toronto Archives.
89 R.W. Leonard to R. Falconer, 21 January 1921, ibid. Leonard added that he was 'very jealous that criticism ... against Professors in the University should never be warranted': ibid. See also Falconer's reply, outlining MacIver's pro-

fessional qualifications: R. Falconer to R.W. Leonard, 22 January 1921, Falconer Papers, University of Toronto Archives, box 65. Annie Besant (1847–1933) was a well-known English theosophist and socialist who became active in Indian politics; see further R. Kumar, *Annie Besant's Rise to Power in Indian Politics, 1914–1917* (New Delhi: Concept Publishing, 1981).
90 R. MacIver to R. Falconer, 27 January 1921, ibid. A brief description of MacIver's response is contained in Greenlee, supra, note 84, at 277–8.
91 (Toronto: J.M. Dent and Sons 1919).
92 See, for example, ibid. at 16–17.
93 Ibid. at 226ff.
94 R.W. Leonard to R. Falconer, 9 December 1921, Falconer Papers, University of Toronto Archives, box 72.
95 R. Falconer to R.W. Leonard, 12 December 1921, ibid.
96 R.W. Leonard to B.E. Walker, 15 December 1921, Walker Papers, box 15, Fisher Rare Book Library, University of Toronto; R.W. Leonard to H.J. Cody, 15 December 1921, Cody Papers, Archives of Ontario.
97 See, for example, 'Professors in politics are read stern lesson by Sir Robert Falconer,' *Globe*, 15 February 1922, 11. See further Horn, supra, note 62, at 70–1, and the newspaper reports cited there.
98 The list of participants is contained in 'Personnel of Party Visiting the West Indies,' *Industrial Canada*, March 1922, 67. For reasons not explained, Colonel and Mrs Leonard, Colonel Arthur Hatch, and Sir Alexander Bertram left the party in Jamaica, one of the first stops, and remained there for the duration of the trip.
99 R.W. Leonard to R. Falconer, 24 April 1922, Falconer Papers, box 72, University of Toronto Archives.
100 B.E. Walker to R. Falconer, 2 March 1922, Walker Papers, Fisher Rare Book Room, University of Toronto, box 35.
101 R.W. Leonard to R. Falconer, 24 February 1923, Willison Papers, box 25, 18335, National Archives of Canada.
102 Ibid. See also Leonard's complaint about communistic lectures at the University of Toronto: R.W. Leonard to R. Falconer, 11 January 1924, Falconer Papers, box 84, University of Toronto Archives, discussed in chapter 2. Robert MacIver held the chair of the department until 1927, when he left for Columbia University. Though Leonard's campaign of vitriol must have affected the decision to leave, MacIver's autobiography (R.M. MacIver, *As a Tale That Is Told: The Autobiography of R.M. MacIver* (Chicago: University of Chicago 1968) does not refer to Reuben Leonard or these events. Nor are they discussed in *The Reminiscences of Robert MacIver* (Columbia University Oral History Collection, Part IV, no. 142, 1971).

103 See, for example, G. Parkin, 'Canadian Ambassador at Washington' (1921) 12 Round Table 170. See further J.C. Weaver, Imperilled Dreams: Canadian Opposition to the American Empire, 1918–1930, PhD Thesis, Duke University (1973) at 45ff.
104 R.W. Leonard to R.L. Borden, 20 July 1921, Newton Rowell Papers, box 11.
105 Ibid. Borden was also sceptical about aspects of the Covenant and the overall efficacy of the League, though the rationale for his views differed from those of Leonard: see further Brown and Cook, supra, note 37, 158, at 288ff. If an additional explanation is needed for Leonard's decision not to join the League of Nations Society, it might be furnished by the fact that Robert MacIver was a member of its executive committee.
106 S. King-Hall, *Chatham House: A Brief Account of the Origins, Purposes, and Methods of the Royal Institute of International Affairs* (London: Oxford University Press 1937) at 1.
107 C.G.D. Roberts and A.R.Turnbull, eds., *A Standard Dictionary of Canadian Biography* (Toronto: Trans-Canada Press, 1934–8), vol. 2, at 241. Cf. L. Curtis to R.W. Leonard, 21 June 1923, Chatham House, 4/Leon: 'Our committee felt that if the British Institute of International Affairs could acquire the house it ought to bear the name of its first and greatest Prime Minister, Lord Chatham who ... did more than anyone to lay the foundations of the British Empire.'
108 Quoted in Roberts and Turnbull, supra, note 107, at 241. Curtis also suggested that 'before the War he [Leonard] had dreamed of finding some permanent way in which he could benefit the British Commonwealth as a whole ...': L. Curtis, 'Lieut.-Colonel R.W. Leonard' (1931) 10 International Affairs 1, at 2.
109 Lavin, supra, note 30, at 172–3. The passage quoted within this quotation is from L. Curtis to R.W. Leonard, 19 July 1923, Chatham House 4/Leon.
110 R.W. Leonard to L. Curtis, 13 August 1923, Chatham House 4/Leon. Leonard continued: 'His present occupation of contributing his memoirs to the Hearst Press does not appeal favourably to me. I don't know what his views might be considered to represent just now.'
111 R.W. Leonard to L. Curtis, 24 July 1923, Chatham House, 4/Leon.
112 R.W. Leonard to L. Curtis, 13 August 1923, Chatham House, 4/Leon.
113 Ibid.
114 'A Canadian Gift,' *The Times*, 16 October 1923, 11. The gift also included 15, 17, and 18 Ormond Yard: Macadam to A.L. Bishop, 30 October 1944., Chatham House, 4/Leon.
115 'The Canadian gift to Britain: names of the donors,' *The Times*, 23 October 1923, 11.

116 Lord Meston, 'Canadian gift to the Empire,' *The Times*, 24 October 1923, 10 (letter). See also R.W. Leonard to W.L.M. King, 15 December 1923, King Papers, box 89, 75560, National Archives of Canada.
117 On this occasion, the headline was more accurate: 'A British Empire gift,' *The Times*, 10 November 1923, 14.
118 Ibid.
119 *The Times*, 31 December 1923, 16. About fifty people attended: R.W. Leonard to L. Curtis, 29 December 1923, Chatham House, 29 December 1923, 4/Leon.
120 T.E. Lawrence to D.G. Hogarth, quoted in J. Wilson, *Lawrence of Arabia: The Authorized Biography of T.E. Lawrence* (London: Heinemann 1989) at 729.
121 R.W. Leonard to L. Curtis, 29 December 1923, Chatham House 4/Leon.
122 T.E. Lawrence to R.W. Leonard, 11 February 1925 (private collection; a copy of this letter is on file at the Faculty of Law, University of Alberta).
123 This is the number contained in the list (in Lawrence's handwriting) held in the Lawrence Papers at the Houghton Library, Harvard University: fms Eng 1252 (356). 'Leonard, Col. R.W.' is listed as subscriber #69. Cf. P.M. O'Brien, *T.E. Lawrence: A Bibliography* (Boston: G.K. Hall 1988) at 39, and 45.
124 Extract of a letter read into the record at the May 1923 meeting of the trustees of Queen's University, quoted in M.C. Tillotson, *Memorandum on the Leonard Foundation Awards*, 15 November 1950, Leonard Foundation Awards and Trust – Terms and Trust, Queen's University Secretariat.
125 Leonard told John Willison that the press in England and the 'big men in London' had been very appreciative but that the response in Canada had been less enthusiastic: R.W. Leonard to J. Willison, 30 November 1923, Willison Papers, box 25, 18337, National Archives of Canada. And in thanking Edmund Walker for arranging the dinner in his honour, he remarked that 'I sometimes feel that in Canada we perhaps do not recognize sufficiently the merits of our citizens': R.W. Leonard to B.E. Walker, 31 December 1923, Walker Papers, Ms. Coll. 1, box 16, Fisher Rare Book Room, University of Toronto.
126 'Colonel R.W. Leonard Dies; Canadian Philanthropist,' New York *Herald Tribune*, 18 December 1930.
127 There were also a number of minor donations: Dalhousie University was given $35,000, which was used for their science library; money was provided to help endow a scholarship at the University of Toronto in honour of the late Maurice Cody; a donation was made to the newly created Banting Research Institute; and money was given to help finance a conference on education. He also donated funds to the YMCA in Cobalt, established an award in 1924 for graduates of Ridley attending Wycliffe, and in 1927 he

provided $5,000 to help in the development of an 'Evangelical Publications Trust' at Wycliffe.
128 Included in the 'Leonard Canadian Collection,' as it is now called, are works by Frank Carmichael, Lawren Harris, A.Y. Jackson, Cornelius Krieghoff, and Tom Thomson.
129 Toronto General Trusts to Board of Governors, Ridley College, quoted in K. Beattie, *Ridley: The Story of a School* (St Catharines: Ridley College 1963) at 465.
130 An attempt by Charles Magrath, chairman of the Hydro-Electric Power Commission, to have R.W. Leonard appointed to the Imperial Privy Council in 1926 failed. So did John Cowan's proposal to have the University of Toronto confer an honorary doctorate on Leonard.
131 'Soldier, engineer, miner dies at St Catharines,' Toronto *Star*, 17 December 1930, 16.
132 See further the obituaries listed in the bibliography.
133 See, for example, Resolution of the Art Gallery of Ontario, 9 March 1931, reported in D.H. McDougall to Mrs R.W. Leonard, 12 March 1931, Archives of the Art Gallery of Ontario.
134 Reproduced in 'Many messages of deepest sympathy,' St Catharines *Standard*, 19 December 1930, at 18.
135 'Col. Leonard dies: Canadian patriot,' New York *Times*, 18 December 1930, 23.
136 'Canadian philanthropist dead,' *Wall Street Journal*, 19 December 1930, 11.
137 *The Times*, 18 December 1930, 16.
138 L. Curtis, 'Lieut.-Colonel R.W. Leonard' (1931) 10 International Affairs 1.
139 A will is a testament to the vulnerability of the human condition and the inevitability of death, and never was this more true than in the case of Reuben Wells Leonard. His will was executed on 4 December 1920, and codicils were added in 1923, 1925, 1928, and 1930. With each one, Leonard's signature deteriorated. The once large bold script was now small, weak, and bent, a metaphor of his relentlessly declining health. The last codicil, completed just five days before his death, is signed only with a jagged, barely decipherable 'X.' In an accompanying affidavit, it was said that while Leonard was too infirm to execute the document properly, he was able to understand the nature and purpose of the document that was presented to him.
140 Most of the estate was in the form of Canadian securities. Over $3 million took the form of shares in the Finance and Development Company, presumably a holding company. The listed value of his shares in Coniagas was only $114,105.

141 It was, at least, important enough to make the news: 'Leonard Fortune is shared widely,' *Globe*, 26 January 1931.
142 The trustees were to pay for all of the carrying charges out of the residue of the estate. The house was valued at $40,250.
143 These involved, mainly, small annuities and gifts for the education of nephews and nieces at the schools contemplated by the Leonard Foundation.
144 Leonard's personal secretary, office manager, and secretary received gratuities of $10,000 and $5,000, respectively, to be drawn from the fund of $50,000.
145 Provision was made for use of the income of the postponed half-share for the education of Arthur Bishop's children: clause 11(a).
146 The five schools were chosen at the annual general meeting of the Leonard Foundation in 1936. They were: Ridley, Wycliffe, Havergal, Queen's, and the University of Toronto.
147 The uses to which this gift was put are described in L. Dickson, *The Museum Makers: The Story of the Royal Ontario Museum* (Toronto: Royal Ontario Museum 1986) at 41. Leonard had been a member of a group known as the 'Ten Friends of the Arts' (along with fellow Round Tabler, Edmund Walker). Members of this groups pledged donations to the Royal Ontario Museum of $500.00 per annum: ibid.
148 See further G. Lonn, *Canadian Profiles* (Toronto: Pitt. Publishing 1965) at 31–2.
149 Lavin, supra, note 30, at 114.
150 Arthur Bishop kept up the association with Curtis, who became the godfather to Bishop's daughter, Judith.
151 See M. Bliss, *A Living Profit: Studies in the Social History of Canadian Business, 1883–1911* (Toronto: McClelland and Stewart 1974) at 32: 'In its ultimate implications the [businessman's] success ethic had little or nothing to do with making money, everything to do with the cultivation of moral character.' See further ibid. at ch. 1, passim.
152 'Scratch a Canadian "colonel" before the military was put through the crucible of the Great War and you often found the rich red blood of a parvenu': M. Bliss, *Northern Enterprise: Five Centuries of Canadian Business* (Toronto: McClelland and Stewart 1987) at 347.

2: The Leonard Foundation Trust in Context

1 'Generous donors of Chatham House win warm tributes,' Toronto *Globe*, 28 December 1923.
2 Recitals 5 and 6 state that the trust is a continuation of the 1920 trust. Recital

200   Notes to pages 53–8

7 acknowledges the advice and assistance given by Mrs Leonard and expresses a desire that her name be associated with the Foundation.
3 These are set out below, in the text accompanying note 5, infra.
4 The list is reproduced in the appendix of this book.
5 See Leonard Foundation Trust deed (1923) at Schedule 'A.'
6 An association was formed in 1928. It is discussed briefly in chapter 3.
7 The deed creates a 'charitable trust,' the nature of which is outlined in chapter 3.
8 See further B. Ziff, *Principles of Property Law*, 2nd ed. (Toronto: Carswell 1996) at 24–7, and the references cited there.
9 Construing the trust as a political statement has an ironic twist. To count as a charitable trust, the trust's purposes cannot be political. A trust is regarded as political if it seeks to further the aims of a particular party, tries to prevent or promote a change in the law, or if it promotes a particular doctrine or policy outlook. The Leonard Foundation Trust does not appear to fall within these categories. At the same time, in a more general sense, philanthropic action is often directed towards political ends, and I will argue below ('Philanthropy') that philanthropy is inherently a political activity. See further M. Chesterman, *Charities, Trusts and Social Welfare* (London: Wiedenfield and Nicholson 1979), ch. 15, passim; L. Sheridan, 'Charity versus Political' (1973) 2 Anglo-American Law Review 47; E. Clark, 'The Limitation on Political Activity,' (1960) 46 Virginia Law Review 439.
10 In particular, *The Origin of the Species* (1859) in which the theory of natural selection is outlined, and *The Descent of Man* (1871) in which human evolution is explained. It should be noted that Darwinism proper could support the view that not just physical but also mental traits could pass through inheritance as part of the struggle to survive. No modifier such as 'social' would be needed to make this argument since it is already inside Darwinian thought.
11 See further M. Hawkins, *Social Darwinism in European and American Thought, 1860–1945* (Cambridge: Cambridge University Press 1997).
12 See C. Berger, *The Sense of Power: Studies in the Ideas of Canadian Imperialism, 1867–1914* (Toronto: University of Toronto Press 1970) at 132.
13 See C.G. Holland, 'Victorian Culture in Canada: The Thought and Intellect of William Dawson LeSueur,' PhD Thesis, University of Toronto 1990, at 79ff; A.B. McKillop, ed., *A Critical Spirit: The Thought of William Lawson LeSueur* (Toronto: McClelland and Stewart 1977) at Part 2, passim.
14 See further A. McLaren, *Our Own Master Race: Eugenics in Canada, 1885–1945* (Toronto: McClelland and Stewart 1990).
15 Raised in New Brunswick, Parkin, like Leonard, turned initially to teaching

as a vocation. Soon after graduating from University of New Brunswick, he served as a school headmaster in the province. A year spent at Oxford (studying classics) had a profound effect on his thinking, and he returned to Canada with a veneration for Oxford, the British private school system, and British imperialism. A stream of important publications followed, including *Imperial Federation: The Problem of National Unity* (1892), in which he described the relationship he foresaw between Canada and the Empire. In 1902 Parkin left again for Oxford, serving as the organizing secretary of the Rhodes Scholarship Trust until 1917. In that year he returned to Canada to become the headmaster of Upper Canada College in Toronto, a post that he held until his death.

16 J.B. Bury, *The Idea of Progress: An Inquiry into its Origins and Growth* (London: Macmillan 1920).
17 See, for example, R. Nisbet, *History of the Idea of Progress* (New York: Basic Books 1980).
18 See further G.A. Almond et al., *Progress and Its Discontents* (Berkeley: University of California Press 1982).
19 P.J. Bowler, *The Invention of Progress: The Victorians and the Past* (Oxford: Basil Blackwell 1989) at 3.
20 As to images of Canada's climate and its relationship to progress, see Berger, supra, note 12, at 129ff.
21 See further Berger, ibid., at ch. 4, passim.
22 And the building of the transcontinental railway was viewed as an act of patriotism: see further A.A. den Otter, *The Philosophy of Railroads: The Transcontinental Railway Idea in British North America* (Toronto: University of Toronto Press 1997); M. Bliss, *A Living Profit: Studies in the Social History of Canadian Business, 1883–1911* (Toronto: McClelland and Stewart 1974) at 13.
23 R.W. Leonard, 'The Scope of Engineering in Canada' (1910) 4(1) Applied Science (new series) 1.
24 R.W. Leonard, 'Retiring President's Address' (1920) 3 Engineering Journal 78.
25 R.W. Leonard to R. Falconer, 21 January 1921, Falconer Papers, box 65, University of Toronto Archives. See also 'Retiring President's Address, supra, note 24, at 178.
26 The key passages of the speech are quoted in chapter 1.
27 W.R. Lawson, *Canada and the Empire* (London: William Blackwood 1911) at 32.
28 G. Smith, *Canada and the Canadian Question* (Toronto: Hunter, Rose 1891).
29 J.S. Ewart, *The Imperial Project and the Republic of Canada* (Toronto: McClelland and Stewart 1917).

30 See generally R.G. Moyles and D. Owram, *Imperial Dreams and Colonial Realities: British Views of Canada, 1880–1914* (Toronto: University of Toronto Press 1988).
31 J. Willison, *Partners in Peace: The Dominion, The Empire and the Republic* (Toronto: Warwick Bros. and Rutter 1923) at 87. See also J. Willison, *Canada in the Empire* (London: Whitefriars 1922) at 15; J. Willison, 'From Month to Month' (1927) 11 Willison's Monthly 445. Likewise, see R.A. Falconer, 'A New Imperial Allegiance' (1916) 15 University Magazine 12, at 17.
32 'Deliberately Planned in Berlin,' Manitoba *Free Press*, 8 August 1914, 11. Likewise, to James Cappon, a supporter of Leonard's ill-fated Queen's project, 'the Empire represents an ideal of high importance for the future of civilization, the attempt to assemble in a higher unity than even that of nationality the forces which maintain and advance the white man's ideals of civilization, his sense of justice, his constitutional freedom, his respect for law and order, his humanity. It is an attempt to transcend the evils of nationality ... without impairing the vigour which the national consciousness gives to a people': quoted in S.E.D. Shortt, *The Search for an Ideal: Six Canadian Intellectuals and Their Convictions in an Age of Transition, 1890–1930* (Toronto: University of Toronto Press 1976) at 74. See also Shortt's discussion of the views of Maurice Hutton, ibid. at 90.
33 L. Curtis to E.J. Kylie, 10 January 1913, quoted in D. Lavin, *From Empire to International Commonwealth: A Biography of Lionel Curtis* (Oxford: Clarendon Press 1995) at 116. 'Even a keen and cultured observer as Mr. Curtis evidently is, broad-minded and high-spirited, cannot altogether avoid the temptation of believing that the Anglo-Saxon has a born right to rule the world': H. Bourassa, *Independence or Imperial Partnership? A Study of the Problem of the Commonwealth by Mr. Lionel Curtis* (Montreal: Le Devoir 1916) at 35.
34 See Willison, *Partners in Peace*, supra, note 31; J.S. Willison, *Anglo-Saxon Amity* (n.p., 1906); R. Falconer, *The United States as a Neighbour* (Cambridge: Cambridge University Press, 1925). See further J.C. Weaver, 'Imperilled Dreams: Canadian Opposition to the American Empire, 1918–1930,' PhD thesis, Duke University 1973, at 72ff.
35 See further R. Bothwell, *Loring Christie: The Failure of Bureaucratic Imperialism* (New York: Garland, 1988) at 34ff. See also Shortt, supra, note 32, at 90, discussing the political views of Maurice Hutton.
36 J.L. Granatstein, *Yankee Go Home: Canadians and Anti-Americanism* (Toronto: HarperCollins 1996) at 77–8.
37 See also 'Canada: Geography and Development' (1923) 13 Round Table 836: 'Before Canada is always the danger of absorption of her people, her busi-

ness, even her national identity, by a country not barred by physical or national obstacles.'
38 Supra, note 36, at 40. See also R. Cuff, 'The Toronto Eighteen and the Election of 1911' (1965) 57 Ontario History 169; W.M. Baker, 'A Case Study of Anti-Americanism in English-Speaking Canada: The Election Campaign of 1911' (1970) 51 Canadian Historical Review 426. Anti-American sentiment near the turn of the century is discussed in N. Penlington, *Canada and Imperialism, 1896–1899* (Toronto: University of Toronto Press 1965) at ch. 14, passim.
39 Supra, note 12.
40 See, for example, W.D. Lighthall, *Canada: A Modern Nation* (Montreal: Witness Print House 1904) at 78. See also Lavin, supra, note 33, at 116, quoting the South African Round Tabler Dougal Malcom.
41 The pre-1986 Leonard Foundation application forms contained an asterisk after the reference to the requirement that applicants be British subjects. The notation reads: 'Applications from Canadian Citizens who otherwise are eligible will be accepted for consideration.' This was treated as a valid interpretation of the deed by Mr Justice McKeown in *Re Canada Trust & Ontario Human Rights Commission* (1987) 42 Dominion Law Reports (4th) 263 (Ontario High Court) at 279.
42 In particular, Berger argues that Canadian imperialists (such as George Denison) tended both to denigrate laissez-faire capitalism and to incorporate the social gospel into their conception of the imperial mission: see Berger, supra, note 12, at 186ff. Leonard did not fit this description: see below ('Philanthropy'). But is Berger correct?
43 In 1912 he joined Sir Edmund Walker and Zebulon Lash (an advocate of imperial federation from Newfoundland) in establishing a fund to support 'the publication of such information and the advocacy of such measures as would uphold Canadian Nationality in connection with the British Empire and maintain Canada's fiscal independence': Agreement dated 5 February 1912, Walker Papers, Fisher Rare Book Room, University of Toronto, box 29B.
44 R.W. Leonard to R.L. Borden, 20 July 1921, Newton Rowell Papers, box 48, 7887, National Archives of Canada.
45 R.W. Leonard to L. Curtis, 13 August 1923, R.W. Leonard Papers, Chatham House, 4/Leon.
46 Ibid.
47 L. Curtis to Devonshire, 17 September 1923, R.W. Leonard Papers, Chatham House, 4/Leon.
48 R.W. Leonard to C.A. Magrath, 16 December 1912, Magrath Papers, vol. 11, file 53, National Archives of Canada. 'The great bulk, dishonest instincts, and

strong hostility of our neighbours, makes a thoughtful Canadian always anxious': Col. George Denison (1895), quoted in D.A. Guthrie, 'The Imperial Federation Movement in Canada,' PhD thesis, Northwestern University 1940, at 111.

49 See, for example, R.W. Lee, 'Canada and the Empire' (1916) 15 University Magazine 233, at 242: 'The British Empire is held together not – "By inky blots and rotten parchment bonds" but by common ideals, traditions, institutions.'

50 See, for example, C.H. Mitchell, 'A Survey of the Empire' in *Empire Club of Canada* (1922) 397. See further Moyles and Owram, supra, note 30, at 236ff.

51 Imperial federation is a term that has been used in a general sense to refer to measures aimed at the strengthening and unifying of the British Empire. It sometimes describes partial federal union, involving commercial, military, or political reorganization. Sometimes it connotes elements of a federal device, such as a multinational assembly or council. In its strictest sense, it means a form of governance in which legislative, executive, and judicial powers are integrated among polities, with a division of powers between the central government and its regional counterparts.

52 (Toronto: Macmillan 1916).

53 See further E.A. Smillie, *Historical Origins of Imperial Federation* (Montreal: n.p., 1910). In 1890 a motion was brought in the Canadian Senate calling for Canadian representation in the British House of Commons and Privy Council: *Senate Debates*, 4th Sess., 16th Parl., 1890, at 256 (per Senator Charles Bouton). The motion was considered over the course of two days, following which it was withdrawn by Senator Boulton.

54 Guthrie, supra, note 48, at 162.

55 S.J. Duncan, *The Imperialist* (1904) (Toronto: McClelland and Stewart ed., 1961). Sara Duncan was a friend of John Willison and she asked for his help in obtaining material on imperial federation as part of her research for the novel: see C. Thomas, 'Canadian Mythologies in Sara Jeannette Duncan's *The Imperialist*' (1977) 12(2) Journal of Canadian Studies 38.

56 See, for example, the English reviews: *The Economist*, 8 July 1916; *Times Literary Supplement*, 25 May 1916, 241; (1916) 32 Law Quarterly Review 335; and these American reviews: (1916) 31 Political Science Quarterly 445; (1917) 25 Journal of Political Economy 396; (1916) 10 American Political Science Review 791. In Canada, Henri Bourassa paid special attention to the book. Several articles on the subject, originally printed in *Le Devoir*, were republished in French and English. The English version is: H. Bourassa, *Independence or Imperial Partnership? A Study of The Problem of the Commonwealth by*

Mr. Lionel Curtis (Montreal: Le Devoir 1916). See also the extensive critique in A.B. Keith, 'The Ideal of an Imperial Constitution' (1916) 36 Canadian Law Times 831; A. Glazebrook, 'Our Future in the Empire,' in J.O. Miller, ed., *The New Era in Canada* (London: Dent 1917) 263; and (1916) 47 Canadian Magazine 342. Following the publication of *The Problem of the Commonwealth*, Zebulon Lash published a short monograph, which was in essence a response to Curtis. In the preface, written by Edmund Walker, it was pointed out that Lash was not a member of the Round Table: see Z.A. Lash, *Defence and Foreign Affairs: A Suggestion for the Empire* (Toronto: Macmillan 1917).

57 See, for example, C.W. Colby, 'Topics of the Day,' University Magazine, February 1916, 6.
58 See V. Massey, *What's Past Is Prologue* (Toronto: Macmillan 1963) at 36.
59 Memorandum issued by the Round Table in Canada for publication in the Canadian press, 10 February 1917.
60 W. Laurier to A. Aylesworth, 15 May 1917, quoted in O.D. Skelton, *The Life and Letters of Sir Wilfrid Laurier* (Toronto: Oxford University Press 1921), vol. 2, at 510.
61 Compare Bothwell's analysis: '... as a group, their exercise of influence was a lamentable failure': R. Bothwell, *Loring Christie: The Failure of Bureaucratic Imperialism* (New York: Garland 1988) at 42.
62 J.G. Greenlee, *Sir Robert Falconer: A Biography* (Toronto: University of Toronto Press 1987) at 311.
63 Quoted in 'To serve Empire truly is to serve mankind,' Toronto *Star*, 23 February 1924, 2.
64 Leonard to Borden, supra, note 44.
65 Quoted in Toronto *Star*, supra, note 63.
66 Leonard to Borden, supra, note 44.
67 See C. Cross, *The Fall of the British Empire* (New York: Coward-McCann 1968) at 171ff.
68 See further N. Stepan, *The Idea of Race in Science: Great Britain, 1800–1960* (Hamden, Conn.: Archon 1982).
69 *Dominion School Geography* (Toronto: Educational School 1910) at 60–1. At least as late as 1924–5, this textbook was authorized for use in Grade 8 classes in Alberta: Alberta Department of Education, *Authorized Textbooks, Grades I-VIII, 1924–25* (n.p., 1924). See further T.J. Stanley, 'White Supremacy and the Rhetoric of Educational Indoctrination,' in J.A. Mangan, ed., *Making Imperial Mentalities: Socialisation and British Imperialism* (Manchester: Manchester University Press 1990).
70 C.S. Eby, 'The True Inwardness of the Yellow Peril,' in J.C. Hopkins, ed., *Empire Club Speeches* (Toronto: William Briggs 1910), 43.

71 See, for example, C.W. Dilke, *Greater Britain* (London: Macmillan 1870) at 572.
72 See R.A. Huttenback, *Racism and Empire* (Ithaca, N.Y.: Cornell University Press 1976) at 15.
73 J. Chamberlain, 'Speech Delivered in Toronto in 1887,' quoted in Skelton, supra, note 60, vol. 2, at 62.
74 Quoted in M. Banton, *Racial Theories* (Cambridge, U.K.: Cambridge University Press 1987) at 76.
75 G. Parkin, *Imperial Federation: The Problem of National Unity* (London: Macmillan 1892) at 1. See also Shortt, supra, note 32, at 90, discussing the work of Maurice Hutton. See also B. Williams, *Cecil Rhodes* (London: Henry Holt 1921; repr. New York: Greenwood Press 1968) at 55.
76 Banton, supra, note 74, at 76.
77 E.D. Cope, *On the Hypothesis of Evolution: Physical and Metaphysical* (New Haven, Conn.: Chatfield 1870) at 31ff.
78 See further R. Cook, *The Regenerators: Social Criticism in Late Victorian English Canada* (Toronto: University of Toronto Press 1985) at 15; J. Dillenberger, *Protestant Thought and Natural Science: A Historical Interpretation* (New York: Doubleday 1960) ch. 8, passim; R.J. Taylor, 'The Darwinian Revolution: The Responses of Four Canadian Scholars,' PhD Thesis, McMaster University, 1976; A.B. McKillop, *A Disciplined Intelligence: Critical Inquiry and Canadian Thought in the Victorian Era* (Montreal: McGill-Queen's University Press 1979) ch. 4, passim; C. Berger, *Science, God, and Nature in Victorian Canada* (Toronto: University of Toronto Press 1983) at 54.
79 Bowler, supra, note 19, at 110.
80 Dominion Bureau of Statistics, *Origin, Birthplace, Nationality and Language of the Canadian People* (Ottawa: F.A. Acland 1929) at 43–4.
81 This was evident within the school system in English Canada. 'The ideal of the Melting pot is one which has never commended itself, for any long time ... to Canadian opinion': G.E. Jackson, 'Race in Canada,' in British Association for the Advancement of Science, ed., *Handbook of Canada* (Toronto: University of Toronto Press 1924), 41. See also C.N. Cochrane and W.S. Wallace, *This Canada of Ours* (National Council of Education 1921) at 173ff. See further H.H. Palmer, 'Reluctant Hosts: Anglo-Canadian Views of Multiculturalism in the Twentieth Century,' in J.R. Malle and J.C. Young, eds., *Cultural Diversity and Canadian Education* (Ottawa: Carleton University Press 1984). See also D. Avery, 'Canadian Immigration Policy, 1896–1919: The Anglo-Canadian Perspective,' PhD thesis, University of Western Ontario, 1973; V. Knowles, *Strangers at our Gates: Canadian Immigration and Immigration Policy, 1540–1997*, rev. ed. (Toronto: Dundurn Press 1997).

82 See, for example, G. Bryce, 'Past and Future of Our Race,' in *Proceedings of the Canadian Club of Toronto* (1911) at 6.
83 *House of Commons Debates*, 7 June 1929, at 3925–57.
84 See, for example, J.S. Woodsworth, *Strangers within Our Gates* (Toronto: F.C. Stephenson 1909). See also J. Nelson, 'Shall We Bar the Yellow Race?' (1922) 35(10) Maclean's 13; R. Connor, *The Foreigner: A Tale of Saskatchewan* (Toronto: Westminster 1909); W.G. Smith, *A Study in Canadian Immigration* (Toronto: Ryerson Press 1920); E.W. MacBride, 'The Various Races of Man' (1906) 5(2) McGill University Magazine 294; J.A. Lindsay, 'National Characteristics' (1929) 9(2) Dalhousie Review 181. Cf. W. Kirkconnell, 'Western Immigration,' Canadian Forum, July 1928, 706–7, arguing against nativist critiques of immigration. See further W.P. Ward, 'The Oriental Immigrant and Canada's Protestant Clergy, 1858–1925' (1974) 22 B.C. Studies 40.
85 See further M. Valverde, *The Age of Light, Soap, and Water: Moral Reform in English Canada, 1885–1925* (Toronto: McClelland and Stewart 1991) ch. 5, passim. Depictions of race in Canadian literature during the period under discussion are assessed in T.L. Craig, 'Attitudes Towards Race in Canadian Prose Fiction in English, 1905–1980,' PhD thesis, University of Toronto, 1982.
86 *House of Commons Debates*, 3rd. Sess., 11th Parl., 3 April 1911 at 6524 (per William Thorburn, MP for Lanark).
87 *House of Commons Debates*, 8 May 1922, 1st Sess., 14th Parl., 1922, vol. 152, at 1509–77. See also *House of Commons Debates*, 14th Parliament, 2nd Sess. (Ottawa: F.A. Acland 1923) vol. 5, at 4648 (19 June 1923).
88 'An influx of Jews puts a worm next the kernel of every fair city where they get a hold ... They are not the material out of which to shape a people holding a national spirit. They remain cosmopolitan while war drains the blood of the solid citizens of a nation ... Canada's police court annals are a disgrace in their constant fining of these habitual lawbreakers, who reckon the difference between fines and bootleggers' profits ... Jews of all countries should be discriminated against as a race by a poll tax': H.R. Murton, 'Canada's Immigration Slogan Mocked at by the Jews,' Toronto *Telegram*, 22 September 1924, 9.
89 Once a neglected topic in Canadian history, the literature concerning the treatment of minorities in Canada is now expansive. See further J. Boyko, *Last Steps to Freedom: The Evolution of Canadian Racism* (Winnipeg: Watson and Dwyer 1995), and the references cited there.
90 See McLaren, supra, note 14, at ch. 3, passim.
91 W.S. Wallace, 'The Canadian Immigration Policy,' Canadian Magazine, February 1908, 360.
92 (Princeton, N.J.: Princeton University Press 1923).

93 P. Sandiford, 'The Inheritance of Talent Among Canadians' (1927) 35 Queen's Quarterly 2.
94 Ibid. at 13.
95 Ibid.
96 Ibid. at 17.
97 Ibid. at 18–19.
98 'To serve Empire truly is to serve mankind,' supra, note 63.
99 'Retiring President's Address,' supra, note 24, at 78. He also suggested that 'we must be very jealous about extending the franchise to alien immigrants who become the ready and fanatical followers of irresponsible, self-seeking agitators': ibid. at 81.
100 Leonard to Borden, supra, note 44.
101 See also Bourassa, supra, note 33, at 35.
102 Based on demographics, the British Empire was overwhelmingly non-White:

United Kingdom	45,365,599
Canada	7,204,838
Australia	4,775,614
New Zealand	1,070,652
South Africa	
white	1,278,025
black	5,958,499
India	312,632,537
Egypt	11,287,359
Sudan	2,600,000
Crown Colonies, etc.	42,437,296
TOTAL	433,574,001

These figures are taken from Curtis, *supra*, note 52, at the chart opposite page 69.
103 (New York: Columbia University Press 1931).
104 W.B. Worsfold, *The Empire on the Anvil* (London: Smith, Elder 1916) at 153–4. See also ibid. at 158.
105 Cheng also reviewed the views of eight others, not included in his general survey, all of whom preferred some measure of representation for India: see Cheng, supra, note 103, at 178–81.
106 See T. MacFarlane, *Within the Empire* (Ottawa, 1891), summarized in Cheng, supra, note 103; L. Raglan, 'A Real Imperial Parliament' (1922) 92 Nineteenth Century and After, summarized in Cheng, supra, note 103, at 145–8. However, it was not always made clear to whom the franchise would be extended in India.
107 Supra, note 52, at 206. See also F.C. de Sumichrast, 'The Leadership of the

Empire,' *Addresses before the Canadian Club of Ottawa* (Ottawa: Mortimer Press, 1911) 62, at 62–3.
108 R. Brand, 'Memorandum on the first part of Round Table Report,' October 1912, quoted in Lavin, supra, note 33, at 116.
109 E. Grigg, 'Draft Introduction to the "Whitsuntide Egg,"' May 1914, quoted in Lavin, supra, note 33, at 116.
110 See further D.C. Ellinwood, 'The Future of India in the British Empire: The Round Table Group Discussions' (1969) 3 Nanyang University Journal 196.
111 See the text accompanying notes 192 to 195, infra.
112 Berger, supra, note 12, at 219ff.
113 H.J. Cody, 'Religious Contributions Toward Imperial Unity,' in J. Castell Hopkins, ed., *Empire Club Speeches, Being Addresses Delivered before the Empire Club during Its Session of 1908–1909* (Toronto: William Briggs 1910) 19, at 22. See also H.J. Cody, 'The Growth and Genius of the British Empire,' *Empire Club of Canada* (1922) 64.
114 'To me the Empire has become a religion': C.A. Magrath, 'Canada and Empire,' in *Addresses Delivered before the Canadian Club, 1911–12* (Ottawa: Mortimer Press 1912) 148, at 151. Compare Philip Kerr's appraisal: '[Lionel Curtis's] God is the British empire and he worships and serves it day and night ... the empire is a noble thing but not fit to be a god': P. Kerr to Lady Astor, 13 April 1915, N. Astor Papers, quoted in Lavin, supra, note 33, at 106.
115 R.B. Bennett, *Empire Club of Canada: Addresses Delivered to Members during the Session of 1912–13 and 1913–14* (Toronto) part 2, at 203.
116 Ibid.
117 Berger, supra, note 12, at 219–26.
118 Statistics Canada, *1991 Census Highlights* (Ottawa: Industry, Science and Technology, Canada 1994) at 105. By 1991, the figure was 36.2 per cent: ibid.
119 Ibid. By 1991, the figure was 45.7 per cent: ibid.
120 R. Perin, *Rome in Canada: The Vatican and Canadian Affairs in the Late Victorian Age* (Toronto: University of Toronto Press 1990) at 236.
121 J.R. Miller, 'Anti-Catholicism in Canada: From the British Conquest to the Great War,' in T. Murphy and G. Stortz, eds., *Creed and Culture: The Place of English-Speaking Catholics in Canadian Society, 1750–1930* (Montreal: McGill-Queen's University Press 1993) 25, at 41.
122 See further R.J.A. Huel, 'J.J. Maloney: How the West was Saved from Rome, Quebec and the Liberals,' in J.E. Foster, ed., *The Developing West* (Edmonton: University of Alberta Press 1983) 219.
123 A.T. Galt, *Civil Liberty in Lower Canada* (Montreal: D. Bentley 1876); A.T. Galt, *Church and State* (Montreal: Dawson 1876).

124 C. Lindsey, *Rome in Canada: The Ultramontane Struggle for Supremacy over the Civil Authority* (Toronto: Lovell Bros 1877).
125 See G.S. Kealey, 'The Orange Order in Toronto: Religious Riot and the Working Class,' in G.S. Kealey and P. Warrian, eds., *Essays in Canadian Working Class History* (Toronto: McClelland and Stewart 1976) 13; M.A. Galvin, 'The Jubilee Riots in Toronto, 1875,' Canadian Catholic Historical Association Report (n.p., 1959) 93.
126 J.T. Watt, 'The Protestant Protective Association in Ontario: A Study in Anti-Catholic Nativism,' MA Thesis, McMaster University 1965, at 25.
127 The litany of Catholic evils is recited in J.R. Miller, 'Anti-Catholic Thought in Victorian Canada' (1985) 66 Canadian Historical Review 474.
128 Christian Guardian, 20 September 1875, quoted in Galvin, supra, note 125, at 105–6.
129 Watt, supra, note 126, at 39.
130 Quoted in Miller, supra, note 127, at 475.
131 See B.F. Hogan, 'The Guelph Novitiate Raid: Conscription, Censorship and Bigotry during the Great War,' in *Canadian Catholic Historical Association: Study Sessions, 1978* (Ottawa: Historia Ecclesiae Catholicae 1979) 57.
132 See further M.G. McGowan, '"We are All Canadians": A Social, Religious and Cultural Portrait of Toronto's English-Speaking Roman Catholics, 1890–1920,' PhD Thesis, University of Toronto, 1988, at 452ff.
133 Quoted in Hogan, supra, note 131, at 61, note 8. See also J.J. Maloney, *Rome in Canada* (Vancouver: Columbia Protestant Publications 1935) at 105.
134 'Rowell scores nationalists,' *Globe*, 7 December 1917, 3.
135 Leonard Foundation Trust deed, at 1 (emphasis added).
136 J. Wild, *Canada and the Jesuits* (Toronto: Canadian Advance 1889) at 71.
137 See further C. Fahey, *In His Name: The Anglican Experience in Upper Canada* (Carleton University Press 1991) ch. 8, passim.
138 C. Gossage, *A Question of Privilege: Canada's Independent Schools* (Toronto: Peter Martin Associates 1977) at 139.
139 Ibid.
140 Dominion Bureau of Statistics, *Annual Survey of Education in Canada, 1924* (Ottawa: F.A. Acland 1926) at 6.
141 The University of New Brunswick is the only non-denominational university that is *not* included in the 1923 list. The reasons for this omission are not apparent. It was added to the list of eligible schools by the General Committee shortly afterwards.
142 In addition, he provided funding for the National Conference on Educational Citizenship, held in 1923.
143 'Retiring President's Address,' supra, note 24, at 78.

144 R.W. Leonard to R. Falconer, 24 April 1922, Falconer Papers, box 72, University of Toronto Archives.
145 R.W. Leonard to R. Falconer, 11 January 1924, Falconer Papers, box 84, University of Toronto Archives. Falconer wrote a placating reply: R. Falconer to R.W. Leonard, 14 January 1924, ibid.
146 R.W. Leonard to R. Falconer, 21 January 1921, Falconer Papers, box 65, University of Toronto Archives.
147 Quoted in Berger, supra, note 12, at 215. Professor Wrong was referring to Rhodes scholars.
148 J. Aikins, 'Address on Opening of Manitoba Law School' (1914) 34 Canada Law Times 1183, at 1189. See also C.R. Fay, 'How Education Strengthens the Links of Empire,' *Empire Club of Canada* (1921) 256.
149 See further J.G. Greenlee, *Education and Imperial Unity, 1901–1926* (New York: Garland 1987).
150 See T.G. August, *The Selling of the Empire: British and French Imperialist Propaganda, 1890–1940* (Westport, Conn.: Greenwood Press 1985) at 113.
151 See further Greenlee, supra, note 149.
152 As to the influences on Rhodes, see R.I. Rotberg, *The Founder: Cecil Rhodes and the Pursuit of Power* (New York: Oxford University Press 1988) at 664–5.
153 G.R. Parkin, *The Rhodes Scholarships* (Toronto: Copp Clark 1912). Parkin was succeeded as secretary by Philip Kerr (Lord Lothian), the London Round Tabler.
154 Ibid. at 12.
155 I mean by this term the exclusive private schools, such as Eton, Harrow, Charterhouse, and so on.
156 This term is discussed in J.A. Mangan, 'Social Darwinism, Sport and English Upper Class Education,' Stadion 7 (1982) 92.
157 'If there is in the British race, as I think there is, a special aptitude for "taking up the white man's burden," it may be ascribed, above all other causes, to the spirit of organised games': J.E.C. Weldon, headmaster at Harrow, quoted in L. James, *The Rise and Fall of the British Empire* (New York: St Martin's Press 1995) at 207. See further J.A. Mangan, *The Games Ethic and Imperialism* (New York: Viking 1986); D. Newsome, *Godliness and Good Learning* (London: John Murray 1961) at 80–2.
158 The view that social Darwinism complemented the ideology of muscular Christianity in the private school systems in England and Canada is presented in D.W. Brown, 'Social Darwinism, Private Schooling and Sport in Victorian and Edwardian Canada,' in J.A. Mangan, ed., *Pleasure, Profit, Proselytism: British Culture and Sport at Home and Abroad, 1700–1914* (London: Frank Cass 1988). See also A. Metcalfe, 'Some Background Influences on

Nineteenth-Century Sport and Physical Education,' Canadian Journal of History of Sport and Physical Education, 5(1) (May 1974) 62–73.
159 Brown, supra, note 158, at 227.
160 See further Stanley, supra, note 69.
161 Quoted in R. Stamp, 'Canadian Identity and the National Identity' in A. Chaiton and N. McDonald, eds., *Canadian Schools and Canadian Identity* (Toronto: Gage Educational 1977) 29, at 34. See also W.L. Grant, *History of Canada* (London: Heineman, rev. ed., 1927) at 435, where the reader is counselled that 'beyond even Canada we must love the world-wide Empire.'
162 See Department of Education (Manitoba), *Empire Day* (1913).
163 It has been suggested that Rhodes was thinking of English-Dutch division in South Africa, not the matter of allowing persons of colour to apply: Rotberg, supra, note 152, at 668.
164 Berger, supra, note 12, at 48.
165 Rhodes had developed a personal rapport with Kaiser Wilhelm through the course of various business dealings in Africa.
166 R.W. Leonard, 'The Scope of Engineering in Canada' (1910) 4 Applied Science: Transactions of the University of Toronto Engineering Society (new series) 1, at 9.
167 The events surrounding that proposed gift are discussed in chapter 1.
168 R.W. Leonard to Principal D.M. Gordon, 22 October 1914, Queen's University Archives.
169 Cf. Berger, supra, note 12, at 262.
170 Among the financial supporters of this organization were Edmund Walker and Featherstone Osler, two Leonard acquaintances. See further Berger, ibid., at 237–8.
171 A.B. McKillop, 'Marching as to War: Elements of Ontario Undergraduate Culture, 1890–1914' in P. Axelrod and J.G. Reid, eds., *Youth, University and Canadian Society: Essays in the Social History of Higher Education* (Montreal: McGill-Queen's University Press 1989) 75, at 84–5; R.M. Stamp, *The Schools of Ontario, 1876–1976* (Toronto: University of Toronto Press 1982) at 92–3.
172 See A. Thompson (a member of the Leonard Foundation General Committee), 'New look needed at foundations,' Winnipeg *Free Press*, 20 November 1982.
173 These developments paralleled somewhat those occurring in England. By 1878, women were being admitted at the University of London and by 1880 both Oxford and Cambridge had two women's colleges. But full student status was at first denied to women in the Oxbridge system. At Oxford, women were allowed to attend lectures (if accompanied by a chaperone) and by 1894 they were permitted to take examinations. However, women at

Oxford were not entitled to receive degrees until 1920 (a factor that must have influenced Rhodes's decision to exclude females from his scholarship program). Cambridge waited until 1948.

174 V. Strong-Boag, *The New Day Recalled: The Lives of Girls and Women in English Canada, 1919–1939* (Toronto: Copp Clark Pitman 1988) at 24. See also Statistics Canada, *Historical Compendium of Education Statistics from Confederation to 1975* (Ottawa, 1978) at 208.
175 Strong-Boag, supra, note 174, at 21.
176 Leonard, supra, note 166, at 4.
177 Strong-Boag, supra, note 174, at 21.
178 P.J. Harrigan, 'The Schooling of Boys and Girls in Canada' (1990) 23 Journal of Social History 803, at 806.
179 See W. Taylor, *A New View of Surface Forces* (Toronto: University of Toronto Press 1925) at 18, for the story of how this association came about.
180 Professor Francie Ostrower's empirical study of philanthropy revealed a similar set of preferences. Among the donors in New York City whom she surveyed in 1987 and 1988, the pattern of giving of large gifts was as follows: education (69.4 per cent of donors giving); culture (42.9 per cent); health (30.6 per cent); social services: (29.4 per cent); churches/temples: (15.5 per cent); animals/environment: (10.7 per cent); rights/advocacy/policy (10.7 per cent); youth (6 per cent): see F. Ostrower, *Why the Wealthy Give: The Culture of Elite Philanthropy* (Princeton, N.J.: Princeton University Press 1995) at 40. These figures were based on the three largest gifts made by approximately eighty-five donors during the twelve months preceding the survey.
181 Including the following: Tourilli Fish and Game Club, Quebec; Mount Royal Club, Montreal; Rideau Club, Ottawa; and National and Engineers' Club, Toronto.
182 Michael Bliss has estimated that in 1910 there may have been somewhere between four and five dozen millionaires in the country: M. Bliss, *Northern Enterprise: Five Centuries of Canadian Business* (Toronto: McClelland and Stewart 1987) at 345.
183 Some exhibited less restraint, such as Sir Henry Pellatt, the Cobalt millionaire who built the ill-fated Casa Loma in Toronto. See further Bliss, ibid. at 347.
184 That honour must surely go to Sir William C. Macdonald, who made his fortune through tobacco. Over the course of his life, Macdonald gave more than $14 million to McGill University alone. See further Bliss, ibid. at 349.
185 The Carnegie Corporation (established in 1911) and the Rockefeller Foundation (1913) provided funding to Canadian causes, and the money

received from these two sources was substantial. Scholarships awarded under the Rhodes Trust (1902) were from the outset made available to Canadians, as were awards under the Royal Commission for the Exhibition of 1851. Private philanthropy organized via a charitable foundation did not become common in Canada until after the Second World War. When the Leonard Foundation was established in 1916, the only comparable Canadian institutions were the Massey Foundation (1898) and the Strathcona Trust (1909).

186 Ostrower, supra, note 180, at 8ff.
187 A. Michaud, 'Distinguishing Non-Donors from Donors: An Exploratory Study of the Determinants of Charitable Giving in Canada,' M.A. Thesis, Concordia University, 1993, at 84.
188 Alice Michaud's study found that 78.9 per cent of donors and 71.8 per cent of non-donors felt that it was appropriate that charities serve as a substitute for government in the provision of some services: ibid. at 136.
189 In a tribute to R.W. Leonard on his death, H.G. Williams, then headmaster of Ridley Lower School, wrote: 'He took the responsibility of riches as he took all his other responsibilities. His money was not to be used for the indulgence of himself or others, but in the highest sense of the word was a trust, and he its administrator': H.G. Williams, 'A Tribute to the Late Col. R.W. Leonard,' *Acta Ridleiana*, Easter 1931, reprinted in K. Beattie, *Ridley: The Story of a School* (St Catharines, Ont.: Ridley College 1963) vol. 2, 1058, at 1060.
190 R.W. Leonard to R. Falconer, 14 July 1917, Falconer Papers, box 48A, University of Toronto Archives.
191 R.W. Leonard to R. Falconer, 28 February 1920, Falconer Papers, box 59, University of Toronto Archives.
192 'Retiring President's Address,' supra, note 24, at 79.
193 See also Cook, supra, note 78; Berger, supra, note 12.
194 Cook, supra, note 78, at 34ff.
195 A.E. Smith, 'Cutting Down an Evil Tree,' *Social Service Congress, Report of the Addresses and Proceedings* (Toronto: Social Services Council of Canada 1914) at 204.
196 'Retiring President's Address,' supra, note 24, at 79. See also W.G. Sumner, *The Challenge of Facts and Other Essays* (New Haven, Conn.: Yale University Press 1914) at 90: 'The millionaires are a product of natural selection, acting on the whole body of men to pick out those who meet the requirement of certain work to be done.'
197 A. Carnegie, *The Gospel of Wealth* (Cambridge, Mass.: Belknap Press, 1962 ed., E.C. Kirkland) at 35.

198 Ibid.
199 Parkin, supra, note 75, at 46.
200 See, for example, 'Bias and the Bequest,' *Globe and Mail*, 29 November 1982, 6 (editorial); L. Smith, 'A benefactor largely forgotten,' St Catharines *Standard*, 21 February 1983. See also 'A Sorry Anachronism,' Toronto *Star*, 12 August 1986 (editorial).
201 On the changing nature of racial discourse, see further F. Reeves, *British Racial Discourse* (Cambridge, U.K.: Cambridge University Press 1983), especially at ch. 6.
202 N. Christie and M. Gauvreau, *A Full-Orbed Christianity: The Protestant Churches and Social Welfare in Canada, 1900–1940* (Montreal: McGill-Queen's University Press 1996) at 19.
203 R.W. Leonard to R. Falconer, 24 February 1923, Willison Papers, box 25, 18335, National Archives of Canada.
204 *University of Manitoba Calender, 1924–1925* (Winnipeg: University of Manitoba 1924) at 220.
205 See, for example, James Darling McCall Scholarship; Charles Alexander Scholarship; Sir William Macdonald Scholarships; Babcock and Wilcox Ltd Scholarship (McGill University) (awards restricted to males); Ursuline College of Arts Scholarships (University of Western Ontario); Loan Scholarship Fund of the University Women's Club; the Fraser Cupin Home Economics Scholarship (University of Manitoba); Royal Victoria College Entrance Scholarships; Hannah Wilard Lyman Exhibition (McGill University) (awards restricted to females).
206 See, for example, 1851 Exhibition Scholarships; Daughters of the Empire Overseas Scholarships (restricted to British subjects); Medical Fellowships of the National Research Council (open to citizens of the United States and Canada); S. Ubukata Fund (University of Toronto) (restricted to Japanese students at the University of Toronto).
207 Supra, note 204, at 235.
208 Thomas Alexander Rowat Scholarship.

3: Leonard under Siege

1. See, for example, Toronto General Trust Corporation to R. Falconer, 26 March 1925, Falconer Papers, box 75, University of Toronto Archives.
2 Leonard Foundation File, Queen's University Archives.
3 J.C. Hopkins, ed., *Canadian Annual Review of Public Affairs for 1923* (Toronto: Canadian Review 1924) at 558. It was noted, however, that these figures were probably too low: ibid. Cf. P. Axelrod, *Making a Middle Class: Student Life in*

English Canada during the Thirties (Montreal: McGill-Queen's University Press 1990) at 27. Annual incomes among skilled and semi-skilled workers in Toronto around this period ranged from approximately $675 ('agricultural labourers') to $1,850 ('manufacturing employees'): Industrial Relations Section, School of Commerce and Administration, *The Economic Welfare of Canadian Employees (Bulletin #4)* (Kingston: Queen's University 1940) at 27. Cf. Dominion Bureau of Statistics, *Sixth Census of Canada, 1921* (Ottawa: F.A. Acland 1927) vol. 3, at xix–xx.

4 Dominion Bureau of Statistics, *Higher Education in Canada, 1936–1938* (Ottawa 1939) at 18–23. Funding in Britain was three times greater per student. In the United States there were twenty-eight times more awards than in Canada. See also Axelrod, supra, note 3, at 26; J. Chernick, 'National Scholarships' (1938) 1(2) Manitoba Arts Review 29.

5 Constitution, Leonard Foundation Association, article 2, Henry Marshall Tory Papers, University of Alberta Archives.

6 In the 1936 Leonard Foundation Association Bulletin, the rationale of the criteria was explained somewhat apologetically by Henry Cody: 'Colonel Leonard believed in the mission of the British Empire and the history of the Empire shows that it has a mission of service. For this reason, and not because he ruled out creed or colour, those who are of British race and Protestant faith are to be the recipients of the scholarships': 'Some Thoughts Gleaned from Dr. Cody's Address,' Leonard Foundation Association Bulletin, March 1936, at 2 [copy on file at the University of Alberta]. The University of Toronto benefited greatly from the Leonard Foundation Trust over the years. On Leonard's death, the university's Senate paid tribute to the Foundation. It was described as the greatest and most enduring of Colonel Leonard's benefactions, and the scholarships were said to be in a class comparable to the Rhodes scholarships: 'Resolution Adopted by the Senate of the University of Toronto on 13 February 1931,' Reuben Wells Leonard Papers, University of Toronto.

7 J.E. Kendle, *The Round Table Movement and Imperial Union* (Toronto: University of Toronto Press 1975) at 217–18.

8 This was the Halibut Treaty, entered into between Canada and the United States.

9 See, for example, *Cunningham & Attorney-General for British Columbia v. Tommey Homma & Attorney-General for Canada,* [1903] Appeal Cases 151 (Privy Council); *Union Colliery Co. of British Columbia v. Bryden,* [1899] Appeal Cases 580 (Privy Council).

10 See, for example, The Chinese Immigration Act, Statutes of Canada, 1923, ch. 38; *Quong-Wing v. The King* (1914) 49 Supreme Court Reports 440. See

further W.S. Tarnopolsky and W.F. Pentney, *Discrimination and the Law*, 2nd ed. (Toronto: Carswell 1985) ch. 1, passim.

11 I will not trace the developments leading up to the enactment of the Charter. On that topic, see further B. Elman, 'Altering the Judicial Mind and the Process of Constitution-Making in Canada' (1990) 28 Alberta Law Review 521.

12 This distinction between the nature of public and private conduct is examined in chapter 4.

13 *Applin* v. *Race Relations Board*, [1974] 2 All England Law Reports 73 (House of Lords) at 89 (*per* Lord Simon), referred to in the factum of Canada Trust in the first hearing of the *Leonard Foundation* case, at 8.

14 See further H.L. Molot, 'The Duty of Business to Serve the Public: Analogy to the Innkeeper's Obligation' (1968) 46 Canadian Bar Review 612.

15 A Scottish court had so held in *Rothfield* v. *North British Railway Co.*, 1920 Sessional Cases 805.

16 (1924) 55 Ontario Law Reports 349 (High Court).

17 Quoted in J.W. St.G. Walker, *'Race,' Rights, and the Law in the Supreme Court of Canada: Historical Case Studies* (Toronto and Waterloo: Osgoode Society and Wilfrid Laurier University Press 1997) at 150.

18 Supra, note 16, at 350 (per Lennox J.).

19 See further Walker, supra, note 17, at 150–1. In *Johnson* v. *Sparrow et al.* (1899) Q.R. 8 B.R. 379, a black patron was refused admission to a theatre after having purchased a ticket. He was awarded damages based on the breach of contract. The grounds for refusal were not regarded as germane. See also *Barnswell* v. *National Amusement* (1914) 21 British Columbia Reports 435. Cf. *Loew's Montreal Theatre* v. *Reynolds* (1919) 30 Quebec King's Bench 459.

20 [1940] Supreme Court Reports 139. A detailed account of this case can be found in Walker, supra, note 17, ch. 3, passim.

21 *Rogers* v. *Clarence Hotel*, [1940] 3 Dominion Law Reports 583 (British Columbia Court of Appeal). O'Halloran J.A. delivered a spirited dissenting opinion. The limits of the common law are also apparent in *King* v. *Barclay & Barclay's Motel* (1960) 31 Western Weekly Reports 451 (Alberta District Court).

22 For a critique of the decision, see B. Laskin, 'Tavern Refusing to Serve Negro – Discrimination' (1940) 18 Canadian Bar Review 314. In an editorial note in the Dominion Law Reports it was suggested that the case 'would appear to be the first authoritative decision on a highly contentious question and is the law's confirmation of the socially enforced inferiority of the coloured races': [1940] 1 Dominion Law Reports 81.

23 *Second UNESCO Statement on Race*, clause 9(b), reproduced in A. Montagu, *Statement on Race*, 3rd ed. (New York: Oxford University Press 1972) at 146.

24 See further R.B. Howe, 'Incrementalism and Human Rights Reform' (1993) 28(3) Journal of Canadian Studies 29.
25 Such as the Insurance Act, Statutes of Ontario 1932, ch. 24, s. 24, which prohibited discrimination on the grounds of race and religion. See generally Tarnopolsky and Pentney, supra, note 10, at ch. 2, passim.
26 Saskatchewan Bill of Rights Act, Statutes of Saskatchewan 1947, chapter 35.
27 The Fair Employment Practices Act, 1951, Statutes of Ontario, 1951, ch. 24 (which prohibited discrimination on the grounds of race, creed, colour, nationality, ancestry, or place of origin); the Female Employees Fair Remuneration Act, 1951, Statutes of Ontario 1951, ch. 26.
28 Statutes of Ontario 1954, ch. 28.
29 The Ontario Anti-Discrimination Commission Act, 1958, Statutes of Ontario 1958, ch. 70.
30 Ontario Human Rights Code, 1961–2, Statutes of Ontario 1961–2, ch. 93.
31 Ontario Human Rights Code, Revised Statutes of Ontario 1990, ch. H.19, s. 1. See also s. 2, which adds 'receipt of public assistance' as a prohibited ground for discrimination in the provision of accommodations, and s. 5, which prohibits discrimination in employment, *inter alia*, on the basis of a 'record of offences.'
32 Ontario Human Rights Code, Statutes of Ontario 1981, ch. 53 (see now Revised Statutes of Ontario 1990, ch. H.19). The preambles in the 1972 and 1981 versions of the code are similar: see Revised Statutes of Ontario 1970, ch. 318; Revised Statutes of Ontario 1980, ch. 340. The first reference to the Universal Declaration of Human Rights is found in the Fair Employment Practices Act, 1951, Statutes of Ontario 1951, ch. 24.
33 (1982) 3 Canadian Human Rights Reporter 9349 (Ontario Board of Inquiry). See also *Bloedel v. Board of Governors of the University of Calgary* (1980) 1 Canadian Human Rights Reporter D/25 (Alberta Board of Inquiry); *Hickling et al. v. Lanark, Leeds & Grenville County Roman Catholic Separate School Board*, unreported, 14 August 1986 (Ontario Board of Inquiry).
34 The history of the doctrine is traced in W.S.M. Knight, 'Public Policy in English Law' (1922) 38 Law Quarterly Review 207. See also P.H. Winfield, 'Public Policy in the English Common Law,' (1928) 42 Harvard Law Review 76; L.F. Moller, 'Some Aspects of the Doctrine of Public Policy' [1947] New Zealand Law Journal 91. The tag 'public policy' was probably first used in *Holman v. Johnson* (1775) 98 English Reports 1120.
35 See generally *Fender v. St. John Mildmay*, [1938] Appeal Cases 1 (House of Lords).
36 It has been suggested that new heads of public policy cannot now be recognized: see, for example, *Wadgery v. Fall*, [1926] 4 Dominion Law Reports 333

(Saskatchewan Court of Appeal) at 335; *Re Millar*, [1938] Supreme Court Reports 1. Cf. J. Phillips, 'Anti-Discrimination, Freedom of Property Disposition, and the Public Policy of Charitable Educational Trusts: A Comment on *Re Canada Trust Company and Ontario Human Rights Commission*' (1990) 9(3) Philanthropist 3, at 23–4.

37 See further K.J. Vandervelde, 'The New Property of the Nineteenth Century: The Development of the Modern Concept of Property,' (1980) 29 Buffalo Law Review 325. See also *Chesterfield* v. *Jannsen* (1751) 26 English Reports 191, in which Lord Hardwicke acknowledged that the doctrine of public policy embraced 'political arguments in the fullest sense of the word.'

38 This well-known metaphor was apparently first used by Mr Justice Burrough in *Richardson* v. *Mellish* (1824) 130 English Reports 294.

39 *Fender* v. *St. John Mildmay*, supra, note 35; *Re Millar*, supra, note 36; *Walkerville Brewing Co. Ltd.* v. *Mayrand*, [1929] 2 Dominion Law Reports 945 (Ontario court of Appeal).

40 See, for example, *Rodrigues* v. *Speyer Bros.*, [1919] Appeal Cases 59 (House of Lords) at 135–6 (per Lord Parmoor).

41 [1945] Ontario Reports 778 (Supreme Court).

42 The nature of covenants running with land and the rules governing them are discussed in B. Ziff, *Principles of Property Law*, 2nd ed. (Toronto: Carswell 1996) at 348ff.

43 Deed of Land, between the St Catharines Improvement Corp. Ltd. and Elizabeth Farster, 4 June 1920 [copy on file at the University of Alberta].

44 Discriminatory covenants had been before Ontario courts before, but the issue of whether these were invalid owing to the doctrine of public policy had never been extensively examined. In *Essex Real Estate Co. Ltd.* v. *Holmes* (1930) 37 Ontario Weekly Notes 392 (High Court) affirmed (1930) 38 Ontario Weekly Notes 69 (Court of Appeal), the covenant read as follows: '... the lands shall not be sold to or occupied by persons not of the Caucasian race nor to Europeans except such as are of the English-speaking countries and the French and the people of French descent.' It was held that the applicant, a Syrian, being of the Caucasian race, was not excluded from purchasing the land by this provision. Public policy was not raised. In *Re Bryers & Morris* (1931) 40 Ontario Weekly Notes 572 (High Court), the covenant read: '... none of the lands shall be used or occupied by, let or sold to negroes or Asiatics, Bulgarians, Austrians, Russians, Serbs, Roumanians, Turks, Armenians, whether British subjects or not, or foreign born Italians, Greeks or Jews.' The question of invalidity (as an undue restraint on alienation) was sidestepped on procedural grounds. In *Re McDougall & Waddell*, [1945] 2 Dominion Law Reports 244 (Ontario High Court), the clause read: 'the said lands ... shall not

at any time be sold to, let to or occupied by any person or persons other than Gentiles (non-Semitic) of European or British or Irish or Scottish racial origin.' It was held that this did not contravene the Racial Discrimination Act, Statutes of Ontario, 1944, ch. 51. The broader public policy argument was not addressed. Invalidity based on public policy arguably may explain a little-known 1911 British Columbia ruling. There, an application was brought to determine whether a covenant that prevented transfers to persons of Japanese or Chinese origin was valid. Hunter C.J. held that the covenant was inoperative and hence could not be registered. No reasons for judgment were given. See further H.S. Robinson, 'Limited Restraints on Alienation' (1950) 8 Advocate 250, at 251, where the short judgment is set out. Other examples of restrictive covenants can be found in Walker, supra, note 17, at 190–1, 398, note 35.

45 It was also argued that the registration of the deed contravened the Racial Discrimination Act, Statutes of Ontario 1944, ch. 51. That act had a narrow scope, prohibiting only the publication or display of representations expressing racial or religious discrimination. Although Mr Justice MacKay said that this argument had merit, it was not made a basis for the decision.

46 Supra, note 41, at 782–3.

47 'Blow to prejudice,' *Globe and Mail*, 2 November 1945, 6. See also G.R. Schmitt, 'Re Wren' (1946) 15 Fortnightly Law Journal 264; 'Covenant against Jew buying land illegal,' Toronto *Star*, 1 November 1945, 1; 'Anti-Semitic land-sale clause declared illegal,' *Globe and Mail*, 1 November 1945, 1. It was estimated that the decision could affect lands valued at $1 million in the city of Hamilton: 'Says $1,000,000 affected in Hamilton property,' Toronto *Star*, 1 November 1945, 1. The *Drummond Wren* case was followed by Mr Justice Barlow in an unreported Ontario decision in 1946: D.A.L. Smout, 'An Inquiry into the Law of Racial and Religious Restraints on Alienation' (1952) 30 Canadian Bar Review 863, at 869.

48 'Re Wren [1945] O.R. 778 – Contributed' (1946) 15 Fortnightly Law Journal 264. The author agreed with the outcome of the case on the basis that the covenant was too vague to be enforced.

49 Ibid.

50 [1948] Ontario Reports 579 (High Court) affirmed [1949] Ontario Reports 503 (Court of Appeal) reversed on other grounds [1951] Supreme Court Reports 64. The case is discussed in detail in Walker, supra, note 17, at ch. 4, passim.

51 [1949] Ontario Reports at 526.

52 Ibid. at 522–3.

53 Ibid. at 523.

54 'Protest ruling in racial case,' *Globe and Mail*, 11 June 1949, 4.
55 See, for example, 'The law should be changed,' Toronto *Star*, 13 June 1949, 6; *Star Weekly*, 27 August 1949.
56 'Should change law Rabbi Feinberg says as covenant upheld,' Toronto *Star*, 10 June 1949, 3.
57 Referred to in the *Star Weekly*, supra, note 55. See also Walker, supra, note 17, at 218 and the accompanying note.
58 'Tolerance and Law,' *Globe and Mail*, 11 June 1949.
59 Conveyancing and Law of Property Amendment Act, 1950, Statutes of Ontario, 1950, ch. 11, s. 1. See now Conveyancing and Law of Property Act, Revised Statutes of Ontario, 1990, chapter C.34, section 22. Manitoba followed the same course: An Act to Amend The Law of Property Act, Statutes of Manitoba, 1950 (1st Sess.), ch. 33, s. 1. See now Law of Property Act, Revised Statutes of Manitoba, 1987, s. 7, as amended.
60 In dissent, Locke J. expressed approval of the judgment of Robertson C.J.O.: [1951] S.C.R. at 80.
61 See *Blathwayt* v. *Cawley*, [1976] Appeal Cases 397 (House of Lords) where property was to be forfeited in the event of a recipient being or becoming a Roman Catholic. *Blathwayt* was followed in *In re Tepper's Will Trusts*, [1987] Chancery 358, where the relevant condition concerned adherence to, and marriage within, the Jewish faith. As to the law of Ireland on point, see A. Lyall, 'Human Rights and Conditional and Determinable Interests in Freeholds' (1987) 22 Irish Jurist (N.S.) 250.
62 The law following the *Leonard* case is discussed in chapter 4.
63 In *Re Kennedy*, [1950] Western Weekly Reports 151 (Manitoba King's Bench), a bequest was made subject to the condition precedent that the donee be 'married to a Protestant of good repute.' The court noted that it was not seriously contended by counsel that this condition, if sufficiently certain, could be found to be void on any other ground: ibid. at 160.
64 See *Blathwayt* v. *Cawley*, supra, note 61, at 429 (per Lord Chelsea).
65 See further P. Butt, 'Testamentary Conditions in Restraint of Marriage' (1977) 8 Sydney Law Review 400; Z. Cowen, 'Religious Restraints in Wills' (1944) 17 Australian Law Journal 374; H.R. Hahlo, 'Jewish Faith and Race Clauses in Wills' (1950) 67 South African Law Journal 231.
66 (1956) 6 Dominion Law Reports (2d) 615 (British Columbia Supreme Court).
67 Ibid. at 619 (per McInnes J.). McInnes J. relied on the authorities concerning the promotion of separation of parent and child. As to gifts that induce spousal separation, see *Re Johnson's Will Trusts*, [1967] Chancery 387.
68 The protection of family integrity has supported a second type of collateral attack on discriminatory gifts. Gifts that seek to influence parental responsi-

bilities have been held to contravene public policy. That principle has been applied where the effect of the gift is to persuade parents, by means of a conditional legacy, to follow a specified religious creed. The case law pertaining to this principle, and doubts as to its continued validity, are presented in *Blathwayt* v. *Baron Cawley*, supra, note 61.

69 See further D.W.M. Waters, *The Law of Trusts in Canada*, 2nd ed. (Toronto: Carswell 1984) at 516ff.
70 Ibid. at 611ff.
71 [1947] 1 Chancery 183.
72 Ibid. at 168.
73 [1966] Chancery 191.
74 See the text accompanying note 127, infra.
75 Supra, note 73, at 206.
76 See further P. Lamek, 'Case Comment on *Re Lysaght*' (1966) 4 Osgoode Hall Law Journal 113; F.H. Newark, 'Trustees Who Dislike the Terms of the Trust' (1966) 17 Northern Ireland Legal Quarterly 123. The reasoning on the question of the dominant, or general, charitable intent seems facile. I regard the assumptions drawn about the settlor's intent to be improbable: See also Phillips, supra, note 36, at 20. Supportive of the ultimate result, neither Lamek nor Newark criticize this aspect of the judgment.
77 Quoted in Walker, supra, note 17, at 244.
78 Quoted in 'MPP raps foundation for racial prejudice,' *Globe and Mail*, 21 February 1956, 8. Sid Blum, secretary of the Toronto Joint Labour Committee for Human Rights, called on the administrator of the trust to seek a way to amend it.
79 H. Allen, 'Won't accept racial clauses – Bissell' , Toronto *Telegram*, 4 February 1960, 14.
80 'Racial bias charged in scholarships,' Toronto *Telegram*, 7 September 1961. In 1967 James Anderson, an anthropologist at the University of Toronto who was conducting research on attitudes toward race, 'shocked his audience' when he read the requirements for the Leonard Foundation scholarship during a talk presented to the World Federalists of Canada: 'Study finds racial, religious bias in Metro youth,' Toronto *Star*, 11 May 1967.
81 F.C. James to city clerk, city of Calgary, 14 September 1961, City Clerk's Office, box 586, file 3947, City of Calgary Archives.
82 H. Cassels to D.V. LePan, 18 May 1965, Registrar's Office, University College, University of Toronto.
83 In 1986 the University of Toronto followed the same approach when a bequest under the will of former Ontario Premier G. Howard Ferguson vested in University College. That gift provided for a scholarship for stu-

dents of 'Anglo-Saxon stock' who lived within a twenty-four kilometre radius of the city of Toronto. An order was obtained deleting the condition as to race.
84 *Re Metcalfe*, [1972] 3 Ontario Reports 598 (High Court). The university did not refer to gender discrimination as a basis for its decision to disclaim: see ibid. at 599.
85 'Male only scholarship is rejected,' *Globe and Mail*, 18 January 1979, 10. In 1972 Queen's University brought an application in relation to a scholarship endowed by James H. Rattray. Under the gift, no student who was a 'Communist, Socialist or Fellow Traveller' could receive an award. It was held that this language was void for uncertainty: *Re Rattray* (1974) 44 Dominion Law Reports (3d) 533 (Ontario Court of Appeal) affirming (1973) 38 Dominion Law Reports (3d) 321 (High Court).
86 A.M. Laverty to F.A. Wansbrough, 18 February 1969. Leonard Foundation Records, Queen's University Secretariat. The resignation was accepted: F.A. Wansbrough to A.M. Laverty, 26 February 1969, ibid.
87 J.J. Deutsch to F.A. Wansbrough, 18 February 1969, ibid.
88 'Terms of Award of Scholarships, Fellowships and Bursaries within the Gift of Queen's University,' Unpublished Report (1969), Queen's University Secretariat.
89 D.W. Lang to J.C. MacLeod, 26 November 1982, Motion Record at 90.
90 Ontario Human Rights Code, Revised Statutes of Ontario 1980, ch. 340, s. 2(1).
91 Ontario Human Rights Code, Statutes of Ontario 1981, ch. 53, s. 1.
92 'Rights board to study bursary,' Toronto *Star*, 10 October 1982, A6.
93 *Hansard, Legislative Assembly of Ontario*, 2nd. Sess., 32 Parl., 22 November 1982, at 5327.
94 Ibid.
95 Ibid. at 5328.
96 J. Walters, 'Private scholarship fund for WASPs doesn't faze Ramsay,' London *Free Press*, 24 November 1982, C3.
97 'Human rights are not for WASPs,' Orillia *Packet and Times*, 6 December 1982, 4. 'When has being part of an ethnic majority become something evil or illegal in this country?': 'Restricted scholarships,' Sault Ste Marie *Star*, 25 November 1982. See also H.F. Barrett, *Globe and Mail*, 1 December 1982, 7 (letter).
98 C. Hoy, 'A discriminating opinion,' Toronto *Sun*, 23 November 1982; C. Hoy, 'WASPs also have rights,' Toronto *Sun*, December, 1982; C. Hoy, 'Pretentious rights code,' Toronto *Sun*, 12 December 1982; C. Hoy, 'Rights turn into wrongs,' Toronto *Sun*, 9 November 1982.
99 'Human wrongs,' Toronto *Sun*, 1 November 1982.

100 Reported in K. Cox, 'Board probing "white race" scholarship,' *Globe and Mail*, 23 October 1982, 1.
101 D.M. Rayside, 'Moral courage,' *Globe and Mail*, 29 October 1982 (letter). For a reply to Rayside, see M. Stanley, 'WASPs need not apply,' *Globe and Mail*, 8 November 1982 (letter).
102 Quoted in M. Doyle, 'School grants for white protestants only,' *Montreal Gazette*, 9 April 1985, A-3.
103 J.C. MacLeod to B. Purcell, 4 February 1986, Motion Record, at 83.
104 Rev. E.W. Scott to G.E. Galbraith, Canada Trust, 29 April 1986, Motion Record, 92, at 93.
105 See further *Hansard, Legislative Assembly of Ontario*, 2nd Sess., 33rd Parl., Wednesday, 28 May 1986, 937–41.
106 By Lindsay Scotten, Toronto *Star*, 9 August 1986.
107 'A sorry anachronism,' Toronto *Star*, 12 August 1986.
108 L. Scotten, 'Woman denied whites-only bursary still feels the hurt,' Toronto *Star*, 16 August 1986, A3. Ms. Goto fell within the preferred classes because her father had served in Canadian army intelligence during the Second World War. She was interviewed by a member of the General Committee: 'I asked the interviewer whether or not I would even be considered, because I'm Japanese. The answer was that I should complete the application, that I might be considered because I'm not black!' She was turned down on the stated ground that her family's income was too high: ibid.
109 'Act now on racist funding: Ubale,' Toronto *Sun*, 10 August 1986.
110 'Shameful discrimination in bursaries,' *Canadian Churchman*, November 1985, 4; 'Update Leonard trust,' *The Anglican*, September 1986, 4.
111 See W. Cooke, 'No favors for Protestant men?' *Canadian Churchman*, January 1986, 5 (letter). See also J. Lynn, 'Let people bequeath to whom they choose,' Toronto *Star*, 18 August 1986, A14 (letter); M. Howell, 'Isn't U. of T.'s bursary for S. Africa racist?' 19 August 1986 (letter); R. Huizinga, 'Ban all discrimination in bursaries, awards,' Toronto *Star*, 16 August 1986, B3 (letter); P.M. Ryan, 'What's wrong with whites-only bursary?' Toronto *Star*, 21 August 1986, A12 (letter).
112 C. Hoy, 'Ill will over last will,' Toronto *Sun*, 12 August 1986.
113 Clause 9 of the trust deed contemplates such action and allows money to be taken from the corpus of the trust to cover the costs of such a proceeding. However, clause 9 also requires that the judge hearing the application meet the criteria for eligibility for membership on the General Committee. In bringing the motion, the trustees did not purport to act under the authority of this provision, but rather under section 60 of the Trustee Act (see now Revised Statutes of Ontario, 1990, ch. T.23) and by virtue of the court's

inherent jurisdiction to supervise charitable trusts. In addition, the question of whether the trial and appellate courts fell within the limitations imposed by clause 9 was never raised (Court of Appeal decision, infra, note 129, at 329). Nor was the validity of such a restriction specifically addressed, though it is (and was) of no effect.

114 See further *Re Rattray*, supra, note 85.
115 The residual clause is discussed in chapter 1.
116 Nine awards listed in the affidavit did not contain meaningful discriminatory restrictions. Some of these were merely endowed by certain religious or ethnic groups. A number of awards indicated that *preference* should be given to a certain class of applicants. These were treated in the same fashion as fully exclusionary restrictions in the affidavit and in the above chart.
117 *Re Canada Trust Co. & Ontario Human Rights Commission* (1987) 42 Dominion Law Reports (4th) 263 (Ontario High Court) [referred to below as *Leonard (No. 1)*].
118 The Ontario Human Rights Commission had pressed a preliminary objection. The commission argued that the court should decline to answer questions relating to the meaning and scope of the Human Rights Code on the basis that such matters fell, in the first instance, within the jurisdiction of the commission (and not the courts). McKeown J. rejected this argument. His ruling on this point was upheld on appeal: see infra, note 129, at 325–6 and 344–6. McKeown J. also held that the terms of the trust did not fail for uncertainty. Applying *Re Selby's Will Trusts*, [1966] 1 Weekly Law Reports 43 (Chancery Division), it was held that the terms were sufficiently precise to allow the General Committee to identify at least some persons who met the criteria. This is all that the law requires in this context. This conclusion was endorsed by Tarnopolsky J.A. on appeal (infra, note 129, at 346–8) but the uncertainty issue was not addressed in the majority judgment.
119 See the cases cited in note 33, supra.
120 Supra, note 117, at 280.
121 Earlier in the judgment, three examples were drawn from the Middleton affidavit: the Wilfrid Laurier Memorial Prizes, awarded at the University of Western Ontario only to English-speaking students or children of naturalized British parents; the Amouney Jassie Memorial Award at the University of Windsor, available to the children of members of the Windsor Islamic Association; and the Dick Cousins Bursary, at Western, which is available to deserving Roman Catholic student-teachers: ibid. at 272.
122 See *Commissioners of Inland Revenue* v. *Raphael et al.*, [1935] Appeal Cases 96 (House of Lords) and *Re McKellar*, [1972] 3 Ontario Reports 16 (High Court) affirmed 3 Ontario Reports 178n (Court of Appeal), both of which are

referred to in *Leonard (No. 1)*, supra, note 117, at 275–6. See also E. Beal, *Cardinal Rules of Legal Interpretation* (Toronto: Carswell 1924) at 184.
123 See *Mackenzie et al. v. Duke of Devonshire*, [1896] Appeal Cases 400 (House of Lords) referred to in *Leonard (No. 1)*, supra, note 117, at 275 and 277.
124 See *Ex parte Dawes* (1886) 17 Queen's Bench Division 275, referred to in *Leonard (No. 1)*, supra, note 117, at 276.
125 Supra, note 117, at 278.
126 See the text accompanying notes 38 to 40, supra.
127 Supra, note 75.
128 For a detailed criticism of the decision, see J.C. Shepherd, 'When the Common Law Fails' (1987) 9 Estates & Trusts Journal 117.
129 *Re Canada Trust Co. & Ontario Human Rights Commission* (1990) 69 Dominion Law Reports (4th) 321 (Court of Appeal) [referred to below as *Leonard (No. 2)*].
130 The presence of Osler J. on the panel is notable. The Oslers had been a prominent family in Toronto at least from the time of the family patriarch, the Anglican minister Reverend Featherstone Lake Osler (1805–95). Over the years, Reuben Wells Leonard had dealings with several members of that family. Henry S. Osler (1862–1933) acted for Leonard in the promotion of Coniagas Mines in 1906, preparing the company prospectus and being the first (nominal) subscriber. Over the next several years the company was involved in two legal disputes that were ultimately resolved at the Court of Appeal level. In both instances, Featherstone Osler, Jr (1838–1924) sat as a member of the court. Additionally, Sir Edmund Osler (1845–1924) served as a member of the Board of Governors at the University of Toronto along with Reuben Leonard. It is, therefore, ironic that a member of the Osler family would preside over the fate of the Foundation.
131 *Leonard (No. 2)*, supra, note 129, at 334.
132 Ibid.
133 Ibid. at 335.
134 Ibid.
135 See the discussion earlier in this chapter, under 'The Ascendancy of Human Rights Protections prior to the *Leonard* case,' Tarnopolsky J.A. discounted the relevance of English law (especially the decision in *Re Lysaght*, supra, note 73). That decision was rendered before the introduction of race relations legislation in England. Moreover, it was observed that the English statute does not contain a prohibition against discrimination based on religion: *Leonard (No.2)*, supra, note 129, at 348.
136 Supra, note 129, at 353, citing *Andrews v. Law Society of British Columbia*, [1989] 1 Supreme Court Reports 143.

137 See Certificates of Assessment of Costs, issued 16 August 1988 (High Court); Certificates of Assessment of Costs, issued 27 May 1991 (Court of Appeal). The Ontario Human Rights Commission did not seek reimbursement for costs.

4: After *Leonard*

1 The Foundation advises potential applicants that students whose family's gross total income exceeds a stated amount (it was $40,000 in 1996) are unlikely to be successful. In 1996 the committee on scholarships was asked to review the current policies relating to the size of awards and the relevance of academic achievement. As part of the process of review, a survey was conducted among Leonard scholars who had received a renewal of their awards. Of the forty-two questionnaires that were sent out, thirty-five were returned. Three questions were posed: 1) 'Do you agree that students who must set up a second residence in order to attend university should receive a greater amount than those who are able to stay at the family home?' (yes: thirty-two; no: three); 2) 'Should the amount of the awards remain as they are and benefit about 140 students each year?' (yes: thirty-two; no: three) 3) Do you agree with the present practice of making awards without ranking academic achievement levels? (yes: twenty-six; no: nine). The committee on scholarships proposed that the criteria and value of the awards not be changed; this recommendation was accepted by the General Committee.
2 R.W. Leonard, 'Retiring President's Address' (1920) 3 Engineering Journal 78 [emphasis added].
3 *Re Canada Trust & Ontario Human Rights Commission* (1987) 42 Dominion Law Reports (4th) 263 (Ontario High Court)[referred to as *Leonard (No. 1)*] at 278.
4 *Re Canada Trust & Ontario Human Rights Commission* (1990) 69 Dominion Law Reports (4th) 321 (Ontario Court of Appeal) [referred to as *Leonard (No. 2)*] at 334–5 [emphasis added].
5 The evidence on the tenor of public opinion relied upon in the Court of Appeal was drawn from the affidavit of Jack MacLeod, the trust officer. MacLeod deposed that he was aware of some thirty articles, letters-to-the-editor, and so on that had appeared since 1975 concerning the trust, and that these were generally critical of the trust. However, this is not an accurate depiction of the public discourse, especially in the early 1980s. I have collected eight editorials critical of the action being taken against the Leonard Foundation (five of which were written by columnist Claire Hoy of the Toronto *Sun*) and eight letters-to-the-editor that adopt the same position (two by Harry F. Barrett of the Canadian Association for Free Expression)

(making 16 in all). On the other side of the debate, I am aware of four editorials and three letters in favour of changing the terms of the trust. There were also five articles that had an anti-Foundation slant (twelve in all).

6 I will not discuss at length the ancillary holdings in the case. In brief, I agree with the findings that the trust was not void for uncertainty, and that the court had jurisdiction to rule on the applicability of the Ontario Human Rights Code. I also agree that the doctrine of *cy-près* was applicable. Contrary to the analysis of Tarnopolsky J.A. (*Leonard (No.2)*, supra, note 129, at 354–5), it is only when the trust is *initially* impracticable or impossible that a general charitable intent must be found in order to invoke the doctrine. Once the trust has been established, all that need be shown is that the trust can continue as a valid charitable instrument after the introduction of the *cy-près* revisions. That was the case here. See further L.A. Turnbull, 'Case Comment: Canada Trust Co. v. Ontario (Human Rights Commission)' (1991) 38 Estates and Trusts Reports 47.

7 See the summary of the Middleton Affidavit in chapter 3.

8 See also Louis Riel Scholarship; National Aboriginal Achievement Awards, open to students of Inuit, Metis, or First Nations ancestry; CN Native Education Awards; Harry A. and Frances Lepofsky Friedman Award, open to Aboriginal and Inuit students at the University of Alberta; Metis Heritage Association Ted Trindell Memorial Scholarship, open to Metis and non-status Indians; Native Women's Association of Canada Awards, open to First Nations and Metis women; Petro-Canada Education Awards for Native Students; Royal Bank Native Student Awards.

9 See also Indo-Canada Cultural Association Bursary, available to a student at the University of Saskatchewan who has either a parent or parents from India or parents of Indo-Canadian ancestry; the Canadian Italian Business and Professional Men's Association, open to students of Italian origin or descent; Lebanese-Syrian-Canadian Association Scholarships, available to students of Lebanese-Syrian descent. Polish Combatants R.C.L. Branch 219 Silver Jubilee Scholarship, for students of Polish ancestry at Lakehead University; Knights of Kaleva Entrance Awards, available at Lakehead for students of Finnish heritage; Jewish Community of Thunder Bay Shomayim Congregation Silver Jubilee Award, available at Lakehead for students of Jewish heritage.

10 See also Alumnae Entrance Scholarships for female students at the University of New Brunswick; Margaret Archibald Memorial Entrance Scholarship at the Technical University of Nova Scotia, under which preference is to be given to women pursuing a career in engineering; Rhea Bray Memorial Bursary, open to women students at the University of Windsor who are resi-

Notes to pages 141–2   229

dents of Essex County; Chatelaine Magazine Entrance Scholarship for Women in Automotive Business at Georgian College; CN Scholarship Program for Women.

11 See also Mature Students Entrance Scholarships, tenable at Concordia University.

12 See also Canadian National Institute for the Blind Awards, open to registered blind or visually impaired students; City of Ottawa Scholarship for Disabled Students.

13 However, the Charter permits derogations from that principle where the governmental measure is shown to impose a reasonable limitation on the basal equality right. In addition, the Charter contemplates that affirmative action may be permissible. Affirmative action is discussed again below, under 'Contested Meanings of Equality,' infra.

14 Note, however, that it has been held that a university's mandatory retirement policy is not reviewable under the Charter: *McKinney* v. *University of Guelph*, [1990] 3 Supreme Court Reports 229. In contrast, the operations of a government-controlled community college were held to be subject to the Charter in *Douglas/Kwantlen Faculty Association* v. *Douglas College*, [1990] 3 Supreme Court Reports 570.

15 As to the effect of an appellate decision that reverses a lower court decision, on different grounds, on the precedential value of the initial decision, see R.W.M. Dias, *Jurisprudence*, 5th ed. (London: Butterworths 1985) at 144–5. After reviewing the authorities, the author concludes that a subsequent court has a good deal of freedom as to how it will treat the prior holding.

16 Ontario Human Rights Commission, *Policy Statement with Respect to Exclusionary Scholarships* (1991).

17 Currently in Ontario, those grounds are as follows: race, ancestry, place of origin, colour, ethnic origin, citizenship, creed, sex, sexual orientation, age, marital status, family status or handicap: Ontario Human Rights Code, Revised Statutes of Ontario, 1990, ch. H.19, s. 1.

18 A third exemption relates to discrimination on the ground of family status. Where an educational subsidy is made available by an employer to employees and their families, the commission views this as acceptable. This position is said to be consistent with the code, which permits an employer to grant or withhold employment or advancement in employment to a family member of a present employer under paragraph 24(1)(d) of the current code: see supra, note 16, at 4–5.

19 Ibid. at 3.

20 Consider, for example, the complaint addressed in *Gregory* v. *Donauschwaben Park Waldheim Inc.* (1990) 13 Canadian Human Rights Reporter D/505

(Ontario Board of Inquiry). The case involved an allegation that the owners of a recreational park contravened the code by restricting the sale of cottages in the park to persons of German origin. The exemption contained in section 18 was found to be applicable. A broad range of social and cultural activities were undertaken in the park. Moreover, it was shown that a majority of the cottage owners participated in these activities. Hence, it was not merely a rural subdivision dressed up to look like a cultural or ethnic club (which would not fall within the exemption). See also *Martinie* v. *Italian Society of Port Arthur* (1995) 24 Canadian Human Rights Reporter D/169 (Ontario Board of Inquiry), where it was held that a club established for use by men of Italian descent was permitted to exclude women.

21 Supra, note 16, at 4.
22 *Oliver* v. *City of Hamilton* (1995) 26 Municipal Planning Law Reports (2d) 278 (Ontario Board of Inquiry).
23 *Baptiste* v. *Napanee & District Rod & Gun Club* (1993) 19 Canadian Human Rights Reporter D/246 (Ontario Board of Inquiry).
24 See, for example, *Floyd* v. *Canada (Employment & Immigration Commission)* (1993) 20 Canadian Human Rights Reporter D/381 (Canadian Human Rights Tribunal).
25 See, for example, *Co-operators General Insurance Co.* v. *Alberta (Human Rights Commission)* (1993) 107 Dominion Law Reports (4th) 298 (Alberta Court of Appeal), leave to appeal to the Supreme Court of Canada refused: 112 Dominion Law Reports (4th) vii.
26 See also J.C. Shepherd, 'When the Common Law Fails' (1987) 9 Estates and Trusts Journal 117, at 125–6.
27 One of the points argued in the case was that 'public policy' should be ascertained as at the time that the trust was created (1923), not as at the date of the hearings (1987, 1990). It seems clear that, had this earlier reference point been adopted, the trust would have been upheld. McKeown J. opted for the latter date. The Court of Appeal took the same approach, as do other Canadian judgments that apply the doctrine. This means that a trust, apparently valid when first created, may cease to be so as times change. Such an approach is not problem-free, since it has a retrospective dimension. The trust, created on the faith of the law as it then stood, is later undone. It is just such a concern that informed Ontario's treatment of racially restrictive covenants in 1950. There, it will be recalled, such covenants were declared by statute to be unlawful (see 'Documentary Discrimination' in chapter 3). But the 1950 act had prospective effect only; existing covenants were unaffected by the measure. Despite this, the approach taken in the *Leonard* case seems correct. First, change is endemic to the law. It is not uncommon for judicial rulings to

unsettle long-established practices, as occurred here. Second, it is important that public policy play a vibrant, curative role. In other words, it is doubtful whether modern-day courts should be required to enforce trust arrangements that are now regarded as repugnant. This reforming function is especially important in the context of charitable trusts, since they may last in perpetuity. Moreover, the retrospective application of the law is minimal in a case such as *Leonard*. It is true that the court is imposing a standard not in existence at the time of the Foundation's creation. However, the impact of the ruling is otherwise purely prospective. The earlier actions of the trustees were not declared to be invalid; no past conduct had now to be undone or rectified.

28 (1996) 139 Dominion Law Reports (4th) 746 (S.C.T.D., Chambers).
29 University Act, Revised Statutes of Prince Edward Island, 1988, ch. U-4, ss. 3(1) and paragraph 4(f).
30 See the earlier discussion of this doctrine in chapter 3.
31 The scholarships are, respectively, the St Dunstan's University Board of Governor's Scholarship, the Rogers-Cairns Scholarships, and the Ivan and Blanche Darrach Bursary.
32 Supra, note 28, at 751 (per MacDonald C.J.T.D.).
33 An order was issued directing the executors to find a suitable trustee to replace the university and to seek a further order approving that selection.
34 See further P. Fitzpatrick, 'Racism and the Innocence of Law' (1987) 14 Journal of Law & Society 119.
35 International Convention on the Elimination of All Forms of Racial Discrimination, A/RES/2106/a(XX), article 2.
36 See text accompanying note 4, supra.
37 For a more extensive analysis of these justifications for private property, see B. Ziff, *Principles of Property Law*, 2nd ed. (Toronto: Carswell 1996) at 8–37. See also J.W. Harris, *Property and Justice* (Oxford: Clarendon Press 1996).
38 See further F.E. Olsen, 'The Family and the Market: A Study of Ideology and Legal Reform,' (1982–3) 96 Harvard Law Review 1497; S.B. Boyd, 'Challenging the Public/Private Divide: An Overview,' in S.B. Boyd, ed., *Challenging the Public/Private Divide: Feminism, Law and Public Policy* (Toronto: University of Toronto Press 1997).
39 J.C. MacLeod to B. Purcell, 4 February 1986, Motion Record, at 83. Likewise, the pre-1986 application forms describe the Leonard Foundation as 'a private Foundation established in 1916 by the late Colonel Reuben Wells Leonard 1860–1930.'
40 (1996) 28 Ontario Reports (3d) 496 (Court of Appeal). Leave to appeal to the Supreme Court of Canada was refused, 12 December 1996.

41 *Fox* v. *Fox Estate* (1994) 5 Estates and Trusts Reports (2d) 174 (Ontario Court (General Division)).
42 Supra, note 40, at 501–2
43 Ibid. at 502. See also *Re Murley Estate* (1995) 405 Atlantic Province Reports 271 (Newfoundland Supreme Court, Trial Division) at 274.
44 On the protean nature of the concept of equality, see generally P. Westen, *Speaking of Equality: An Analysis of the Rhetorical Force of 'Equality' in Moral and Legal Discourse* (Princeton, N.J.: Princeton University Press 1990); J.R. Pennock and J.W. Chapman, eds., *Nomos IX: Equality* (New York: Atherton Press 1967); A. Gutmann, *Liberal Equality* (Cambridge, U.K.: Cambridge University Press 1980).
45 This term is taken from S. Fish, *There's No Such Thing as Free Speech and It's a Good Thing Too* (New York: Oxford University Press 1994) at 11.
46 Canadian Charter of Rights and Freedoms, ss. 15(2).
47 Ontario Human Rights Code, Revised Statutes of Ontario, 1990, ch. H.23, s. 14. See further C. Sheppard, *Study Paper on Litigating the Relationship Between Equity and Equality* (Toronto: Ontario Law Reform Commission 1993). See also M.A. Drumbl and J.D.R. Craig, 'Affirmative Action in Question: A Coherent Theory of Section 15(2)' (1997) 4 Review of Constitutional Studies 80.
48 See, for example, M. Loney, *The Pursuit of Division: Race, Gender and Preferential Hiring in Canada* (Montreal: McGill-Queen's University Press 1998).
49 As to the case law concerning affirmative action under human rights law, see generally R.W. Zinn and P.R. Brethour, *The Law of Human Rights in Canada* (Aurora, Ont.: Canada Law Book, looseleaf) at Part 15:30.
50 [1966] Chancery 191.
51 See Sex Discrimination Act, 1975, ch. 65, s. 78, which sets out the procedures for deleting gender discrimination in trusts.
52 Race Relations Act, 1968, ch. 71, s. 9.
53 Race Relations Act, 1976, ch. 74, s. 34.
54 Section 43.
55 The Equal Protection Clause, the 14th Amendment to the United States Constitution, provides that 'no State shall ... deny to any person within its jurisdiction the equal protection of the laws.'
56 *Shelley* v. *Kraemer*, 334 United States Reports 1 (1948). As to the use of the equality protections to abridge property rights, see further *Pennsylvania et al.* v. *Board of Directors of City Trusts of the City of Philadelphia*, 353 United States Reports 230 (1957); *Sweet Briar Institute* v. *Button*, 280 Federal Supplement 312 (United States District Court, Virginia, 1967); *Evans* v. *Newton*, 382 United States Reports 296 (1966); Cf. *Evans* v. *Abney*, 396 United States Reports 435

(1970); *Mills* v. *Philadelphia Acting Through Board of City Trustees*, 144 Atlantic Reporter 2d 728 (1958).

57 See further 'Validity and Effect of Gift for Charitable Purposes Which Excludes Otherwise Qualified Beneficiaries Because of Their Race or Religion,' (1969) 25 American Law Reports 3d 736; 'Validity of charitable gift or trust containing gender restrictions on beneficiaries,' (1991) 90 American Law Reports 4th 836.

58 See, for example, *Shapiro* v. *Columbia Union National Bank and Trust Co.*, 576 South Western Reporter 2d 310, certiorari denied 444 United States Reports 831 (1978).

59 See further *In re Kempf's Will*, 297 New York Supplement 307, affirmed 16 North Eastern Reporter 2d 123 (1938).

60 See, for example, *Howard Saving Institution* v. *Peep*, 170 Atlantic Reporter 2d 39 (New Jersey Supreme Court, 1961). *Cy-près* was applied on the ground of impracticality in *Coffee* v. *William Marsh Rice University*, 408 South Western Reporter 2d 269 (Texas Court of Appeals, 1966), and in *Re Estate of Hawley*, 223 NYS2d 803 (1961). This is the same as the approach taken in the English case of *Re Lysaght*, [1966] Chancery 191, discussed in chapter 3. Exceptionally, the uncertainty of the trust terms has been used as a basis for removing discriminatory restrictions. Two such cases, decided shortly after the American Civil War, involved gifts to blacks: *Needles* v. *Martin*, 33 Md. 609 (trust for the education of 'free coloured persons'); *Grimes' Executors* v. *Martin*, 35 Ind. 198 (1871) (trust for the education of 'coloured children').

61 It should be noted that a shadow of doubt has been cast over the validity of private scholarship programs (that is, those that are exempt from scrutiny on constitutional grounds). In *Bob Jones University* v. *United States*, 461 United States Reports 574 (1983), an issue arose as to whether a private educational institution with a discriminatory admissions policy could claim certain federal tax exemptions. The United States Supreme Court held that, in order to fit within the tax exemptions, the institution had to confer a public benefit, and that racially discriminatory private schools violate fundamental public policy and so do not meet that standard. However, the Supreme Court did not go so far as to hold that discriminatory charitable trusts were void. Nor did the court purport to affect the functioning of the university.

62 The literature on the American law concerning affirmative action is extensive. Two helpful offerings are: N. Capaldi, 'The Liberal Paradigm in Affirmative Action Law,' (1998) 43 Loyola Law Review 525; 'Symposium, Affirmative Action: Diversity of Opinions,' (1997) 68 University of Colorado Law Review 833.

63 See *Shaw et al. v. Reno et al.*, 113 Supreme Court Reporter 2816 (1993). A less rigorous standard has been applied to gender-based discrimination. The state action must have an 'exceedingly persuasive justification.' Moreover, it must be shown that the action advances important government objectives and is substantially related to the achievement of those objectives: *United States v. Virginia et al.*, 518 United States Reports 515 (1996).
64 See further Y. Garfield, 'Squaring Affirmative Action Policies with Judicial Guidelines: A Model for the Twenty-First Century,' (1996) 22 Journal of College & University Law 895.
65 38 F.3d 147 (4th Cir. 1994) certiorari denied 115 S.Ct. 2001 (1995). See further R. Wells and J. Strope, 'The Podberesky Case and Race-Based Financial Aid,' (1996) 26 Journal of Student Financial Aid 33; Editorial, 'Set scholarship standard,' *The Oregonian*, 5 April 1995, B10.
66 The decision has placed in jeopardy the validity of hundreds of affirmative action scholarships in the United States. Included among these is the Leslie V. Forte Scholarship, established at Northern Virginia Community College by private donors in honour of the college's first black English professor. It is available only to minority students. Following the *Podberesky* decision, a white student at the college filed a complaint with the United States Department of Education. After conducting a review, the department's Office of Civil Rights concluded that the Forte awards contravened its policy on race-based aid (which is informed by the office's understanding of the case law) and the *Podberesky* ruling. The Forte awards were then suspended. See further P. Healy, 'Education Department Sends Strong Warning on Race-Exclusive Scholarships,' Chronicle of Higher Education, 31 October 1997, A47.

Epilogue

1 C. Gillis, 'Shy philanthropist made no waves in the class of "79,"' Edmonton Journal, 5 April 1997, A1.
2 C. Friesen, 'No outcry over scholarships for Chinese students at U,' Edmonton Journal, 12 April 1997, A15 (letter). Letters in support of the Chan gift followed: E. Johnson, 'Award conditions common,' Edmonton Journal, 16 April 1997, A13 (letter); A. Chu, 'All awards discriminate,' Edmonton Journal, 19 April 1997, A15 (letter); K. Schiltroth, 'Improving calibre of students,' Edmonton Journal, 21 April 1997, A11 (letter).
3 See, for example, T.R. Machan, *Generosity: Virtue in Civil Society* (Washington, D.C.: Cato 1998), where it is argued that the welfare state erodes the concept of private property and inhibits acts of kindness and generosity. See also

G. Himmelfarb, *The De-Moralization of Society: From Victorian Virtues to Modern Values* (New York: Vintage Books 1994).

4 See further M. Horn, *Academic Freedom in Canada: A History* (Toronto: University of Toronto Press 1999) ch. 12, passim.

5 See further P. Knapp et al., *The Assault on Equality* (Westport, Conn.: Praeger 1996).

6 N. Stepan, *The Idea of Race in Science: Great Britain 1800–1960* (London: Macmillan 1982); M. Kohn, *The Race Gallery: The Return of Race Science* (London: Jonathan Cape 1995). See also K. Malik, *The Meaning of Race: Race, History and Culture in Western Society* (New York: New York University Press 1996); E. Barkan, *The Retreat of Scientific Racism: Changing Concepts of Race in Britain and the United States Between the World Wars* (Cambridge, U.K.: Cambridge University Press 1992).

7 A.R. Jensen, 'How Much Can We Boost IQ and Scholastic Achievement?' (1969) 33 Harvard Educational Review 1.

8 R.J. Herrnstein and C. Murray, *The Bell Curve: Intelligence and Class Structure in American Life* (New York: Free Press 1994).

9 Rushton found as follows: 'Across time, country, and circumstance, African descended people show similarities that differentiate them from Caucasoids who, in turn, show similarities differentiating them from Orientals ... The racial gradient of Oriental-white-black occurs on multifariously complex dimensions. From brain size, intelligence, and personality to law abidingness, social organization, and reproductive morphology, Africans and Asians average at opposite ends of the continuum, with Caucasian populations falling intermediately': J.P. Rushton, *Race, Evolution, and Behavior: A Life History Perspective* (New Brunswick, N.J., Transaction Publishers 1995) at 259, 262.

10 See, for example, S.J. Gould, *The Mismeasure of Man*, rev. ed. (New York: Norton 1996). See also the literature referred to in note 12, infra.

11 J.P. Rushton, 'The Bell Curve Debate: History, Documents, Opinions,' Current, September 1997, 35. See also K. Lamb, 'The Problem of Equality' (1995) 20 Journal of Social, Political and Economic Studies 467; P. Stretesky, 'The "Problem of Equality" Revisited: A Response to Kevin Lamb' (1997) 20 Journal of Social, Political and Economic Studies 467; K. Lamb, 'The "Problem of Equality" Revisited: A reply to Stretesky' (1997) 22 Journal of Social, Political and Economic Studies 205.

12 For a sampling of some of the literature provoked by *The Bell Curve*, see, S. Fraser, ed., *The Bell Curve Wars: Race, Intelligence and the Future of America* (New York: Basic Books 1995); C.S. Fischer et al., *Cracking the Bell Curve Myth* (Princeton, N.J.: Princeton University Press 1996); Knapp et al., supra, note 5;

R. Sternberg, *Intelligence, Heredity and Environment* (New York: Columbia University Press 1997); B. Devlin, ed., *Intelligence, Genes, and Success: Scientists Respond to the Bell Curve* (New York: Springer 1997); J.L. Kincheloe et al., eds., *Measured Lies: The Bell Curve Examined* (New York: St Martin's Press 1996); R. Jacoby and N. Glauberman, eds., *The Bell Curve Debate: History, Documents, Opinions* (New York: Times Books 1995); C. Jencks and M. Phillips, eds., *The Black-White Test Score Gap* (Washington, D.C.: Brookings Institute Press 1998); L.A. Jacobs, 'Equal Opportunity, Natural Inequalities and Racial Disadvantage: The Bell Curve and its Critics' (1999) 29 Philosophy of Social Science 121. Other recent critical accounts of race science include: M. Kohn, *The Race Gallery: The Return of Racial Science* (London: Vintage 1996); A. Corcos, *The Myth of Human Races* (East Lansing: Michigan State University Press 1997).

13 See also R.G. Newby, ed. 'The Bell Curve: Laying Bare the Resurgence of Scientific Racism' (1995) 39(1) American Behavioral Science (special issue).

14 See further P. Kitcher, *The Lives to Come: The Genetic Revolution and Human Possibilities* (New York: Simon and Schuster 1996). See also E. Landers, 'Genetics in the 21st Century' (1999) 10 Human Genome News 13.

15 See further S.O.Y. Keita and R.A. Kittles, 'The Persistence of Racial Thinking and the Myth of Racial Divergence' (1997) 99 American Anthropologist 534, at 537ff, and the studies cited there.

16 See E.M. Miller, 'Review and Extension of "Heredity and Humanity"' (1996) 21 Journal of Social, Political and Economic Studies 349, at 354ff., and the studies referred to there.

17 See also B. Myers, 'The Bell Curve and the New Social Darwinism' (1996) 60 Science & Society 195.

18 Rushton is discussed, and his academic freedom defended, in D. Bercuson et al., *Petrified Campus: The Crisis in Canada's Universities* (Toronto: Random House 1997) at 96–9.

Select Bibliography

A. ARCHIVAL MATERIALS

Art Gallery of Ontario Archives
Sir Robert Laird Borden Papers, National Archives of Canada
Henry John Cody Papers, Archives of Ontario
Coniagas Mines Ltd Papers, Cobalt Mining Museum
Lionel Curtis Papers, Bodleian Library, Oxford University
Sir Robert Falconer Papers, University of Toronto
Joseph Flavelle Papers, National Archives of Canada
Arthur Glazebrook Papers, National Archives of Canada
William Lyon Mackenzie King Papers, National Archives of Canada
T.E. Lawrence Papers, Houghton Library, Harvard University
Leonard Foundation Records, Canada Trust, Toronto
Reuben Wells Leonard Diary (1897), Private Collection
Reuben Wells Leonard Papers, Chatham House, London, England
Reuben Wells Leonard Papers, Special Collections, St Catharines Public Library
Reuben Wells Leonard Papers (Clipping File) University of Toronto Archives
Reuben Wells Leonard Student and Alumnus Records, Royal Military College of Canada Archives
Reuben Wells Leonard, Military Records, National Archives of Canada
Charles A. Magrath Papers, National Archives of Canada
Queen's University Archives

Ridley College Archives
Newton Rowell Papers, National Archives of Canada
Henry Marshall Tory Papers, Bruce Peel Special Collections, University of
    Alberta
University College, University of Toronto, Registrar's Office Records
Sir B. Edmund Walker Papers, Fisher Rare Book Room, University of Toronto
Sir John Willison, National Archives of Canada
Hume Wrong Papers, National Archives of Canada
Wycliffe College Archives

B. INTERVIEWS AND PERSONAL CORRESPONDENCE

Valerie Bishop
Susannah Crassweller
Judith M.M. Perry
Silvio Sauro, Honorary Secretary of the Leonard Foundation

C. GOVERNMENT REPORTS

Alberta Department of Education, *Authorized Textbooks, Grades I–VII, 1924–25*
    (n.p., 1924)
Canada, Dept. of Mines, *Gold in Canada, 1933* (Ottawa: Patenaude 1933)
– *Gold Occurrences in Ontario East of Lake Superior* (Ottawa: Patenaude 1936)
Canadian Battlefields Memorials Commission, *Canadian Battlefields Memorials*
    (Ottawa: F.A. Acland 1929)
Commission of Conservation (Canada), *Lands, Fisheries and Game, Minerals*
    (Ottawa: Mortimer 1911)
Dominion Bureau of Statistics, *Sixth Census of Canada, 1921* (Ottawa: F.A. Acland
    1927), vol. 3
– *Annual Survey of Education in Canada, 1924* (Ottawa: F.A. Acland 1926)
Ontario Bureau of Mines, *19th Annual Report* (Toronto: L.K. Cameron 1910)
– *27th Annual Report* (Toronto: A.T. Wigress 1910)
Ontario Human Rights Commission, *Policy Statement with Respect to Exclusionary
    Scholarships* (1991)
Report of the National Transcontinental Railway Investigating Commission (Ottawa:
    King's Printer 1914)

D. BOOKS AND ARTICLES

Aikins, J. 'Address on Opening of Manitoba Law School' (1914) 34 Canada Law
    Times 1183

Almond, G., et al., eds. *Progress and Its Discontents* (Berkeley: University of California Press 1982)
Anderson, J.T.M. *The Education of the New Canadian: A Treatise on Canada's Greatest Educational Problem* (Toronto: J.M. Dent 1918)
Angus C., and B. Griffin. *We Lived a Life and Then Some: The Life and Death of a Mining Town* (Toronto: Between the Lines 1996)
Atherton, W.H. *Canadian Unity to Win the War* (Montreal: Canadian Unity and Win the War League 1917)
August, T.G. *The Selling of the Empire: British and French Imperialist Propaganda, 1890–1940* (Westport: Greenwood Press 1985)
Avery, D. *'Dangerous Foreigners': European Immigrant Workers and Radicalism in Canada, 1896–1932* (Toronto: McClelland and Stewart 1979)
Axelrod, P. *Making a Middle Class: Student Life in English Canada during the Thirties* (Montreal: McGill-Queen's University Press 1990)
Axelrod, P., and J.G. Reid, eds. *Youth, University and Canadian Society: Essays in the Social History of Higher Education* (Kingston: McGill-Queen's University Press 1989)
Bailey, A.G. 'The Historical Setting of Sara Duncan's *The Imperialist*' (1973) 11(3) Journal of Canadian Fiction 205
Baker, W.M. 'A Case Study of Anti-Americanism in English-Speaking Canada: The Election of 1911' (1950) 51 Canadian Historical Review 426
Baldwin, D. 'A Study in Social Control: The Life of the Silver Miner in Northern Ontario' (1977) 2 Labour/Le Travailleur 79
– 'The Development of an Unplanned Community: Cobalt, 1903–1914' (1978) 18 Plan Canada 17
Bannister, R.C. *Social Darwinism: Science and Myth in Anglo-American Social Thought* (Philadelphia: Temple University Press 1979)
Banton, M. *The Idea of Race* (London: Tavistock 1977)
– *Racial Theories* (Cambridge, U.K.: Cambridge University Press, 1987)
Barkan, E. *The Retreat of Scientific Racism: Changing Concepts of Race in Britain and the United States Between the World Wars* (Cambridge, U.K: Cambridge University Press 1992)
Bayard, R.H. *Anti-Americanism in Canada and the Abortive Reciprocity Agreement of 1911* (Ann Arbour, Mich.: University Microfilms 1971)
Beattie, K. *Ridley: The Story of a School* (St Catharines: Ridley College 1963)
Bell, L.M., and K.E. Bray. *Women of Action: St. Catharines and Area, 1876–1976* (St Catharines: Local Council of Women 1976)
Bennett, R.B. *Empire Club of Canada: Addresses Delivered to Members during the Sessions of 1912–1913 and 1913–1914* (Toronto) Part 2, 203
Berger, C., ed. *Imperialism and Nationalism, 1884–1914: A Conflict in Canadian Thought* (Toronto: Copp Clark 1969)

- *The Sense of Power: Studies in the Ideas of Canadian Imperialism 1867–1914* (Toronto: University of Toronto Press 1970)
- *Science, God and Nature in Victorian Canada* (Toronto: University of Toronto Press 1983)

Bissell, C. *The Young Vincent Massey* (Toronto: University of Toronto Press 1981)

Bliss, M. *A Living Profit: Studies in the Social History of Canadian Business, 1883–1911* (Toronto: McClelland and Stewart 1974)
- *A Canadian Millionaire: The Life and Business Times of Sir Joseph Flavelle, Bart., 1858–1939* (Toronto: Macmillan 1978)
- *Northern Enterprise: Five Centuries of Canadian Business* (Toronto: McClelland and Stewart 1987)

Bolaria, B.S., and P.S. Li. *Racial Oppression in Canada*, 2nd ed. (Toronto: Garamond Press 1988)

Bolt, C. *Victorian Attitudes to Race* (London: Routledge and Kegan Paul 1971)

Borden, H., ed. *Robert Laird Borden: His Memoirs* (Toronto: Macmillan 1938)

Borden, R.L. *Canada in the Commonwealth: From Conflict to Co-operation* (Oxford: Clarendon Press 1929)

Bothwell, R. *Loring Christie: The Failure of Bureaucratic Imperialism* (New York: Garland 1988)

Bourassa, H. *Independence or Imperial Partnership? A Study of the Problem of the Commonwealth by Mr. Lionel Curtis* (Montreal: Le Devoir 1916)

Bowler, P.J. *The Invention of Progress: The Victorians and the Past* (Oxford: Basil Blackwell 1989)

Boyko, J. *Last Steps to Freedom: The Evolution of Canadian Racism* (Winnipeg: Watson and Dwyer 1995)

Bradley, R.N. *Racial Origins of English Character* (London: George Allen and Unwin 1926)

Bray, R.M. '"Fighting as an Ally": The English-Canadian Patriotic Response to the Great War' (1980) 61 Canadian Historical Review 141
- 'A Conflict of Nationalisms: The Win the War and National Unity Convention, 1917' (1980–1) 15(4) Journal of Canadian Studies 18

Brigham, C.C. *A Study of American Intelligence* (Princeton, N.J.: Princeton University Press 1923)

Brooke-Taylor, J.D.A. 'Racial and Religious Covenants' (1978) 42 Conveyancer & Property Lawyer 24

Brown, D.W. 'Social Darwinism, Private Schooling and Sport in Victorian and Edwardian Canada,' in J.A. Mangan, ed., *Pleasure, Profit, Proselytism: British Culture and Sport at Home and Abroad, 1700–1914* (London: Frank Cass 1988)

Brown, R.C. *Robert Laird Borden: A Biography* (Toronto: Macmillan 1975)

Brown, R.C., and R. Cook. *Canada: 1896–1921: A Nation Transformed* (Toronto: McClelland and Stewart 1974)
Bruner, A. 'The Genesis of Ontario's Human Rights Legislation: A Study in Law Reform' (1979) 37 University of Toronto Faculty Law Review 236
Bury, J.B. *The Idea of Progress* (1920) (New York: Dover Publications, 1955 ed.)
Burley, D.G. *A Particular Condition in Life: Self-Employment and Social Mobility in Mid-Victorian Brantford, Ontario* (Montreal: McGill-Queen's University Press 1994)
Byers, M. *Havergal: Celebrating a Century, 1894–1994* (Toronto: Boston Mills Press 1994)
Calvin, D.D. *Queen's University at Kingston: The First Century of a Scottish-Canadian Foundation* (Kingston, Ont.: Queen's University 1941)
Capaldi, N. 'The Liberal Paradigm in Afifrimative Action Law' (1988) 43 Loyola Law Review 525
'Captain R.W. Leonard's Gig Infantry' in Royal Military College Club of Canada, Proceedings of the 26th Annual Meeting (1909) 261
Carnegie, A. *The Gospel of Wealth* (Cambridge, Mass.: Belknap Press, 1962 ed., E.C. Kirkland)
Carrington, P. *The Anglican Church of Canada: A History* (Toronto: Collins 1963)
Chaiton, A., and N. McDonald, eds. *Canadian Schools and Canadian Identity* (Toronto: Gage Educaitonal 1977)
'Chatham House: Study of Foreign Relations' (1929) 8 Royal Institute of International Affairs Journal 413
Cheng, S.C-Y. *Schemes for the Federation of the British Empire* (New York: Columbia University Press 1931)
Chesterman, M.R. *Charities, Trusts and Social Welfare* (London: Weidenfield and Nicholson 1979)
Chipman, W. 'The Empire at the Cross-Roads' (1923–4) 3 Dalhousie Review 317
Christie, N., and M. Gauvreau. *A Full-Orbed Christianity: The Protestant Churches and Social Welfare in Canada, 1900–1940* (Montreal: McGill-Queen's University Press 1996)
Cochrane, C.N., and W.S. Wallace. *This Canada of Ours: An Introduction to Canadian Civics* (Toronto: National Council of Education 1926)
Cody, H.J. 'Religious Contributions Toward Imperial Unity,' in J. Castell, ed., *Empire Club Speeches, Being Addresses Delivered Before the Empire Club During its Session of 1908–1909* (Toronto: William Briggs 1910) 19
– 'The Growth and Genius of the British Empire,' *Empire Club of Canada* (1922) 64
Colby, C.W. 'Topics of the Day,' University Magazine, February 1916, 6

Cole, D. 'John S. Ewart and Canadian Nationalism' *Canadian Historical Association Report* (1969) 66
Colquhoun, A.H.U. *Press, Politics and People* (Toronto: Macmillan 1935)
Connor, R. *The Foreigner: A Tale of Saskatchewan* (Toronto: Westminster 1909)
Cook, R. *The Politics of John W. Dafoe and the Free Press* (Toronto: University of Toronto Press, 1971)
– *The Regenerators: Social Criticism in Late Victorian English Canada* (Toronto: University of Toronto Press 1985)
Cope, E.D. *On the Hypothesis of Evolution: Physical and Metaphysical* (New Haven, Conn.: Chatfield 1870)
Corcos, A. *The Myth of Human Races* (East Lansing: Michigan State University Press 1997)
Cross, C. *The Fall of the British Empire 1918–1968* (New York: Coward-McCann 1968)
Cuff, R. 'The Toronto Eighteen and the Election of 1911' (1965) 57 *Ontario History* 169
Curtis, L.G. *The Problem of the Commonwealth* (Toronto: Macmillan 1916)
Dale, J.A., ed. *Education and Life* (Toronto: Oxford University Press 1924)
Demolins, E. *Anglo-Saxon Superiority: To What Is It Due?* (Toronto: Musson Book 1899, trans. L. Bert)
Den Otter, A.A. *The Philosophy of Railways: The Transcontinental Railway Idea in British North America* (Toronto: University of Toronto Press 1997)
Denison, G.T. *The Struggle for Imperial Unity* (London: Macmillan 1909)
Dilke, C. *Greater Britain* (London: Macmillan 1870)
Dillenberger, J. *Protestant Thought and Natural Science: A Historical Interpretation* (New York Doubleday 1960)
Dominion School Geography (Toronto: Educational Book 1910)
Donelly, M.S. 'J.W. Dafoe and Lionel Curtis – Two Concepts of the Commonwealth' (1990) 8 *Political Studies* 170
Drumbl, M.A., and J.D.R. Craig. 'Affirmative Action in Question: A Coherent Theory of Section 15(2)' (1997) 4 *Review of Constitutional Studies* 80
Duncan, H.G. *Race and Population Problems* (New York: Longmans, Green 1929)
Duncan, S.J. *The Imperialist* (1904) (Toronto: McClelland and Stewart, ed., 1961)
Eayrs, J. 'The Round Table Movement in Canada, 1909–1920' (1957) 38 *Canadian Historical Review* 1
Eby, C.S. 'The True Inwardness of the Yellow Peril,' in J.C. Hopkins, ed., *Empire Club Speeches* (Toronto: William Briggs 1910) 43
Edinborough, A., ed. *The Enduring World: A Centennial of Wycliffe College* (Toronto: University of Toronto Press 1978)

Ellinwood, D.W.C. 'The Future of India in the British Empire: The Round Table Group Discussions, 1912' (1969) 3 Nanyang University Journal 196

Elliot, S.R. *Scarlet to Green: A History of Intelligence in the Canadian Army* (Toronto: Canadian Intelligence and Security Association 1981)

England, R. *The Central European Immigrant in Canada* (Toronto: Macmillan 1929)

Ewart, J.S. 'A Perplexed Imperialist' (1907–8) 15 Queen's Quarterly 90

Facy, C.R. 'How Education Strengthens the Links of Empire' *Empire Club of Canada* (1921) 256

Fahey, C. *In His Name: The Anglican Experience in Upper Canada, 1791–1854* (Ottawa: Carleton University Press 1991)

Falconer, R.A. 'A New Imperial Allegiance' (1916) 15 University Magazine 12

– *The United States as a Neighbour* (Cambridge, U.K.: Cambridge 1925)

Fitzpatrick, P. 'Racism and the Innocence of Law' (1987) 14 Journal of Law & Society 119

Ford, A.R. *A Path Not Strewn With Roses: One Hundred Years of Women at the University of Toronto, 1884–1984* (Toronto: University of Toronto Press 1985)

Fowler, M. *Redney: A Life of Sara Jeannette Duncan* (Toronto: Anansi 1983)

Fraser, S., ed. *The Bell Curve Wars: Race, Intelligence and the Future of America* (New York: Basic Books 1995)

Galt, A.T. *Church and State* (Montreal: Dawson 1876)

– *Civil Liberty in Lower Canada* (Montreal: D. Bentley, Printer, 1876)

Galvin, M. 'The Jubilee Riots in Toronto, 1975,' Canadian Catholic Historical Association Report (1959) 93

Garner, J.F. 'Racial Restrictive Covenants in England and the United States' (1972) 35 Modern Law Review 478

Gastil, R.D. *Progress: Critical Thinking About Historical Change* (Westport, Conn.: Praeger 1993)

Gibson, F.W. *Queen's University, vol. II, 1917–1961* (Montreal: McGill-Queen's University Press 1983)

Glassman, C.D. '*In re Estate of Wilson*: Judicial Reformation of Discriminatory Charitable Trusts' (1985) 5 Pace L. Rev. 433

Glazebrook, G.P. deT. *Sir Edmund Walker* (Toronto: Oxford University Press, 1933)

– *A History of Transportation in Canada* (Toronto: McClelland and Stewart ed., 1964)

– *A History of Canadian Political Thought* (Toronto: McClelland and Stewart ed., 1966)

Goldstein, A. 'Racial Restrictive Covenants' (1951) 9 University of Toronto Faculty Law Review 30

Gossage, C. *A Question of Privilege: Canada's Independent Schools* (Toronto: Peter Martin Associates 1977)

Gould, S.J. *The Mismeasure of Man*, rev. ed. (New York: Norton 1996)

Granatstein, J.L. *Yankee Go Home? Canadians and Anti-Americanism* (Toronto: HarperCollins 1996)

Granatstein, J.L., and J.M. Hitsman. *Broken Promises: A History of Conscription in Canada* (Toronto: Oxford University Press 1977)

Grant, G.M. *Imperial Federation* (Winnipeg: Manitoba Free Press 1890)

Grant, W.L. History of Canada (London: Heinemen, rev. ed., 1927)

Greenlee, J.G. *Sir Robert Falconer* (Toronto: University of Toronto Press 1988)

– *Education and Imperial Unity, 1901–1926* (New York: Garland 1987)

Gregory, J.W. *The Menace of Colour*, 2nd ed. (London: Seeley, Service 1925)

Guest, D. *The Emergence of Social Security in Canada*, 2nd ed., rev. (Vancouver: University of British Columbia Press 1985)

Halperin, V. *Lord Milner and the Empire: The Evolution of British Imperialism* (London: Odhams Press 1952)

Harris, R.S. *A History of Higher Education in Canada 1663–1960* (Toronto: University of Toronto Press 1976)

Hawkins, M. *Social Darwinism in European and American Thought, 1860–1945* (Cambridge: U.K.: Cambridge University Press 1997)

Herrnstein R.J., and C. Murray. *The Bell Curve: Intelligence and Class Structure in American Life* (New York: Free Press 1994)

Hillberg, L.E. '*In re Estate of Wilson*: Constitutional and Trust Law Tests for the Validity of Gender-Restricted Scholarship Trusts' (1984) 12 Hastings Constitutional Law Quarterly 127

Himmelfarb, G. *The De-Moralization of Society: From Victorian Virtues to Modern Values* (New York: Vintage Books 1994)

The History of the County of Brant, Ontario (Toronto: Warne, Beers 1883)

Hofstadter, R. *Social Darwinism in American Thought*, rev. ed. (Boston: Beacon Press 1944)

Hogan, B. *Cobalt: Year of the Strike, 1919* (Cobalt: Highway Book Shop 1978)

Hore, R.E. 'The Coniagas Mine, Cobalt, Ontario' (1913) 95 Engineering and Mining Journal 981

– ed. *Canadian Mining Manual* (Toronto: Mines Publishing 1914)

Horn, M. *Academic Freedom in Canada: A History* (Toronto: University of Toronto Press 1999)

Howe, R.B. 'The Evolution of Human Rights Policy in Onatario' (1991) 24 Canadian Journal of Political Science 793

– 'Incrementalism and Human Rights Reform' (1993) 28(3) Journal of Canadian Studies 29

Huel, R.J.A. 'J.J. Maloney: How the West was Saved from Rome, Quebec and the Liberals,' in J.E. Foster, ed., *The Developing West* (Edmonton: University of Alberta Press 1983) 219

Hurd P., and A. Hurd. *A New Empire Partnership* (London: John Murray 1915)

Huttenback, R.A. *Racism and Empire* (Ithaca, N.Y.: Cornell University Press 1976)

Jackson, G.E. 'Race in Canada,' in British Association for the Advancement of Science, ed., *Handbook of Canada* (Toronto: University of Toronto Press 1924) 41

James, L. *The Rise and Fall of the British Empire* (New York: St Martin's Press 1995)

Javits, J. 'Restraints upon Alienation – Conditions and Covenants Not to Sell or Lease to Individuals of Particular Classes' (1932–3) 10 New York University Law Quarterly Review 381

Jenkins, D.R. 'The Corps of Guides, 1903–1914' (1996) 5(2) Canadian Military History 88

Jensen, A.R. 'How Much Can We Boost IQ and Scholastic Achievement?' (1969) 33 Harvard Educational Review 1

Johnson (Tekahionwake) P. *Flint and Feather: The Complete Poems* (Toronto: Musson Book 1920)

Johnston, C.M. *Brant County: A History 1784–1945* (Toronto: Oxford University Press 1967)

Johnston, H.H. 'Some Problems of the Empire,' in *Addresses Delivered before the Canadian Club of Ottawa, 1914–15* (Ottawa: Rella L. Crain 1915) 45

Jones, G. *Social Darwinism and English Thought* (Sussex: Harvester 1980)

The Jubilee Volume of Wycliffe College (Toronto: Wycliffe College 1927)

Kealey, G.S. 'The Orange Order in Toronto: Religious Riot and the Working Class,' in G.S. Kealey and P. Warrian, eds., *Essays in Canadian Working Class History* (Toronto: McClelland and Stewart 1976)

Keith, A.B. 'The Ideal of an Imperial Constitution' (1916) 36 Canadian Law Times 831

– *Imperial Unity and the Dominions* (Oxford: Clarendon Press 1916)

Kendle, J.E. *The Round Table Movement and Imperial Union* (Toronto: University of Toronto Press 1975)

Kennedy, D. 'Imperial History and Post-Colonial Theory' (1996) 24 Journal of Imperial and Commonwealth History 345

Kennedy, S. *The Pan-Angles: A Consideration of the Federation of the Seven English-Speaking Nations* (New York: Longman's, Green 1915)

King-Hall, S. *Chatham House: A Brief Account of the Origins, Purposes, and Methods of the Royal Institute of International Affairs* (London: Oxford University Press 1937)

Knapp, P., et al. *The Assault on Equality* (Westport, Conn.: Praeger 1996)

Knight, W.S.M. 'Public Policy in English Law' (1938) 38 Law Quarterly Review 207
Knowles, V. *Strangers at Our Gates: Canadian Immmigration and Immigration Policy* (Toronto: Dundurn Press 1997)
Kohn, M. *The Race Gallery: The Return of Racial Science* (London: Vintage 1996)
Kymlicka, W. *Finding Our Way: Rethinking Ethnocultural Relations in Canada* (Toronto: Oxford University Press 1998)
Lamb, K. 'The Problem of Equality' (1995) 20 Journal of Social, Political and Economic Studies 467
– 'The "Problem of Equality" revisited: A Reply to Stretesky' (1997) 22 Journal of Social, Political and Economic Studies 205
Lamek, P. 'Case Comment on *Re Lysaght*' (1966) 4 Osgoode Hall Law Journal 113
Lash, Z.A. *Defence and Foreign Affairs: A Suggestion for the Empire* (Toronto: Macmillan 1917)
Laskin, B. 'Tavern Refusing to Serve Negro – Discrimination' (1940) 18 Canadian Bar Review 314
Lavin, D. *From Empire to International Commonwealth: A Biography of Lionel Curtis* (Oxford: Clarendon Press 1995)
Lawson, W.R. *Canada and the Empire* (London: William Blackwood 1911)
LeBoudrais, D.M. *Metals and Men: The Saga of Canadian Mining* (Toronto: McClelland and Stewart 1957)
Lee, R.W. 'Canada and the Empire' (1916) 15 University Magazine 233
Levin, M. *Why Race Matters: Race Differences and What They Mean* (Westport, Conn.: Praeger 1997)
Levitt, J. *A Vision Beyond Reach: A Century of Images of Canadian Destiny* (Ottawa: Deneau 1982)
Lighthall, W.D. *Canada, A Modern Nation* (Montreal: Witness Print House 1904)
Lindsay, J.A. 'National Characteristics' (1929) 9(2) Dalhousie Review 181
Lindsey, C. *Rome in Canada* (Toronto: Lovell Bros 1877)
Loney, M. *The Pursuit of Division: Race, Gender and Preferential Hiring in Canada* (Montreal: McGill-Queen's University Press 1998)
Lonn, G. *Canadian Profiles* (Toronto: Pitt Publishing 1965)
– *The Mine Finders* (Toronto: Pitt Publishing 1966)
Lutsky, L. 'National Policy and the Dead Hand: The Race-Conscious Trust' (1973) 112 Trusts & Estates 554
MacBride, E.W. 'The Various Races of Man' (1906) 5(2) McGill University Magazine 294
MacDonald, R.H. *The Language of Empire: Myths and Metaphors of Popular Imperialism, 1880–1918* (Manchester: Manchester University Press 1994)
Machan, T.R. *Generosity: Virtue in Civil Society* (Washington, D.C.: Cato 1998)

McIntyre, W.D. *The Commonwealth of Nations: Origins and Impact, 1869–1971* (Minneapolis: University of Minnesota Press 1971)
MacIver, R.M. *Labour in the Changing World* (Toronto: J.M. Dent and Sons 1919)
– *As a Tale That Is Told: The Autobiography of R.M. MacIver* (Chicago: University of Chicago Press 1968)
Magrath, C.A. *Canada's Growth and Some Problems Affecting It* (Ottawa: Mortimer 1910)
– 'Canada and the Empire,' in *Addresses Delivered before the Canadian Club of Ottawa, 1911–12* (Ottawa: Mortimer, 1912)
Magubane, B.M. *The Round Table Movement: Its Influence on the Historiography of Imperialism* (Harare, Zimbabwe: Snapes Trust 1994)
Malik, K. *The Meaning of Race: Race, History and Culture in Western Society* (New York: New York University Press 1996)
Maloney, J.J. *Rome in Canada* (Vancouver: Columbia Protestant Publications 1935)
Mangan, J.A. 'Social Darwinsim, Sport and English Upper-class Education' Stadion 7 (1982) 93
– *The Games Ethic and Imperialism* (New York: Viking 1986)
Marlow, J. *Cecil Rhodes: Anatomy of Empire* (London: Paul Elek 1972)
Massey, V. *What's Past Is Prologue* (Toronto: Macmillan 1963)
Masters, D.C. *Protestant Church Colleges in Canada*: A History (Toronto: University of Toronto Press 1966)
– *Henry John Cody: An Outstanding Life* (Toronto: Dundurn Press 1995)
Mavor, J. *Niagara in Politics* (New York: E.P. Dutton 1925)
McKillop, A.B., ed. *A Critical Spirit: The Thought of William Dawson LeSueur* (Toronto: McClelland and Stewart 1977)
– *A Disciplined Intelligence: Critical Inquiry and Canadian Thought in the Victorian Era* (Montreal: McGill-Queen's University Press 1979)
– 'Marching as to War: Elements of Ontario Undergraduate Culture, 1890–1914,' in P. Axelrod and J.G. Reid, eds., *Youth, University and Canadian Society: Essays in the Social History of Higher Education* (Montreal: McGill-Queen's University Press 1989)
– *Matters of Mind: The University in Ontario, 1791–1951* (Toronto: University of Toronto Press 1994)
McLaren, A. *Our Own Master Race: Eugenics in Canada, 1885–1945* (Toronto: McClelland and Stewart 1990)
Miller, E.M. 'Review and Extension of "Heredity and Humanity"' (1996) 21 Journal of Social, Political and Economic Studies 349
Miller, J.R. 'Anti-Catholic Thought in Victorian Canada' (1985) 66 Canadian Historical Review 474

- 'Anti-Catholicism in Canada: From the British Conquest to the Great War,' in T. Murphy and G. Stortz, eds., *Creed and Culture: The Place of English-speaking Catholics in Canadian Society, 1750–1930* (Montreal: McGill-Queen's University Press 1993) 25
Milner, A. *Speeches Delivered in Canada in the Autumn of 1908* (Toronto: William Tyrrell 1909)
- *The Nation and the Empire* (London: Constable 1913)
Mitchell, C.H. 'A Survey of the Empire,' in *Empire Club of Canada* (1922) 397
Moller, L.F. 'Some Aspects of the Doctrine of Public Policy' (1947) 23 New Zealand Law Journal 91
Molot, H.L. 'The Duty of Business to Serve the Public: Analogy to the Innkeeper's Obligation' (1968) 46 Canadian Bar Review 612
Montagu, A. *Statement on Race*, 3rd ed. (New York: Oxford University Press 1972)
Moore, J.R. *The Post-Darwinian Controversies: A Study of the Protestant Struggle to Come to Terms with Darwin in Great Britain and America, 1870–1900* (Cambridge, U.K.: Cambridge University Press 1979)
Moore, P.B. *St. Thomas' Saints: The First Hundred Years* (St Catharines, St Thomas' Church 1976)
Morris, P.M. ed. *The Canadian Patriotic Fund: A Record of its Activities from 1914 to 1919* (n.d, n.p.)
Moyles, R.G., and D. Owram. *Imperial Dreams and Colonial Realities: British Views of Canada, 1880–1914* (Toronto: University of Toronto Press 1988)
Murphy, J.P. *Yankee Takeover at Cobalt!* (Cobalt: Highway Book Shop 1977)
Neatby, H. *Queen's University, vol. I, 1841–1917* (Montreal: McGill-Queen's University Press 1978)
Nelson, J. 'Shall We Bar the Yellow Race?' (1922) 35(10) Maclean's 13
Newark, F.H. 'Trustees Who Dislike the Terms of the Trust' (1966) 17 Northern Ireland Legal Quarterly 123
Newton, A.P., ed. *The Empire and the Future* (London: Macmillan 1916)
Nimocks, W. *Milner's Young Men: The Kindergarten in Edwardian Imperial Affairs* (Durham: Duke University Press 1968)
Nisbet, R. *History of the Idea of Progress* (New York: Basic Books 1980)
Nunn, K.B. 'Law as a Eurocentric Enterprise' (1997) 15 Law and Inequality Review 323
Ostrower, F. *Why the Wealthy Give: The Culture of Elite Philanthropy* (Princeton, N.J.: Princeton University Press 1995)
Palmer, H. *Patterns of Prejudice: A History of Nativism in Alberta* (Toronto: McClelland and Stewart 1982)
Parkin, G.R. *Imperial Federation: The Problem of National Unity* (London: Macmillan 1892)

- *Round the Empire* (London: Cassell 1898)
- 'The Relations of Canada and the United States,' in J.C. Hopkins, ed., *Empire Club Speeches* (Toronto: William Briggs 1910) 157
- *The Rhodes Scholarships* (Toronto: Copp Clark 1912)
- 'Canadian Ambassador at Washington' (1921) 12 Round Table 170

Paul, E.F., et al., eds. *Beneficence, Philanthropy and the Public Good* (Oxford: Basil Blackwell 1987)

Penlington, N. *Canada and Imperialism, 1896–1899* (Toronto: University of Toronto Press 1965)

Pennock, J.R., and J.W. Chapman. *Nomos IX: Equality* (New York: Atherton Press 1967)

Perin, R. *Rome in Canada: The Vatican and Canadian Affairs in the Late Victorian Age* (Toronto: University of Toronto Press 1990)

Phillips, J. 'Anti-Discrimination, Freedom of Property Dispositions, and the Public Policy of Charitable Educational Trusts: A Comment on *Re Canada Trust Compnay and Ontario Human Rights Commission*' (1990) 9(3) Philanthropist 3

Portfolio of the Underground Workings of Canada's Producing and Near-Producing Gold Mines (Toronto: Financial Publishing Digest 1936)

Preston, R.A. *Canada's R.M.C.* (Toronto: University of Toronto Press 1969)

Prang, M. *N.W. Rowell: Ontario Nationalist* (Toronto: University of Toronto Press 1975)

Pulker, E. *We Stand on Their Shoulders: The Growth of Social Concern in Canadian Anglicanism* (Toronto: Anglican Book Centre 1986)

Quigley, C. 'The Round Table Groups in Canada, 1908–38' (1962) 43 Canadian Historical Review 204
- *The Anglo-American Establishment* (New York: Books in Focus 1981)

'Re Wren [1945] O.R. 778 – Contributed' (1946) 15 Fortnightly Law Journal 264

Reese, T.R. *History of the Royal Commonwealth Society, 1868–1968* (London: Oxford University Press 1968)

Reeves, F. *British Racial Discourse* (Cambridge: Cambridge University Press 1983)

Reville, F.D. *History of the County of Brant* (Brantford, Ont.: n.p., 1920)

The Riel Rebellion of 1885 (Montreal, n.p., n.d.)

Robin, M. *Shades of Right: Nativist and Fascist Politics in Canada, 1920–1940* (Toronto: University of Toronto Press 1992)

Robinson, H.S. 'Limited Restraints on Alientation' (1950) 8 Advocate 250

Rosenfeld, M. *Affirmative Action and Justice* (New Haven, Conn.: Yale University Press 1991)

Rotberg, R.I. *The Founder: Cecil Rhodes and the Pursuit of Power* (New York: Oxford University Press 1988)

Rowell, N.W. *The British Empire and World Peace* (London: Humphrey Milford 1922)
Runnalls J.L., et al., *A Century with the St. Catharines General Hospital* (St Catharines, St Catharines General Hospital 1974)
Rushton, J.P. *Race, Evolution and Behavior: A Life History Perspective* (New Brunswick, N.J.: Tranaction Publishers 1995)
Sandiford, P. 'The Inheritance of Talent Among Canadians' (1927) 35 Queen's Quarterly 2
Sayers, J.D. *Can the White Race Survive?* (Washington, D.C.: Independent Publishing 1929)
Schmitt, G.R. 'Re Wren' (1946) 15 Fortnightly Law Journal 263
Schneewind, J.B. ed. *Giving: Western Ideas of Philanthropy* (Bloomington: Indiana University Press 1996)
Seeley, J. *The Expansion of England* (London: Macmillan 1911)
Sheppard, C. *Study Paper on Litigating the Relationship Between Equity and Equality* (Toronto: Ontario Law Reform Commission 1993)
Shepherd, J.C. 'When the Common Law Fails' (1987) 9 Estates and Trusts Journal 117
Shipman, P. *The Evolution of Race* (New York: Simon and Schuster 1994)
Shortt, S.E.D. *The Search for an Ideal: Six Canadian Intellectuals and the Convictions in an Age of Transition, 1890–1930* (Toronto: University of Toronto Press 1976)
Skelton, O.D. *The Life and Letters of Sir Wilfrid Laurier* (Toronto: Oxford University Press 1921)
Smillie, E.A. *Historical Origins of Imperial Federation* (Montreal: n.p., 1910)
Smith, A.E. 'Cutting Down an Evil Tree,' in *Social Service Congress* (Toronto: Social Services Council of Canada 1914) 204
Smith, G. *Canada and the Canadian Question* (Toronto: Hunter, Rose 1891)
Smith, P. *Harvest from the Rock: A History of Mining in Ontario* (Toronto: Macmillan 1986)
Smith, W.G. *A Study in Canadian Immmigration* (Toronto: Ryerson Press 1920)
– *Building the Nation: A Study of Some Problems Concerning the Churches' Relation to Immigrants* (Toronto: Canadian Council of the Missionary Education Movement 1922)
Smout, D.A.L. 'An Inquiry into the Law of Racial and Religious Restraints on Alienation' (1952) 30 Canadian Bar Review 863
Solski, M., and J. Smaller. *Mine Mill: The History of the International Mine, Mill and Smelter Workers Since 1895* (Ottawa: Steel Rail Publishing 1984)
Speer, R.E. *Of One Blood: A Short Study of the Race Problem* (New York: Council of Women for Home Missions and Missionary Education Movement 1924)
Stamp, R.M. 'Canadian Identity and the National Identity,' in A. Chaiton and

N. McDonald, eds. *Canadian Schools and Canadian Identity* (Toronto: Gage Educational Publishing 1977) 29
Stanley, T.J. 'White Supremacy and the Rhetoric of Educational Indoctrination,' in J.A. Mangan, ed., *Making Imperial Mentalities: Socialisation and British Imperialism* (Manchester: Manchester University Press 1990)
Stepan, N. *The Idea of Race in Science: Great Britain 1800–1960* (London: Macmillan 1982)
Sternberg, R. *Intelligence, Heredity and Environment* (New York: Columbia University Press 1997)
Stoddard, L. *The Rising Tide of Color Against White World-Supremacy* (London: Chapman and Hall 1923)
Stretesky, P. 'The "Problem of Equality" Revisited: A Response to Kevin Lamb' (1997) 20 Journal of Social, Political and Economic Studies 467
Strong-Boag, V. *The New Day Recalled: Lives of Girls and Women in English Canada, 1919–1939* (Toronto: Copp Clark Pitman 1988)
Stuart, R.C. 'Review Essay: Anti-Americanism in Canadian History' (1997) 27 American Review of Canadian Studies 293
de Sumichrast, F.C. 'The Leadership of the Empire,' in *Addresses Delivered before the Canadian Club of Ottawa, 1910* (Ottawa: Mortimer 1911) 62
Sumner, W.G. *The Challenge of Facts and Other Essays* (New Haven, Conn.: Yale University Press 1914)
Swanson, S.R. 'Discriminatory Charitable Trusts: Time for a Legislative Solution' (1986) 48 University of Pittsburgh Law Review 153
'Symposium, Affirmative Action: Diversity of Opinions' (1997) 68 University of Colorado Law Review 833
Tarnopolsky, W.S., and W.F. Pentney. *Discrimination and the Law*, 2nd ed. (Toronto: Carswell 1985) (looseleaf)
Tausky, T.E. *Sara Jeannette Duncan: Novelist of Empire* (Port Credit, Ont.: P.D. Meany Publishers 1980)
Thomas, C. 'Canadian Social Mythologies in Sara Jeanette Duncan's *The Imperialist*' (1977) 12(2) Journal of Canadian Studies 38
Thornton, M. *The Liberal Promise: Anti-Discrimination Legislation in Australia* (Melbourne: Oxford University Press 1990)
Thro, W.E. 'The Constitutional Problem of Race-Based Scholarships and a Practical Solution' (1996) 111 Education Law Reporter 625
Townsley, B.F. *Mine-Finders* (Toronto: Saturday Night Press 1935)
Underhill, F.H. *The British Commonwealth: An Experiment in Co-operation Among Nations* (Durham, N.C.: Duke University Press 1956)
'Validity of Charitable Gift or Trust Containing Gender Restrictions on Beneficiaries' (1991) 90 American Law Reports 4th 836

'Validity and Effect of Gift for Charitable Purposes Which Excludes Otherwise Qualified Beneficiaries Because of Their Race or Religion' (1969) 25 American Law Reports 3d 736
Valverde, M. *The Age of Light, Soap, and Water: Moral Reform in English Canada, 1885–1925* (Toronto: McClelland and Stewart 1991)
Wagar, W.W. *Good Tidings: The Belief in Progress from Darwin to Marcuse* (Bloomington: Indiana University Press 1972)
Waldie, J. *Brant County: The Story of Its People* (Brantford, Ont.: Brant Historical Society 1984–5)
Walker, B.E. 'Practical Imperialism,' in W. Clark, ed., *Empire Club Speeches* (Toronto: William Briggs 1904) 203
Walker, J.W. St.G. *'Race,' Rights, and the Law in the Supreme Court of Canada: Historical Case Studies* (Toronto and Waterloo: Osgoode Society and Wilfrid Laurier University Press 1997)
Wallace, W.S. 'The Canadian Immigration Policy,' *Canadian Magazine*, February 1908, 360
Ward, W.P. 'The Oriental Immigrant and Canada's Protestant Clergy, 1858–1925' (1974) 22 B.C. Studies 40
– *White Canada Forever: Popular Atitudes and Public Policy Toward Orientals in British Columbia*, 2nd ed. (Montreal: McGill-Queen's University Press 1990)
Watkin, T.G. 'Discrimination and Charity' (1981) 45 Conveyancer and Property Lawyer 131
Wells, R., and J. Strope. 'The Podberesky Case and Race-Based Financial Aid' (1996) 26 Journal of Student Financial Aid 33
Westen, P. *Speaking of Equality: An Analysis of the Rhetorical Force of 'Equality,' in Moral and Legal Discourse* (Princeton, N.J.: Princeton University Press 1990)
Wetherell, M., and J. Potter. *Mapping the Language of Racism: Discourse and the Legitimation of Exploitation* (New York: Columbia University Press 1992)
Wild, J. *Canada and the Jesuits* (Toronto: Canadian Advance, 1889)
Williams, B. *Cecil Rhodes* (London: Henry Holt 1921; repr. New York: Greenwood Press 1968)
Willison, J.S. *Anglo-Saxon Amity* (n.p., 1906)
– *Partners in Peace: The Dominion, the Empire and the Republic* (Toronto: Warwick Bros and Rutter 1923)
– *Sir George Parkin: A Biography* (London: Macmillan 1929)
Winfield, P.H. 'Public Policy in the English Common Law' (1928) 42 Harvard Law Review 76
Winks, R. *The Blacks in Canada: A History*, 2nd ed. (Montreal: McGill-Queen's University Press 1997)

Woodsworth, J.S. *Strangers within Our Gates, or Coming Canadians* (Toronto: F.C. Stephenson 1909)
Worsfold, W.B. *The Empire on the Anvil* (London: Smith, Elder 1916)
Wurtele, E.F. *Royal Military College Club of Canada Reference Book* (1892)

E. NEWSPAPERS AND MAGAZINES

Allen, H. 'Won't accept racial clauses – Bissell,' Toronto *Telegram*, 4 February 1960, 14
'Anti-Semitic land-sale clause declared illegal,' *Globe and Mail*, 1 November 1945, 1
'The award of the Sir John Kennedy medal to Lieu.-Colonel R.W. Leonard' (1929) 12 Engineering Journal 163
Barrett, H.F. 'Blatant bias suggested in treatment of WASPs,' *Globe and Mail*, 1 December 1982 (letter)
– 'Reverse discrimination,' *Globe and Mail*, 10 December 1982 (letter)
Benjafield, G. 'The 'Y' and Leonard,' St Catharines *Downtowner*, July/August 1991, 3
'Bias and the bequest,' *Globe and Mail*, 29 November 1982 (editorial)
'"Bill and Dan" sent on the hunt for their "Hindenburg Line"' Toronto *Telegram*, 21 March 1917, 16
'Blow to prejudice,' *Globe and Mail*, 2 November 1945, 6 (editorial)
'Brantford and Brant County men who have made good elsewhere,' Brantford *Expositor*, 26 May 1928, 13
'A British Empire gift,' *The Times*, 10 November 1923, 14
'The Canadian Club: new premises opened by Mackenzie King,' *The Times*, 10 November 1923, 9
'A Canadian gift,' *The Times*, October 16, 1923, 11
'The Canadian gift to Britain: names of the donors,' *The Times*, 23 October 1923, 11
Chernick, J. 'National scholarships' 1(2) (1938) *Manitoba Arts Review* 29
Chu, A. All awards discriminate,' Edmonton Journal, 19 April 1997, A15 (letter)
Claridge, T. 'Court quashes exclusive terms of scholarships for WASPS,' *Globe and Mail*, 26 April 1990, A1
'Cobalt has made 25 millionaires – steel directors to meet next Friday,' Montreal *Star*, 14 April 1909, 12
'Cobalt tied up by strike,' Northern Miner, 26 July 1919, 1
Cooke, W. 'No favors for Protestant men?' *Canadian Churchman*, January 1986 (letter)
'Col. Leonard,' Toronto *Star*, 2 January 1924

'Col. Leonard's further gift to St. Catharines Hospital,' *Mail and Empire*, 4 December 1924

'Col. R.W. Leonard, a distinguished son,' Brantford *Expositor*, 26 July 1924, 13

Colby, C.W. 'Topics of the Day,' University Magazine, February 1916

'Covenant against Jew buying land illegal,' Toronto *Star*, 1 November 1945, 1

Cox, K. 'Board probing "white race" scholarship,' *Globe and Mail*, 23 October 1982, 1

Crowe, P. 'Tory has "deep south mentality": Liberal,' Toronto *Star*, 23 November 1982

Dawson, A. 'Act now on racist funding: Ubale,' Toronto *Sun*, 10 August 1986

'Deliberately Planned in Berlin' Manitoba *Free Press*, 8 August 1914

Doyle, M. 'School grants for white Protestants only,' Montreal *Gazette*, 9 April 1985, A-3

Fagan, D. 'Whites-only scholarship does not violate law, judge rules,' *Globe and Mail*, 12 August 1987, A14

Fenell, T. 'The silencers: a new wave of repression is sweeping through the universities,' *Maclean's*, 27 May 1991, 40

Forsyth, P. 'Bursary founder admired in his day,' St Catharines *Standard*, 26 April 1990, 9

Friesen, C. 'No outcry over scholarships for Chinese students at U,' Edmonton *Journal*, 12 April 1997, A15 (letter)

'Funding ruling stalls,' Toronto *Sunday Sun*, 19 December 1982

'General Hughes says Canada will soon have 157,000 men under arms,' St Catharines *Standard*, 16 June 1915, 1

'Gift of Col. R.W. Leonard,' *Mail and Empire*, 2 June 1924

Gillis, C. 'Shy philanthropist made no waves in class of "79,"' Edmonton *Journal*, 5 April 1997

Greer, N. 'Discriminating against WASPs,' Peterborough *Examiner*, 16 December 1982 (letter)

'Health of Lt.-Col. Leonard reported as much improved,' *Globe*, 6 December 1924

Healy, P. 'Education Department sends strong warning on race-exclusive scholarships,' *Chronicle of Higher Education*, 31 October 1997, A47

'Historic convocation,' *Queen's Review* 4(8) (November 1930), 274

Howell, M. 'Isn't U. of T.'s bursary for S. Africa racist?' 19 August 1986 (letter)

Hoy, C. 'Rights turn into wrongs,' Toronto *Sun*, 9 November 1982

– 'A discriminating opinion,' Toronto *Sun*, 23 November 1982

– 'WASPs also have rights,' Toronto *Sun*, December 1982

– 'Pretentious rights code,' Toronto *Sun*, 12 December 1982

– 'Ill will over last will,' Toronto *Sun*, 12 August 1986

Hull, G. 'Human rights officials question scholarship,' *Queen's Journal*, 29 October 1982, 1
'Human rights are not for WASPs,' Orillia *Packet and Times*, 6 December 1982 (editorial)
'Human wrongs,' Toronto *Sun*, 1 November 1982 (editorial)
Huzinga, R. 'Ban all discrimination in bursaries, awards,' Toronto *Star*, 16 August 1986 (letter)
Jones, D. 'Benefactor had shy style,' Toronto *Star*, 25 May 1985
Lavigne, Y. 'Racial tie to bequest "unacceptable,"' *Globe and Mail*, 23 October 1986
'The law should be changed,' Toronto *Star*, 13 June 1949, 6 (editorial)
'Legacy of scholarships being investigated,' North Bay *Nugget*, 23 October 1982
'Legislation for professional engineers' (1919) 2 Engineering Journal 458
'Leonard home to be torn down shortly,' St Catharines *Standard*, 4 January 1938, 14
'Lieut.-Col. Leonard not crtically ill,' *Mail and Empire*, 6 December 1924
Lynn, J. 'Let people bequeath to whom they choose,' Toronto *Star*, 18 August 1986 (letter)
McRae, J.A. 'Banner of Bolshevism behind strike of miners in northern district,' *Saturday Night*, 16 August 1990
Makin, K. 'Lawyer defends whites-only scholarship,' *Globe and Mail*, 20 March 1987, A14
'Male-only scholarship bequest rejected,' *Globe and Mail*, 18 January 1979
'Many messages of deepest sympathy,' St Catharines *Standard*, 19 December 1930, 1
Meston, Lord 'Canadian gift to the empire,' *The Times*, 24 October 1923, 10 (letter)
'Mine operators' side of Cobalt Strike,' *Northern Miner*, 30 August 1919, 1
'MPP raps foundation for racial prejudice' *Globe and Mail*, 21 February 1956
'Mrs. R. Leonard passes away,' *Globe*, 13 September 1935
Murton, H.R. 'Canada's immigration slogan mocked at by the Jews,' Toronto *Telegram*, 22 September 1924, 9
'Personnel of party visiting the West Indies,' *Industrial Canada*, March 1922, 67
Post-strike conditions at the Cobalt Mines,' 13 September 1919, 1
'Professors in politics are read stern lesson by Sir Robert Falconer,' *Globe*, 15 February 1922, 11
'Promising week ends nowhere,' *Northern Miner*, 23 August 1919, 1
'Protest ruling in racial case,' *Globe and Mail*, 11 June 1949, 4
'Queen's University and the Leonard gift,' Kingston *Standard*, 25 April 1914, 4
'Radicals appear to gain ground in Cobalts strike,' *Saturday Night*, 6 September 1919, 18

'Racial bias charged in scholarships,' Toronto *Telegram*, 7 September 1961
Rayside, D.M. 'Moral courage,' *Globe and Mail*, 29 October 1982
'Reorganization of Queen's University with important changes now probable,' Toronto *News*, 16 April 1914, 1
'Restricted scholarships,' Sault Ste Marie *Star*, 25 November 1982 (editorial)
'Rights board to study bursary,' Toronto *Star*, 25 October 1982
'Rights code and bequests,' Oshawa *Times*, 25 November 1982 (editorial)
'Rights code could fight school fund,' *Globe and Mail*, 23 November 1982
'Rowell scores nationalists,' *Globe*, 7 December 1917, 3
'Rules governing the award of the Leonard medal' (1918) 1 Engineering Journal 291
Ryan, P.M. 'What's wrong with whites-only bursary?' Toronto *Star*, 21 August 1986 (letter)
'Says German case complete,' Toronto *Star*, 14 October 1914, 2
'Says $1,000,000 affected in Hamilton property,' Toronto *Star*, 1 November 1945, 1
Schiltroth, K. 'Improving calibre of students,' Edmonton *Journal*, 1997 April A11 (letter)
'Scholarship for "White Race" ruled discriminatory by court,' St Catharines *Standard*, 25 April 1990, 1
'Scholarship fund is racial issue?' Sudbury *Star*, 29 November 1982 (editorial)
Scotten, L. 'Whites-only scholarship is labelled "repugnant,"' Toronto *Star*, 9 August 1986, A1
– 'Woman denied whites-only bursary still feels the hurt,' Toronto *Star*, 16 August 1986
'Set scholarship standard,' *The Oregonian*, 5 April 1995, B10
'Shameful discrimination in bursaries,' *Canadian Churchman*, November 1985
'Should change law[,] Rabbi Feinberg Says[,] as covenant upheld,' Toronto *Star*, 10 June 1949, 3
Smith, L. 'A benefactor largely forgotten,' St Catharines *Standard*, 21 February 1983
Stanley, M. 'WASPs need not apply,' *Globe and Mail*, 8 November 1982 (letter)
'Study finds racial, religious bias in Metro youth,' Toronto *Star*, 11 May 1967
'Sunday will decide,' *Northern Miner*, 6 September 1919, 1
Thompson, A. 'New look needed at foundations,' Winnipeg *Free Press*, 20 November 1982
'Tolerance and law,' *Globe and Mail*, 11 June 1949 (editorial)
'To serve empire truly is to serve mankind' Toronto *Star*, 23 February 1924
'Trust for white Protestants upheld,' St Catharines *Standard*, 12 August 1987, 4
'Update Leonard trust,' *The Anglican*, September 1986, 4
'Veterans sum up cobalt strike situation,' *Northern Miner*, 9 August 1919, 1

Select Bibliography 257

Walters, J. 'Private scholarship fund for WASPs doesn't faze Ramsay,' London *Free Press*, 24 November 1982, C3
'WASPs-only scholarships under investigation,' St Catharines *Standard*, 23 October 1982
Wetherbe, S. 'Catholic rights,' *Globe and Mail*, 20 December 1982 (letter)
'What the miners turned down,' *Northern Miner*, 16 August 1919, 1
Willison, J. 'From month to month' (1927) 11 Willison's Montly 445
Wright, S.W. 'Private scholarships for minorities challenged,' *Black Issues in Higher Education*, 1 May 1997, 14

F. R.W. LEONARD'S PUBLICATIONS

'The Spring Hill Collieries' (1888) 2 Transactions of the Society of Civil Engineering 404
'Another Graduate's Views' (1894–5) 4 Canadian Magazine 431
'Masonry Pier Moved by Ice and Replaced' (1898) 12 Transactions of the Canadian Society of Civil Engineers 131
'Railway Fencing' (1903) 17 Transactions of the Canadian Society of Civil Engineers 329
'Gig Infantry,' in Proceedings of the Military College Club of Canada (1904) 145
'Gig Infantry,' in Proceedings of the 25th Annual Meeting of the Royal Military College Club of Canada (1908) 403
'Principal Railway Systems of Canada from a National Point of View' Proceedings of the Royal Military College Club of Canada (1902) 144
'Some Experiments on Loss of Heat from Iron Pipes' (1904)
'The Scope of Engineering in Canada' (1910) 4(1) Applied Science (new series) 1
'Nickel-Copper Steel' (1918) 32 Transactions of the Canadian Society of Civil Engineers 361
'Economic and Strategic Aspects of Enlargement of the Welland Canal and of Construction of the Georgian Bay Ship Canal' (1916) 30 Transactions of the Canadian Society of Civil Engineers 197
'The Mining and Metallurgy of Cobalt Silver-Ores' (1919) 2 Engineering Journal 86
'President Leonard's Message' (1919) 2 Engineering Journal 728
'Retiring President's Address' (1920) 3 Engineering Journal 78

G. OBITUARIES

'"All sunshine makes a desert" Said Cobalt Pioneer Miner,' *Northern Miner*, 15 January 1931, 2

'Canadian engineer and philanthropist passed away,' Truro *News*, 17 December 1930
'Canadian philanthropist dead,' *Wall Street Journal*, 19 December 1930, 11
'Col. Leonard dead,' New Glasgow *News*, 17 December 1930
'Col. Leonard died today at St Catharines,' Woodstock *Sentinel-Review*, 17 December 1930
'Col. Leonard dies; Canadian patriot,' New York *Times*, 18 December 1930, 23
'Col. Leonard, engineer, dies,' London *Free Press*, 18 December 1930
'Col. Leonard, philanthropist, noted engineer, dies in St Catharines,' Toronto *Telegram*, 17 December 1930
'Col. Leonard, St. Kitts, dead,' Windsor *Border Cities Star*, December 1930
'Col. Leonard's death is widely lamented,' Toronto *Globe*, 18 December 1930
'Col. R. Leonard, philanthropist, dies in Ontario,' Winnipeg *Tribune*, 17 December 1930
'Col. Reuben Leonard is called by death,' *Mail and Empire*, 18 December 1930
'Col. Reuben Leonard, veteran of 1885, Dies,' Manitoba *Free Press*, 18 December 1930, 2
'Col. R.W. Leonard died today at his home in St. Catharines,' Stratford *Beacon Herald*, 17 December 1930
'Col. R.W. Leonard, dies in Ontario,' Edmonton *Journal*, 17 December 1930, 2
'Col. R.W. Leonard dies; Canadian philanthropist,' New York *Herald Tribune*, 18 December 1930
'Col. R.W. Leonard, philanthropist, dies at St Kitts,' Niagara Falls *Review*, 17 December 1930
'Colonel Reuben Wells Leonard,' *Canadian Churchman*, December 1930
'Colonel Reuben Wells Leonard, M.E.I.C.,' *Canadian Railway and Marine World*, January 1931, 29
'Colonel R.W. Leonard,' *Industrial Canada*, January 1930
Curtis, L. 'Lieut.-Colonel R.W. Leonard' (1931) 10 International Affairs 1
'Death of a great Canadian and imperialist,' *Mail and Empire*, 18 December 1930
'Death removes Col. R.W. Leonard,' St Catharines *Standard*, 17 December 1930, 1
'Final tribute is paid to Colonel Leonard,' Toronto *Globe*, December 1930
'Financier dead, Port Arthur *News Chronicle*,' 20 December 1930
'A great Canadian,' Vancouver *Province*, 18 December 1930
'The late Colonel Leonard,' Montreal *Gazette*, 18 December 1930
'The late Colonel Leonard,' Manitoba *Free Press*, 19 December 1930
'Lieutenant-Colonel Leonard,' *The Times*, 18 December 1930, 16
'Lieut-Col. R.W. Leonard,' *Canadian Mining and Mettallurgical Bulletin*, January 1931

'Lieut. Col. R.W. Leonard passes away at 70 years,' Ottawa *Citizen*, 18 December 1930
'Lt.-Col. Leonard taken by death,' Port Hope *Guide*, 18 December 1930
'Lt.-Col. R. Leonard Canadian engineer is dead at 70,' Ottawa *Journal*, 17 December 1930
'Many messages of deepest sympathy,' St Catharines *Standard*, 19 December 1930
'A noted Brantfordite,' Brantford *Expositor*, 17 December 1930
'Philanthropist is borne to rest,' Woodstock *Sentinel-Review*, 22 December 1930
'Prominent public figure passes in Col. R.W. Leonard,' Montreal *Gazette*, 18 December 1930
Queen's Review, 5(1) (January 1931), 34
'Reuben Wells Leonard, M.E.I.C.' 14 (1931) Engineering Journal
R.M.C. Review, June 1931, 89
'Soldier, engineer, miner dies at St Catharines,' Toronto *Star*, 17 December 1930, 16
'St Catharines philanthropist died this morning,' Oshawa *Times*, 17 December 1930
'A useful life is closed,' Toronto *Globe*, 18 December 1930

H. UNPUBLISHED THESES

Avery, D.H. 'Canadian Immigration Policy and the Alien Question, 1896–1919: The Anglo-Canadian Perspective,' PhD thesis, University of Western Ontario 1973
Bagnall, J.C. 'The Ontario Conservatives and the Development of Anti-Discrimination Policy, 1944–1962,' PhD thesis, Queen's University 1984
Cook, 'T.G. Apostle of Empire: Sir George Parkin and Imperial Federation,' PhD thesis, Queen's University 1977
Craig, T. 'Attitudes Toward Race in Canadian Prose Fiction,' PhD thesis, University of Toronto 1982
Eagle, J.A. 'Sir Robert Borden and the Railway Problem in Canadian Politics 1911–1920,' PhD thesis, University of Toronto 1972
Guthrie, D.A. 'The Imperial Federation Movement in Canada,' PhD thesis, Northwestern University 1940
Holland, C.G. 'Victorian Culture in Canada: The Thought and Intellect of William LeSueur,' PhD thesis, University of Toronto 1990
Lee, M.D. 'Imagining the Empire: Political and Non-Political Societies and the Vision of a United Empire,' PhD thesis, University of Nebraska (Lincoln) 1993
McGowan, M.G. '"We Are All Canadians": A Social, Religious and Cultural

Portrait of Toronto's English-Speaking Roman Catholics, 1890–1920,' PhD thesis, University of Toronto 1988
McLaughlin, K.M. 'Race, Religion and Politics: The Election of 1896 in Canada,' PhD thesis, University of Toronto 1974
MacLean, G.R. 'The Imperial Federation Movement in Canada, 1884–1902,' PhD thesis, Duke University 1958
Michaud, A. 'Distinguishing Non-donors from Donors: An Exploratory Study of the Determinants of Charitable Giving in Canada,' MA thesis, Concordia University 1993
Taylor, R.J. 'The Darwinian Revolution: The Responses of Four Canadian Scholars,' PhD thesis, McMaster University 1976
Vipond, M. 'National Consciousness in English-Speaking Canada in the 1920s: Seven Case Studies,' PhD thesis, University of Toronto 1974
Watt, J.T. 'The Protestant Protective Association in Ontario: A Study in Anti-Catholic Nativism,' MA thesis, McMaster University 1965
Weaver, J.C. 'Imperilled Dreams: Canadian Opposition to the American Empire (1918–1930),' PhD thesis, Duke University 1973

Table of Statutes

CANADA

Canadian Bill of Rights, Statutes of Canada 1960, c. 44; repr. Revised Statutes of Canada 1985, App.III
Canadian Charter of Rights and Freedoms, s. 15. Part I of the Constitution Act, 1982, being Schedule B to the Canada Act 1982 (U.K.), 1982, c.11
The Chinese Immigration Act, Statutes of Canada, 1923, ch. 38
Constitution Act, 1867 (U.K.), 30 & 31 Vict., c. 3, reprinted in R.S.C. 1985, App. II, No. 5

MANITOBA

An Act to Amend The Law of Property Act, Statutes of Manitoba, 1950 (1st Sess.), ch. 33, s. 1
Law of Property Act, Revised Statutes of Manitoba, 1987, s. 7, as amended.

ONTARIO

Conveyancing and Law of Property Amendment Act, 1950, Statutes of Ontario, 1950, ch. 11, s. 1
Conveyancing and Law of Property Act, Revised Statutes of Ontario, 1990, ch. c.34
The Fair Employment Practices Act, 1951, Statutes of Ontario 1951, ch. 24.

The Female Employees Fair Remuneration Act, 1951, Statutes of Ontario 1951, ch. 26
The Insurance Act, Statutes of Ontario 1932, ch. 24
The Ontario Anti-Discrimination Commission Act, 1958, Statutes of Ontario 1958, ch. 70
Ontario Human Rights Code, 1961–2, Statutes of Ontario 1961–2, ch. 93
Ontario Human Rights Code, Statutes of Ontario 1981, ch. 53
Ontario Human Rights Code, Revised Statutes of Ontario 1990, ch. H.19
Racial Discrimination Act, Statutes of Ontario, 1944, ch. 51

SASKATCHEWAN

Saskatchewan Bill of Rights, Statutes of Saskatchewan, 1947, ch. 35

ENGLAND

Race Relations Act, 1968, ch. 71, s. 9
Race Relations Act, 1976, ch. 74, ss. 34, 43
Sex Discrimination Act, 1975, ch. 65, s. 78

UNITED STATES

Bill of Rights, 14th Amendment, United States Constitution

Table of Cases

Andrews v. *Law Society of British Columbia*, [1989] 1 Supreme Court Reports 143
Applin v. *Race Relations Board*, [1974] 2 All England Law Reports 73 (House of Lords)
Baptiste v. *Napanee and District Rod and Gun Club* (1993) 19 Canadian Human Rights Reporter D/246 (Ontario Board of Inquiry)
Barnswell v. *National Amusement* (1914) 21 British Columbia Reports 435 (Court of Appeal)
Blathwayt v. *Baron Cawley*, [1976] Appeal Cases 397(House of Lords)
Bloedel v. *Board of Governors of the University of Calgary* (1980) 1 Canadian Human Rights Reporter D/25 (Alberta Board of Inquiry)
Bob Jones University v. *United States* (1983) 461 United States Reports 574
Re Bryers and Morris (1931) 40 Ontario Weekly Notes 572 (High Court)
Re Canada Trust Co. and Ontario Human Rights Commission (1987) 42 Dominion Law Reports (4th) 263 (Ontario High Court) [referred to in the text as *Leonard (No. 1)*]
Re Canada Trust Co. and Ontario Human Rights Commission (1990) 69 Dominion Law Reports (4th) 321 (Court of Appeal) [referred to in the text as *Leonard (No. 2)*]
Chesterfield v. *Jannsen* (1751) 26 English Reports 191
Christie v. *York*, [1940] Supreme Court Reports 139
Coffee v. *William Marsh Rice University*, 408 South Western Reporter 2d 269 (Texas Court of Appeals, 1966)
Commissioners of Income Tax v. *Pemsel*, [1891] Appeal Cases 1 (House of Lords)

Commissioners of Inland Revenue v. *Raphael et al.*, [1935] Appeal Cases 96 (House of Lords)
Coniagas Mines Ltd. v. *Town of Cobalt* (1907) 20 Ontario Law Reports 622 (Court of Appeal)
Co-operators General Insurance Co. v. *Alberta (Human Rights Commission)* (1993) 107 Dominion Law Reprots (4th) 298 (Alberta Court of Appeal) leave to appeal to the Supreme Court of Canada refused: 112 Dominion Law Reports (4th) vii
Cunningham and Attorney-General for British Columbia v. *Tommey Homma and Attorney-General for Canada*, [1903] Appeal Cases 151 (Privy Council)
Ex parte Dawes (1886) 17 Queen's Bench Division 275
Re Dominion Hall Trust, [1947] 1 Chancery 183
Douglas/Kwantlen Faculty Association v. *Douglas College*, [1990] 3 Supreme Court Reports 570
Re Drummond Wren, [1945] Ontario Reports 778 (High Court)
Re Estate of Hawley (1961) 223 New York Supplement 803
Essex Real Estate Co. Ltd. v. *Holmes* (1930) 37 Ontario Weekly Notes 392 (High Court) affirmed (1930) 38 Ontario Weekely Notes 69 (Court of Appeal)
Evans v. *Abney* (1970) 396 United States Reports 435
Evans v. *Newton*, 382 United States Reports 296 (166)
Fender v. *St John Mildmay*, [1938] Appeal Cases 1 (House of Lords)
Floyd v. *Canada (Employment and Immigration Commission)* (1993) 20 Canadian Human Rights Reporter D/381 (Canadian Human Rights Tribunal)
Fox v. *Fox Estate et al.* (1996) 28 Ontario Reports (3d) 496 (Court of Appeal) reversing (1994) 5 Estates and Trusts Reports (2d) 174 (Ontario General Division) leave to appeal to the S.C.C. refused: December 12, 1996
Franklin v. *Evans* (1924) 55 Ontario Law Reports 349 (High Court)
Gregory v. *Donauschwaben Park Waldheim Inc.* (1990) 13 Canadian Human Rights Reporter D/505
Grimes' Executors v. *Martin* (1871) 35 Indiana Reports 198
Hickling et al. v. *Lanark, Leeds and Grenville County Roman Catholic Separate School Board*, Unreported, 14 August 1986 (Ontario Board of Inquiry)
Holman v. *Johnson* (1775) 98 English Reports 1120
Howard Saving Institution v. *Peep*, 170 Atlantic Reporter 2d 39 (New Jersey Supreme Court, 1961)
Re Hurshman (1956) 6 Dominion Law Reports (2d) 615 (British Columbia Supreme Court)
Johnson v. *Sparrow et al.*(1899) Q.R. 8 B.R. 379
Re Johnson's Will Trusts, [1967] Chancry 387
In re Kempf's Will (1938) 2897 New York Supplement 307, affirmed 16 North Eastern Reporter 2d 123

Re Kennedy, [1950] Western Weekly Reports 151 (Manitoba King's Bench)
King v. *Barclay and Barclay's Motel* (1960) 31 Western Weekly Reprots 451 (Alberta District Court)
Loew's Montreal Theatre v. *Reynolds* (1919) 30 Quebec Kings Bench 459
Re Lysaght, [1966] Chancery 191
Re McDougall and Waddell, [1945] 2 Dominion Law Reports 244 (High Court)
Re McKellar, [1972] 3 Ontario Reports 16 (High Court) affirmed 3 Ontario Reports 178n (Court of Appeal)
Mackenzie et al. v. *Duke of Devonshire*, [1896] Appeal Cases 400 (House of Lords)
McKinney v. *University of Guelph*, 1990] 3 Supreme Court Reports 229
Martinie v. *Italian Society of Port Arthur* (1995) 24 Canadian Human Rights Reproter D/169
Re Metcalfe, [1972] 3 Ontario Reports 598 (High Court)
Re Millar, [1938] Supreme Court Reports 1
Mills v. *Philadelphia Acting Through Board of City Trustees* (1958) 144 Atlantic Reporter 2d 728
Needles v. *Martin*, 33 Maryland Reports 609
Re Noble and Wolf, [1948] Ontario Reports 549 (High Court) affirmed [1949] Ontario Reports 503 (Court of Appeal) reversed [1951] Supreme Court Reports 64
Oliver v. *City of Hamilton* (1995) 26 Municipal Planning Law Reports (2d) 278 (Ontario Board of Inquiry)
Pennsylvania et al. v. *Board of Directors of City Trusts of the City of Pennsylvania* (1957) 353 United States Reports 230
Podberesky v. *Kirwin* (1995) 38 Federal Reporter 3d147 (4th Circuit, 1994) certiorari denied 115 Supreme Court Reporter 2001
Quong-Wing v. *The King* (1914) 49 Supreme Court Reports 440
Re Ramsden Estate (1996) 139 Dominion Law Reports (4th) 746 (Prince Edward Island Supreme Court, Chambers)
Re Rattray, (1974) 44 Dominion Law Reports (3d) 533 (Ontario Court of Appeal) affirming (1973) 38 Dominion Law Reports (3d) 321 (High Court)
Rawala et al. v. *DeVry Institute of Technology* (1982) 3 Canadian Human Rights Reporter 9349 (Ontario Board of Inquiry)
Richardson v. *Mellish* (1824) 130 English Reports 294
Rodrigues v. *Speyer Bros.*, [1919] Appeal Cases 59 (House of Lords)
Rogers v. *Clarence Hotel*, [1940] 3 Dominion Law Reports 583 (British Columbia Court of Appeal)
Rothfield v. *North British Railway Co.*, 1920 Sessional Cases 805
Re Selby's Will Trusts, [1966] 1 Weekly Law Reports 43 (Chancery Division)

Shapiro v. *Columbia Union National Bank and Trust Co.* (1978) 576 South West Reporter 2d 310, certiorari denied 444 United States Reports 831
Shaw et al. v. *Reno et al.* (1993) 113 Supreme Court Reporter 2816
Shelley v. *Kraemer* (1948) 334 United States Reports 1
Sweet Briar Institute v. *Button*, 280 Federal Supplement 312 (United States District Court, Virginia, 1967)
Re Tepper's Will Trust, [1987] Chancery 358
Union Colliery Co. of British Columbia v. *Bryden*, [1899] Appeal Cases 580 (Privy Council)
United States v. *Virginia et al.* (1996) 518 United States Reports 515
Wadgery v. *Fall*, [1926] 4 Dominion Law Reports 333
Walkerville Brewing Co. v. *Mayrand*, [1929] 2 Dominion Law Reports 945 (Ontario Court of Appeal)

Index

academic freedom, 35, 36, 50, 164
Acadia University, 83, 90
affirmative action, 7, 135, 142, 147, 156–8, 229n13
Aikins, James, 84
Aklavik, Northwest Territories, 45
Alberta Human Rights Commission, 121
All Souls College. *See* Oxford University
American Bill of Rights, 159, 160, 161, 232n55
American Federation of Labor, 32
American law: concerning discriminatory trusts, 159–61
American Protective Association, 80
Anderson, James, 222n80
Anglican, The, 126
Anglican Church of Canada, 93, 116, 124, 125
Anglicanism, 97; high church, 82–3; low church, 12, 82–3, 149
Anglican Theological College, 55

Anglo-Saxon race, 71, 72, 76, 78, 79, 86
anti-Americanism, 6, 63–5, 96
anti-Catholicism, 6, 79–81, 82, 96–7, 115, 117
anti-Semitism, 74, 111–14, 117, 143, 165, 207n88
Arnold, Thomas, 86
arsenic, 18, 29
Art Gallery of Ontario, 48, 50
Art Gallery of Toronto, 45, 48, 91
Aryan Nations, 148, 150
Association for Civil Liberties, 114
Association of Universities and Colleges of Canada, 136
Aylesworth, John B., 113

Banting Research Foundation, 46,
Banting Research Institute, 197n127
Barfoot, Walter, 100
Barrett, Harry F., 227n5
Beer, Frank, 191n33
Bell Curve, The, 165
Bennett, R.B., 73, 79, 96

Berger, Carl, 6, 9, 10, 63–4, 78–9, 203n42
Bertram, Alexander, 195n98
Besant, Annie, 35, 195n89
Bill of Rights. *See* American Bill of Rights; Canadian Bill of Rights; Saskatchewan Bill of Rights
Bishop, Arthur Leonard, 20, 31, 40, 46, 47, 48–9, 54, 98, 100, 102, 128, 199n150
Bishop, Edith, 20
Bishop, Francis J., 19, 20
Bishop, Judith, 199n150
Bishop, Leonard, 20, 48, 128
Bishop's College, 83
Bishop Strachan School for Young Ladies, 82, 83
Bliss, Michael, 199nn151–2, 213n182
Blum, Sidney, 222n78
Blumenbach, Johann Friedrich, 71
Bolshevik Revolution, 34
Borden, Robert Laird, 4, 5, 22, 23, 27, 29, 31, 37, 38, 50, 63, 67, 68, 81, 101, 193–4n74, 195n105
Borden and Elliot, 127, 129
Bourassa, Henri, 202n33, 204–5n56
Bowler, Peter, 60
Boy Scouts, 47, 49, 88
Brand, Lord, 77
Brant, County of, Ontario, 12, 13
Brantford, Ontario, 4, 12, 48, 50, 83
Brantford Collegiate Institute, 13
Brigham, Carl, 74, 165
British-American Shipbuilding Company, 31
British Columbia Department of Labour, 121
British Commonwealth of Nations, 65, 69–70, 101
British Empire, 3, 6, 11, 21–2, 24, 27, 29, 38, 39, 41, 42, 43, 44, 50, 53, 57, 61–70, 76, 78–9, 80, 85, 86, 87, 88, 89, 90, 95, 101, 116, 131, 164; composition of, 76, 208n102; decline of, 70, 101; justifications of, 61–3; Leonard Foundation Trust and, 61–70; reform of, 21–2, 66–9, 76–8. *See also* imperial federation
British Empire League (BEL), 21, 66–7
British Institute of International Affairs. *See* Royal Institute of International Affairs
Brotherhood Week, 118
Buckley, Denys B., 117
Bury, J.B., 59

Calgary City Council, 119
Cambridge University, 212–13n173
Campbell, John, 28
Canada: British Empire and, 27, 61, 62–9; development and progress of, 60; ethnic composition of, 73; foreign relations and, 37–8, 68, 69, 101; immigration policies in, 73–4; Leonard Foundation Trust deed and, 3, 64; R.W. Leonard's contributions to, 5, 48, 166; racism in, 9, 33, 73–5; railway development in, 22–3; religious composition of, 79
Canada First Movement, 63–4
Canada Trust, 124
Canada Trust Co. & Ontario Human Rights Commission, Re (*Leonard Foundation Trust* case), 4, 7, 9, 10, 109, 127–35, 136; analysis of, 137–9, 141, 143, 144–5, 146–51, 153–4, 155–6, 161, 162; appeal judgment in, 4, 132–5, 136, 137, 141, 144–6, 147, 148, 149, 150, 166, 225n113, 225n118, 228n6, 230–1n27; award of

Index 269

costs in, 135; implications of, 136–62; initiation of, 7, 127; judgment at first instance in, 4, 129–32, 138, 141–4, 149, 230n27; parties to, 127–8; preliminary motion in, 127–8; press coverage of, 7, 122–4, 126–7, 139, 145, 227n5
Canadian Association for Free Expression, 227n5
Canadian Battlefields Memorials Commission, 32
Canadian Bill of Rights, 104
Canadian Charter of Rights and Freedoms, 104, 105, 124, 135, 141, 151, 156, 159, 229nn13–14
Canadian Churchman, 126
Canadian Defence League, 89
Canadian Encyclopaedia, 4
Canadian Expeditionary Force, 89
Canadian Home Journal, 81
Canadian Hydro-Electric Power Company, 15
Canadian Magazine, 74
Canadian Manufacturers' Association, 37, 191n33
Canadian Military Institute, 47
Canadian National Institute for the Blind, 32
Canadian nationalism, 6, 63–4
Canadian Officers' Training Corps (COTC), 24, 27, 50, 89
Canadian Pacific Railway, 14,
Canadian Patriotic Fund, 27, 30
Canadian Red Cross, 27, 30, 46, 49
Canadian Round Table Movement. *See* Round Table Movement
Canadian Society of Civil Engineers, 20
Cape Breton Railway, 14
Capon, Anthony, 124, 125

Cappon, James, 26, 202n32
Carleton University, 100
Carnegie, Andrew, 47, 58, 94
Carnegie Corporation, 213–14n185
Cassels, Brock, 120
Cassels Brock and Blackwell, 127
Catholicism. *See* anti-Catholicism; Roman Catholicism
Catton, Elizabeth. *See* Leonard, Elizabeth
Chamberlain, Joseph, 72
Chan, Charles, 163
charitable trusts, 57, 78, 95, 115–17, 135, 202n9. *See also* cy-près, doctrine of
Chatham, Earl of, 38
Chatham House, 38–42, 46, 49, 50, 51, 52, 56, 61, 64, 91. *See also* Royal Institute of International Affairs
Chatham House speech, 41–2, 64
Cheng, Seymour, 76–7
Chown, George, 26
Christianity, 6, 57, 58, 72, 78–83, 86, 93, 95. *See also* Anglicanism; Leonard Foundation Trust deed (1923), criteria under; muscular Christianity; Protestantism; religion; Roman Catholicism
Christie, Loring, 191n33
Christie v. *York*, 106, 107, 152
Church of England Deaconess and Missionary Training House, 47, 55
Civilization: advancement of. *See* progress
Coalition government. *See* Union government
cobalt (mineral), 18, 29
Cobalt, Ontario, 16, 17, 18, 19, 97, 197n127; R.W. Leonard's reputation in, 19, 49; mayor of, 19; miners'

strike of (1919), 32–3, 37; silver production in, 17–18
Coburg, Ontario, 12
Cochrane, Frank, 26
Cody, Florence L., 119
Cody, Henry J., 36, 52, 79, 100, 119, 216n6
Cody, Maurice, 197n127
collegiate institutes, 55
Collins, Henry, 5
Colonial Auxiliary Forces Officers' Decoration, 32
Commonwealth. *See* British Commonwealth of Nations
Coniagas Mines Ltd, 5, 20, 26, 34, 45, 46, 48, 49, 51, 57, 85, 91, 97, 164, 226n130; First World War, during, 29–31; formation of, 18; profits of, 18; strike at, 32–3
Coniagas Reduction Company, 18, 19, 29
Coniaurum Mines Ltd, 45
conscription, 29, 81
Constitution Act, 1867, 104
Convention on the Elimination of All Forms of Discrimination Against Women, 134
Co-operative Commonwealth Federation (CCF), 107–8, 118
Cope, Edward Drinker, 72
Copps, Sheila, 122
Corps of Guides, 15–16, 24, 27, 192n56
Cowan, John, 198n130
craniology, 72. *See also* race science
Cumberland Railway and Coal Company, 14
Curtis, Lionel George, 4, 21, 22, 28, 38–43, 46, 49, 58, 62, 64, 65, 66–8, 59, 77, 85, 199n150
Curzon, Lord, 41

cy-près: doctrine of, 116, 117, 127, 134, 135, 138, 146, 160, 228n6, 233n60. *See also* charitable trusts; deviation, equitable doctrine of

Dalhousie College and University, 55, 83, 90, 197n127
Darwin, Charles, 58
Darwinism, 72, 86. *See also* social Darwinism
Davis, Henry H., 100, 106
DeCew Falls, 15
Denison, George, 63, 80, 203n42, 203–4n48
Derby, Lord, 38
Deutsch, John, 120
Devonshire, Duke of, 39, 40, 50
discrimination: forms of, 5, 7, 8, 9, 74, 105–18, 147–8
Dominion Hall Trust, Re, 116–17
Dominion School Geography, 71
Drummond Wren, Re, 110–12, 113, 114
Duncan, Sara Jeannette, 6, 12, 67, 204n55

Eby, C.S., 71
Edgehill School for Girls, 55
Edward, Prince of Wales, 4, 40, 41, 46
election: of 1911, 23, 63; of 1917, 29, 81
Electric Steel and Engineering Ltd, 31
Emanuel College, 55
Empire Club of Canada, 71
Empire Day, 87
Encyclopaedia of Canada, 4
Encyclopaedia Canadiana, 4
Engineering Institute of Canada, 32, 46, 54
English law: concerning discrimination, 105–6, 116–17, 118, 158–9, 162
English Speaking Union (ESU), 39, 40

Equal Rights Association, 80
equality: conceptions of, 7, 9, 10, 103, 104, 138, 139, 147–62
equitable deviation, 160. *See also* cyprès, doctrine of
eugenics, 58, 75
Ewart, John, 61

facilities: meaning of under human rights law, 109, 130, 143
Falconer, Robert, 4, 21, 28, 34, 35, 36, 37, 50, 62, 84, 97, 194–5n89
Feinberg, Abraham, 114
females: eligibility of, under the Leonard Foundation Trust, 3, 52, 53, 89–91, 145; participation of, in education, 90–1, 212–13n173
Ferguson, G. Howard, 222n80
Financial Post, 84
First World War, 5, 22, 26, 27–32, 44, 61, 62, 63, 65, 69, 73, 81, 89, 91, 101
Flavelle, Joseph, 4, 41, 50, 62, 92, 192n49
Fleming, Sandford, 50, 92
Forbes, Kenneth, portrait by, 51
Foreign Office, 41
Fortnightly Law Journal, 112
Fox Estate, Re, 154
Franklin, W.V., 106
Franklin v. Evans, 106, 152
freedom of religion, 148, 149
freedom of speech and expression, 148, 149
Frost, Leslie, 118

Galt, Alexander, 80
General Committee. *See* Leonard Foundation Trust deed (1923), General Committee under
George, Lloyd, 40

Germany, 27, 28, 31, 62, 64, 81, 88
gig infantry, 15, 16
Girl Guides, 47
Gladstone, William, 38
Glazebrook, Arthur, 21
Globe and Mail, 112, 114
Gordon, Daniel M., 25, 26
Gospel of Wealth, The, 94
Goto, Edy, 126, 224n108
Grace Church, 12, 50, 83
Grace Mission, 32, 45, 50
Grand Trunk Pacific Railway, 23, 34, 49
Grand Trunk Railway, 22
Great War. *See* First World War
Greenlee, James, 68
Grey, Earl, 41, 50
Griffith H.C., 100
Grigg, Edward, 78
grubstaking, 16
Guthrie, Donald, 127

Halibut Treaty, 216n8
Harvard Educational Review, 165
Hatch, Arthur, 195n98
Havergal College, 55, 82, 83, 102, 199n146
Henderson, William T., 113
Herrnstein, Richard, 165
Hersey, Milton, 16, 17, 18, 19, 20
high church. *See* Anglicanism
high schools, 55
Hogg, Frederick D., 113
Hope, John A., 113
Hoy, Claire, 123, 126–7, 227n5
Hughes, Sam, 31, 193n74
Human Genome Project, 165–6
human rights protections: development of, 104–18
Hurshman, Re, 115

Hutton, Maurice, 202nn32, 35

immigration. *See* Canada, immigration policies in
Imperial Conference (1923), 101
Imperial Conference (1926), 101
Imperial Conference (1930), 101
Imperial Education Conference, 85
imperial federation: R.W. Leonard and, 6, 68–70, 96; meaning of, 6, 21, 65, 66, 204n51; race and, 76–8; schemes for, 66–7, 76–7; support in Canada for, 96. *See also* British Empire; *Problem of the Commonwealth, The*; Round Table Movement
Imperial Federation League, 63, 66
Imperial Studies Conference, 85
Imperial Studies Movement, 85
Imperial War Conference, 101
imperialism. *See* British Empire
Imperialist, The. See Duncan, Sara Jeannette
India, 77
innkeeper's liability: discrimination and, 105–6
intelligence testing, 74–5, 165–6
International Affairs, 46
International Convention on the Elimination of All Forms of Racial Discrimination, 134, 148
International Covenant on Civil and Political Rights, 134
International Mine, Mill and Smelter Workers Union, 32
International Workers of the World (Wobblies), 33
Isbister Scholarships, 97

J.B.6, 16, 17, 18, 19

J.B.7, 16, 17, 18, 45
James, F. Cyril, 119, 120
Jensen, Arthur, 165
Jones, H.V.F., 191n33
Jubilee Riot, 80

Kakabeka Falls, 15
Kendle, James, 4
Kennedy Medal: award to R.W. Leonard of, 46
Kerr, Philip, 191n34, 209n114, 211n153
Khaki University, 27, 83, 88
kindergarten, 21
King, William Lyon Mackenzie, 41, 42, 50, 67
King's College, 83
King's Collegiate School, 55
Kingston School of Mining, 20, 25, 83
Kingston *Standard*, 25
Kolyn, Al, 121
Kylie, Edward, 191n33

Labour in the Changing World. See MacIver, Robert
Lagden, Godfrey, 85
Lang, Daniel, 121
Lash, Zebulon A., 203n42, 205n56
Laurier, Wilfrid, 22, 23, 29, 60, 68
Laval University, 83
Laverty, Marshall, 120
Lavin, Deborah, 39
law: discrimination, concerning, 7, 9, 10, 74, 96, 104–18, 121, 129–35, 139–62; narrative, as, 10. *See also* human rights protections, development of; Ontario Human Rights Code; public policy, doctrine of
Lawrence, T.E., 4, 42
Lawson, W.R, 61

League of the Empire, 21, 85
League of Nations, 38, 69, 75–6, 96, 101
League of Nations Society of Canada, 38, 96, 196n105
Lenin, Vladimir I., 35
Leonard, Elizabeth (*née* Catton), 12
Leonard, Francis Henry, 12
Leonard, Kate (*née* Rowlands), 14, 24, 39, 41, 45, 46, 47, 48, 49, 50, 52, 54, 55, 83, 98, 100, 189n11, 195n98, 200n2
Leonard, Reuben (grandfather), 12
Leonard, Reuben Wells, 3–8, 9, 10, 11, 12–51, 52, 54, 56–8, 59, 67, 68–70, 75–6, 81, 82–97, 98, 100, 101, 102, 105, 112, 131, 138, 155, 163, 164, 166, 194n75, 89, 195n98, 197n125, 208n99, 226n130; anti-American views of, 6, 64–5, 96; anti-Catholicism and, 6, 82, 96–7; benefactions of, 3, 8, 24–6, 27, 32, 38, 43, 44–5, 47–8, 50, 91, 192nn43–4, 55, 197–8n127, 199n147, 203n42, 210n142; Brantford years, 12–13; British Empire, views on, 3, 6, 41–2, 57, 61, 64–6, 68–70; career of, 4, 5, 13–51; Chatham House, gift of, 38–42; Coniagas Mines, and, 16–19, 20, 21, 26, 29–31, 32–3, 45; Corps of Guides and, 15–16, 27; Curtis, Lionel and, 21, 28, 38–43, 49, 68, 69; death of, 8, 46; education of, 13–14; education, views on, 57, 83–4; engineering career of, 5, 13, 14, 16, 190n28; First World War and, 27–32; illness of, 44, 46, 198n139; imperial federation, views on, 6, 68–70; 'In These Times' statement, 30–1; labour, views on, 33, 34–5, 37; Leonard Foundation, establishment of, 3, 43–4, 52; marriage of, 14; military service of, 5, 14–16, 27, 49, 81; military training, views on, 56–7, 88–9; National Transcontinental Railway Commission (NRTC), and 22–3, 24, 26–7, 37; obituaries of, 8, 46; opinions about, 8; philanthropy and, 3, 5, 11, 20, 24, 27, 57, 91–5; progress, views on, 3, 6, 11, 57, 59, 60–1; Queen's University, proposed gift to, 24–6, 43–4; race, views on, 3, 6, 8, 11, 38, 57, 70, 72, 75–6, 78, 138, 155, 164; religion, views on, 3, 6, 78, 82–3, 93, 96–7; Round Table Movement and, 4, 21, 22, 24, 28, 29, 35, 38, 67, 68; source of wealth of, 16–19; speech at Chatham House by, 41–2; teacher, career as, 13; university governance and, 20, 24, 26, 27, 28, 83; will of, 47–8, 102, 127, 128, 198–9nn139–47; writings on, 4–5
Leonard Field, 50
Leonard Foundation, 4, 6–7, 8–9, 47, 48, 51, 52, 70, 75, 78, 95, 98, 102, 103, 136, 137, 150, 151, 152, 166, 222n80; application forms, 70, 118, 120, 126, 130, 136, 203n41; awards granted by, 99–100, 103, 136–7; controversy surrounding, 4, 7, 51, 118–35; establishment of, 3, 27, 43, 52; participants in, 4, 54, 100, 106, 120, 123; trustee of, 56, 124, 127. *See also* Leonard Foundation Trust deed (1923)
Leonard Foundation Association, 56, 95, 100, 144, 216n6
Leonard Foundation Trust case. *See* Canada Trust Co. & Ontario Human Rights Commission, Re

274 Index

Leonard Foundation Trust deed (1916), 27, 43, 52, 144, 214n185
Leonard Foundation Trust deed (1920), 43, 52, 144
Leonard Foundation Trust deed (1923), 3, 4, 5–6, 7, 11, 43–4, 47, 52–6, 95, 97, 100, 101, 103, 104, 136, 157–8, 164, 166, 200n9; affirmative action, and, 157–8; autobiography, as, 5, 56–7; British Empire and, 61, 64, 70; Canada, and, 64; clause 9 of, 229–30n113; criteria under, 3, 53–4, 56, 70, 78; dispositive document, as, 5, 56; education and, 83–91; females and, 3, 52, 53, 89–91, 145; General Committee under, 4, 54, 56, 70, 78, 90, 98, 102, 120, 123, 124, 125, 136, 157, 210n141, 224n108, 225n118, 227n1, 224n108; honorary secretary under, 54; meaning of, 11, 56–97; monetary value of, 3, 8, 43, 56, 102; need and, 53, 90, 95, 157, 227n1; philanthropy and, 93, 95; political tract, as, 6, 57–8, 200n36; preferred classes under, 53–4, 57, 78, 90, 135, 136–7, 224n108; progress and, 59–61; race and, 70, 72, 75, 76; recitals of, 3, 43, 52–3, 78, 108, 118, 130–1, 132–3, 144, 145, 199–200n2; religion and, 78, 79, 82–4; revision of, 4, 134–5, 136; scholarship, subcommittee on, under, 54, 227n1; selection of institutions under, 54–6, 83, 136; social Darwinism and, 6, 57, 75, 95; time capsule, as 5–6, 58–9; trustees' duties under, 54, 56, 229–30n113; validity, of, 4, 6, 127–35; values contained in, 59–97
Leonard Hall, 50

Leonard Hotel and Motel, 50
Leonard House, 102
Leonard Library. *See* Wycliffe College
Leonard Medal, 32
Leonard Nurse's Home, 45, 50
Leonard's Coffee Pot, 50
LeSueur, William, 58
Lincoln County Victory Loan Campaign, 27
Lincoln Regiment, 46
Lindsey, Charles, 80
Linneaus, Carolus, 70, 71
Longwell, Alex, 16, 17, 18, 19, 20
low church. *See* Anglicanism
Loyalists, 63
Lysaght, Re, 117, 132, 158

McCarthy, D'Alton, 80
MacDonald, Donald, 118
Macdonald, John A., 14, 40
Macdonald, William C., 213n184
Macdonald College, 55
Macdonald Institute, 55
McGill University, 13, 55, 83, 89, 90, 97, 119, 120, 213n184
MacIver, Robert, 33–7, 44, 61, 84, 87, 97, 164, 194–5n89, 195n102, 196n105
MacKay, J. Keiller, 111, 220n45
McKeown, William P., 129–32, 138, 141, 143, 155–6, 162, 203n41, 225n118, 230n27
MacLeod, Jack Cummings, 128, 227n5
McMaster University, 83
MacRae, Robert, 124, 125
Magrath, Charles A., 198n130, 209n114
Manitoba *Free Press*, 62
Massey, Vincent, 21, 191n34
Massey Foundation, 214n185
Meston, Lord, 41

Michaud, Alice, 214n188
Michipicoten, Ontario, 15
Middlesex Regiment (2nd), 31
Middleton, Frederick, 14
Middleton, William, 128
Middleton affidavit, 129, 139–40, 225nn116, 121
Midland Battalion (militia), 14
military training, 11, 24, 44, 54, 55, 88, 89
Militia, Canadian Department of, 4, 5, 14, 15, 25, 26
Miller, Willet G., 17, 18
millionaires: in Canada, 20, 92, 213n182; social Darwinism and, 73, 214n196
Milner, Alfred, 21
Mining and Metallurgical Institute of Canada, 54
Mitchell, Charles H., 100
Montreal *Gazette*, 25, 124
Montreal and Ottawa Short Line, 15
Moore, A.T., 97
Mount Allison University, 83, 90
Mount Royal Club, 213n181
multiculturalism, 7, 73, 135
Murchison, Lorne, 6
Murray, Charles, 165
muscular Christianity, 6, 86, 95

NAFTA, 164
National Conference on Educational Citizenship, 210n142
National and Engineers' Club, 213n181
National Transcontinental Railway Commission (NRTC), 22–3, 24, 26–7, 37
New College. *See* Oxford University
New York Central Railway, 14

New York *Times*, 46
Niagara Falls hydro-electric power project, 5, 15, 48
nickel, 18, 29, 31
Noble & Wolf, Re, 112–15
North-West Rebellion (1885) 5, 14, 48, 49, 81
nurses training schools, 55

Ontario: development of human rights protections in, 108–9; imperialism and school system in, 87
Ontario Agricultural College, 55
Ontario Department of Education, 87
Ontario Human Rights Code, 7, 108, 109, 118, 121, 124, 126, 127, 129–30, 134, 139, 141–4, 154, 155, 225n118, 228n6, 229nn17, 18
Ontario Human Rights Commission, 7, 121, 122, 123, 124, 126, 128, 141–3, 151–2, 162, 225n118, 227n137
Ontario legislature, 118, 121
Orange Order, 80
Orillia *Packet and Times*, 123
Osler, Edmund, 92, 226n130
Osler, Featherstone (1838–1924), 212n170, 226n130
Osler, Featherstone Lake (1805–95), 226n130
Osler, Henry S., 226n130
Osler, John H. 132, 138, 226n130
Osler family, 50, 226n130
Ostrower, Francie, 213n180
Ottawa Normal School, 13
Oxford University, 21, 33, 85, 87, 201n15, 212–13n173; All Souls College, 21, 85; New College, 85

Page, Walter, 39, 40, 64

Page Library, 40, 64
Parent, S.-N., 23
Paris Peace Conference, 21, 38, 39
Parkin, George, 58, 63, 72, 85, 95–6, 200–1n15, 211n153
Peers, Michael, 126
Pellatt, Henry, 213n183
Perin, Roberto, 79
Peterson, David, 125
philanthropy, 10–11, 91–5, 138, 164; Christianity and, 78, 93; R.W. Leonard and, 3, 4, 5, 8, 20, 24, 32, 39, 44–5, 47–8, 49–50, 58, 91, 93–5; political significance of, 92–3; social Darwinism and, 94; social significance of, 91–2, 200n9
Podberesky v. Kirwin, 161
Policy on Race Relations, 125–6, 134
Policy Statement with Respect to Exclusionary Scholarships, 141–3
Porcupine, Ontario, 33, 45
post-colonial discourse analysis, 11
Preferred classes. *See* Leonard Foundation Trust (1923), preferred classes under
Prince of Wales. *See* Edward, Prince of Wales
private property. *See* property rights
privatization: education and, 164
Problem of the Commonwealth, The; controversy surrounding, 67–8; thesis of, 66, 77. *See also* Curtis, Lionel George
progress, 3, 6, 11, 43, 53, 59–61, 62, 70, 71, 72, 95
property rights, 7, 10, 138, 148, 149–54, 164
Protestant Defence Alliance, 80
Protestant Protective Association, 80, 81, 82

Protestant schools, 55
Protestantism, 6. *See also* Leonard Foundation Trust deed (1923), criteria under; public policy, legal doctrine of, 7, 109–10, 111, 130, 132, 133, 137, 139, 141, 144–6, 230–1n27
public/private distinction, 150–4
public schools, 55, 136
Public Trustee (Ontario), 128
Purcell, Borden, 126

Quebec, 23, 29, 80, 81,82, 88, 193n66
Queen's University, 4, 8, 13, 16, 48, 50, 83, 90, 199n146; gift of land to, 44, 50; honorary doctorate awarded at, 46, 48; R.W. Leonard, as trustee at, 20, 26, 83, 92; Leonard Foundation and, 8, 55, 102, 120–1; military halls of residence at, proposal for, 24–6, 44, 50, 88–9. *See also* Kingston School of Mining

race, 3, 5, 6, 9, 10, 70–8; British Empire and, 76; imperial reform and, 76–8; Leonard Foundation Trust deed and, 70, 71, 72, 76; R.W. Leonard's views on, 3, 6, 8,11, 38, 57, 70, 72, 75–6, 78, 138, 155, 164; meaning of, 71; public discourse about, 73–4, 96; social Darwinism and, 57, 166; theories of, 70–3. *See also* Canada, racism in
'Race,' *Rights, and the Law in the Supreme Court of Canada. See* Walker, James
race science, 6, 72, 74, 75, 138, 164–6
racial discrimination. *See* discrimination, forms of
Ramsay, Russell, 122
Ramsden Estate, Re, 145–6

Index   277

Rawala et al. v. DeVry Institute of Technology, 109
Rayside, David, 123–4
reciprocity, 63
recitals. *See* Leonard Foundation Trust deed (1923), recitals of
Red Cross. *See* Canadian Red Cross
Redlington Rock Drill Company, 19, 29
Reich, Platon, 28, 35, 192n58, 194n83
religion, 78–83, 148–9; Canada, in, 79; Empire and, 78–9; Leonard Foundation Trust and, 78, 79, 82–3. *See also* Anglicanism; anti-Catholicism; anti-Semitism; freedom of religion; Protestantism; Roman Catholicism
religion-based restrictions in wills, 115, 153–4
restrictive covenants: discrimination and, 111–15, 219–20n44
Rhodes, Cecil, 58, 85–90, 96, 212nn163, 165, 213n173
Rhodes House, 87
Rhodes scholarship, 58, 63, 216n6; difference between Leonard Foundation Trust and, 85–90; nature of, 85; Quebec and, 88; revision of, 159
Rhodes Scholarship Trust, 201n15, 214n185
Rideau Club, 213n181
Ridley College, 4, 20, 46, 49, 50, 51, 82, 83, 86, 91, 100, 197n127; donations to, 45, 199n146; Leonard Foundation Trust and, 52, 55, 102; scholarships at, 50, 102; transformation of, 102
Riel, Louis, 14, 81
Riel Rebellion (Riel Resistance). *See* North-West Rebellion (1885)

Robertson, Robert S., 113, 114
Robins, Sidney L., 132–4, 135, 137, 138, 144, 145, 148, 150, 162
Rockefeller, John D., 47
Rockefeller Foundation, 213–14n185
Roman Catholicism, 79–82, 87, 142. *See also* anti-Catholicism
Rome in Canada. See Lindsey, Charles
Rothesay Collegiate School, 55, 86
Round Table Movement, 4, 24, 58, 65–6, 67, 97, 205n56; Canadian group of, 21, 22, 28, 29, 35, 38, 67, 68; R.W. Leonard and, 21, 22, 49, 67; London group of, 68, 77, 85 membership of, 21, 22; nature of, 21; origins of, 21, 65; *The Problem of the Commonwealth* and, 28, 67–8. *See also* imperial federation
Rowell, Newton, 81
Rowlands, Kate. *See* Leonard, Kate
Royal Air College of Canada, 55, 87
Royal Canadian Military Institute. *See* Canadian Military Institute
Royal Colonial Institute (RCI), 21, 40, 85
Royal Commission for the Exhibition of 1851, 214n185
Royal Institute of International Affairs, 38–42, 46, 49, 64. *See also* Chatham House
Royal Military College of Canada, 4, 13–14, 15, 16, 20, 24, 25, 49, 52, 54, 55, 57, 83, 88
Royal Naval College, 52, 55, 88
Royal Ontario Museum, 48, 91, 128, 132, 199n147
Rugby School, 86
Rushton, J. Philippe, 165, 166, 235n9
Russell, John, portrait by, 51
Rutland Canadian Railway, 14

278 Index

St Andrews' College, 55
St Catharines, Ontario, 4, 15, 18, 19, 20, 21, 32, 48, 50, 51, 83, 91, 102, 111, 116
St Catharines General and Marine Hospital, 27, 45, 50
St Dunstan's University, 83
St Francis Xavier, 83
St Joseph's College, 83
St Lawrence and Adirondack Railway Company, 15
St Thomas' Anglican Church, 19, 20, 21, 45, 46, 50, 83, 116, 192n44
Sandiford, Peter, 75
Saskatchewan Bill of Rights, 108
Saskatoon Legal Assistance Clinic, 121
Schemes for the Federation of the British Empire. See Cheng, Seymour
scholarships: availability of, 100, 102–3; Ontario Human Rights Code, and, 139–44; social history and, 11; types of, 117, 119–20, 129, 140–1, 159–61, 215nn205, 206, 208, 222–3n80, 223n85, 225n121, 228–9nn8–12. *See also* Rhodes scholarship
Schroeder, Walter F., 113
Scott, Edward W., 124, 126
Scully, Hugh, 191n33
Second World War, 49, 104, 105, 107, 116, 159, 164, 214n185
Sense of Power, The. See Berger, Carl
services: meaning of under human rights law, 109, 129–30, 141, 143
Seven Pillars of Wisdom. See Lawrence, T.E.
Seven Years' War, 38–9
Shaver Hospital for Chest Diseases, 50, 192n44

silver, 16, 17–18, 29, 30
Skelton, O.D., 26
Smith, Goldwin, 61, 62, 67
Smuts, Jan, 40, 69
social Darwinism, 95, 96, 138, 164, 166; athletics and, 86; Leonard Foundation Trust and, 6, 57, 75, 95; nature of, 57–8; philanthropy and, 94; race and, 72–3, 75; religious belief and, 72
social gospel, 93, 203n42
social historiography, 10–11
Social Service Council, 93
social welfare state, 11, 93, 97, 164
Sommerville, William, 127, 128
South Africa, 21, 22, 76, 212n163
Spencer, Herbert, 58, 96
Springbank, 19, 20, 44, 46, 47, 102, 111
Spring Hill Collieries, 14
Stackhouse, Reginald, 100, 123, 124
Statute of Westminster, 1931, 101
Strathcona, Lord, 89
Strathcona Trust, 89, 214n185
Study of American Intelligence, A. See Brigham, Carl
Sudbury, Ontario, 15
Sumner, William, 58, 214n196

Tarnopolsky, Walter S., 132, 134–5, 138, 144, 151, 152, 162, 225n118, 226n135, 228n6
Taylor, Wilson, 91
Temiskaming, Ontario, 50–1
Temiskaming Mine Managers' Association, 33, 34
Temiskaming and Northern Ontario Railway, 16
Ten Friends of the Arts, 199n147
Thorold, Ontario, 18
Times, The, 41, 46

Toronto General Trusts Corporation, 20, 47, 49, 56, 124
Toronto *News*, 26
Toronto *Star*, 46, 69, 75, 114, 126
Toronto *Sun*, 123, 126, 227n5
Toronto *Telegram*, 46
Tory, Henry Marshall, 100
Tourilli Fish and Game Club, 40, 213n181
Treaty of Versailles, 101
Trethewey, William G., 16, 17, 20
Trethewey Mine, 45. *See also* J.B.7
Trinity College, 28, 82, 83
Trinity College School, 82, 83
trust deed. *See* Leonard Foundation Trust deeds (1916), (1920), (1923)

Ubale, Bhausheb, 126
uncertainty: invalidity of documents due to, 110, 111, 127, 225n118, 228n6
Union Government, 29, 37
United Nations Educational, Scientific, and Cultural Organization (UNESCO) Statement on Race, 107
United States, 15, 27, 31, 62, 63, 64, 67, 69, 88, 96, 159–62. *See also* anti-Americanism
Universal Declaration of Human Rights, 107
University of Alberta, 56, 83, 100, 119, 121, 163
University of British Columbia, 56, 83, 121
University College (Toronto), 119, 222n80
University of Manitoba, 56, 83, 97, 120
University of Montreal, 83
University of New Brunswick, 83, 201n15, 210n141
University of Ottawa, 83
University of Prince Edward Island, 145–6
University of Saskatchewan, 56, 83
University of Toronto, 27, 28, 33–7, 44, 50, 52, 55, 68, 75, 83, 84, 90, 100, 102, 119, 121, 124, 191n33, 216n6, 222n80; Board of Governors of, 20, 21, 27, 83, 92, 226n130; gifts to, 37, 48, 197n127, 199n146
University of Toronto Schools, cadet corps of, 192n44
University of Western Ontario, 55, 83, 89, 121, 165, 166
Upper Canada College, 55, 210n15

Vanderbilt, George, W., 47
Ventures Ltd, 45
Victoria Lawn Cemetery, 46
Victoria University (Toronto), 83, 90
Victorian League, 85
Victorian Order of Nurses, 24
Volunteers' Decoration, 31

Walker, B. Edmund, 21, 35, 36, 37, 42, 50, 92, 197n125, 199n147, 203n42, 205n56, 212n170
Walker, James, 10
Wallace, W.S., 74
Wall Street *Journal*, 46
Welland, Ontario, 31, 97
Welland Canal, 18, 91
Wells, Julia Anne, 12
Western Canadian Colonization Association, 32
Western Federation of Miners, 32–3
Western University. *See* University of Western Ontario

white man's burden, 56, 211n157
will. *See* Leonard, Reuben Wells, will of
Williams, H.G., 214n189
Willison, John S., 21, 62, 192n49, 197n125, 204n55
Winnipeg General Strike, 32, 34
Win-the-War Movement, 29
World War I. *See* First World War
World War II. *See* Second World War
Worsfold, Basil, 77

Wrong, George, 21, 84
Wycliffe College, 4, 20, 47, 83, 100, 123, 197–8n127, 199n146; Leonard Foundation and, 8, 51, 55, 102; Leonard Library of, 45, 50

York Club, 52
Young Men's Christian Association (YMCA), 44, 50, 197n127
Young Women's Christian Association (YWCA), 24, 44

PUBLICATIONS OF THE OSGOODE SOCIETY FOR CANADIAN LEGAL HISTORY

1981 David H. Flaherty, ed., *Essays in the History of Canadian Law: Volume I*
1982 Marion MacRae and Anthony Adamson, *Cornerstones of Order: Courthouses and Town Halls of Ontario, 1784–1914*
1983 David H. Flaherty, ed., *Essays in the History of Canadian Law: Volume II*
1984 Patrick Brode, *Sir John Beverley Robinson: Bone and Sinew of the Compact*
      David Williams, *Duff: A Life in the Law*
1985 James Snell and Frederick Vaughan, *The Supreme Court of Canada: History of the Institution*
1986 Paul Romney, *Mr. Attorney: The Attorney General for Ontario in Court, Cabinet, and Legislature, 1791–1899*
      Martin Friedland, *The Case of Valentine Shortis: A True Story of Crime and Politics in Canada*
1987 C. Ian Kyer and Jerome Bickenbach, *The Fiercest Debate: Cecil A. Wright, the Benchers, and Legal Education in Ontario, 1923–1957*
1988 Robert Sharpe, *The Last Day, the Last Hour: The Currie Libel Trial*
      John D. Arnup, *Middleton: The Beloved Judge*
1989 Desmond Brown, *The Genesis of the Canadian Criminal Code of 1892*
      Patrick Brode, *The Odyssey of John Anderson*
1990 Philip Girard and Jim Phillips, eds., *Essays in the History of Canadian Law: Volume III – Nova Scotia*
      Carol Wilton, ed., *Essays in the History of Canadian Law: Volume IV – Beyond the Law: Lawyers and Business in Canada, 1830–1930*
1991 Constance Backhouse, *Petticoats and Prejudice: Women and Law in Nineteenth-Century Canada*
1992 Brendan O'Brien, *Speedy Justice: The Tragic Last Voyage of His Majesty's Vessel* Speedy
      Robert Fraser, ed., *Provincial Justice: Upper Canadian Legal Portraits from the Dictionary of Canadian Biography*
1993 Greg Marquis, *Policing Canada's Century: A History of the Canadian Association of Chiefs of Police*
      F. Murray Greenwood, *Legacies of Fear: Law and Politics in Quebec in the Era of the French Revolution*
1994 Patrick Boyer, *A Passion for Justice: The Legacy of James Chalmers McRuer*
      Charles Pullen, *The Life and Times of Arthur Maloney: The Last of the Tribunes*
      Jim Phillips, Tina Loo, and Susan Lewthwaite, eds., *Essays in the History of Canadian Law: Volume V – Crime and Criminal Justice*
      Brian Young, *The Politics of Codification: The Lower Canadian Civil Code of 1866*

1995 David Williams, *Just Lawyers: Seven Portraits*
Hamar Foster and John McLaren, eds., *Essays in the History of Canadian Law: Volume VI – British Columbia and the Yukon*
W.H. Morrow, ed., *Northern Justice: The Memoirs of Mr Justice William G. Morrow*
Beverley Boissery, *A Deep Sense of Wrong: The Treason Trials and Transportation to New South Wales of Lower Canadian Rebels after the 1838 Rebellion*
1996 Carol Wilton, ed., *Essays in the History of Canadian Law: Volume VII – Inside the Law: Canadian Law Firms in Historical Perspective*
William Kaplan, *Bad Judgment: The Case of Mr Justice Leo A. Landreville*
F. Murray Greenwood and Barry Wright, eds., *Canadian State Trials: Volume I – Law, Politics, and Security Measures, 1608–1837*
1997 James W. St.G. Walker, *'Race,' Rights, and the Law in the Supreme Court of Canada: Historical Case Studies*
Lori Chambers, *Married Women and Property Law in Victorian Ontario*
Patrick Brode, *Casual Slaughters and Accidental Judgments: Canadian War Crimes and Prosecutions, 1944–1948*
Ian Bushnell, *A History of the Federal Court of Canada, 1875–1992*
1998 Sidney Harring, *White Man's Law: Native People in Nineteenth-Century Canadian Jurisprudence*
Peter Oliver, *'Terror to Evil-Doers': Prisons and Punishments in Nineteenth-Century Ontario*
1999 Constance Backhouse, *Colour-Coded: A Legal History of Racism in Canada, 1900–1950*
G. Blaine Baker and Jim Phillips, eds., *Essays in the History of Canadian Law: Volume VIII – In Honour of R.C.B. Risk*
Richard W. Pound, *Chief Justice W.R. Jackett: By the Law of the Land*
David Vanek, *Fulfilment: Memoirs of a Criminal Court Judge*
2000 Barry Cahill, *The Thousandth Man: A Biography of James McGregor Stewart*
A.B. McKillop, *The Spinster and the Prophet*
Beverley Boissery and F. Murray Greenwood, *Uncertain Justice: Canadian Women and Capital Punishment*
Bruce Ziff, *Unforeseen Legacies: Reuben Wells Leonard and the Leonard Foundation Trust*